SOURCES IN BRITISH POLITICAL HISTORY 1900–1951

Volume 3

Sources in British Political History 1900 – 1951

compiled for the British Library of
Political and Economic Science by
CHRIS COOK

with

Philip Jones
Josephine Sinclair
Jeffrey Weeks

Volume 3

A Guide to the Private
Papers of Members
of Parliament: A–K

First published 1977 by
THE MACMILLAN PRESS LTD
London and Basingstoke
Associated companies in New York
Dublin Melbourne Johannesburg and Madras

ISBN 0 333 15038 4

Printed in Great Britain by
UNWIN BROTHERS LTD Woking and London

Contents

Foreword

This is the third in the series of volumes reporting the results of a survey of twentieth-century British political archives. It has been undertaken by the British Library of Political and Economic Science with the support of the Social Science Research Council.

The project originated from a meeting of archivists, historians and librarians, held in October 1967 on the initiative of Nuffield College, Oxford, which appointed a Political Archives Investigation Committee (whose membership is listed on p. x) to explore the possibility of making a major effort to locate and list modern British political manuscripts and encourage their preservation.

With the assistance of a grant from the Social Science Research Council a two-year pilot project, directed by Dr Cameron Hazlehurst, was begun at Nuffield College in 1968, with the object of locating the papers of Cabinet Ministers who held office between 1900 and 1951. The same Committee acted as a steering committee for the project. This enquiry was an undoubted success; and Dr Hazlehurst's guide to the papers of Cabinet Ministers was published in 1974.[1]

In view of the favourable outcome of the pilot project, the Committee had no hesitation in recommending that a more comprehensive survey should be undertaken; and particularly bearing in mind the bibliographical facilities and geographical convenience of London, as well as the number of scholars active in relevant fields working in the London School of Economics, it proposed that this phase of the investigation should be carried out under the auspices of the British Library of Political and Economic Science.

A generous grant was accordingly made to that Library by the Social Science Research Council; and on 1 October 1970 a research team directed by Dr C. P. Cook began work on a six-year project intended to locate the papers of all persons and organisations influential in British politics between 1900 and 1951, encourage their preservation, and publish guides.

The records of political parties, societies, institutions and pressure groups were described in the first volume in this series.[2] The second volume was concerned with the private papers of senior public servants, diplomats and military personnel.[3]

The third and fourth volumes have been devoted to reporting the findings of a comprehensive search that has been made for the papers of all Members of the House of Commons.[4] The fifth volume will deal with the papers of selected writers, intellectuals and propagandists.[5]

D. A. Clarke
British Library of Political and Economic Science

[1] C. Hazlehurst and C. Woodland, *A Guide to the Papers of British Cabinet Ministers, 1900–1951* (London: Royal Historical Society, 1974).

[2] C. Cook (and others), *Sources in British Political History, 1900–1951, Vol. 1: A Guide to the Archives of Selected Organisations and Societies* (London: Macmillan, 1975).

[3] C. Cook (and others), *Sources in British Political History, 1900–1951, Vol. 2: A Guide to the Private Papers of Selected Public Servants* (London: Macmillan, 1975).

[4] For the second part of this survey, see C. Cook (and others), *Sources in British Political History, 1900–1951, Vol. 4: A Guide to the Private Papers of Members of Parliament: L–Z*.

[5] C. Cook and J. Weeks, *Sources in British Political History, 1900–1951, Vol. 5: A Guide to the Private Papers of Selected Writers, Intellectuals and Propagandists*.

Acknowledgements

This book, like its predecessors, could not have been compiled without a large grant from the Social Science Research Council and the help and guidance of Derek Clarke, the Librarian of the British Library of Political and Economic Science. It would be impossible to thank by name all the people without whose help this volume either would not have appeared or would have looked very different. I am, however, indebted to the following:

Maurice Bond, M.V.O. O.B.E., Clerk of the Records at the House of Lords; D. S. Porter of the Bodleian Library, Oxford; Christine Kennedy of Nuffield College, Oxford; A. E. B. Owen of Cambridge University Library; Daniel Waley, Keeper of Manuscripts at the British Library; J. K. Bates, Secretary of the National Register of Archives (Scotland); J. S. Ritchie at the National Library of Scotland; Sir John Ainsworth, Bt, at the National Library of Ireland; and G. M. Griffiths at the National Library of Wales. The Keeper and the staff at the Public Record Office, and their colleagues at the Northern Ireland Public Record Office, have given generously of their time.

A variety of related projects have been involved in work closely associated with our own. Particular thanks are due to Michael Rush of the University of Exeter; Joyce Bellamy and Professor John Saville at the University of Hull (whose *Dictionary of Labour Biography* has been of invaluable assistance); Iain MacDougall, Secretary of the Scottish Society for the Study of Labour History, and Hywel Francis of the South Wales Miners Library, University College, Swansea.

Many repositories, though not primarily interested in collecting the papers of Members of Parliament, have material of relevance. Particular thanks are due to the staffs of the Bodleian Library, Rhodes House Library, the House of Lords Record Office, the Imperial War Museum, the Liddell Hart Centre for Military Archives, Churchill College, Cambridge, the India Office Library, the Middle East Centre at St Antony's College, Oxford, King's College, Cambridge and the University of Warwick. The compilation of any biographical register of M.Ps and Ministers relies heavily on the existing reference publications of Fred Craig and David Butler. The staff at Transport House, Conservative Central Office and Liberal headquarters also co-operated in the survey. The archivists of local record offices, many company archivists and a host of local reference librarians must also be warmly thanked. I have relied heavily on suggestions, advice and information supplied by colleagues and friends, both at the London School of Economics and elsewhere. I should like to thank especially David Bebbington, David Bovey, Stephen Brooks, Susan Bruley, Philip Bull, Martin Ceadel, Janet Druker, Chris Howard, George Jones, Stephen Koss, Ian Nish, John Ramsden, Angela Raspin, David Rolf, Martin Sieff, Richard Storey, Paul Sturges and Philip Woods.

I have also received much help and advice from members of the steering committee, both past and present. In addition, Dr Davis and the staff of the Historical Manuscripts Commission, whose work is so closely associated with our own, have been of continuous assistance. The pioneering work done by Cameron Hazlehurst and Christine Woodland has also helped in the production of this book.

Last, but by no means least, the compilation of this book has been a team effort, and my very warm thanks are due to my colleagues and co-authors, Philip Jones, Josephine Sinclair and Jeffrey Weeks. Most of the typing for the survey was done with unfailing energy and kindness by Eileen Pattison, with additional secretarial help from Jean Ali.

CHRIS COOK

Members of the Political Archives Investigation Committee

Mr John Brooke, formerly Historical Manuscripts Commission (1967 –) (Chairman, 1972 –)
Mr D. A. Clarke, British Library of Political and Economic Science (1967 –)
Dr C. P. Cook, Historical Manuscripts Commission (1970 –)
Mr Martin Gilbert, Merton College, Oxford (1967–70)
Dr R. M. Hartwell, Nuffield College, Oxford (Chairman, 1967–72)
Dr Cameron Hazlehurst, Nuffield College, Oxford (1967–70)
Professor A. Marwick, The Open University (1972 –)
Dr H. M. Pelling, St John's College, Cambridge (1967 –)
Dr John Roberts, Merton College, Oxford (1973 –)
Mrs Felicity Strong, formerly Historical Manuscripts Commission (1967 –)
Mr A. J. P. Taylor, Magdalen College, Oxford (1972 –)
Professor D. C. Watt, London School of Economics and Political Science (1967 –)
Mr Jeffrey Weeks, British Library of Political and Economic Science (1975 –)
Dr Edwin Welch, Churchill College, Cambridge (1967–71)

Introduction

1. Scope of the Survey

The third and fourth volumes in this series are concerned with the surviving private papers of all Members of Parliament from the General Election of September 1900 to the fall of the Attlee Government in the election of October 1951. These two volumes attempt to include every M.P. elected during this period, together with every holder of a ministerial appointment. The survey, however, did *not* attempt to trace the papers of every member of the House of Lords, only of those who had held ministerial office.[1] However, all elected M.P.s (including the Sinn Fein members returned in 1918) have been included to provide within two volumes the only comprehensive biographical list of M.P.s which currently exists for the period 1900 to 1951.

2. The Reports

The reports which appear in the following pages are necessarily very brief. Biographical details are restricted to a concise note detailing the person's party affiliation, the constituency for which he sat and any ministerial office held. Where appropriate, important aspects of a person's career have been briefly noted if these are of particular relevance, but in every case researchers are urged to use entries in this Guide in conjunction with the appropriate entries in *Who's Who*, *Who Was Who* and the *Dictionary of National Biography*.

These reports attempt only to describe briefly the extent and nature of those collections of private papers which have survived. Where it has been found that no private papers exist, this information has been included. Reference has not usually been made to published biographies, memoirs or other such works. In addition, whilst reference has often been made to the relevant papers of an individual to be found in another collection, such cross-referencing could only be done for a selection of the most important collections. Researchers are again most strongly urged to consult the Personal Index at the National Register of Archives. This computer print-out, which is up-dated annually, may also be consulted at the British Library, the Bodleian Library and Cambridge University Library.

In many instances, the reader will note that entries in this volume have no accompanying text describing surviving papers. This normally means that, despite attempts to trace a surviving member of the family (or indeed a solicitor still in touch with the family), no names of possible contacts could be established. In virtually every case (as is outlined below), the will and act of probate of the person concerned was consulted, but with no success in the search for a surviving relative. However, researchers willing to undertake the arduous task of tracing a widow's will (or the will of the major beneficiary) might well succeed in eliciting a contact. With only limited reserves of time and manpower, the survey could obviously not go to these lengths, except for a very few of the more important members.

3. Research Procedure

This volume (and the fourth volume) have between them attempted to describe the surviving papers of some 3800 individuals. Many of these M.P.s were often at Westminster for only one parliament; some, indeed, sat for even less time. Especially after such landslide elections as 1906, 1918, 1931 and 1945, an individual M.P. lost his seat in the succeeding election and rapidly disappeared from public life. To attempt to trace the relatives and descendants of so many individuals of such varied backgrounds has been an Herculean task.

The research procedure adopted involved, in the first instance, the collation of information on record at the National Register of Archives and at a number of repositories in this country, the United States and the Commonwealth. For persons whose papers were not known to be deposited, reference was made to the standard reference works, such as *Who Was Who, Kelly's Handbook* and *Burke's Peerage*. More specialist publications, such as the *Dictionary of Labour Biography* (compiled by Joyce Bellamy and John Saville) and the various yearbooks produced by the political parties, were extensively consulted. There has been close liaison with research projects in related fields: particular mention must be made of the survey of Scottish Labour records.[2]

Where possible, as a result of this research, a letter of inquiry was sent to a surviving relative or a close contact. Over 2000 such letters were despatched. In addition, several hundred more letters were sent out as a result of visits made to the Principal Probate Registry at Somerset House to consult wills and probate acts. In many cases, this enabled contacts to be made with the surviving family, executor or solicitors. Lack of time and resources meant that a second visit to Somerset House to search for further contacts was not possible in most cases.

Despite these efforts, there are still many M.P.s included in this volume for whom the survey had no knowledge of whether any private papers were extant. In these cases, as explained earlier, no text appears below the entry for the individual M.P. In the case of M.P.s still alive, and indeed in some cases still active in politics, the absence of any text indicates that, failing any definite information, any surviving papers are presumed to be still with the individual concerned.

No comprehensive attempt was made in this survey to trace the surviving papers of former Irish Nationalist members, whilst virtually no effort was made to trace papers of former Sinn Fein or Republican members still in private hands. However, much effort was devoted to finding details of the collections of such papers in the National Library of Ireland, or in the Public Record Office of Northern Ireland. These details are included in the text. In addition, an appendix on Irish archives (see pp. 269–276) summarises the most useful sources for students working in this area and explains certain of the complexities of the Irish archive scene. The symbol * after each Irish entry refers the user to this appendix.

For those persons in this volume who held ministerial office, any personal collections of papers surviving at the Public Record Office (i.e. the Private Office series of papers) have where possible been included in this guide. In addition, Private Office collections still retained by the relevant government department are also described. It must be remembered, however, that certain Private Office series at the Public Record Office are *not* arranged by person, for example, the Ministry of Education series (Ed. 24 and Ed. 136) and Ministry of Labour and National Service series (Lab. 25).

Finally, it cannot be emphasised too strongly that, although this volume has attempted (with the exceptions mentioned) a thorough and comprehensive search for papers, it is utterly unavoidable that considerable omissions still remain. For any number of reasons it may not be possible to include details of papers of certain figures who should be included. It may be impossible to trace a family; an address may change; illness or incapacity may prevent a reply to an inquiry; papers may be in store and details thus not available. In such circumstances, omissions are inevitable. Equally, the information presented here may change; papers may be lost, destroyed, found or deposited. In particular, the addresses of custodians of papers will frequently change. For this reason, where the address of a person mentioned in the text can be obtained from the current *Who's Who* or similar sources, constantly up-dated, it is not cited in the text.

For all these instances, the editors of this book merely ask that, if scholars obtain additional information to that included here, they would inform them so that this information may be added to the project's findings.

4. Availability of Papers

The mention of the existence of private papers in this volume in no way implies that these collections are necessarily available for research. Where papers are *known* to be closed to scholars, an attempt has been made to incorporate this information. For all collections in libraries and record offices, a preliminary letter to the appropriate archivist is very strongly advised. For collections in private hands, a letter is absolutely essential; no research worker should expect private collections necessarily to be opened up for his work. A letter of thanks to such custodians of private papers is also a matter of common courtesy. Scholars are reminded again of the law of copyright – and, in particular, that copyright lies with the writer of a letter, not the recipient.

5. Arrangement

The entries in this guide have, in general, been arranged alphabetically, under the last known name of the person concerned. Where a family name differs from the title subsequently chosen by a peer, a cross-reference has been given in the text. The two volumes have thus attempted to be completely self-indexing. Hyphenated names are usually found under the last half of the surname (e.g. for Talbot-Smith, see Smith).

6. Abbreviations and Symbols

The use of the symbol * (referring the user to Appendix 1) is described above. In addition, to save needless repetition, standard abbreviations have been used for certain titles, party affiliations and appointments. A Life Peer has been styled Baron. Otherwise, titles have been abbreviated as follows: D (Duke); M (Marquess); E (Earl); Vt (Viscount); B (hereditary Baron); and Bt (Baronet). The British Library of Political and Economic Science is referred to throughout as BLPES, whilst the earlier volumes in this series are referred to as *Sources* with the appropriate volume and page reference.

Frequent reference is made in this volume to the survey of Cabinet Ministers' papers undertaken by Cameron Hazlehurst and Christine Woodland at Nuffield College, Oxford. This volume (*A Guide to the Papers of British Cabinet Ministers, 1900–1951*) is referred to in this book as Hazlehurst and Woodland.

7. Further Information

Deposits of papers too recent to be included in this volume are recorded in the annual list of Accessions to Repositories published by H.M. Stationery Office for the Historical Manuscripts Commission. More detailed unpublished lists of archives both in repositories and libraries and in the custody of their originators may often be found in the National Register of Archives maintained by the Historical Manuscripts Commission, Quality House, Quality Court, Chancery Lane, London WC2A 1HP, where known alterations and additions to the information given in this volume will be recorded.

It is hoped that the information in this volume is correct at the time of going to press, but apart from the possible changes mentioned earlier, it must be remembered that many details of papers were often supplied by persons whose knowledge of the records was imperfect, by librarians who had not yet been able to catalogue records fully, or by scholars whose interests might be limited to certain aspects of their research. Both the British Library of Political and Economic Science and the Historical Manuscripts Commission would be grateful to be informed of alterations, additions and amendments.

Notes

1 Many members of the House of Lords, will of course, be found in other volumes in this series. The papers of senior diplomats, colonial officials and civil servants who received peerages were discussed in Volume 2, whilst, for example, many of the press lords will appear in Volume 5.

2 This survey of records of the Labour movement in Scotland, conducted by Ian

MacDougall, the secretary of the Scottish Committee of the Society for the Study of Labour History, has published an *Interim Bibliography of the Scottish Working Class Movement* (1965). MacDougall's extensive *Catalogue of Some Labour Records in Scotland and Some Scots Records Outside Scotland* will be invaluable. This work not only covers the primary sources and collections of private papers known to survive, but also published records, writings and reports. The book's sections comprise (1) Friendly Societies, (2) Co-operation, (3) Political Movements from the 18th Century onwards, (4) Trade Unionism, (5) Miscellaneous groups and organisations, (6) Newspapers and periodicals, and (7) Leaders, rank and file, associates and forerunners of the Working Class movement. A comprehensive index of subjects, persons and places has been included in this major work.

Private Papers A – K

ABERCONWAY, 1st B
Sir Charles Benjamin Bright McLaren, 1st Bt (1850–1934)

M.P. (Lib.) Stafford, 1880–6; Bosworth, 1892–Jan 1910.

The present (3rd) Lord Aberconway says he knows of no surviving papers relating to the parliamentary careers of the 1st and 2nd Lords Aberconway.

ABERCONWAY, 2nd B
Henry Duncan McLaren (1879–1953)

M.P.(Lib.) Staffordshire West, 1906–Jan 1910; Bosworth, Dec 1910–22.

See above. Papers of Christabel, Lady Aberconway, wife of the 2nd Baron, are preserved at the British Library (Add.Mss 52432–5, and 52550–6). These comprise 11 volumes of letters to Lady Aberconway and include correspondents such as H. H. Asquith and his wife, Margot, H. G. Wells, Samuel Courtauld, G. B. Shaw, etc.

ABERCORN, 3rd D of
James Albert, M of Hamilton (1869–1953)*

M.P. (Con.) Londonderry, 1900–13.
Treasurer, H.M. Household, 1903–5. Governor of Northern Ireland, 1922–45.

Abercorn's son, the 4th Duke, knows of no surviving political papers. The Abercorn family papers are in the Northern Ireland Public Record Office. These, however, appear to contain no relevant political material. Relevant material may be found in the P. L. Gell, British South Africa Company papers (see NRA 5438).

ABERTAY, 1st B
Sir Charles Coupar Barrie (1875–1940)

M.P. (Lib.) Elgin Burghs, 1918; Banffshire, 1918–24; Southampton (Nat.Lib.), 1931–40.

No family contact was established. Surviving records of the National Liberals are described in *Sources*, Vol. 1, pp. 183–4.

ABRAHAM, William (1840–1914)*

M.P. (Irish Nat.) Limerick West, 1885–92; Cork N.E., 1893–Jan 1910; Dublin Harbour, Jan 1910–15.

Efforts to contact Abraham's son proved unsuccessful.

ABRAHAM, William (1842–1922)

M.P. (Lib.Lab.) Rhondda Valley, 1885–1918; (Lab.) Rhondda West, 1918–20.

Full biographical details are given in the *Dictionary of Labour Biography*, Vol. I, p.4. *Mabon* by E. W. Evans (Cardiff, 1959) mentions certain papers in the care of the family. It proved impossible to trace these. Dr Evans, now of the University of Hull, states that these were in any case of biographical rather than political interest. Reference should be made to the records of the South Wales Miners housed in the Library of University College, Swansea.

ACKROYD, Thomas Raven (1861–1946)

M.P. (Lib.) Manchester Moss Side, 1923–4.

It proved impossible to contact any members of Ackroyd's family, and the Manchester Trustee Office of Barclays Bank, which administered the estate, had no relevant records.

ACLAND, Sir Francis Dyke, 14th Bt (1874–1939)

M.P. (Lib.) Richmond (Yorks.), 1906–Jan 1910; Cornwall N.W., Dec 1910–22; Tiverton, 1923–4.
Financial Secretary, War Office, 1908–10. Parliamentary Under-Secretary, Foreign Affairs, 1911–15.Parliamentary Secretary, Board of Agriculture, 1915–16.

Acland family papers have been deposited at Devon Record Office. These may include a few papers relating to Sir Francis Dyke Acland. Sir F. D. Acland's son, Sir Richard Acland, Bt, Sprydon, Broadclyst, Exeter, Devon, has retained certain other papers relating to his father. These will eventually join the family papers in Devon Record Office. Correspondence with Austen Chamberlain regarding Anglo-German relations (1898–1914) can be found in the Chamberlain papers at Birmingham University Library.

ACLAND, Sir Richard Thomas Dyke, 15th Bt (1906–   ).

M.P. (Lib., later Common Wealth) Barnstaple, 1935–45; (Lab.) Gravesend, 1947–55.

Sir Richard Acland has given his surviving papers to the Library of the University of Sussex. Most of these relate to his activities in Common Wealth during World War II, with correspondence, 1940–5; a typescript diary, with letters and documents, kept from March 1943 to August 1945; a collection of press cuttings about Common Wealth and a small collection of election addresses.

ACTON, 2nd B
Sir Richard Maximilian Dalberg-Acton, 2nd Bt (1870–1924)

Diplomat.
Lord in Waiting, 1905–15.

The Dalberg-Acton family papers are in the care of the Hon. Richard Gerald Acton. One box file of papers, consisting of correspondence, memoranda, etc. relates to the 2nd Lord Acton's diplomatic career, particularly as Consul-General in Zurich, 1917–19. Enquiries should be directed to Lord Acton's daughter, Hon. Mrs Douglas Woodruff, Marcham Priory, nr Abingdon, Berks. Correspondence (1918) can be found in the Hardinge Papers at Cambridge University Library.

ADAIR, Rear-Admiral Thomas Benjamin Stratton (1861–1928)

M.P. (Con.) Shettleston, 1918–22.

ADAM, William Augustus (1865–1940)

M.P. (Con.) Woolwich, Jan–Dec 1910.

It did not prove possible to trace any of Adam's heirs. Frederic Hall & Co., solicitors, of Folkestone, who acted in his estate, were unable to provide any contacts.

ADAMS, David (1871–1943)

M.P. (Lab.) Newcastle West, 1922–3; Consett, 1935–43.

A small collection of papers was placed by David Adams' son in the Tyne and Wear Archives

Department. This consists of articles by and about Adams, certain records of his council work and several press cuttings.

ADAMS, David Morgan (1875–1942)

M.P. (Lab.) Poplar South, 1931–42.

Efforts to contact the widow proved unsuccessful.

ADAMS, (Harold) Richard (1912–   )

M.P. (Lab.) Balham and Tooting, 1945–50; Wandsworth Central, 1950–5.
Lord Commissioner of the Treasury, 1949–51.

ADAMS, (Samuel) Vyvyan Trerice (1900–51)

M.P. (Con.) Leeds West, 1931–45.

The papers of Vyvyan Adams are preserved at BLPES. The collection consists of correspondence; typescripts of speeches and articles; and press cuttings. The chief interest of the collection of correspondence lies in its usefulness as an index of constituency opinion during the 1930s, particularly in view of Adams' opposition to the policy of Appeasement. The bulk of the correspondence dates from 1933, and in addition to letters received, includes copies of Adams' replies to his correspondents. There are however relatively few letters from leading politicians. Adams' career after 1945 is reflected in a collection of private correspondence. Copies of Adams' speeches, including typescripts and notes, and drafts of pamphlets and books by him are further useful indications of his political interests. In addition, Adams preserved a very good series of press-cutting books, (he subscribed to an agency) and these are particularly substantial for the 1930s.

ADAMS, William Thomas (1884–1949)

M.P. (Lab.) Hammersmith South, 1945–9.

No papers have been traced. For full biographical details of his career see *Dictionary of Labour Biography*, Vol. I, p. 11.

ADAMSON, Janet (Jennie) Laurel (1882–1962)

M.P. (Lab.) Dartford, 1938–45; Bexley, 1945–6.
Parliamentary Secretary, Ministry of Pensions, 1945–6.

A very small collection of formal letters of appointment and some press cuttings is retained by Mrs Adamson's daughter, Mrs Kemp, 63 The Ridings, Surbiton, Surrey. Mrs Adamson's other daughter, Mrs H. E. Redgrave, knows of no further material.

ADAMSON, William (1863–1936)

M.P. (Lab.) Fife West, Dec 1910–31.
Secretary of State for Scotland, 1924 and 1929–31.

No collection of papers is known to survive. For details of members of the family approached, see Hazlehurst and Woodland, p. 1.

ADAMSON, William Murdoch (1881–1945)

M.P. (Lab.) Cannock, 1922–31, 1935–45.
Junior Lord of the Treasury, 1941–4.

Adamson's daughters, Mrs H. E. Redgrave and Mrs E. Kemp, know of no relevant papers.

ADDISON, 1st Vt
Christopher Addison (1869–1951)

M.P. (Lib.) Hoxton, Jan 1910–22; (Lab.) Swindon, 1929–31; 1934–5.
Parliamentary Secretary, Board of Education, 1914–15; Ministry of Munitions, 1915–16. Minister of Munitions, 1916–17; Reconstruction, 1917–19. President of the Local Government Board, 1919. Minister of Health, 1919–21. Minister without Portfolio, 1921. Parliamentary Secretary, Ministry of Agriculture and Fisheries, 1929–30. Minister of Agriculture and Fisheries, 1930–1. Secretary of State for Dominion Affairs, 1945–7; for Commonwealth Relations, 1947. Lord Privy Seal, 1947–51. Paymaster-General, 1948–9. Lord President of the Council, 1951.

The papers of Lord Addison at the Bodleian Library, Oxford (ref. Addison Papers), together with letters of condolence on his death (ref. Ms Eng. lett. d. 332) and the diaries of Lady Addison (ref. Reserved Ms 109 1–3) are fully described in Hazlehurst and Woodland, p. 1.

ADKINS, Sir William Ryland Dent (1862–1920)

M.P. (Lib.) Middleton, 1906–23.

Viscount Rochdale, the son of 1st Baron Rochdale, a principal beneficiary of Sir Ryland Adkins' estate, knows of no surviving papers. It was not possible to trace any close relations.

AGNEW, Sir Andrew Noel, 9th Bt (1850–1928)

M.P. (Lib.Un.) Edinburgh South, 1900–6.

Sir Fulque Agnew, Bt, (nephew) knows of no surviving papers. Lady Agnew stated that a list of family papers has been given to the Scottish Record Office, but it seems that no relevant material is among these papers.

AGNEW, Sir George William, 2nd Bt (1852–1941)

M.P. (Lib.) Salford West, 1906–18.

Mr G. K. Agnew (grandson) writes that very little material survived the bombing of the family home, Rougham Manor, in 1940. Some family and estate papers that did survive contain nothing of political importance relating to Sir G. W. Agnew, Bt. These papers have been deposited in Suffolk Record Office (Bury St Edmunds Branch).

AGNEW, Sir Peter Garnett, 1st Bt (1900–   )

M.P. (Con.) Camborne, 1931–50; Worcestershire South, 1955–66.

AILWYN, 1st B
Sir Ailwyn Edward Fellowes (1855–1924)

M.P. (Con.) Huntingdonshire North, 1887–1906.
President of the Board of Agriculture, 1905.

Hazlehurst and Woodland, p.52, record that few papers apart from a volume of speeches have been traced. A scrapbook (1887–1906) can be found in the Cambridgeshire Record Office at Huntingdon.

AINSWORTH, Charles Anderton (1874–1956)

M.P. (Con.) Bury, 1918–35.

Letters of Administration were granted to Ainsworth's widow. It was not possible to trace her, or their two sons and daughter. The solicitors who acted in the estate were unable to provide any further relevant information.

AINSWORTH, Sir John Stirling, 1st Bt (1844–1923)

M.P. (Lib.) Argyllshire, 1903–18.

Ainsworth's grandson, Sir John Ainsworth, Bt, knows of no papers, and believes that none have survived.

AIRD, Sir John, 1st Bt (1833–1911)

M.P. (Con.) Paddington North, 1887–1906.

Sir John's grandson, Sir John Aird, Bt, knows of no relevant papers.

AIREDALE, 1st B
Sir James Kitson (1835–1911)

M.P. (Lib.) Colne Valley, 1892–1907.

There is a small selection of Airedale papers (the remainder being presumed lost) housed in the Archives Department, Sheepscar Library, Leeds LS7 3AP (ACC 1138). This consists of a bundle of letters, 1884–1942, which appear to have been selected for signatures, and a photograph album. There is no trace of the Gladstone letters concerning the 1880 Leeds election which were reputed to have been used by Morley. In addition, three press-cutting books, 1895–1921, have been placed in the reference department of the Sheepscar Library.

AIRLIE, 12th E of
David Lyulph Gore Wolseley Ogilvy, Lord Ogilvy (1893–1968)

Lord in Waiting, 1926–9.
Lord Chamberlain to the Queen (later Queen Mother), 1937–65.

AITCHISON, Lord
Craigie Mason Aitchison (1882–1941)

M.P. (Lab., later Nat.Lab.) Kilmarnock, 1929–33.
Lord Advocate for Scotland, 1929–33.

Aitchison's widow acted as his executor. It was not possible to trace her or their two sons.

AITKEN, Sir (John William) Max, 2nd Bt (1910–   )

M.P. (Con.) Holborn, 1945–50.
Chairman, Beaverbrook Newspapers Ltd.

The Beaverbrook papers now in the House of Lords Record Office may contain relevant information.

AITKEN, Sir (William) Maxwell, 1st Bt, see BEAVERBROOK, 1st B

AITKEN, Sir William Traven (1905–64)

M.P. (Con.) Bury St Edmunds, 1950–64.

The surviving papers of Sir William Aitken, few in number, are in the care of his widow, Hon. Lady Aitken, 47 Phillimore Gardens, London W8.

ALBEMARLE, 8th E of
Arnold Allan Cecil Keppel, Vt Bury (1858–1942)

M.P. (Con.) Birkenhead, 1892–4.
Lord in Waiting, 1922–4.

The 9th Earl of Albemarle states that he knows of no political papers, either of the 8th Earl or of his predecessors.

ALBERY, Sir Irving James (1879–1967)

M.P. (Con.) Gravesend, 1924–5.

Mr Michael Albery (son), 9 Old Square, Lincoln's Inn, London WC2A 3SR, has custody of his father's papers, which include correspondence and a few press cuttings. These chiefly relate to his theatrical interests or to personal matters, and contain few references to political affairs.

ALBU, Austen Harry (1903–)

M.P. (Lab.) Edmonton, 1948–Feb 1974 .
Minister of State, Department of Economic Affairs, 1965–7.

Mr Albu has retained various papers relating to his political career, including press cuttings and correspondence relating to the Socialist League; a similar file relating to the Labour Spain Committee; material relating to discussions held within the Socialist Clarity Group; three box files of correspondence relating to the Control Commission of Germany, 1946–7; various notes for speeches and Fabian pamphlets; and constituency correspondence. Mr Albu has deposited the latter in BLPES.

ALDEN, Sir Percy (1865–1944)

M.P. (Lib.) Tottenham, 1906–18; (Lab.) Tottenham South, 1923–4.

It did not prove possible to contact members of Alden's family. A biography of Alden appears in *Dictionary of Labour Biography* Vol. III, pp. 3–5. Material relating to Alden can be found in the Labour Party archive.

ALDENHAM, 2nd B
Hon. Alban George Henry Gibbs (1846–1936)

M.P. (Con.) City of London, 1892–1906.

Relevant papers may be found in the archives of Anthony Gibbs and Sons Ltd at the Guildhall Library, London. These include various 'family' letters by and to Alban Gibbs and Vicary Gibbs, 1883–1905 (ref. Ms 11021/29 and 30); and a copy out-letter book of Gibbs , mainly relating to business matters, 1874–1936 (ref. Ms 11039); a file of 'private' letters written by Vicary Gibbs from Australian branches of the firm to Alban Gibbs and others, mainly relating to business matters. together with some replies, 1883–4. Gibbs' activities are also extensively recorded in the business archive itself e.g. in the Directors' general copy out-letter books, 1907–35 (ref. Ms 11041/1–6: and the special copy out-letter books, 1881–1922 (ref. Ms 11042/1–2). Further miscellaneous papers can be found in the Hereford Record Office.

ALDINGTON, 1st B
Sir Toby (Austin Richard William) Low (1914–)

M.P. (Con.) Blackpool North, 1945–62.
Parliamentary Secretary, Ministry of Supply, 1951–4. Minister of State, Board of Trade, 1954–7.

Lord Aldington states that he has not yet collected together or analysed his personal records.

ALEXANDER OF HILLSBOROUGH, 1st E
Albert Victor Alexander (1885–1965)

M.P. (Lab. and Co-op.) Sheffield Hillsborough, 1922–31, 1935–50.
Parliamentary Secretary, Board of Trade, 1924. 1st Lord of the Admiralty, 1929–31; 1940–May 1945; August 1945–6. Minister without Portfolio, Oct–Dec 1946. Minister of Defence, 1946–50. Chancellor of the Duchy of Lancaster, 1950–1.

Alexander's papers, at Churchill College, Cambridge, and the papers of his agent, Alderman Dr Albert Ballard, in Sheffield Public Library, are described in Hazlehurst and Woodland, pp. 2–3.

ALEXANDER, Ernest Edward (1872–1946)

M.P. (Con.) Leyton East, 1922–3, 1924–9.

Messrs Stilgoes, solicitors to the executors, were unable to help; and no heirs could be traced.

ALEXANDER, Maurice (1889–1945)

M.P. (Nat.Lib.) Southwark S.E., 1922–3.

Efforts to trace persons named in the will and act of probate proved unsuccessful. Simmonds, Church, Rackman, solicitors, who acted in the estate, were unable to supply any relevant information.

ALEXANDER, Brigadier-General Sir William (1874–1954)

Military career; served European War, 1914–18. Controller of Aircraft Supply and Production, 1917–19; Director General of Purchases, 1919–20.
M.P. (Con.) Glasgow Central, 1923–45.

Efforts to trace the family have been unsuccessful. All personal effects were left to Thornton Properties, St Brelade, Jersey, C.I.

ALINGTON, 2nd B
Humphrey Napier Sturt (1859–1919)

M.P. (Con.) Dorset East, 1891–1904.

The Hon. Mrs G. G. Marten, granddaughter of Lord Alington, knows of no surviving papers.

ALLAN, Sir Henry Spencer Moreton Havelock-, 2nd Bt (1872–1953)

M.P. (Lib.) Bishop Auckland, Jan 1910–18.

Surviving records of the Havelock-Allan family are held in the North Yorkshire County Record Office at Northallerton, and the Durham County Library at Darlington. No papers of the 2nd Baronet are known to exist. Relevant material can be found in the papers of T. A. Pease, 1st Baron Gainford, at Nuffield College, Oxford.

ALLAN, Sir William (1837–1903)

M.P. (Lib.) Gateshead, 1893–1903.

Richardsons, Westgarth & Co. Ltd of Wallsend, the company of which Allan was a director, knows of no relevant information.

ALLEN, Arthur Acland (1868–1939)

M.P. (Lib.) Christchurch, 1906–Jan 1910; Dunbartonshire, Dec 1910–18.

Members of his family believe that no papers survive. See also Charles Peter Allen.

ALLEN, Arthur Cecil (1887–   )

M.P. (Lab.) Bosworth, 1945–59.

Mr Allen says that he retained no political papers.

ALLEN, Charles Peter (1861–1930)

M.P. (Lib.) Stroud, 1900–18.

A small collection of letters, of a largely formal nature, from correspondents such as W. E. Gladstone, H. H. Asquith and Winston Churchill, is in the care of C. P. Allen's daughter, Mrs Spreckley, Holly Cottage, Powick, Worcester. Copies of these papers are available in the Modern Records Centre, University of Warwick Library.

ALLEN, Sir John Sandeman- (1865–1935)

M.P. (Con.) Liverpool West Derby, 1924–35.

Lady Margaret Sandeman-Allen, daughter-in-law of John Sandeman-Allen, knows of no papers.

ALLEN, John Sandeman- (1892–1949)

M.P. (Con.) Birkenhead West, 1931–45.

See above.

ALLEN, Sir Ronald Wilberforce (1889–1936)

M.P. (Lib.) Leicester South, 1923–4.

Wilberforce Allen, the firm of solicitors in which Sir Ronald was a senior partner, had no information regarding papers. Sir Ronald's executor died some years previously, and the firm had no contact with his family.

ALLEN, Sydney Scholefield (1898–1974)

M.P. (Lab.) Crewe, 1945–Feb 1974.

Scholefield Allen retained few of his papers. All that survives with his widow, of 1 Kara Lodge, 14 Newton Grove, Bedford Park, London W4, is a small collection of letters and other items that he considered of particular personal interest. Mrs Scholefield Allen has kept a diary which comments on current political events but this is not currently available.

ALLEN, William (1870–1945)

M.P. (Lib.) Newcastle-under-Lyme, 1892–1900; (Con.) Burslem, 1931–5.

Allen's son and a solicitor acted as his executors. It did not prove possible to trace either of these for further information.

ALLEN, William Edward David (1901–73)*

M.P. (Ulster Un., later New Party) Belfast West, 1929–31.

Mr D. S. Bruce-Edwards, Whitechurch House, Cappagh, Co. Waterford, former secretary of

W. E. D. Allen, states that in accordance with instructions in Allen's will, all his political and personal papers were destroyed on his death. His literary material, however, was bequeathed to the Bodleian Library, Oxford.

ALLEN, Sir William James (1866–1947)*

M.P. (Un.) Armagh North, 1917–22; Armagh, 1922–47.

ALLENDALE, 1st Vt
Wentworth Canning Blackett Beaumont (1860–1923)

M.P. (Lib.) Hexham, 1895–1907.
Vice Chamberlain, H. M. Household, 1905–7. Captain of the Yeomen of the Guard, 1907–11. Lord in Waiting, 1911–16.

See below.

ALLENDALE, 2nd Vt
Hon. Wentworth Henry Canning Beaumont (1890–1956)

Lord in Waiting, 1931–2; 1937–45; 1954–6.

The present (3rd) Viscount Allendale says that apart from a few personal photographs, he has no papers relating to either the 1st or the 2nd Viscount, and believes that none were kept.

ALLERTON, 1st B
William Lauries Jackson (1840–1917)

M.P. (Con.) Leeds North, 1880–1902.
Financial Secretary, Treasury, 1885–6 and 1886–91. Chief Secretary for Ireland, 1891–2.

The present (3rd) Lord Allerton knows of no papers.

ALLHUSEN, (Augustus) Henry Eden (1867–1925)

M.P. (Con.) Salisbury, 1897–1900; Hackney Central, 1900–6.

Mrs M. Stewart-Mackenzie (daughter), Westburton Place, Pulborough, Sussex RH20 1HD has two albums of press cuttings relating to her father's two victorious election campaigns. The bulk of the papers was disposed of by Mrs Allhusen in 1925.

ALLIGHAN, Garry (b. 1900)

M.P. (Lab.) Gravesend, 1945–7.

ALLSOPP, Hon. George Higginson (1846–1907)

M.P. (Con.) Worcester, 1885–1906.

Allsopp's nephew, Mr Samuel Allsopp, believes that no papers survived.

ALNESS, 1st B
Robert Munro (1868–1955)

M.P. (Lib.) Wick Burghs, 1910–18; Roxburghshire and Selkirkshire, 1918–22.
Secretary of State for Scotland, 1916–22.

Lady Alness (widow) knows of no papers. See Hazlehurst and Woodland, p. 111.

ALPASS, Joseph Herbert (1873–1969)

M.P. (Lab.) Bristol Central, 1929–31, Thornbury, 1945–50.

Mr H. J. Hampden Alpass (son), Coombe Dingle House, 95 Coombe Lane, Bristol BS9 2AR, has a small collection of material relating to his father's career, including press cuttings and occasional letters, largely of a formal nature.

ALPORT, Baron
Cuthbert James McCall Alport (1912–   )

Director, Conservative Political Centre, 1945–50.
M.P. (Con.) Colchester, 1950–61.
Assistant Postmaster General, 1955–7. Parliamentary Under-Secretary, Commonwealth Relations, 1957–9. Minister of State, Commonwealth Relations, 1959–61.High Commissioner, Federation of Rhodesia and Nyasaland, 1961–3.

Lord Alport says that he proposes to leave his papers to the Skinners' Library, City University.

ALSTEAD, Robert (1873–1946)

M.P. (Lib.) Altrincham, 1923–4.

Professor Stanley Alstead (son) believes that no relevant papers have survived.

ALTHORP, 1st Vt, see SPENCER, 6th E

ALTRINCHAM, 1st B
Sir Edward William Maclean Grigg (1879–1955)

M.P. (Lib.) Oldham, 1922–5; (Nat.Con.) Altrincham, 1933–45.
Governor, Kenya, 1925–31.
Parliamentary Secretary, Ministry of Information, 1939–40. Financial Secretary, War Office, 1940. Joint Parliamentary Under-Secretary, War Office, 1940–2. Minister Resident, Middle East, 1944–5.

Hazlehurst and Woodland, pp. 66–7, give details of the papers which survive with Mr John Grigg, Lord Altrincham's son, 32 Dartmouth Row, London SE10. Copies of many of these papers are available at the Bodleian Library, Oxford, and at the Douglas Library, Queens University, Kingston, Ontario.

ALVERSTONE, 1st Vt
Sir Richard Everard Webster, 1st Bt (1842–1915)

M.P. (Con.) Launceston, 1885; Isle of Wight, 1885–1900.
Attorney-General, 1885–Feb 1886; Aug 1886–92; 1895–1900.

It appears that no papers survive. For details of persons contacted see Hazlehurst and Woodland, p. 148.

ALVINGHAM, 1st B
Robert Daniel Thwaites Yerburgh (1889–1955)

M.P. (Con.) Dorset South, 1922–9.

Efforts to contact the present (2nd) Lord Alvingham were not successful.

AMBROSE, Robert (b. 1855)*

M.P. (Irish Nat.) Mayo West, 1893–Jan 1910.

AMERY, (H.) Julian (1919–   )

M.P. (Con.) Preston, 1950–66; Brighton Pavilion, 1969–
Parliamentary Under-Secretary, War Office, 1957–8; Colonial Office, 1958–60. Secretary of State for Air, 1960–2. Minister of Aviation, 1962–4; Public Building and Works, Jun–Oct 1970. Minister for Housing and Construction, Department of the Environment, 1970–2. Minister of State, Foreign and Commonwealth Office, 1972–4.

AMERY, Leopold Charles Maurice Stennett (1873–1955)

M.P. (Con.) Birmingham South, 1911–18; Birmingham Sparkbrook, 1918–45.
Parliamentary Under-Secretary, Colonies, 1919–21. Parliamentary and Financial Secretary, Admiralty, 1921–2. 1st Lord of the Admiralty, 1922–4. Secretary of State for the Dominions, 1925–9; for India, 1940–5.

L. S. Amery's papers, in the care of his son, Rt.Hon. Julian Amery, M.P., 112 Eaton Square, London SW1, are described in Hazlehurst and Woodland, p. 3, and consist of c. 230 box files of papers and 40 volumes of diary.

AMMON, 1st B
Charles George Ammon (1875–1960)

M.P. (Lab.) Camberwell North, 1922–31, 1935–44.
Parliamentary and Financial Secretary, Admiralty, 1924, 1929–31. Government Chief Whip, House of Lords, 1945–9.

Lord Ammon's papers have been deposited in Hull University Library. The collection includes correspondence dating from the late nineteenth century; diaries for various years in the 1920s, 1930s and 1950s; early drafts of Ammon's autobiography; press cuttings, c. 1914 to the 1950s; election literature; details of trips to Africa, Canada and China; papers relating to the National Dock Labour Board; and various articles and lectures. Ammon's diaries, 1938–9, 1947, and scrapbooks containing press cuttings and photographs are available in Southwark Central Reference Library, Kennington District Library, Walworth Road, London SE17.

AMULREE, 1st B
Sir William Warrender Mackenzie (1860–1942)

Secretary of State for Air, 1930–1.

A small collection of papers - correspondence, 1925–37, and desk diaries - has been deposited in the Bodleian Library, Oxford (ref. Dep. c 384–391, d. 07), and is described in Hazlehurst and Woodland, p. 98.

AMWELL, 1st B
Frederick Montague (1876–1966)

M.P. (Lab.) Islington West, 1923–31, 1935–47.
Parliamentary Under-Secretary, Air, 1929–31. Parliamentary Secretary, Ministry of Transport, 1940–1; Ministry of Aircraft Production, 1941–2.

Private Office papers (AVIA 9) can be found at the Public Record Office. No other information was available.

ANCASTER, 2nd E of
Gilbert Heathcote-Drummond-Willoughby, Lord Willoughby de Eresby (1867–1951)

M.P. (Con.) Horncastle, 1894–1911.
Parliamentary Secretary, Ministry of Agriculture, 1921–2. Lord Great Chamberlain of England, 1937–50.

The 3rd Earl of Ancaster knows of no relevant papers. The Ancaster family papers which are deposited in Lincolnshire Archives Office contain occasional references to the 2nd Earl's political career. The permission of the present Earl is necessary for use of any records later than 1910.

ANCASTER, 3rd E of
Gilbert James Heathcote-Drummond-Willoughby, Lord Willoughby de Eresby (1907–)

M.P. (Con.) Rutland and Stamford, 1935–50.

Rt. Hon. the Earl of Ancaster states that he retained no papers relating to his parliamentary career.

ANDERSON, Lord
Andrew Macbeth Anderson (1862–1936)

M.P. (Lib.) Ayrshire North Jan 1910–11.
Solicitor-General, Scotland, 1911–13.

Lord Anderson's son, Mr A. M. Anderson, says that his father left no relevant papers regarding his career.

ANDERSON, Sir Alan Garrett (1877–1952)

M.P. (Con.) City of London, 1935–40.
Controller of Railways, Ministry of War Transport, 1941–5; and Chairman of Railway Executive.

A collection of papers is held at the Public Record Office (PRO 30/68). These consist largely of papers relating to Anderson's work on government committees. Further material survives in the care of Sir Alan's son, Sir Colin Anderson, Admiral's House, Hampstead Grove, London, NW3. The papers cover a wide range of subjects, including business affairs, his parliamentary career, educational matters, railways, food supply, hospitals, the Bank of England and personal affairs.

ANDERSON, Alexander (1888–1954)

M.P. (Lab.) Motherwell, 1945–54.

ANDERSON, Frank (1889–1959)

M.P. (Lab.) Whitehaven, 1935–59.

The career of Frank Anderson is described in *Dictionary of Labour Biography*, Vol. I, pp. 24–5. This mentions Anderson's extensive collection of correspondence. Efforts to trace the present whereabouts of these papers proved unsuccessful. The Public Library and Museum, Lowther Street, Whitehaven, Cumbria, has a collection of press cuttings relating to Anderson's work as M.P. for Whitehaven.

ANDERSON, George Knox (1854–1941)

M.P. (Con.) Canterbury, 1918.

Enquiries should be directed to Anderson's daughter, Mrs P. Cobb, who lives in Maidstone, Kent.

ANDERSON, Sir John, see WAVERLEY, 1st Vt

ANDERSON, William Crawford (1877–1919)

M.P. (Lab.) Sheffield Attercliffe, 1914–19.

A biographical sketch of Anderson is included in the *Dictionary of Labour Biography*, Vol. II, pp. 11–15. This lists various sources, but no substantial collection of papers seems to have survived.

ANDREWS, Joseph Ormond (1873–1909)

M.P. (Lib.) Barkston Ash, 1905–6.

ANGELL, Sir (Ralph) Norman (1874–1967)

Journalist and publicist.
M.P. (Lab.) Bradford North, 1929–31.

The personal papers and library of Sir Norman Angell are deposited at Ball State University, Muncie, Indiana, U.S.A. The personal collection includes ·correspondence, manuscripts, and newspaper articles, and may be consulted on application to the Department of History. Miscellaneous letters and papers, including correspondence with Gilbert Murray and W. A. White, and mss of articles and essays are available in Columbia University Library, New York.

ANNAND, James (1843–1906)

M.P. (Lib.) Aberdeenshire East, 1906 (elected Jan, died 6 Feb).

Annand's son, Mr J. B. Annand, Little Brooms, Rotherfield, nr Crowborough, Sussex, has in his possession four books of press cuttings for the period 1895–1906. No correspondence has survived, apart from a few letters of condolence written after James Annand's death.

ANNESLEY, 1st B, see VALENTIA, 11th Vt

ANSON, Sir William Reynell, 3rd Bt (1843–1914)

M.P. (Con.) Oxford University, 1899–1914.
Parliamentary Secretary, Board of Education, 1902–5.

The Anson family papers are in the care of Sir Peter Anson, Bt, Rosefield, Rowledge, Farnham, Surrey. However, no papers relating to the career of Sir William Anson appear to have survived in this collection. At the Public Record Office, the Board of Education Private Office Papers (Ed. 24) contain some papers of Sir William Anson, 1902–5.

ANSTRUTHER, Henry Torrens (1860–1926)

M.P. (Lib.Un.) St Andrew's District, 1886–1903.
Junior Lord of the Treasury, 1895–1903.

Anstruther's grandson knows of no papers, and knows of none in the care of his family.

APPLIN, Reginald Vincent Kempenfelt (1869–1957)

M.P. (Con.) Enfield, 1924–9, 1931–5.

It proved impossible to trace Applin's widow, and the Executor and Trustee Department of Lloyds Bank Ltd, who acted in his estate, had no relevant information.

APSLEY, Lord
Allen Algernon Bathurst (1895–1942)

M.P. (Con.) Southampton, 1922–9; Bristol Central, 1931–42.

A number of Lord Apsley's papers are in the care of his eldest son, Rt. Hon. Earl Bathurst. However, the bulk of the papers relating to Lord Apsley's political activities are in the care of his other son, Hon. George Bathurst. Access to these papers is restricted.

APSLEY, Lady
Violet Emily Mildred Bathurst (d. 1966)

M.P. (Con.) Bristol Central, 1943–5.

Lady Apsley's papers, roughly sorted into chronological order, are in the care of her son, Hon. George Bathurst. Access to these papers is restricted.

ARBUTHNOT, Gerald Archibald (1872–1916)

M.P. (Con.) Burnley, Jan–Dec 1910.

It did not prove possible to contact the descendants of executors mentioned in the will and act of probate.

ARBUTHNOT, Sir John Sinclair Wemyss, 1st Bt. (1912–)

M.P. (Con.) Dover, 1950–64.

Sir John Arbuthnot has preserved a certain amount of material, including a number of letters from leading politicians, and ecclesiastical and business figures; a full set of press cuttings from 1935; and records of a more formal nature.

ARCHDALE, Sir Edward Mervyn, 1st Bt (1853–1943)*

M.P. (Con.) Fermanagh North, 1898–1903, 1916–21.
Minister of Agriculture and Commerce, Northern Ireland, 1921–5; of Agriculture, 1925–33.

Certain papers relating to Archdale are deposited in the Northern Ireland Public Record Office. These include family memoirs (DI/639), a letter book and 1885 agent's correspondence (D1390/26/7); various documents relating to electoral preparations, 1899–1900 (D1390/26/1–17); political correspondence 1917, 1918 (D627/431, 432); and various other individual items.

ARCHIBALD, 1st B
George Archibald (1898–1975)

Captain, Yeomen of the Guard, and Government Deputy Chief Whip, 1951.

Lord Archibald stated that he retained no papers.

ARKWRIGHT, Sir John Stanhope (1872–1954)

M.P. (Con.) Hereford, 1900–12.

A collection of papers survives in the care of Hereford Record Office and comprises correspondence, 1907–12; various items concerning parliamentary business; political pamphlets; and papers relating to various political clubs and societies. For the period of World War 1 there are papers and correspondence dealing with food production, agricultural problems and recruitment of forces, notes on current affairs, and newspaper cuttings.

ARMAGHDALE, 1st B
Sir John Brownlee Lonsdale, 1st Bt (1850–1924)*

M.P. (Con.) Mid Armagh, 1900–18.
Hon. Secretary, Irish Unionist Party, 1901–16; Chairman, 1916–18.

Certain relevant papers are deposited in the Northern Ireland Public Record Office. Amongst these are records of the firm of Joshua E. Peel & Son, solicitors, including letter books of Armaghdale's political agent, 1886–1916.

ARMITAGE, Robert (1866–1944)

M.P. (Lib.) Leeds North, 1906–18; Leeds Central, 1918–22.

Simpson Curtis & Co., solicitors, of Leeds, who acted in the estate, had no relevant information and the Yorkshire Archaeological Society and Leeds City Library similarly had no information. Records of the Leeds Liberal Federation and the Yorkshire Liberal Federation for the relevant period are deposited in Leeds Archives Department.

ARMSTRONG, William Charles Heaton- (1853–1917)

M.P. (Lib.) Sudbury, 1906–17.

Enquiries should be directed to Mr T. M. R. Heaton-Armstrong (grandson), Couligarton, Aberfoyle, via Stirling, Scotland.

ARNOLD, 1st B
Sydney Arnold (1878–1945)

M.P. (Lib.) Holmfirth, 1912–18; Penistone, 1918–21.
Parliamentary Under-Secretary, Colonies, Jan–Nov 1924. Paymaster-General, 1929–Mar 1931.

Hazlehurst and Woodland, p. 5, describe a very small collection in the care of Arnold's nephew, Gerald Arnold Esq., c/o Messrs Seal Arnold & Co., Cavendish House, 30 Pall Mall, Manchester M60 2QX.

ARNOTT, John (1871–1942)

M.P. (Lab.) Hull S.W., 1929–31.

J. H. Milner & Son, solicitors of Leeds, who acted in the estate, had no information regarding Arnott. He was one time Lord Mayor of Leeds, but the Leeds Archives Department had no information.

ARROL, Sir William (1839–1913)

M.P. (Lib.Un.) Ayrshire, 1895–1906.

Contact was established with Sir William Arrol & Co. Ltd, Engineers, 85 Dunn Street, Glasgow G40. They retained contact with members of Arrol's family. However, no papers came to light.

ARUNDEL, E. of, see NORFOLK

ASHBOURNE, 1st B
Edward Gibson (1837–1913)*

M.P. (Con.) Dublin University, 1875–85.
Attorney-General, Ireland, 1877–80. Lord Chancellor, Ireland, 1886, 1886–92, 1895–1905.

A considerable collection of papers, deposited in the House of Lords Record Office, and including personal and legal papers, election and other political material, and diaries, is described in Hazlehurst and Woodland, pp. 60–1.

ASHBY ST LEDGERS, see WIMBORNE, 1st Vt

ASHCOMBE, 2nd B
Hon. Henry Cubitt (1867–1947)

M.P. (Con.) Reigate, 1892–1906.

Reigate Conservative records, some dating from 1869, have been deposited in Surrey Record Office.

ASHER, Alexander (1835–1905)

M.P. (Lib.) Elgin Burghs, 1881–1905.
Solicitor-General for Scotland, 1881–5, 1886, 1892–4.

ASHFIELD, 1st B
Sir Albert Henry Stanley (1874–1948)

M.P. (Con.) Ashton-under-Lyne, 1916–20.
President of the Board of Trade, 1916–19.

Hazlehurst and Woodland, p. 138, were unable to trace any papers.

ASHLEY, Wilfrid William, see MOUNT TEMPLE, 1st B

ASHTON OF HYDE, 1st B
Thomas Gair Ashton (1855–1933)

M.P. (Lib.) Hyde, 1885–6; Luton, 1895–1911.

The present (2nd) Lord Ashton of Hyde says he knows of no papers relating to his father's career.

ASHTON, Sir Hubert (1898–   )

M.P. (Con.) Chelmsford, 1950–64.

No information on papers was available. Certain records of the Chelmsford Conservative Association dating from 1924 have been retained by the Association.

ASKE, Sir Robert William, 1st Bt (1872–1954)

M.P. (Lib., later Lib. Nat.) Newcastle East, 1923–4, 1929–45.

Neither Sir Robert's son, Rev. Sir Conan Aske, Bt, nor his daughter, Miss Audrey Aske, know of any surviving papers.

ASSHETON, Ralph, see CLITHEROE, 1st B

ASQUITH, Herbert Henry, see OXFORD AND ASQUITH, 1st E of

ASTBURY, Frederick Wolfe (1872–1954)

M.P. (Con.) Salford West, 1918–23, 1924–9, 1931–5.

Mrs Gwendolyn MacClancy, ward of F. W. Astbury, knows of no papers.

ASTBURY, Sir John Meir (1860–1939)

M.P. (Lib.) Southport, 1906–Jan 1910.

Sir John Astbury's stepdaughter, Mrs H. Hunter-Rodwell, knows of no papers and believes that none have survived.

ASTOR, 2nd Vt
Hon. Waldorf Astor (1879–1952)

M.P. (Con.) Plymouth, Dec 1910–19.
Parliamentary Secretary, Ministry of Food, 1918–19; Local Government Board, 1919–21.

Lord Astor's papers are deposited in Reading University Library. They include correspondence files, 1902–52; papers relating to Cliveden, 1893–1952; press cuttings and other records relating to Plymouth, 1911–52; Chatham House papers, 1930–53; Christian Science correspondence, 1920–51; and papers on religion, 1922–51. Until 1982 the permission of the Astor Trustees is necessary for access to these papers; enquiries should be directed to the archivist at Reading University Library.

ASTOR, 3rd Vt
William Waldorf Astor (1907–66)

M.P. (Con.) Fulham East, 1935–45; High Wycombe, 1951–2.

No information on papers was available.

ASTOR, Viscountess
Nancy Witcher Astor (1879–1964)

M.P. (Con.) Plymouth Sutton, 1919–45.

The papers of Lady Astor - a substantial collection - are deposited in Reading University Library. They include correspondence and various other papers, and cover the period 1900–64. Amongst the papers is a collection of political papers and correspondence, 1919–45; material relating to nursery schools, 1931–64; general papers, including material on Christian Science, World War I; letters of condolence on the death of Lord Astor, 1952; family papers, 1906–63; papers relating to American relatives, 1907–46; letters from 'Eminent people', 1905–60 (including letters from the Royal Family, A. J. Balfour, J. M. Barrie, Hilaire Belloc, Lord Curzon, Geoffrey Dawson, J. L. Garvin, T. E. Lawrence, Sean O'Casey, G. B. and Charlotte Shaw, etc.); and sundry papers, 1919–59, which include non-Parliamentary speeches, articles and messages, address books and diaries, the draft of an autobiography, papers relating to Royal visits and entertainment, various publications and press cuttings.

ASTOR OF HEVER, 1st B
Hon. John Jacob Astor (1886–1971)

Chief Proprietor of *The Times*, 1922–66.
M.P. (Con.) Dover, 1922–45.

Such personal papers of Lord Astor as survive are in the care of his family. Enquiries should be directed to the present (2nd) Lord Astor of Hever. Two boxes of Astor's papers, one of which includes appointment diaries, 1944–62, are retained in the archive of *The Times* (see *Sources*, Vol. 1, p. 258).

ASTOR, Hon. Michael Langhorne (1916–)

M.P. (Con.) Surrey East. 1945–51.

Mr Michael Astor states that he has kept no papers relating to his period in Parliament.

ATHOLL, 8th D of
John George Stewart-Murray, M of Tullibardine (1871–1942)

M.P. (Con.) Perthshire West, Jan 1910–17.
Lord Chamberlain, 1921–2.

See below.

ATHOLL, Katharine Marjory, Duchess of (1874–1960)

M.P. (Con.) Kinross and West Perthshire 1923–38.

Parliamentary Secretary, Board of Educaton, 1924–9.

The Blair Atholl papers have been listed by the NRA (Scotland) to whom enquiries should be directed. The papers of Katharine, Duchess of Atholl include correspondence as Parliamentary Secretary to the Board of Education, 1924–9. There is also considerable material on Scottish Home Rule, 1920–35; Indian affairs 1933–7; and on Conservative organisation, 1938–9. There is also material on Romania. Czechoslovakia and the Little Entente, 1936–9. There is much constituency material, including minutes of constituency meetings. Correspondence on the Spanish Civil War also figures largely, with letters from A. D. Lindsay, Philip Noel Baker and Lords Lloyd, Cranborne and Plymouth. There is also a mass of family and personal letters. For further details, see NRA 19071.

ATKEY, Sir Albert Reuben (1867–1947)

M.P. (Con.) Nottingham Central, 1918–22.

Papers are deposited in Nottingham Central Library, South Sherwood Street, Nottingham N61 4DA, and consist of Atkey's correspondence as an M.P., 1918–22; papers as Lord Mayor of Nottingham, 1929–30; records of Atkey's bicycle and motor car business, 1898–1948; and personal papers, including diaries (1885, 1936–45), correspondence and photographs, 1885–1947.

ATKINSON, 1st B
John Atkinson (1844–1932)

M.P. (Con.) Londonderry North, 1895–1905.
Solicitor-General, Ireland, 1889–92. Attorney-General, Ireland, 1892, 1895–1905.

It did not prove possible to contact the widows of Atkinson's sons, nor any other surviving members of the family.

ATKINSON, Hon. Sir Cyril (1874–1967)

M.P. (Con.) Altrincham, 1924–33.

Sir Cyril's son, Rt. Hon. Sir Fenton Atkinson, knows of no surviving papers.

ATTENBOROUGH, Walter Annis (1850–1932)

M.P. (Con.) Bedford, Jan–Dec 1910.

Messrs Stanley Attenborough and Sons, solicitors in the estate, had no relevant information.

ATTEWELL, Humphrey Cooper (1894–1972)

M.P. (Lab.) Harborough, 1945–50.

ATTLEE, 1st E
Clement Richard Attlee (1883–1967)

M.P. (Lab.) Limehouse, 1922–50; Walthamstow West, 1950–5.
Parliamentary Under-Secretary for War, 1924. Chancellor of the Duchy of Lancaster, 1930–1.
Postmaster General, 1931. Lord Privy Seal, 1940–2. Secretary of State, Dominion Affairs,
1942–3. Lord President of the Council, 1943–5. Deputy Prime Minister, 1942–5. Prime
Minister, 1945–51.

Papers at University College, Oxford, Churchill College, Cambridge, and in the care of Mr Kenneth Harris, are described in Hazlehurst and Woodland, pp. 6–7.

AUSTIN, 1st B
Sir Herbert Austin (1866–1941)

M.P. (Con.) Birmingham King's Norton, 1918–24.

Lord Austin's son-in-law, Colonel A. C. R. Waite, believes that no papers have survived.

AUSTIN, Herschel Lewis (1911–)

M.P. (Lab.) Stretford, 1945–50.

AUSTIN, Sir John, 1st Bt (1824–1906)

M.P. (Lib.) Osgoldcross, 1886–1906.

Neither Sir John's grandchildren nor his great-grandchildren knew of any surviving papers.

AVON, 1st E of
Sir (Robert) Anthony Eden (1897–)

M.P. (Con.) Warwick and Leamington, 1923–57.
Parliamentary Under-Secretary, Foreign Affairs, 1931–3. Lord Privy Seal, 1933–5. Minister
without Portfolio for League of Nations Affairs, 1935. Secretary of State for Foreign Affairs,
1935–8, 1940–5, 1951–5. Secretary of State for Dominion Affairs, 1939–40; for War,
May–Dec 1940. Prime Minister, 1955–7.

Lord Avon will eventually deposit his papers in Birmingham University Library. See Hazlehurst
and Woodland, p. 49. Private Office papers (1936–45), now at the Foreign and Commonwealth
Office, will be made available at the Public Record Office.

AWBERY, Stanley Stephen (1888–1969)

M.P. (Lab.) Bristol Central, 1945–64.

A collection of diaries, letters, papers, press cuttings and articles, c. 1908–68, has been deposited in the Glamorgan County Record Office. The diaries consist of numerous appointments diaries, 1920–68, and a full diary for 1939–45 covering Awbery's work as Port Labour Inspector for South Wales Ports, 1941–2, and his period as prospective parliamentary candidate for Bristol Central (1940–5). Letters and papers include material relating to Labour Party selection conferences at Forest of Dean (1929), Ashton-under-Lyne (1931); the Campaign for Moral Re-armament (c. 1958), and the Ambatielos (Greek prisoners) affair (1963). Correspondents include E. Bevin, A. Deakin, Stafford Cripps, Dom Mintoff. Awbery's career as M.P., is well covered, with his visits to Malaysia, E. Germany, Algeria, as a member of Parliamentary delegations, especially prominent. There is also a collection of election addresses and cuttings for Bristol c. 1945–59. The archive also includes Labour Party and I.L.P. ephemera from the 1908–26 period, various articles on both labour and local history written by Awbery, and a collection of photographs. Correspondence on colonial affairs can be found in the Fabian Colonial Bureau papers at Rhodes House Library, Oxford.

AYLES, Walter Henry (1879–1953)

M.P. (Lab.) Bristol North, 1923–4; 1929–31; Southall, 1945–50; Hayes and Harlington, 1950–3.

AYLESTONE, 1st B
Herbert William Bowden (1905–   )

M.P. (Lab.) Leicester South, 1945–50; Leicester. S.W., 1950–67.
Assistant Government Whip, 1949–50. Lord Commissioner of the Treasury, 1950–1. Opposition Chief Whip, 1955–64. Lord President of the Council and Leader of the House of Commons, 1964–6. Secretary of State, Commonwealth Affairs, 1966–7.
Chairman, Independent Broadcasting Authority, 1967–75.

Lord Aylestone has retained many of his papers but these are not currently available.

BACON, Baroness
Alice Martha Bacon (1911–   )

M.P. (Lab.) Leeds N.E., 1945–55; Leeds S.E., 1955–70.
Minister of State, Home Office, 1964–7; Department of Education and Science, 1967–70.

Baroness Bacon destroyed many of her papers. The remainder, consisting of unsorted private papers, correspondence, diaries and press cuttings, she intends to leave to the Library of the University of Leeds.

BAGLEY, Edward Albert Ashton (1876–1961)

M.P. (Con.) Farnworth, 1918–22.

Mr J. E. Risebrook, executor to Bagley, states that his widow, who died in 1972, destroyed all his papers and records shortly after his death in 1961.

BAGOT, 4th B
William Bagot (1857–1932)

Lord in Waiting, 1895–1901.

The Bagot papers, at Levens Hall, Kendal, contain no relevant material.

BAGOT, Sir Josceline FitzRoy, 1st Bt.[1] (1854–1913)

M.P. (Con.) Westmorland South, 1892–1906; Kendal, Jan 1910–13.

The Bagot family papers are housed at Levens Hall, nr. Kendal, Cumbria. It seems, however, that few papers relate directly to the activities of Josceline FitzRoy Bagot or his wife Theodosia Bagot, who actively supported her husband in his election campaigns. Several volumes of press cuttings do survive and these contain references to Bagot's career.

1 Josceline Bagot died before the passing under the Great Seal of the Patent of Baronetage and therefore never used his title.

BAILEY, Eric Alfred George Shackleton (1905–   )

M.P. (Con.) Manchester Gorton, 1931–5.

Contact with Mr Bailey, who was living in Australia, was not established.

BAILEY, Sir James (1840–1910)

M.P. (Con.) Walworth, 1895–1906.

Information available in the will and act of probate was not sufficient to enable relatives to be contacted.

BAILLIE, Sir Adrian William Maxwell, 6th Bt (1898–1947)

M.P. (Con.) Linlithgow, 1931–5; Tonbridge, 1937–45.

Sir Adrian Baillie's son, Sir G. G. H. Baillie, Bt, states that he has no papers relating to his father's political career.

BAIN, James Robert (1851–1913)

M.P. (Con.) Egremont, 1900–6.

Messrs Helder, Roberts & Co., solicitors, who acted in the estate, had no relevant information.

BAIRD, John (1906–65)

M.P. (Lab.) Wolverhampton East, 1945–50; Wolverhampton N.E., 1950–64.

Mrs Baird (widow) knows of no relevant papers. Relevant minute books of the Wolverhampton Labour Party are in the care of Professor G. Jones at the London School of Economics.

BAIRD, John George Alexander (1854–1917)

M.P. (Con.) Glasgow Central, 1886–1906.

Mrs Edith Brown Lindsay (daughter), Colstoun, Haddington, Scotland EH41 4PA, believes that no papers survive; and this was confirmed by other members of the family.

BAIRD, Sir John Lawrence, 2nd Bt, see STONEHAVEN, 1st Vt

BAKER, Francis Edward Noel- (1920–   )

M.P. (Lab.) Brentford and Chiswick, 1944–50; Swindon, 1955–68.

Mr Francis Noel-Baker has retained a large amount of diaries and papers dating from 1945. These are at his home in Greece, and will in due course be used in a book by him.

BAKER, Harold Trevor (1877–1960)

M.P. (Lib.) Accrington, Jan 1910–18.
Financial Secretary to the War Office, 1912–13.

It is believed that Baker's papers were destroyed by his sister.

BAKER, Sir John (1828–1909)

M.P. (Lib.) Portsmouth, 1892–1900, 1906–9.

It is believed that no papers survive.

BAKER, John (1867–1939)

M.P. (Lab.) Wolverhampton Bilston, 1924–31.

Messrs Russell Jones & Walker, solicitors, who acted in the estate, were unable to provide any family contacts. The Iron and Steel Trades Confederation (of which Baker was for many years an official), Swinton House, 324 Gray's Inn Road, London WC1X 8DD, has a small file of papers relating to Baker's work as a parliamentary candidate and M.P., including documents relating to election expenses, agents reports, notes on campaigns, etc.

BAKER, Joseph Allen (1852–1918)

M.P. (Lib.) Finsbury East, 1906–18.

Joseph Baker's son, Rt. Hon. Philip Noel-Baker, believes that all papers were destroyed during World War II.

BAKER, Peter Arthur David (1921–   )

M.P. Con.) Norfolk South, 1950–4.

Peter Baker was expelled from the House of Commons on 17 December, 1954. No information on papers was forthcoming.

BAKER, Philip J. Noel- (1889–   )

M.P. (Lab.) Coventry, 1929–31; Derby, 1936–50; Derby South, 1950–70.
Parliamentary Secretary, Ministry of War Transport, 1942–5. Minister of State, Foreign Office, 1945–6. Secretary of State for Air, 1946–7; Commonwealth Relations, 1947–50. Minister of Fuel and Power, 1950–1.

Hazlehurst and Woodland, p. 8, state that a large collection of papers remains with Mr Noel-Baker. The material is not open for inspection. League of Nations correspondence (1918–19) is available at the Public Record Office (FO 800/249). Private Office papers (1950–1) will be placed in the Public Record Office.

BAKER, Sir Randolf Littlehales, 4th Bt (1879–1959)

M.P. (Con.) Dorset North, Jan 1910–18.

Sir Randolf's daughter, Mrs W. H. Gibson Fleming, Ranston, Blandford, Dorset, has a small collection of letters written by her father. These date from the World War I period and largely consist of letters to members of his family (particularly his aunt) written from the Western Front. Also surviving is a small folder of North Dorset election literature, 1910.

BAKER, Walter John (1876–1930)

M.P. (Lab.) Bristol East, 1923–30.
Assistant General Secretary, Union of Post Office Workers.

Efforts to contact members of Baker's family proved unsuccessful. The Union of Post Office Workers has a bulky file of material relating to his parliamentary work on the cable and wireless organisation of the 1920s. Details of U.P.W. papers can be found in *Sources*, Vol. 1, p. 270.

BALCARRES, Lord, see CRAWFORD AND BALCARRES

BALDOCK, John Markham (1915–)

M.P. (Con.) Harborough, 1950–9.

Leicestershire Record Office has an important collection of Constituency Association records (*Sources*, Vol. 1, p. 67).

BALDWIN OF BEWDLEY, 1st E
Stanley Baldwin (1867–1947)

M.P. (Con.) Worcestershire West, 1908–18; Bewdley, 1918–37.
Joint Financial Secretary, Treasury, 1917–21. President of the Board of Trade, 1921–2. Chancellor of the Exchequer, 1922–3. Prime Minister, 1923–4, 1924–9, 1935–7. Lord President of the Council, 1931–5.

The bulk of Baldwin's papers is held in Cambridge University Library. Hazlehurst and Woodland, pp. 8–9, describe this collection and the other personal papers which remained with the family at Bushey House, Apperley, Glos.

BALDWIN OF BEWDLEY, 2nd E
Oliver Ridsdale Baldwin, Viscount Corvedale (1899–1958)

M.P. (Lab.) Dudley, 1929–31; Paisley, 1945–7.
Governor and C-in-C., Leeward Islands, 1948–50.

A collection of Earl Baldwin's papers is retained by Mr Richard Payne, The Giffords, Crowmarsh, Wallingford, Berks. It covers most aspects of Baldwin's interests and political activities. A substantial part of the papers concerns Baldwin's long-standing interest in the affairs of Armenia (he was a Lieutenant-Colonel in the Armenian army in the Russo-Armenian War of 1921), and includes letters from members of the Armenian resistance, correspondence with government departments, and an interesting typescript note by Baldwin describing his undercover work on Armenia in the early years of World War II. Baldwin's similar interest in the 'Assyrian Christian' problem of Northern Mesopotamia (Iraq) in the early 1920s is also reflected by correspondence with Agha Petros and other resistance leaders, and with government ministers. Another small group of correspondence and papers covers his parliamentary activities and includes letters from many prominent politicians, and also covers his interest in establishing a permanent parliamentary committee to investigate complaints against government departments. A file of papers, and another of press cuttings, relate to Baldwin's controversial period as Governor of the Leeward Islands. Baldwin's non-political interests are reflected in a number of personal and family letters; and by manuscript drafts and typescripts of his various publications.

BALDWIN, Alfred (1841–1908)

M.P. (Con.) Bewdley, 1892–1908.

The Baldwin family has in its possession a small quantity of press cuttings and letters relating to Alfred Baldwin.

BALDWIN, Sir Archer Ernest (1883–1966)

M.P. (Con.) Leominster, 1945–59.

BALFOUR, 1st E
Sir Arthur James Balfour (1848–1930)

M.P. (Con.) Hertford, 1874–85; Manchester East, 1885–1906; City of London, 1906–22. President, Local Government Board, 1885–6. Secretary of State for Scotland, 1886–7. Chief Secretary for Ireland, 1887–91. 1st Lord of the Treasury, 1891–2 and 1895–1905, and Prime Minister, 1902–5. 1st Lord of the Admiralty, 1915–16. Secretary of State for Foreign Affairs, 1916–19. Lord President of the Council, 1919–22 and 1925–9.

The British Library (Add MSS 49683–49962) holds the bulk of Balfour's papers. A further assortment of material remains at the family home, Whittingehame, in Scotland, and enquiries should be addressed to the National Register of Archives (Scotland). Papers on foreign affairs (1916–22) can be found at the Public Record Office (FO 800/199–217), together with Balfour's Irish papers (PRO 30/60, 1–13). A letter album (1882–93) survives at Duke University, Durham, North Carolina, and the important papers of J. S. Sandars, Balfour's private secretary, 1892–1915, are housed in the Bodleian Library, Oxford. Further details of these collections are given in Hazlehurst and Woodland, pp. 9–11.

BALFOUR, 2nd E of
Gerald William Balfour (1853–1945)

M.P. (Con.) Leeds Central, 1885–1906.
Chief Secretary for Ireland, 1895–1900. President of the Board of Trade, 1900–5. President of the Local Government Board, 1905.

The papers, which are described in Hazlehurst and Woodland, pp. 11–12, remain in the family home at Whittingehame, and arrangements for inspection may be made with the National Register of Archives (Scotland). A further series of papers is at the Public Record Office (PRO 30/60).

BALFOUR OF BURLEIGH, 6th B
Sir Alexander Hugh Bruce (1849–1921)

Parliamentary Secretary, Board of Trade, 1889–92.
Secretary of State for Scotland, 1895–1903.

The present (8th) Lord Balfour of Burleigh has a collection of his grandfather's papers (Hazlehurst and Woodland, pp. 21, 166). Arrangements for inspection should be made with the National Register of Archives (Scotland). The collection comprises personal and political correspondence, including drafts and copies, 1886–1920; Cabinet papers and confidential prints, mostly concerning fiscal questions, 1898–1903; pamphlets, memoranda, press cuttings and other papers. Many leading politicians are included among the correspondents, and the main subject groups include Church of Scotland affairs, Scottish Office brochures, 1902–3; Free Trade and the Cabinet crises of 1903, 1910–11, the 1909 Budget, the Parliament Bill and related issues, 1909–11; trade between Canada and the West Indies, 1909–10; Clyde Munitions Workers, 1915–16; and the Committee on Industrial Policy after the war, 1916–18.

BALFOUR OF INCHRYE, 1st B
Harold Harington Balfour (1897–)

M.P. (Con.) Isle of Ely, 1929–45.
Parliamentary Under-Secretary, Air, 1938–44. Minister Resident in West Africa, 1944–5.

Lord Balfour has given a copy of his Moscow Diary, 1941, to the Imperial War Museum. This is a personal account of the Anglo-American Mission to Moscow, 21 Sep–10 Oct 1941. Certain other papers and personal letters and memoranda were handed by the Beaverbrook Library to the House of Lords Record Office.

BALFOUR, Alfred (1885–1963)

M.P. (Lab.) Stirling and Clackmannan West, 1945–59.

BALFOUR, Charles Barrington (1862–1921)

M.P. (Con.) Hornsey, 1900–7.

Family papers relating to C. B. Balfour and his four sons are retained at Newton Don, Kelso, Scotland. A small group of letters to C. B. Balfour and an album of press cuttings relating to his electoral campaigns in Hornsey survive in this collection. The Scots Guards Museum at Wellington Barracks possesses his diary and letters home written during the Tel-el-Kebir campaign of 1882. The letters were also published in Vol. LI, No. 206 of *Journal of the Society for Army Historical Research.*

BALFOUR, George (1872–1941)

M.P. (Con.) Hampstead, 1918–41.

Mr H. G. Balfour (son), Oaklands, Pootings, nr Edenbridge, Kent, has a small collection of papers relating to his father's career. Amongst these is a small group of correspondence, 1911–40, containing letters generally of a formal nature. Also in the collection is an interesting 21 pp. biographical memoir, describing both Balfour's business career, where he was a pioneer in the electricity supply industry, and his parliamentary work.

BALFOUR, Kenneth Robert (1863–1936)

M.P. (Con.) Christchurch, 1900–6.

Attempts to contact the son were unsuccessful.

BALFOUR, Sir Robert, 1st Bt (1844–1929)

M.P. (Lib.) Glasgow Partick, 1906–22.

Miss Nancy Balfour, O.B.E. (granddaughter), 36E Eaton Square, London SW1, knows of no relevant political papers.

BALNIEL, Lord, see CRAWFORD AND BALCARRES

BANBURY OF SOUTHAM, 1st B
Sir Frederick George Banbury, 1st Bt (1850–1936)

M.P. (Con.) Peckham, 1892–1906; City of London, 1906–24.

It is believed that no papers survive with the present Baron Banbury of Southam.

BANES, George Edward (1828–1907)

M.P. (Con.) West Ham South, 1886–92, 1895–1906.

It did not prove possible to make any relevant contact.

BANFIELD, John William (1875–1945)

M.P. (Lab.) Wednesbury, 1932–45.
General Secretary, Amalgamated Union of Operative Bakers and Confectioners, 1940–5.

Banfield had two sons; it proved impossible to contact either. Milners, Curry & Gaskell, solicitors, who acted in Banfield's estate, had no further information. Records of the Bakers Union are described in *Sources*, Vol. 1, p. 18.

BANKS, Cyril (1901–69)

M.P. (Con., later Independent), Pudsey, 1950–9.

Mrs Gladys Banks (widow) has retained certain papers which are not made available for research purposes.

BANKS, Sir Reginald Mitchell- (1880–1940)

M.P. (Con.) Swindon, 1922–9, 1931–4.

Attempts to contact the family were unsuccessful.

BANNER, Sir John Sutherland Harmood-, 1st Bt (1847–1927)

M.P. (Con.) Everton, 1905–24.

BANNERMAN, Sir Henry Campbell- (1836–1908)

M.P. (Lib.) Stirling Burghs, 1868–1908.
Financial Secretary, War Office, 1871–4 and 1880–2. Parliamentary Secretary, Admiralty, 1882–4. Chief Secretary for Ireland, 1884–5. Secretary of State for War, 1886 and 1892–5. Prime Minister, 1905–8.

The papers in the British Library (Add.Mss 41206–52, 52512–21) are described in Hazlehurst and Woodland, pp. 12–13.

BANTON, George (1856–1932)

M.P. (Lab.) Leicester East, 1922, 1923–4.

BARCLAY, Sir (Robert) Noton (1872–1957)

M.P. (Lib.) Manchester Exchange, 1923–4.

Miss E. H. Barclay (daughter), Far Hills, Mottram, Alderley Edge, Cheshire, knows of no papers relating to her father's parliamentary career. All that survive with her are papers relating to Sir Noton Barclay's other activities, and to his personal affairs. It appears that no further papers remain with other members of the family.

BARCLAY, Sir Thomas (1853–1941)

M.P. (Lib.) Blackburn, Jan–Dec 1910.

Stephenson Harwood & Tatham, solicitors, acted in the English estates of Sir Thomas and Lady

Barclay. They had no information concerning the present whereabouts of the daughter of Sir Thomas Barclay.

BARING, Sir Godfrey, 1st Bt (1871–1957)

M.P. (Lib.) Isle of Wight, 1906–Jan 1910; Barnstaple, 1911–18.

Sir Charles Baring, Bt (son), states that his father's diaries, correspondence and press cuttings were destroyed following his death in 1957.

BARING, Hon. Guy Victor (1873–1916)

M.P. (Con.) Winchester, 1906–16.

Mrs G. H. C. Wakefield (granddaughter), Bramdean House, Alresford, Hants, has a collection of miscellaneous papers relating to her father's career.

BARKER, George (1858–1936)

M.P. (Lab.) Abertillery, 1921–9.

The *Dictionary of Labour Biography*, Vol. I, pp. 37–8, describes Barker's career, but uses only printed sources. It seems that no manuscript material survives.

BARKER, Sir John, 1st Bt (1840–1914)

M.P. (Lib.) Maidstone, 1900–6; Penryn and Falmouth, 1906–Jan 1910.

John Barker & Co. Ltd, of Kensington, the firm which Sir John founded, knows of no relevant papers.

BARKER, Robert Hewitt (1887–1961)

M.P. (Ind.) Sowerby, 1918–22.

BARLOW, Sir (Clement) Anderson Montague-, 1st Bt (1868–1951)

M.P. (Con.) Salford South, Dec 1910–23.
Parliamentary Secretary, Ministry of Labour, 1920–2. Minister of Labour, 1922–4.

Hazlehurst and Woodland, p 13, found that no papers have survived, apart from certain travel diaries (after 1924) which are preserved in Rhodes House Library, Oxford. Papers of the Royal Commission on the Location of Industry (1938), of which Montague-Barlow was Chairman, are in the Public Record Office (H.L.G. 27).

BARLOW, Sir John Denman, 2nd Bt (1898–   )

M.P. (Nat.Lib.) Eddisbury, 1945–50; (Con.) Middleton and Prestwich, 1951–66.

Records of the Middleton and Prestwich Conservative Association can be found in Lancashire Record Office.

BARLOW, Sir John Emmott, 1st Bt (1857–1932)

M.P. (Lib.) Frome, 1892–5; 1896–1918.

BARLOW, Percy (1867–1931)

M.P. (Lib.) Bedford, 1906–Jan 1910.

BARNARD, Sir Edmund Broughton (1856–1930)

M.P. (Lib.) Kidderminster, 1906–Jan 1910.

Messrs Ginn & Co., solicitors in the estate, knew of no relevant contacts.

BARNBY, 2nd B
Hon. Francis Vernon Willey (1884–   )

M.P. (Con.) Bradford South, 1918–22.

Rt. Hon. Lord Barnby stated that he retained no papers relating to his parliamentary career.

BARNES, Alfred (1887–1975)

M.P. (Lab.Co-op.) East Ham South, 1922–31 and 1935–55.
Minister of Transport, 1945–51.

Hazlehurst and Woodland, p. 14, found that Mr Barnes kept no papers. Ministry of Transport Private Office papers are available at the Public Record Office (MT 62/125–129).

BARNES, George Nicoll (1859–1940)

M.P. (Lab.) Glasgow Blackfriars, 1906–18; Glasgow Gorbals, 1918–22.
Minister of Pensions, 1916–17. Minister without Portfolio, 1917–20.

Hazlehurst and Woodland, p. 14, found that no papers have survived.

BARNES, Harry (1870–1935)

M.P. (Co.Lib.) Newcastle East, 1918–22.
Secretary, Cobden Club.

Mr S. W. Alexander, MBE, a former colleague of Barnes in the Cobden Club, knew of no papers. The records of the Cobden Club are described in *Sources*, Vol. 1, p. 44. These are now deposited in West Sussex Record Office.

BARNETT, Sir Richard Whieldon (1863–1930)

M.P. (Con.) St Pancras West, 1916–18; St Pancras S.W., 1918–29.

Mr W. B. Creasser, Plot D, Warren Edge, Park Avenue, Radlett, Herts, godson of Sir Richard, knows of no papers. He stated that no members of the family survive. Wadham College, Oxford, was a beneficiary of the will, but they know of no papers.

BARNSTON, Sir Harry, Bt (1870–1929)

M.P. (Con.) Eddisbury, 1910–29.
Comptroller, H. M. Household, 1921–4, 1924–8.

Sir Harry Barnston's great nephew, P. E. T. Barnston, knows of no papers relating to his great-uncle's career. None were discovered in Sir Harry's home where Mr Barnston now lives.

BARR, James (1862–1949)

M.P. (Lab.) Motherwell, 1924–31; Coatbridge, 1935–45.

Correspondence relating to the Gold Coast is available in the Fabian Colonial Bureau records at Rhodes House Library, Oxford.

BARRAN, Sir John Nicholson, 2nd Bt (1872–1952)

M.P. (Lib.) Hawick Burghs, 1909–18.

Sir J. N. Barran's son, Sir John Barran, Bt, says that no papers of interest were discovered after his father's death.

BARRAN, Sir Rowland Hirst (1858–1949)

M.P. (Lib.) Leeds North, 1902–18.

Sir John Barran, 3rd Bt, (nephew) was unable to supply information. Records of the Leeds Liberal Federation are deposited in Leeds City Library (Archives Department).

BARRAND, Arthur Rhys (1861–1941)

M.P. (Co.Lib.) Pudsey and Otley, 1918–22.

Attempts to contact members of the family prove unavailing.

BARRATT, Sir Francis Layland-, 1st Bt (1860–1933)

M.P. (Lib.) Torquay 1900–Dec 1910; St Austell, 1915–18.

Mr D. Howard (grandson) knows of no surviving papers relating to his grandfather.

BARRIE, Sir Charles Coupar, see ABERTAY, 1st B

BARRIE, Hugh T. (1860–1922)*

M.P. (Con.) Londonderry North, 1906–22.
Vice-President, Department of Agriculture and Technical Instruction, Ireland, 1919–22.

Certain papers are available at the Northern Ireland Public Record Office, including political correspondence 1917 (D 627/430), correspondence with H. de F. Montgomery, 1918 (D 627/432), and letters to Carson, 1918 (D 1507/1/1918/30.31.48. 50.52). Correspondence relating to the Irish Convention can be found in the Sir Horace Plunkett papers.

BARRY, Edward (b. 1852)*

M.P. (Irish Nat.) Cork South, 1892–Jan 1910.

BARRY, Sir Francis Tress, 1st Bt (1825–1907)

M.P. (Con.) Windsor, 1890–1906.

Sir F. T. Barry's great grandson, Major Sir Rupert Barry, Bt, knows of no papers. The Berkshire Archaeological Society, of which Sir Francis was an active member was also unable to assist.

BARRY, Redmond (1866–1913)*

M.P. (Lib.) Tyrone North, 1907–11.
Solicitor-General, Ireland, 1905–9. Attorney-General, Ireland, 1909–11. Lord Chancellor, Ireland, 1911–13.

Redmond Barry's daughter-in-law, Lady Barry, has no records apart from an album of obituary notices.

BARSTOW, Percy Gott (1883–1969)

M.P. (Lab.) Pontefract, 1941–50.

BARTLETT, (Charles) Vernon (Oldfeld) (1894–   )

Broadcaster and journalist.
M.P. (Ind. Prog.) Bridgwater, 1938–50.

Vernon Bartlett has deposited his papers in the Library of the University of Sussex. The bulk of these consist of scripts of broadcast talks, 1928–33, and for the period during and after World War II. The first series of talks largely cover international affairs, particularly the rise of Nazism; the second form an 'unofficial' picture of domestic life in Britain during the war. Besides these scripts, Mr Bartlett retained little apart from several box files of correspondence. Few papers survive relating to his membership of the House of Commons. The British Library has purchased a number of letters, including letters from prominent politicians (Add. Mss 59500–01).

BARTLETT, Sir Ellis Ashmead- (1849–1902)

M.P. (Con.) Suffolk (Eye), 1880–5; Sheffield Ecclesall, 1885–1902.
Civil Lord of the Admiralty, 1885–6; 1886–92.

Relevant correspondence (1883–4) can be found in the Iddesleigh papers (NRA list 5873). Certain records of the Ecclesall Constituency Association survive in the offices of the Sheffield Conservatives (*Sources,* Vol. 1, p. 70).

BARTLETT, Ellis Ashmead- (1881–1931)

M.P. (Con.) Hammersmith North, 1924–6.

No relevant papers have been discovered. Earlier records of the local Conservatives can be found in the London Borough of Hammersmith Public Libraries.

BARTLEY, Sir George Christopher Trout (1842–1910)

M.P. (Con.) Islington North, 1885–1906.

Efforts to trace members of Bartley's family proved unsuccessful.

BARTLEY, Patrick (1909–56)

M.P. (Lab.) Chester-le-Street, 1950–6.

L. Mulcahy, Smith & Co., solicitors, who acted in the estate, had no current contact with members of the family.

BARTON, Sir (A) William (1862–1957)

M.P. (Lib.) Oldham, Jan 1910–18; (Co.Lib.) 1918–22.

William & Glyn's Trust Company Ltd, Manchester, were in touch with a member of the family on behalf of this survey; however, no information regarding papers came to light.

BARTON, Basil Kelsey (1879–1958)

M.P. (Con.) Hull Central, 1931–5.

Mr Derek Barton (nephew) 49 Godfrey Street, London SW3, has a small collection of papers, though little relates to Basil Barton's political career.

BARTON, Clarence (1892–1957)

M.P. (Lab.) Wembley South, 1945–50.

Barton's widow was his sole executrix. Their only child was killed in 1943. It proved impossible to establish any contacts.

BARTON, Robert Childers (b. 1881)*

M.P. (Sinn Fein), 1918–22.

BATEMAN, Arthur Leonard (1879–1957)

M.P. (Con.) Camberwell North, 1931–5.

According to information supplied by Messrs. Simon, Haynes, Zucker & Cassels, solicitors, Bateman's daughter and only surviving relative knows of no papers.

BATEY, Joseph (1867–1949)

M.P. (Lab.) Spennymoor, 1922–42.

Joseph Batey's niece, Councillor Mrs L. G. Jordison, stated that she knew of no papers in the family. The *Dictionary of Labour Biography*, Vol. II, pp. 31–3, gives biographical details but makes no reference to manuscript sources.

BATH, 5th M of
Thomas Henry Thynne, Vt Weymouth (1862–1946)

M.P. (Con.) Frome, 1886–92, 1895–6.
Parliamentary Under-Secretary, India Office, 1905. Master of the Horse, 1922–4.

A small collection of papers relating to the 5th Marquess' career is retained at Longleat, Warminster, Wilts. Enquiries should be directed to the Librarian at Longleat.

BATH, 6th M of
Henry Frederick Thynne, Vt Weymouth (1905–)

M.P. (Con.) Frome, 1931–5.

The Marquess of Bath states that he retained no papers relating to his parliamentary career.

BATHURST, Hon. Allen Benjamin (1872–1947)

M.P. (Con.) Cirencester, 1895–1906; Jan 1910–18.

Lady Ann Bathurst says that her father-in-law's papers were destroyed.

BATHURST, Sir Charles, see BLEDISLOE, 1st Vt

BATTLEY, John Rose (1880–1952)

M.P. (Lab.) Clapham, 1945–50.

Mr J. R. Battley retained a large collection of papers which represent fully his business and political activities. The main part of the collection is filed into 50 box files, each clearly labelled. Some of the files contain correspondence, notes and memoranda dealing with Battley's work on the London County Council, to which he was elected in 1938; many others contain correspondence and details of his involvement with pacifist and temperance organisations, as well as with his parliamentary work. One large box deals with the Clapham Labour Party. The remainder of the files contain much business and personal material. In addition to the box files there are 21 folders of speeches, 1909–45, nine volumes of annotated engagement diaries, 1938–45 and three volumes of press cuttings. The collection is currently with his son, Mr Bernard Battley, 39 Old Town, Clapham, London SW4.

BAXTER, Sir (Arthur) Beverley (1891–1964)

M.P. (Con.) Wood Green, 1935–50; Southgate, 1950–64.
Editor-in-Chief and Director, *Daily Express*, 1929–33.

Certain of Sir Beverley Baxter's papers are in the care of his son, Mr Clive Baxter, c/o *Financial Post*, Suite 311–51 Sparks Street, Ottawa, Ontario, Canada K1P 5E3. These consist of certain press cuttings, a file of letters, generally of a formal nature, from famous personalities, and certain letters from Lord Beaverbrook. Records of the Wood Green Conservative Association are now deposited in the Greater London Record Office (Middlesex Records).

BAYFORD, 1st B
Sir Robert Arthur Sanders, 1st Bt (1867–1940)

M.P. (Con.) Bridgwater, Jan 1910–23; Wells, 1924–9.
Parliamentary Under-Secretary, War Office, 1921–2. Minister of Agriculture and Fisheries, 1922–4.

The Conservative Research Department has Lord Bayford's diary (Feb 1910–Apr 1935), and correspondence remains with his daughter, Hon. Mrs Vera Butler, Kentisheare House, Cullompton, Devon EX15 2BR. Further particulars appear in Hazlehurst and Woodland, p. 127.

BAYLEY, Thomas (1846–1906)

M.P. (Lib.) Chesterfield, 1892–1906.

A grandson, Mr G. N. B. Huskinson, lives near Nottingham. No information on papers was available.

BEACH, Sir Michael Edward Hicks, see ST ALDWYN, 1st E

BEACH, Hon. Michael Hugh Hicks, see QUENINGTON, Vt

BEACH, William Frederick Hicks (1841–1923)

M.P. (Con.) Tewkesbury, 1916–18.

Mr W. W. Hicks Beach, grandson of W. F. Hicks Beach, has none of his grandfather's papers. Family papers of the Earls of St Aldwyn, which are mainly held in the Gloucestershire Record Office, are described in Hazlehurst and Woodland, p. 14.

BEACH, William Whitehead Hicks (1907–   )

M.P. (Con.) Cheltenham, 1950–64.

Mr W. W. Hicks Beach has retained none of his papers.

BEACH, William Wither Bramston (1826–1901)

M.P. (Con.) Andover, 1857–1901.

Some papers have been deposited in the Gloucestershire Record Office including personal correspondence of Beach and his wife, 1850–1901, newspaper cuttings and printed papers for the late nineteenth and early twentieth century, and election papers.

BEALE, Sir William Phipson, 1st Bt (1839–1922)

M.P. (Lib.) Ayrshire South, 1906–18.

Family papers remain with Mrs Anne Beale, Drumlamford, Barrhill, by Girvan, Ayrshire KA26 ORB.

BEAMISH, Rear Admiral Tufton Percy Hamilton (1874–1951)

Assistant to Chief of War Staff, Admiralty, 1912–13. Naval Assistant to 1st Sea Lord, Aug–Nov 1914. Commands, World War I; service at Admiralty, 1917–19.
M.P. (Con.) Lewes, 1924–31, 1936–45.

Churchill College, Cambridge, has a collection of some eight boxes of papers. Special conditions of access apply.

BEAMISH, Sir Tufton Victor Hamilton, see CHELWOOD, Baron

BEASLEY, Peter (b. 1885)*

M.P. (Sinn Fein) Kerry East, 1918–22.

BEATTIE, Francis (1885–1945)

M.P. (Con.) Glasgow Cathcart, 1942–5.

No relevant contacts could be established. Mr Edward Taylor, present M.P. for Glasgow Cathcart, stated that the constituency knew of no relevant material.

BEATTIE, John (1886–1960)*

M.P. (Ind. Lab.) Belfast West, 1943–55.
Leader of Parliamentary Labour Party, Northern Ireland.

Records of the Northern Ireland Labour Party are in Northern Ireland Public Record Office. These contain many papers relating to Beattie. The Northern Ireland Labour Club, 40 Waring Street, Belfast, has a collection of election material much of which relates to his campaigns.

BEATTY, 2nd E
David Field Beatty, Vt Borodale (1905–72)

M.P. (Con.) Peckham, 1931–6.
Joint Parliamentary Secretary, Air Ministry, 1945.

Enquiries should be directed to Mrs Diane Nutting (widow), Chicheley Hall, Newport Pagnell, Bucks.

BEAUCHAMP, 7th E
William Lygon, Vt Elmley (1872–1938)

Governor, New South Wales, 1899–1901. Lord President of the Council, 1910 and 1914–15. 1st Commissioner of Works, 1910–14.

Hazlehurst and Woodland, p. 94, found that the present (8th) Earl Beauchamp of Madresfield Court, Malvern, Worcs, has only a collection of scrapbooks relating to his father's career. The Mitchell Library, Sydney, has a diary he kept while Governor of New South Wales and a substantial collection of correspondence relating to the question of the Federation in 1900.

BEAUCHAMP, 8th E
William Lygon, Vt Elmley (1903–   )

M.P. (Lib.) Norfolk East, 1929–31; (Lib.Nat.), 1931–8.

Earl Beauchamp states that he has no papers relating to his political career.

BEAUCHAMP, Sir Brograve Campbell, 2nd Bt (1897–1976)

M.P. (Con.) Walthamstow East, 1931–45.

See below.

BEAUCHAMP, Sir Edward, 1st Bt (1849–1925)

M.P. (Lib.) Lowestoft, 1906–Jan 1910; Dec 1910–22.

Enquiries regarding papers should be directed to the executors of Sir Brograve Beauchamp, Bt.

BEAUMONT, Hubert (d. 1948)

M.P. (Lab.) Batley and Morley, 1939–48.

Efforts to contact the family were unsuccessful.

BEAUMONT, Hon. Hubert G. (1864–1922)

M.P. (Lib.) Eastbourne, 1906–Jan 1910.

Lord Beaumont of Whitley states that to the best of his knowledge there are no papers relating to his grandfather in the possession of the family.

BEAUMONT, Michael Wentworth (1903–58)

M.P. (Con.) Aylesbury, 1929–38.

Such papers as survive are in the care of Mrs M. W. Beaumont (widow), Harristown House, Brannockstown, Co. Kildare, Ireland.

BEAUMONT, Hon. Ralph Edward Blackett (1901–   )

M.P. (Con.) Portsmouth Central, 1931–45.

Mr Beaumont has retained no relevant papers.

BEAUMONT, Wentworth Canning Blackett, see ALLENDALE, 1st Vt

BEAUMONT, Hon. Wentworth Henry Canning, see ALLENDALE, 2nd Vt

BEAVERBROOK, 1st B
Sir William Maxwell Aitken, 1st Bt (1879–1964)

M.P. (Con.) Ashton-under-Lyne, Dec 1910–16.
Chancellor of the Duchy of Lancaster and Minister of Information, 1918–19. Minister of Aircraft Production, 1940–1. Minister of State, May–June, 1941. Minister of Supply, 1941–2; War Production, Feb 1942. Lord Privy Seal, 1943–5.

Several hundred boxes of Beaverbrook's papers are now deposited in the House of Lords Record Office. For further details see Hazlehurst and Woodland, p. 2. Private Office papers (AVIA 11 and AVIA 9) can be found at the Public Record Office.

BECHERVAISE, Albert Eric (1884–1966)

M.P. (Lab.) Leyton East, 1945–50.

No family contact was established.

BECK, Sir (Arthur) Cecil Tyrrell (1878–1932)

M.P. (Lib.) Wisbech, 1906–Jan 1910; Saffron Walden, Dec 1910–22.
Junior Lord of the Treasury, 1915. Vice Chamberlain, H.M. Household, 1915–17. Parliamentary Secretary, Ministry of National Service and Reconstruction, 1917–19.

BECKER, Harry Thomas Alfred (1892–   )

M.P. (Ind. later Ind.Con.) Richmond, 1922–4.

Mr Harry Becker, now resident in the United States, has retained no substantial collection of papers, but has retained certain press cuttings.

BECKETT, Ernest William, see GRIMTHORPE, 2nd B

BECKETT, John Warburton (1894–1964)

M.P. (Lab.) Gateshead, 1924–9; Peckham, 1929–31.

Some papers survive in the care of his widow, Mrs D. A. Beckett, c/o Flat 6, 18–24 Warwick Way, London SW1V 1RX. These include certain correspondence and press cuttings, and an unpublished autobiography written in 1938 and dealing with the inter-war period.

BECKETT, Hon. Sir (William) Gervase, 1st Bt (1866–1937)

M.P. (Con.) Whitby, 1906–22; Leeds North, 1923–9.

Sir Martyn Beckett, Bt, has no papers relating to his father's political career. Records of the Leeds Conservatives dating from 1925, including press cuttings, are deposited in Leeds City Library.

BEECH, Francis William (1885–1969)

M.P. (Con.) Woolwich West, 1943–5.

The papers consist of six volumes of press cuttings, interspersed with personal honours, photographs, etc. They are at present in the care of Mr F. W. Beech's widow, Mrs Phyllis Beech, 6 Shelley Court, Parkleys, Ham Common, Richmond, Surrey, and will eventually be given to his grandson, Mr David Crawford, Merville, North Parade, Llandudno, Gwynedd.

BEECHMAN, Nevil Alexander (1896–1965)

M.P. (Lib.Nat.) St Ives, 1937–50.
Junior Lord of the Treasury, 1943–5. Chief Whip, Liberal National Party, 1942–5.

Efforts to contact the family were unsuccessful. Records of the Liberal Nationals are described in *Sources*, Vol. 1, pp. 183–4.

BEIT, Sir Alfred Lane, 2nd Bt (1903–   )

M.P. (Con.) St Pancras S.E., 1931–45.

Sir Alfred has retained few papers. The surviving material consists of printed articles and copies of speeches, chiefly concerned with financial and imperial affairs.

BELCHER, John William (1905–64)

M.P. (Lab.) Sowerby, 1945–9.
Parliamentary Secretary, Board of Trade, 1946–8.

Attempts to contact the family produced no information. A daughter, Mrs Mumford, now lives in St Leonards-on-Sea.

BELISHA, Isaac Leslie Hore-, see HORE-BELISHA, 1st B

BELL, Sir (Arthur) Clive Morrison-, 1st Bt (1871–1956)

M.P. (Con.) Honiton, Jan 1910–31.

A small collection was retained by Sir Clive's widow, Hon. Lady Morrison-Bell, Harbour House, Burnham Overy, Staithe, King's Lynn, Norfolk. The chief items are 24 chapters of unpublished autobiography, and two press-cutting albums, relating particularly to Sir Clive's advocacy of 'Tariff Walls'. These are now deposited in the House of Lords Record Office.

BELL, Ernest Fitzroy Morrison- (1871–1960)

M.P. (Con.) Mid-Devon, 1908–Jan 10; Dec 1910–18.

A small collection of Morrison-Bell papers is deposited in the Devon Record Office, Concord House, South Street, Exeter, EX1 1DX. It consists of a bundle of papers, chiefly election material, including newspaper cuttings, telegrams, correspondence and circulars. In addition, there are two scrapbooks of press cuttings dealing with the Mid-Devon election of 1908.

BELL, James (1872–1955)

M.P. (Lab.) Ormskirk, 1918–22.

Letters of Administration were granted to Bell's son, whom it proved impossible to trace.

BELL, Joseph Nicholas (d. 1922)

M.P. (Lab.) Newcastle upon Tyne East, 1922. (A by-election was held in Jan 1923.)

Efforts to contact persons mentioned in the will and act of probate proved unsuccessful.

BELL, Richard (1854–1930)

General Secretary, Amalgamated Society of Railway Servants, 1897–1910.
M.P. (Lab.) Derby, 1900–Jan 1910.

No substantial collection of papers is known. The *Dictionary of Labour Biography*, Vol. II, pp. 34–9 gives biographical details. Certain relevant papers may be found in the archives of the Labour Party (e.g. LP/Con/06). Records of the Amalgamated Society of Railway Servants are described in *Sources*, Vol. 1, p. 199. These records are now in the Modern Records Centre, University of Warwick Library.

BELL, Ronald McMillan (1914–   )

M.P. (Con.) Newport, May–July, 1945; Buckinghamshire South, 1950–Feb 1974; Beaconsfield, Feb 1974–.

Mr Bell doubts whether he has much relevant material.

BELL, William Cory Heward (1875–1961)

M.P. (Con.) Devizes, 1918–23.

Major M. W. H. Bell (son) knows of no relevant surviving papers relating to his father's political career.

BELLAIRS, Carylon Wilfroy (1871–1955)

M.P. (Lib., later Con.) King's Lynn, 1906–Jan 1910; Maidstone, 1915–31.

A collection of papers, relating to both his naval career and his political work, is deposited in McGill University Library, Montreal, Quebec, Canada. This comprises correspondence, 1889–1951; miscellaneous files, 1905–46; notes, 1879–1945; press cuttings, 1902–50, and scrapbooks 1898–1939.

BELLAMY, Albert (1871–1931)

M.P. (Lab.) Ashton-under-Lyne, 1928–31.
President, Amalgamated Society of Railway Servants, 1911–13. First President, National Union of Railwaymen, 1913–17.

Efforts to trace Bellamy's heirs proved unsuccessful. The records of the Amalgamated Society of Railway Servants and of the National Union of Railwaymen are described in *Sources*, Vol. 1, p. 199. These records are now in the Modern Records Centre, University of Warwick Library.

BELLENGER, Frederick John (1894–1968)

M.P. (Lab.) Bassetlaw, 1935–68.
Financial Secretary, War Office, 1945–6. Secretary of State for War, 1946–7.

Hazlehurst and Woodland, p. 15, found that Mr R. C. Bellenger was unable to be of any assistance regarding his father's papers.

BELLOC, (Joseph) Hilaire (Pierre) (1870–1953)

Author, critic and poet.
M.P. (Lib.) Salford South, 1906–Dec 1910.

Robert Speaight, who wrote the official biography of Belloc (1957) and edited his *Letters* (1958) stated that he found little in Belloc's private papers relating to his Parliamentary career. Mr Speaight had access to all the private papers that the literary executors knew of. Mrs Jebb (daughter), King's Land, Shipley, Horsham, Sussex, retains certain papers. Belloc's literary mss and some letters are now housed in the Library of the University of Texas. Correspondence relating to the Marconi scandal can be found in the Herbert Samuel papers. Some 41 letters and an article are among the Sarolea Papers in Edinburgh University Library. Correspondence with Lady Astor can be found in the Astor Papers at Reading University Library.

BELPER, 2nd B
Hon. Henry Strutt (1840–1914)

M.P. (Lib.) Derbyshire, 1868–74; Berwick, 1880–5.
Captain, Gentlemen at Arms, 1895–1906.

Attempts to contact the present Lord Belper were not successful.

BELSTEAD, 1st B
Sir Francis John Childs Ganzoni, 1st Bt (1882–1958)

M.P. (Con.) Ipswich, 1914–23; 1924–37.

Lord Belstead's son, the present (2nd) Lord Belstead, was unable to provide any information.

BENN, Anthony (Neil) Wedgwood (1925–) [1]

M.P. (Lab.) Bristol S.E., 1950–July 1960; Aug 1963–
Postmaster General, 1964–6. Minister of Technology, 1966–70. Secretary of State for Industry, 1974–5; Energy, 1975–.

Mr Benn is to make arrangements for the eventual deposit of his working papers.

[1] Mr Benn succeeded his father as 2nd Viscount Stansgate in 1960. He renounced the title in 1963.

BENN, Sir Arthur Shirley, 1st Bt, see GLENRAVEL, 1st B

BENN, Captain Sir Ion Hamilton, 1st Bt (1863–1961)
Naval career.
M.P. (Con.) Greenwich, Jan 1910–22.

A small collection of papers relating to Sir Ion Benn's naval career, particularly during World War I, is available in the National Maritime Museum.

BENN, Sir John Williams, 1st Bt (1850–1922)

M.P. (Lib.) Westminster St George's East, 1892–5; Devonport, 1904–Jan 1910.

Thirteen volumes of newspaper cuttings, interspersed with occasional letters, draft speeches, posters, election material, photographs, etc. largely concerned with Sir J. W. Benn's work on the London County Council, survive in the care of Benn Brothers Ltd, Bouverie House, 154 Fleet Street, London EC4A 2DL.

BENN, William Wedgwood, see STANSGATE, 1st Vt

BENNETT OF EDGBASTON, 1st B
Sir Peter Frederick Blaker Bennett (1880–1957)

Director-General of Tanks and Transport, Ministry of Supply, 1939–40. Director-General of Emergency Services Organisation, M.A.P.; 1940–1. Chairman, Automatic Gun Board, 1941–4.
M.P. (Con.) Birmingham Edgbaston, 1940–53.
Parliamentary Secretary, Ministry of Labour, 1951–2.

The executors of Lady Bennett (widow) were unable to supply information regarding papers.

BENNETT, Sir Albert James, 1st Bt (1872–1945)

M.P. (Lib.) Mansfield, 1922–3; (Con:) Nottingham Central, 1924–30.
Member of Mechanical Transport Board, War Office; Leather Control Board; Controller of Propaganda for South and Central America, Ministry of Information, in World War II.

Mr Michael Bennett and his brother, Sir Ronald Bennett, Bt, grandsons of Sir A. J. Bennett, have no papers relating to their grandfather.

BENNETT, Air Vice-Marshal Donald Clifford Tyndall (1910–)

R.A.F. career.
M.P. (Lib.) Middlesbrough West, 1945–8.

The Air Vice-Marshal stated that such papers as he had retained were unsorted and of little value.

BENNETT, Sir Ernest Nathaniel (1868–1947)

M.P. (Lib.) Woodstock, 1906–Jan 1910; (Lab.) Cardiff Central, 1929–31; (Nat.Lib.) 1931–45. Assistant Postmaster General, 1932–5.

No large corpus of material appears to survive with the family. Enquiries should be directed to Sir Ernest's son, Sir Frederic Bennett, M.P.

BENNETT, Henry Currie Leigh- (1852–1903)

M.P. (Con.) Chertsey, 1897–1903.

The researchers failed to trace members of the family. Papers of C. A. Whitmore, M.P., who was one of Leigh-Bennett's executors, are believed lost.

BENNETT, Sir Henry Honeywood Curtis- (1879–1936)

M.P. (Con.) Chelmsford, 1924–6.

The Chelmsford Conservatives have retained certain constituency records dating from 1924.

BENNETT, Dr Reginald Frederick Brittain (1911–)

M.P. (Con.) Gosport and Fareham, 1950–Feb 1974; Fareham, Feb 1974–

BENNETT, Sir Thomas Jewell (1852–1925)

Principal Proprietor, *The Times of India*.
M.P. (Con.) Sevenoaks, 1918–23.

No information on papers was forthcoming. The Trust Division of Lloyds Bank Ltd, who administered the estate, had no knowledge of papers.

BENNETT, William (1873–1937)

M.P. (Lab.) Battersea South, 1929–31.

BENNETT, Sir William Gordon

M.P. (Con.) Glasgow Woodside, 1950–5.

BENSON, Sir George (1889–1973)

M.P. (Lab.) Chesterfield, 1929–31, 1935–64.

BENTHAM, Dr Ethel (d. 1931)

M.P. (Lab.) Islington East, 1929–31.

Relevant papers can be found in the Labour Party archive including items relating to the War Emergency Workers National Committee and correspondence (1926–7) concerning the miners (LP/Min./19/30–43).

BENTHAM (George) Jackson (1863–1929)

M.P. (Lib.) Gainsborough, Jan 1910–18.

Mr Peter Bentham Oughtred, J.P. (grandson), Raby Lodge, Brough, North Humberside HU15 1HL, believes that few relevant papers have survived.

BENTINCK, Lord Henry Cavendish-, see CAVENDISH-BENTINCK

BERESFORD, 1st B
Admiral Lord Charles William de la Poer Beresford (1846–1919)

M.P. (Con.) Waterford, 1874–80; Marylebone East, 1885–9; York, 1897–9; Woolwich, 1902–3; Portsmouth, Jan 1910–16.
Junior Lord of the Admiralty, 1886–8.
C-in-C., Mediterranean Fleet, 1905–7; Channel Fleet, 1907–9.

A few papers are available in Duke University, North Carolina. Some papers concerning the Portsmouth Naval Reviews (1886–8) are at the National Maritime Museum. A further substantial amount of correspondence can be found in the Ardagh papers (PRO 30/40) at the Public Record Office.

BERKELEY, Reginald Cheyne (1890–1935)

Playwright.
M.P. (Lib.) Nottingham Central, 1922–4.

Mr Humphry Berkeley (son) believes that no private papers survive, though he has a manuscript of his father's best known play, *The Lady with the Lamp*.

BERNAYS, Robert Hamilton (1902–45)

M.P. (Lib.) Bristol North, 1931–6; (Lib.Nat.) 1936–45.
Parliamentary Secretary, Ministry of Health, 1937–9; Ministry of Transport, 1939–40.

Mrs Bernays, J.P. (widow), The Down House, Tockington, nr Bristol BS12 4PG has retained a substantial collection of files relating to her husband's career.

BERRIDGE, Sir Thomas Henry Devereux (1857–1924)

M.P. (Lib.) Warwick and Leamington, 1906–Jan 1910.

BERRY, (Geoffrey) Lionel, see KEMSLEY, 2nd Vt

BERRY, Sir George Andreas (1853–1940)

M.P. (Con.) Scottish Universities, 1922–31.

Neither Sir George Berry's surviving daughter, Mrs N. M. G. Denis-Sanders, nor his niece, Miss M. E. Berry, know of any surviving papers.

BERRY, Henry (1883–1956)

M.P. (Lab.) Woolwich West, 1945–50.

The Woolwich Labour Party has retained a number of records dating back to 1903. Mrs W. E. Cooper (daughter) 14 Tonbridge Rd., Teston, Maidstone, Kent ME18 5BU, has further relevant information.

BERRY, Hon. John Seymour, see CAMROSE, 2nd Vt

BERTRAM, Julius (1866–1944)

M.P. (Lib.) Hitchin, 1906–Jan 1910.

Attempts to contact the son were unsuccessful.

BESSBOROUGH, 9th E of
Sir Vere Brabazon Ponsonby, Vt Duncannon (1880–1956)

M.P. (Con.) Cheltenham, Jan–Dec 1910; Dover, 1913–20.
Governor-General, Canada, 1931–5.

The present (10th) Earl of Bessborough, Stansted Park, Rowlands Castle, Hants PO9 6DK, son of the 9th Earl, has a substantial collection of his father's papers. This is not generally available and requests for access to the collection will be considered on their merits.

BESWICK, Baron
Frank Beswick (1912–   )

M.P. (Lab.Co-op.) Uxbridge, 1945–59.
Parliamentary Secretary, Ministry of Civil Aviation, 1950–1. Lord in Waiting, 1965. Parliamentary Under-Secretary, Commonwealth Office, 1965–7. Captain, Gentlemen at Arms, and Government Chief Whip, House of Lords, 1967–70. Minister of State, Department of Industry, and Deputy Leader, House of Lords, 1974–5.

Lord Beswick has retained certain material relating to various aspects of his career, including the Kenya trials, 1946; the London Airport decision, 1950; and the British Steel Corporation.

BETHEL, Albert (1874–1935)

M.P. (Con.) Eccles, 1924–9.

Efforts to trace Bethel's heirs proved inconclusive. Records of the Eccles Conservative Association are deposited in Lancashire Record Office.

BETHELL, 1st B
Sir John Henry Bethell, 1st Bt (1861–1945)

M.P. (Lib.) Romford, 1906–18; East Ham North, 1918–22.

See below.

BETHELL, Sir Thomas Robert (1867–1957)

M.P. (Lib.) Maldon, 1906–Jan 1910.

The present (4th) Lord Bethell knows of no papers relating to his great-uncle, Sir T. R. Bethell, or to his brother, the 1st Baron Bethell.

BETTERTON, Sir Henry Bucknall, 1st Bt, see RUSHCLIFFE, 1st B

BEVAN, Aneurin (1897–1960)

M.P. (Lab.) Ebbw Vale, 1929–60.
Minister of Health, 1945–51. Minister of Labour and National Service, 1951.

The papers, which are not available for research, are in the care of the Rt. Hon. Mr Michael

Foot, M.P. Hazlehurst and Woodland, p. 16, provide no details of the collection. A transcript of an interview with Sir Archie Lush, long-time agent for Bevan, is available at the South Wales Miners' Library, University College, Swansea.

BEVAN, Stuart James (d. 1935)

M.P. (Con.) Holborn, 1928–35.

Stuart Bevan's daughter, who was contacted on our behalf by Messrs Farmer & Co., solicitors, believes that no relevant papers have survived.

BEVERIDGE, 1st B
Sir William Henry Beveridge (1879–1963)

Director of Labour Exchanges, 1909–16. Assistant General Secretary, Munitions, 1915–16.
Second Secretary, later Permanent Secretary, Food, 1916–19.
Director, London School of Economics, 1919–37.
Master, University College, Oxford, 1937–45.
M.P. (Lib.) Berwick-on-Tweed, 1944–5.
Chairman of Interdepartmental Committee on Social Insurance and Allied Services, 1941–2.

A substantial collection of Beveridge's papers is preserved at BLPES. The papers have been catalogued with the aid of a grant from the Social Science Research Council, and a handlist and catalogue is available. The papers have been catalogued into a number of categories. Categories I and II consist of personal and family papers, and a substantial collection of family, general and personal correspondence. Category III relates to unemployment and Labour Exchanges, and includes notes, correspondence, papers, lectures, memoranda, government reports, etc. Category IV covers Beveridge's activities during World War I, and includes memoranda, correspondence, notes, drafts, office minutes, etc. relating to his work at the Ministry of Munitions, 1915–16, the Manpower Distribution Board, Reconstruction, the *History of the Ministry of Munitions*, and the Ministry of Food, 1916–19. Category V covers Beveridge's work in the Universities, as Director of the London School of Economics, as Vice Chancellor of the University of London and as Master of University College, Oxford, and again includes a considerable amount of correspondence as well as lecture notes, business papers, memoranda, etc. Category VI relates to Beveridge's political activities. This grouping includes correspondence, speech notes and press cuttings relating to his election as an M.P. in 1944; correspondence concerning his work in Parliament, and related papers; papers of the Liberal Party Organisation Campaign Committee, 1945; Beveridge's Election Diary; related correspondence; and material relating to his membership of the House of Lords from 1946. Category VII, 'Other Interests and Activities', brings together material relating to the Health Service and Old Age, New Towns, Population and Fertility, Weather Periodicity, and World Government. Category VIII covers Beveridge's works on Government Reports: the Royal Commission on the Coal Industry, 1925; the Unemployment Statistics Committee, 1934–44; the Sub-committee (of the Committee of Imperial Defence) on Food Rationing, 1936; the Manpower Survey, 1940; Fuel Rationing Enquiry, 1942; most important, the interdepartmental committee of 1941–2 which produced the Beveridge Report; and the Broadcasting Committee, 1949–50. All of these groupings include correspondence, papers, reports, memoranda, etc. Category IX covers Beveridge's published and unpublished works (including lectures and speeches). Category X covers pamphlets and offprints; Category XI 'Visits Abroad'; and XII covers a large collection of press cuttings, dating from 1870.

BEVIN, Ernest (1881–1951)

M.P. (Lab.) Wandsworth Central, 1940–50; Woolwich East, 1950–1.
Minister of Labour and National Service, 1940–5. Secretary of State for Foreign Affairs, 1945–51. Lord Privy Seal, 1951.

Churchill College, Cambridge, has a collection of Bevin's wartime papers. Papers relating to foreign affairs will be made available in due course in the Private Office Class FO 800 at the Public Record Office. Hazlehurst and Woodland, pp. 16–17, note that none of these papers are open to researchers. Certain papers, reflecting his work as a trade union official in the inter-war period, are available at the Modern Records Centre, University of Warwick Library.

BEVINS, John Reginald (1908–)

M.P. (Con.) Liverpool Toxteth, 1950–64.
Parliamentary Secretary, Ministry of Works, 1953–7; Ministry of Housing and Local Government, 1957–9. Postmaster General, 1959–64.

BHOWNAGREE, Sir Mancherjee Merwanjee (1851–1933)

M.P. (Con.) Bethnal Green N.E., 1895–1906.

By the terms of his will, personal letters were to be destroyed, while political and business letters were to be disposed of at the discretion of Bhownagree's son. It was not possible to verify whether papers were destroyed.

BIGLAND, Alfred (1855–1936)

M.P. (Con.) Birkenhead East, Dec 1910–22.

Messrs Layton & Co., solicitors of Liverpool, who acted in the estate, had no relevant information. Bigland's son died before World War II, and no other contacts were forthcoming.

BIGNOLD, Sir Arthur (1839–1915)

M.P. (Lib.Un.) Wick Burghs, 1900–Jan 1910.

Efforts to trace heirs proved unsuccessful. Records of the Liberal Unionist Party in Scotland are housed in the Glasgow offices of the Conservative Party (see *Sources*, Vol. 1, p. 151).

BIGWOOD, James (d. 1919)

M.P. (Con.) Finsbury East, 1885–6; Brentford, 1886–1906.

Bigwood's son, J. E. C. Bigwood, was sole executor of his estate. He and his heirs were not traced.

BILL, Charles (1843–1915)

M.P. (Con.) Leek, 1892–1906.

The Bill family papers were deposited in Staffordshire County Record Office by Mrs P. Clifford (*née* Bill) of Farley Hall. The collection includes some 90 letters to Charles Bill together with estate and personal material (see NRA 6841).

BILLING, Noel Pemberton (1880–1948)

Royal Naval Air Service, 1914–16.
M.P. (Ind.) Hertfordshire East, 1916–21.

It is believed that some papers may survive with the family.

BILLSON, Sir Alfred (1839–1907)

M.P. (Lib.) Barnstaple, 1892–5; Halifax, 1897–1900; Stafford N.W., 1906–7.

A few letters to Billson have been deposited in Liverpool Record Office. Other material can be found in the George Melly papers (NRA 16027).

BING, Geoffrey Henry Cecil (1909–)

M.P. (Lab.) Hornchurch, 1945–55.
Assistant Government Whip, 1945–6. Attorney-General of Ghana, 1957–61. Adviser to President of Ghana, 1961–6.

BINGHAM, George Charles, see LUCAN, 5th E of

BINGLEY; 1st B
George Richard Lane-Fox (1870–1947)

M.P. (Con.) Barkston Ash, 1906–31.
Parliamentary Secretary for Department of Mines, 1922–4, 1924–8.

Mr George Lane-Fox (grandson), Bramham Park, Wetherby, West Yorkshire LS23 6ND, has a series of diaries, marked 'No. 1 Diary'. These are essentially a personal journal of his grandfather's everyday activities, with brief comments on national issues. The diaries cover the period 1894–1946, with a gap, July 1910–late 1913. The Bramham papers deposited with Leeds City Libraries, Archives Department, appear to contain no relevant material. The Minute Books of the Barkston Ash Conservative Association, 1895–1933, are also deposited with Leeds City Archives.

BINNS, Joseph (1900–)

M.P. (Lab.) Gillingham, 1945–50.
Chairman of Public Works Loans Board, 1970–2.

BIRCH, (Evelyn) Nigel Chetwode, see RHYL, Baron

BIRCHALL, Sir John Dearman (1875–1941)

M.P. (Con.) Leeds N.E., 1918–40.

Major P. D. Birchall of Cotswold Farm, Cirencester, Glos, has retained a collection of papers relating to his father's career. The papers consist of personal letters; diaries, mainly of engagements, 1897–1915; and press cuttings, 1918–40. These relate both to his parliamentary career, and to his work as 2nd Church Estates Commissioner, 1923–4, 1925–9.

BIRD, Sir Alfred Frederick, 1st Bt (1849–1922)

M.P. (Con.) Wolverhampton West, Jan 1910–22.

Enquiries may be directed to Viscomtesse de Mauduit de Kervern, L'Ermitage Sainte Helene, Plan de Grasse, A.M. France; and to Mr R. R. Bird, of Sevenoaks, Kent (grandchildren). Records of the Wolverhampton West Conservatives, dating from 1908, are in the care of Professor George Jones, London School of Economics.

BIRD, Ernest Roy (1883–1933)

M.P. (Con.) Skipton, 1924–33.

Lady Nelson (daughter), 19 Acacia Road, London NW8, has an album, largely consisting of press cuttings, referring to two election campaigns when he stood unsuccessfully for Lambeth, and to his activities at Skipton, 1924–33.

BIRD, Sir Robert Bland, 2nd Bt (1876–1960)

M.P. (Con.) Wolverhampton West, 1922–9.

It is believed that surviving papers would be with Sir Robert's daughter, the Viscomtesse de Mauduit de Kervern, L'Ermitage Sainte Helene, Plan de Grasse, A.M. France.

BIRD, Sir William Barrott Montfort (1855–1950)

M.P. (Con.) Chichester, 1921–3.

Sir William Bird left all his personal papers and diaries to his partner, Mr John Venning, who is believed to have destroyed them later. Sir William's nephew knows of no papers surviving elsewhere. A full collection of records relating to the Chichester Conservative Association is deposited in West Sussex Record Office (*Sources*, Vol. 1, p. 66).

BIRKENHEAD, 1st E of
Sir Frederick Edwin Smith, 1st Bt (1872–1930)

M.P. (Con.) Liverpool Walton, 1906–18; Liverpool West Derby, 1918–19. Solicitor-General, 1915. Attorney-General, 1915–19. Lord Chancellor, 1919–22. Secretary of State for India, 1924–8.

Papers of the first Earl are described in Hazlehurst and Woodland, pp. 133–4. They are in the care of the family, and are not generally made available.

BIRKENHEAD, 2nd E of
Frederick Winston Furneux Smith, Vt Furneux (1907–75)

Lord in Waiting, 1938–40; 1951–5.
Biographer and historian.

Papers are retained by the family.

BIRKETT, 1st B
Sir (William) Norman Birkett (1883–1962)

Advocate. Lord Justice of Appeal, 1950–7.
M.P. (Lib.) Nottingham East, 1923–4, 1929–31.

The present Lord Birkett (son), has various papers relating to his father's career. Amongst these are diaries, largely containing brief notes and engagements; and a large number of press-cutting books which relate mainly to the pre-World War II period, and to famous trials in which Birkett appeared as counsel. Other papers include correspondence and notebooks. Access to the papers is restricted. H. Montgomery Hyde's biography *Norman Birkett* (1964) has made use of these papers.

BIRNAM, Hon.Lord
Sir (Thomas) David King Murray (1884–1955)

M.P. (Con.) Midlothian North, 1943–5.
Solicitor-General for Scotland, 1941–5.

BIRRELL, Augustine (1850–1933)

M.P. (Lib.) Fife West, 1889–1900; Bristol North, 1906–18.
President of the Board of Education, 1905–7. Chief Secretary for Ireland, 1907–16.

The Bodleian Library, Oxford, has a small collection of Birrell's papers. Other personal papers are held in the Library of Liverpool University. Details of the papers, and regulations concerning access, are given in Hazlehurst and Woodland, pp. 17 and 166. Papers of A. P. Magill, Birrell's secretary, are also in the Bodleian Library.

BISHOP, Sir (Frank) Patrick (1900–72)

M.P. (Con.) Harrow Central, 1950–64.

Enquiries should be directed to Mr James Bishop (son), 11 Willow Road, London NW3.

BLACK, Alexander William (1859–1906)

M.P. (Lib.) Banffshire, 1900–Dec 1906.

BLACK, Sir Arthur William (1863–1947)

M.P. (Lib.) Biggleswade, 1906–18.

Mr J. H. Mervill, the last surviving trustee of Sir Arthur Black's estate, knows of no papers. He believes that Black's only daughter, Miss E. M. S. Black, destroyed a number of personal papers; others were put in store. Miss Black has since died, and Mr Mervill had no further information concerning the whereabouts of papers. Messrs J. A. Simpson & Coulby, solicitors in the estate, had no further information.

BLACK, Sir Cyril Wilson (1902–   )

M.P. (Con.) Wimbledon, 1950–70.

Sir Cyril Black states that he has no papers relating to his early years in Parliament.

BLACK, John Wycliffe (1862–1951)

M.P. (Lib.) Harborough, 1923–4.

J. W. Black's daughter says she is unable to find any useful material relating to her father's political career. A fine set of records of the Harborough Liberal Association, including minutes from 1891, have survived c/o 16 Main Street, Kirby Muxloe, Leicester. These records contain references to J. W. Black's political career.

BLACKBURN, (Albert) Raymond (1915–   )

M.P. (Lab.) Birmingham King's Norton, 1945–50; (Ind.) Birmingham Northfield, 1950–1.

BLACKFORD, 2nd B
Hon. Glyn Keith Murray Mason (1887–1972)

M.P. (Con.) Croydon North, 1922–40.

The present (3rd) Lord Blackford states that his father retained no papers relating to his career.

BLADES, Hon. Lord
Daniel Patterson Blades (1888–1959)

Solicitor-General for Scotland, 1945–7.

Efforts to trace heirs proved unavailing.

BLADES, Sir George Rowland, 1st Bt, see EBBISHAM, 1st B

BLAIR, Sir Reginald, 1st Bt (1881–1962)

M.P. (Con.) Bow and Bromley, 1912–22; Hendon, 1935–45.
Chairman, London Municipal Society, 1919–29.

Sir Reginald's daughter is now dead and no family contact was established. Records of the London Municipal Society are described in *Sources*, Vol, 1, pp. 156–7.

BLAKE, Hon. Edward (1833–1912)*

Liberal M.P. in Canada, 1867–91.
Prime Minister, Ontario, 1871–2. Minister of Justice, Attorney-General, Canada, 1875–7.
President of the Council, Canada, 1877–8.
M.P. (Irish Nat.) Longford South, 1892–1907.

The Blake family papers are in the Public Archives of Ontario, Toronto. The collection includes the family and legal correspondence of Edward Blake, 1848–1912; papers and speeches on Canadian and Irish politics as well as miscellaneous newspaper clippings and printed material.

BLAKE, Sir Francis Douglas, 1st Bt (1856–1940)

M.P. (Co.Lib.) Berwick-on-Tweed, 1916–22.

The Blake family papers are housed in the Northumberland Record Office (ref. NRO 580/1–32). Most of these are concerned with estate and family matters, dating back to the seventeenth century. There are only a small number of items relating to Sir Francis Blake, including a letter from Sir Henry Campbell-Bannerman offering him a baronetcy in 1907.

BLAKENHAM, 1st Vt
Hon. John Hugh Hare (1911–)

M.P. (Con.) Woodbridge, 1945–50; Sudbury and Woodbridge, 1950–63.
Minister of State for Colonial Affairs, 1955–6. Secretary of State for War, 1956–8. Minister of Agriculture, Fisheries and Food, 1958–60. Minister of Labour, 1960–3. Chancellor of the Duchy of Lancaster, 1963–4.

The Viscount Blakenham states that he has kept no records.

BLAKER, Sir Reginald, 2nd Bt (1900–)

M.P. (Con.) Spelthorne, 1931–45.

BLANE, Thomas Andrew (1881–1940)

M.P. (Con.) Leicester South, 1918–22.

BLEDISLOE, 1st Vt
Sir Charles Bathurst (1867–1958)

M.P. (Con.) Wilton, Jan 1910–18.
Parliamentary Secretary, Food, 1916–17. Parliamentary Secretary, Agriculture 1924–8. Governor-General, New Zealand, 1930–5.

A collection of papers relating to Lord Bledisloe's career is retained at the family home, Lydney Park, Gloucester. It includes a box of political and general correspondence, 1900–1950s, covering topics such as Unionist Agricultural Policy, Food Supply, Imperial affairs, etc., with letters from a wide range of political contacts; a box of papers and pamphlets on the genealogy of the Bathurst family, and the history of the Lydney area; and smaller boxes containing notes on New Zealand affairs; notes on the military defence of the Gloucester area, 1940; agricultural matters, and personal affairs. Enquiries concerning these records should be directed to the present Viscount Bledisloe.

BLENKINSOP, Arthur (1911–   )

M.P. (Lab.) Newcastle-upon-Tyne East, 1945–59; South Shields, 1964–
Parliamentary Secretary, Ministry of Pensions, 1946–9; Ministry of Health, 1949–51.

Mr Blenkinsop doubts whether he has any papers which would be of historical significance.

BLINDELL, Sir James (1884–1937)

M.P. (Lib.) Holland-with-Boston, 1929–31; (Lib.Nat.) 1931–7.
Assistant Whip, 1931–2. Junior Lord of the Treasury and Chief Whip to Liberal National Party, 1932–7.

The surviving records of the National Liberals are described in *Sources*, Vol. 1, pp. 183–4.

BLISS, Joseph (1853–1939)

M.P. (Lib.) Cockermouth, 1916–18.

Information available at the Principal Probate Registry was not sufficient to lead to any relevant contacts.

BLUNDELL, Francis Nicholas (1880–1936)

M.P. (Con.) Ormskirk, 1922–9.

Mrs H. Whitlock Blundell (daughter), Crosby Hall, Blundellsands, Liverpool L23 4VA, has a collection of her father's papers. This includes personal and business papers and letters and souvenirs from World War I. Amongst the more political papers are notes on agricultural problems and some material on the Catholic Relief Bill, a visit to Canada in 1927, a few letters on the Civil War in Spain, and a good deal of material concerning the foundation of the Lancashire Federation of Rural Friendly Societies.

BLUNDELL, Henry Blundell-Hollinshead- (1831–1906)

M.P. (Con.) Ince, 1885–92, 1895–1906.

A member of the family who was contacted knew of no papers.

BLYTHE, Ernest (b. 1889)*

M.P. (Sinn Fein) Monaghan North, 1918–22.

BLYTON, Baron
William Reid Blyton (1899–   )

M.P. (Lab.) Houghton-le-Spring, 1945–64.

BOARDMAN, Harold (1907–   )

M.P. (Lab.) Leigh, 1945–

BOLAND, Harry (d. 1922)*

M.P. (Sinn Fein) Roscommon South, 1918–22.

BOLAND, John Puis (b. 1870)

M.P. (Irish Nat.) Kerry South, 1900–18.

BOLES, Dennis Coleridge (1885–1958)

M.P. (Con.) Wells, 1939–51.

The local Conservative Association has retained certain constituency records. No personal papers have been discovered.

BOLES, Sir Dennis Fortescue, 1st Bt (1861–1935)

M.P. (Con.) Somerset West, 1911–18; Taunton, 1918–21.

Attempts to contact the present baronet were not successful.

BOLST, Clifford Charles Alan Lawrence Erskine- (1878–1946)

M.P. (Con.) Hackney South, Aug 1922–3; Blackpool, 1931–5.

Messrs Gould & Swayne, solicitors of Glastonbury, Somerset, who acted in Erskine-Bolst's estate, were unable to be of assistance. They had no knowledge of any surviving members of the family. Records of the Blackpool Conservatives are deposited in Lancashire Record Office.

BOLTON, 5th B
Hon. William George Algar Orde-Powlett (1869–1944)

M.P. (Con.) Richmond (Yorks), Jan 1910–18.

It was not possible to make contact with the present (7th) Lord Bolton, the grandson of the 5th Lord Bolton.

BOLTON, Thomas Dolling (1841–1906)

M.P. (Lib.) Derbyshire N.E., 1886–1906.

Bolton's sole executor was a cousin, now presumed dead. No contacts were established.

BOND, Edward (1844–1920)

M.P. (Con.) Nottingham East, 1895–1906.

Neither Lady Pooley (whose husband was a nephew of Bond's) nor Mr Peter Pooley (great-nephew) know of any relevant papers.

BONDFIELD, Margaret Grace (1873–1953)

M.P. (Lab.) Northampton, 1923–4; Wallsend, 1926–31.
Parliamentary Secretary, Ministry of Labour, 1924. Minister of Labour, 1929–31.

Hazlehurst and Woodland, p. 17, were unable to locate any papers.

BONWICK, Alfred James (1883–1949)

M.P. (Lib.) Chippenham, 1922–4.

BOOTH, Alfred (1893–1965)

M.P. (Lab.) Bolton East, 1950–1.

Mrs S. M. Ramsay (daughter) understands that no papers, apart from appointments diaries, were found after Alfred Booth's death.

BOOTH, Frederick Handel (1867–1947)

M.P. (Lib.) Pontefract, Dec 1910–18.

BOOTHBY, Baron
Sir Robert John Graham Boothby (1900–)

M.P. (Con.) Aberdeenshire East, 1924–58.
Parliamentary Secretary, Ministry of Food, 1940–1.

Lord Boothby states that he has kept a small collection of papers only. These are not made available.

BORODALE, Vt, see BEATTY, 2nd E

BORWICK, George Oldroyd (1879–1964)

M.P. (Con.) Croydon North, 1918–22.

BOSCAWEN, Sir Arthur Sackville Trevor Griffith- (1865–1946)

M.P. (Con.) Tonbridge, 1892–1906; Dudley, Dec 1910–21; Taunton, 1921–2.
Parliamentary Secretary, Ministry of Agriculture and Fisheries, 1919–21. Minister of Agriculture and Fisheries, 1921–2. Minister of Health, 1922–3.

The small collection of papers in the Bodleian Library, described in Hazlehurst and Woodland, p. 18, deals mainly with the affairs of 1922.

BOSSOM, Baron
Sir Alfred Charles Bossom, 1st Bt (1881–1965)

M.P. (Con.) Maidstone, 1931–59.

Hon. Sir Clive Bossom, Bt, (son) knows of no papers. Lord Bossom was Chairman of the S.E. Area Provincial Conservative and Unionist Association, 1949–52. Records of the S.E. Area are retained at Conservative Central Office and are described in *Sources*, Vol. 1, pp. 63–4. The records of the Maidstone Conservative Association, dating from 1885, are deposited in the Kent Archives Office.

BOTTOMLEY, Arthur George (1907–)

M.P. (Lab.) Chatham, 1945–50; Rochester and Chatham, 1950–9; Middlesbrough East, 1962–
Parliamentary Under-Secretary, Dominions Office, 1946–7. Secretary for Overseas Trade, Board of Trade, 1947–51. Secretary of State for Commonwealth Affairs, 1964–6. Minister of Overseas Development, 1966–7.

Some correspondence relating to Arthur Bottomley's work at the Dominions Office, 1946–7, is available at the India Office Library. This material relates to the transfer of power in Burma. Other material has been retained by Mr Bottomley, including papers pertaining to India, Rhodesia, the Havana Trade Conference and the Yugoslav Trade Agreement.

BOTTOMLEY, Horatio William (1860–1933)

M.P. (Lib.) Hackney South, 1906–12; (Ind.) 1918–22. (Bottomley was expelled from the House of Commons, 18 Sep 1922.)

Printed circular letters in connection with Bottomley's financial enterprises, 1920–3, are in the care of Mrs N. V. Wicks, 27 Ferncroft Avenue, Eastcote, Middlesex (NRA list 4678). Certain correspondence relating to his candidature at Hackney South can be found in the Labour Party Archive (LPL/ISL/08/13–36).

BOULNOIS, Edmund (1838–1911)

M.P. (Con.) Marylebone East, 1889–1906.

The City of Westminster Libraries (Marylebone Library) has relevant material.

BOULTON, Alexander Claude Forster (1862–1949)

M.P. (Lib.) Ramsey, 1906–Jan 1910.

The solicitors who acted in the estate knew of no papers. It was not possible to establish a family contact. The papers of the English-Speaking Union, of which Boulton was joint founder, are described in *Sources*, Vol. 1, p. 92.

BOULTON, Sir William Whytehead, 2nd Bt (1873–1949)

M.P. (Con.) Sheffield Central, 1931–45.
Junior Lord of the Treasury, 1940–2. Vice Chamberlain, H.M. Household, 1942–4.

Sheffield Conservatives have retained a number of records, some of which have been deposited in Sheffield Central Library. No personal papers are known to survive.

BOURKE, Major Sir (Edward Alexander) Henry Legge-, see LEGGE-BOURKE

BOURNE, Robert Croft (1888–1938)

M.P. (Con.) Oxford City, 1924–38.

It is believed that Bourne retained no papers. Neither his widow, nor his daughter, Lady Bolitho, nor his son, Mr R. M. A. Bourne, know of any surviving records.

BOUSFIELD, William Robert (1854–1943)

M.P. (Con.) Hackney North, 1892–1906.

Bousfield's son died in 1958. It proved impossible to trace any further contact.

BOWATER, Sir T. Vansittart, 1st Bt (1862–1938)

Lord Mayor of London, 1913–14.
M.P. (Con.) City of London, 1922–3; 1924–38.

The Guildhall Library has relevant material on City of London politics, but no personal records are known.

BOWDEN, George Robert Harland (d. 1927)

M.P. (Con.) Derbyshire N.E., 1914–18.

BOWDEN, Herbert William, see AYLESTONE, Baron

BOWDLER, (William) Audley (1884–1969)

M.P. (Lib.) Holderness, 1922–3.

Mr J. C. A. Bowdler (son), states that his father destroyed his papers shortly before he died.

BOWEN, (Evan) Roderic (1913–   )

M.P. (Lib.) Cardigan, 1945–66.

BOWEN, Sir (John) William (1876–1965)

General Secretary, Union of Post Office Workers.
M.P. (Lab.) Crewe, 1929–31.

Sir J. W. Bowen's family know of no relevant papers. The records of the Union of Post Office Workers are described in *Sources*, Vol. 1, p. 270.

BOWER, Norman A. H. (1907–   )

M.P. (Con.) Harrow West, 1941–51.

BOWER, Commander Robert Tatton (1894–1975)

M.P. (Con.) Cleveland, 1931–45.

BOWERMAN, Charles William (1851–1947)

M.P. (Lab.) Deptford, 1906–31.
Secretary, Trades Union Congress, 1911–23.

A substantial amount of correspondence can be found in the Labour Party archive (refs. LRC; LP.GC; WNC. and WNC/Add; LP/PRO/13/1–30; LP/DUB/13/58–62; LP/JB/11/1). The records of the London Society of Compositors (now part of the National Graphical Association) of which Bowerman was General Secretary, 1892–1906, are deposited in the Modern Records Centre, Warwick University, and are described in *Sources*, Vol. 1, p. 179. Records of the T.U.C. are described in *Sources*, Vol. 1, pp. 261–5.

BOWLES, Baron
Francis George Bowles (1902–70)

M.P. (Lab.) Nuneaton, 1942–64.
Captain of the Yeomen of the Guard, 1965–70.

A very few papers remain with Lady Bowles (widow), 88 St James's Street, London SW1, to whom any enquiries should be addressed.

BOWLES, George Frederic Stewart (1877–1955)

M.P. (Con.) Norwood, 1906–Jan 1910.

BOWLES, Sir Henry Ferryman, 1st Bt (1858–1948)

M.P. (Con.) Enfield, 1889–1906; 1918–22.

Enquiries should be directed to Mr Derek Parker Bowles (grandson), White Oak House, Highclere, Newbury, Berks.

BOWLES, Thomas Gibson (1844–1922)

M.P. (Lib.) King's Lynn, 1892–1906; Jan–Dec 1910.

The family were unable to supply information regarding papers. Certain relevant material is contained in the Sir J. A. Kempe Collection at Duke University, Durham, North Carolina.

BOWYER, Sir George Edward Wentworth, 1st Bt, see DENHAM, 1st B

BOYCE, Sir (Harold) Leslie, 1st Bt (1895–1955)

M.P. (Con.) Gloucester, 1929–45.
Lord Mayor of London, 1951–2.

BOYD OF MERTON, 1st Vt
Alan Tindal Lennox-Boyd (1904–   )

M.P. (Con.) Mid Bedfordshire, 1931–60.
Parliamentary Secretary, Ministry of Labour, 1938–9; Ministry of Home Security 1939; Ministry of Food, 1939–40; Ministry of Aircraft Production, 1943–5. Minister of State, Colonial Affairs, 1951–2. Minister of Transport and Civil Aviation, 1952–4. Secretary of State for the Colonies, 1954–9.

Viscount Boyd states that he has promised his papers, relatively few in number, to Churchill College, Cambridge, subject to the views of his wife and sons on his death. Viscount Boyd has made extensive tape recordings relating to his career, and these are retained at St Antony's College, Oxford. Private Office papers (AVIA 9) are in the Public Record Office.

BOYD-CARPENTER, Baron
John Archibald Boyd-Carpenter (1908–   )

M.P. (Con.) Kingston-upon-Thames, 1945–72.
Financial Secretary to the Treasury, 1951–4. Minister of Transport and Civil Aviation, 1954–5; Pensions and National Insurance, 1955–62. Chief Secretary to the Treasury and Paymaster-General, 1962–4.
Chairman, Civil Aviation Authority, 1972–

Lord Boyd-Carpenter says he has retained certain papers which might be of historic interest.

BOYD-ORR, 1st B
John Boyd Orr (1880–1971)

Nutritionist and scientist. Director-General, United Nations Food and Agricultural Organisation, 1945–8.
M.P. (Ind.) Scottish Universities, 1945–6.

The surviving papers of Lord Boyd-Orr have been given to the National Library of Scotland. It appears that Boyd-Orr destroyed most of his incoming correspondence, and the bulk of the papers consists of typescripts of manuscripts of talks, articles, etc. (sometimes with covering letters). Amongst the surviving letters are 204 from various correspondents (1948–64), 29 letters of condolence to Lady Boyd-Orr in 1971, and drafts of 9 letters by Boyd-Orr (1950–1). A manuscript volume survives, containing mostly economic and political notes and quotations (1956–67). There is also a bound volume of newspaper cuttings relating to Boyd-Orr's visit to South America (1947) and miscellaneous press cuttings (1947–58). Correspondence relating to Africa (1929–39) can be found in the Lothian papers at the Scottish Record Office.

BOYLE OF HANDSWORTH, Baron
Sir Edward Charles Gurney Boyle, 3rd Bt (1923–   )

M.P. (Con.) Handsworth, Nov 1950–70.
Parliamentary Secretary, Ministry of Supply, 1954–5. Economic Secretary to the Treasury, 1955–6. Parliamentary Secretary, Ministry of Education, 1957–9. Financial Secretary to the Treasury, 1959–62. Minister of Education, 1962–4. Minister of State, Department of Education and Science, 1964.
Vice Chancellor, Leeds University, 1970–

BOYLE, Daniel (1859–1925)*

M.P. (Irish Nat.) Mayo North, Jan 1910–18.

BOYLE, Sir Edward, 1st Bt (1849–1909)

M.P. (Con.) Taunton, 1906–9.

Lord Boyle of Handsworth (grandson), The University, Leeds LS2 9JT, has certain papers of his grandfather. These are unsorted.

BOYLE, James (1863–1936)*

M.P. (Irish Nat.) Donegal West, 1900–2.

BOYLE, William Lewis (1859–1918)

M.P. (Lib.Un.) Mid-Norfolk, Jan 1910–18.

Three volumes of press cuttings, intermingled with letters, correspondence, etc., concerning W. L. Boyle's career, have been placed by his family in Norfolk and Norwich Record Office.

BOYTON, Sir James (1855–1926)

M.P. (Con.) Marylebone East, Jan 1910–18.

Boyton was a director of the firm of Elliot Son & Boyton, estate agents. They were unable to supply any information.

BRABAZON OF TARA, 1st B
John Theodore Cuthbert Moore-Brabazon (1884–1964)

M.P. (Con.) Chatham, 1918–29; Wallasey, 1931–42.
Parliamentary Secretary, Ministry of Transport, 1923–4, and 1924–7. Minister of Transport, 1940–1. Minister of Aircraft Production, 1941–2.

The papers (1906–64) at the Royal Air Force Museum are described in Hazlehurst and Woodland, p. 18. Private Office papers (AVIA 9) can be found at the Public Record Office.

BRABNER, Rupert Arnold (1911–45)

M.P. (Con.) Hythe, 1939–45.
Joint Parliamentary Under-Secretary, Air, 1944–5.

BRABOURNE, 5th B
Hon. Michael Herbert Rudolph Knatchbull (1895–1939)

M.P. (Con.) Ashford, 1931–3.
Governor, Bombay, 1933–7, and Bengal, 1937–9. Acting Viceroy of India, 1938.

The Knatchbull family archives are deposited on loan at the Kent Archives Office. This collection includes few papers relating to the 5th Baron Brabourne apart from some letters concerning his candidature at Ashford, his election success and his succession to the Barony. Further papers are held by the India Office Library. This large collection includes papers and correspondence on Bombay and Bengal, volumes of bound correspondence while Lord Bradbourne was acting as Viceroy, files, bundles of miscellaneous papers, engagement books and copies of speeches. Principal correspondents include successive Viceroys and Secretaries of State for India, Lord Erskine, the 11th Earl of Scarbrough, Viscount Waverley and R. A. Butler (now Lord Butler of Saffron Walden).

BRACE, William (1856–1947)

M.P. (Lab.) Glamorgan South, 1906–18; Abertillery, 1918–20.
Parliamentary Under-Secretary, Home Department, 1915–18. Chief Labour Adviser to Department of Mines, 1920–7.

A biography of Brace appears in *Dictionary of Labour Biography*, Vol. 1, pp. 51–3. This mentions no Mss. The records of the South Wales Miners Federation, of which Brace was once President, are deposited in the Library of University College Swansea. See *Sources*, Vol. 1, pp. 197–8.

BRACKEN, 1st Vt
Brendan Rendall Bracken (1901–58)

M.P. (Con.) Paddington North, 1929–45; Bournemouth, 1945–50; Bournemouth East, 1950–1.
Minister of Information, 1941–5. 1st Lord of the Admiralty, 1945.

Hazlehurst and Woodland, p. 19, found that no papers have survived.

BRACKENBURY, Henry Langton (1868–1920)

M.P. (Con.) Louth, Jan–Dec 1910; 1918–20.

Lt-Col Robert Brackenbury (son) knows of no papers.

BRADDOCK, Elizabeth (Bessie) Margaret (1899–1970)

M.P. (Lab.) Liverpool Exchange, 1945–70.

Liverpool City Libraries established that both Mr and Mrs Braddock threw papers away regularly; and the papers that existed in 1970 were destroyed following damage to Mrs Braddock's office. All that survived after Mrs Braddock's death were the papers of her husband which have been deposited with the Merseyside Record Office (acc. 2335). The most outstanding of these relate to Mr Braddock's dispute with the Executive Committee of the Communist Party of Great Britain concerning the role of the Central Commission. Through this, Mr and Mrs Braddock resigned from the Communist Party.

BRADDOCK, Thomas (1887–   )

M.P. (Lab.) Mitcham, 1945–50.

BRADFORD, 5th E of
Orlando Bridgeman, Vt Newport (1873–1957)

Lord in Waiting, 1919–24.

Family muniments are housed at the family home, Weston Park, Shifnal, Salop TF11 8LE. Lists are available at the National Register of Archives.

BRADWELL, Baron
Thomas Edward Neil Driberg (1905–76)

M.P. (Ind.) Maldon, 1942–5; (Lab.) 1945–55; Barking, 1959–Feb 1974.

Lord Bradwell retained an important collection of papers. Enquiries should be directed to his agents, David Higham Associates.

BRADY, P. J. (b. 1868)*

M.P. (Irish Nat.) Dublin, St Stephen's Green, Jan 1910–18.

BRAINE, Sir Bernard Richard (1914–   )

M.P. (Con.) Billericay, 1950–5; Essex S.E., 1955–
Parliamentary Secretary, Ministry of Pensions and National Insurance, 1960–1. Parliamentary Under-Secretary, Commonwealth Relations, 1961–2. Parliamentary Secretary, Ministry of Health, 1962–4.

Sir Bernard Braine has retained a substantial collection of papers covering his political activities, the bulk of the material referring to his career since 1950. The papers include correspondence, press cuttings and photocopies of material which Sir Bernard judges to be of interest.

BRAINTREE, 1st B
Sir Valentine George Crittall (1884–1961)

M.P. (Lab.) Maldon, 1923–4.

Certain records of the Maldon Labour Party are desposited in the Labour Party archive at Transport House.

BRAITHWAITE, Sir Albert Newby (1893–1959)

M.P. (Con.) Buckrose, 1926–45; Harrow West, 1951–9.

Lady Braithwaite (widow), 9 The Meadows, Portsmouth Road, Guildford, Surrey GU2 5DT, has a press-cuttings book, but knows of no other relevant papers.

BRAITHWAITE, Sir Joseph Gurney, 1st Bt (1895–1958)

M.P. (Con.) Sheffield Hillsborough, 1931–5; Holderness, 1939–50; Bristol N.W., 1950–5. Parliamentary Secretary, Transport and Civil Aviation, 1951–3.

BRAMALL, Sir (Ernest) Ashley (1916–   )

M.P. (Lab.) Bexley, 1946–50.
Leader of the Inner London Education Authority, 1970–

Sir Ashley states that he has never made a policy of retaining papers. The only ones he now has are those relating to his work at County Hall, and some papers of his constituency Labour Party.

BRAMSDON, Sir Thomas Arthur (1857–1935)

M.P. (Lib.) Portsmouth, May-Oct 1900, 1906–Jan 1910; Portsmouth Central, 1918–22, 1923–4.

BRANCH, James (1845–1918)

M.P. (Lib.) Enfield, 1906–Jan 1910.

Efforts to contact heirs and his firm proved unsuccessful.

BRAND, Hon. Arthur George (1853–1917)

M.P. (Con.) Wisbech, 1891–5, 1900–6.
Treasurer, H.M. Household, 1894–5.

Brand's great-nephew, the present (5th) Viscount Hampden, has been unable to trace any surviving papers.

BRASS, Sir William (b. 1886)

M.P. (Con.) Clitheroe, 1922–45.

Records of the Clitheroe Conservative Association are deposited in the Lancashire Record Office (*Sources*, Vol. 1, p. 66). No personal papers were discovered.

BRASSEY OF APETHORPE, 1st B
Sir Henry Leonard Campbell Brassey, 1st Bt (1870–1958)

M.P. (Con.) Northampton North, Jan 1910–18; Peterborough, 1918–29.

Records of the Northampton Conservatives (deposited in Northamptonshire Record Office) date from 1925 only. Peterborough Conservatives have records dating from 1898. A collection of material relating to the Brassey family is in Hastings Public Library but this contains no relevant material. It is believed that the family know of no papers.

BRASSEY, Albert (1844–1918)

M.P. (Con.) Banbury, 1895–1906.

Banbury Conservatives have no records prior to 1913.

BRASSEY, Robert Bingham (1875–1946)

M.P. (Con.) Banbury, Jan–Dec 1910.

See above.

BREESE, Charles Edward (1867–1932)

M.P. (Co.Lib.) Caernarvonshire, 1918–22.

The papers of C. E. Breese are located in the National Library of Wales (N.L.W. Mss 9471–89). The collection includes correspondence addressed to Breese as an M.P., and other miscellaneous correspondence addressed to C. E. and Edward Breese; records relating to the supply of soldiers for agricultural work in 1916; papers and correspondence relating to Crown and Common Lands in Wales; and newspaper cuttings relating to North Wales.

BRENTFORD, 1st Vt
Sir William Joynson-Hicks, 1st Bt (1865–1932)

M.P. (Con.) Manchester North West, 1908–Jan 1910; Brentford, 1911–18; Twickenham, 1918–29.
Parliamentary Secretary, Overseas Trade Department, 1922–3. Postmaster and Paymaster-General, 1923. Financial Secretary, Treasury, 1923. Minister of Health, 1923–4. Secretary of State for Home Affairs, 1924–9.

The present (3rd) Viscount Brentford of Newick Park, Sussex, has a few papers only. These are not available for research (Hazlehurst and Woodland, p. 75).

BRIANT, Frank (1865–1934)

M.P. (Lib.) Lambeth North, 1918–29; 1931–4.

Mr A. Parsons, whose father was a close friend of Briant's, knew of no papers. Briant was Superintendent of the Alford House Institute for Men and Boys for some forty-six years. Alford House was contacted but had no information.

BRIDGEMAN, 1st Vt
William Clive Bridgeman (1864–1935)

M.P. (Con.) Oswestry, 1906–29.
Parliamentary Secretary, Ministry of Labour, 1916–19; Board of Trade, 1919–20; Board of Trade (Mines Department), 1920–2. Secretary of State for Home Affairs, 1922–4. 1st Lord of the Admiralty, 1924–9.

The present (2nd) Viscount Bridgeman, Leigh Manor, Minsterley, Salop, has a collection of his father's papers. Restrictions concerning availability, and other details, are given in Hazlehurst and Woodland, p. 19.

BRIDPORT, 3rd Vt
Rowland Arthur Herbert Nelson Hood (1911–69)

Lieutenant-Commander, Royal Navy (Emergency List).
Lord in Waiting, 1939–40.

The present Viscount was not able to supply information.

BRIGG, Sir John (1834–1911)

M.P. (Lib.) Keighley, 1895–1911.

Correspondence (1894–1911), mainly relating to the 1902 Education Act can be found in the Brigg family papers in Keighley Public Library (NRA 6338).

BRIGGS, (W. J.) Harold (1870–1945)

M.P. (Con.) Manchester Blackley, 1918–23; 1924–9.

The Public Trustee acted in the estate and forwarded a letter to representatives of the family. No information was made available.

BRIGHT, Allan Heywood (1862–1941)

M.P. (Lib.) Oswestry, 1904–6.

Mrs Elizabeth Lloyd (daughter), Barton Court, Colwall, Malvern, Worcs WR13 6HN, knows of no papers apart from a scrapbook of reports of her father's speeches.

BRISCOE, Richard George (1893–1957)

M.P. (Con.) Cambridgeshire, 1923–45.

R. G. Briscoe's nephew, Mr M. G. M. Bevan, knows of no relevant papers. His uncle, in fact, made a habit of destroying the majority of his papers.

BRISE, Sir Edward Archibald Ruggles-, 1st Bt see RUGGLES-BRISE, Sir Edward Archibald, 1st Bt

BRISTOL, 4th M of
Rear Admiral Lord Frederick William Fane Hervey (1863–1951)

Naval career.
M.P. (Con.) Bury St Edmunds, 1906–7.

Family papers are held at the Suffolk Record Office (Bury St Edmunds Branch). The material includes correspondence, mainly of a family nature, with the 4th Marquess and others who were active in public life. Unfortunately, there are few papers relating to Bristol's political career in the House of Commons and later in the Lords.

BRITTAIN, Sir Harry E (1873–1974)

M.P. (Con.) Acton, 1918–29.

A very few papers, including some correspondence and ephemera, have been deposited on loan in BLPES. Papers on the Tariff Commission, of which Sir Harry was a founder member are also located at BLPES. See *Sources*, Vol. 1, p. 252.

BRITTON, George Bryant (1863–1929)

M.P. (Co.Lib.) Bristol, 1918–22.
Lord Mayor of Bristol, 1920–1.

Mr J. H. Britton (son), Shortwood Lodge, Pucklechurch, nr Bristol BS17 3PF, has very few papers relating to his father's political career. The firm of which G. B. Britton was founder is now part of the Ward White Group Ltd of Bristol. It has no papers, but a history has been published; *Cobblers' Tale* (Bristol, 1951; revised ed. 1963) and this contains many references to Britton's work.

BROAD, Francis Alfred (1874–1956)

M.P. (Lab.) Edmonton, 1922–31, 1935–45.

Mr M. J. Broad (grandson), knows of no papers.

BROAD, Thomas Tucker (b. 1863)

M.P. (Co.Lib.) Clay Cross, 1918–22.

BROADBENT, John (1872–1938)

M.P. (Con.) Ashton-under-Lyne, 1931–5.

Col John Broadbent's daughter, Mrs M. H. Connery, knows of no surviving papers.

BROADBRIDGE, 1st B
Sir George Thomas Broadbridge, 1st Bt (1869–1952)

Lord Mayor of London, 1936–7.
M.P. (Con.) City of London, 1938–45.

BROADHURST, Henry (1840–1911)

M.P. (Lib.) Stoke-upon-Trent, 1880–5; Bordesley, 1885–6; Nottingham, 1886–92; Leicester, 1894–1906.
Parliamentary Under-Secretary, Home Department, 1886.

Seven volumes of correspondence to Broadhurst, 1873–1911, which include letters from leading politicians, such as Gladstone, Henry Fawcett, John Morley, Rosebery, etc., are preserved at the BLPES. Also at BLPES is a typescript, with Mss corrections, of H. Hopkinson's unpublished 'Life of Henry Broadhurst; with a selection from his correspondence' (c. 1925). A note on Broadhurst's career appears in *Dictionary of Labour Biography*, Vol. II, pp. 62–8.

BROADLEY, Henry Broadley Harrison- (1853–1914)

M.P. (Con.) Howdenshire, 1906–14.

Mrs D. Harrison-Broadley, Tickton Grange, nr Beverley, Humberside, states that surviving papers are deposited in the Record Office at Beverley but these are chiefly estate papers.

BROCKET, 2nd B
Hon. Arthur Ronald Nall Nall-Cain (1904–67)

M.P. (Con.) Liverpool Wavertree, 1931–4.

Lord Brocket's family was unable to provide any information relating to papers.

BROCKLEBANK, Sir (Clement) Edmund Royds (1882–1949)

M.P. (Con.) Nottingham East, 1924–9; Liverpool Fairfield, 1931–45.

No family contact was established.

BROCKLEHURST, John Fielden, see RANKSBOROUGH, 1st B

BROCKLEHURST, Colonel William Brocklehurst (1851–1929)

M.P. (Lib.) Macclesfield, 1906–18.

Neither Mrs J. H. Dent-Brocklehurst (whose husband was a cousin of Colonel Brocklehurst's) nor Mrs Lettice Miller (great-niece) know of any surviving papers.

BROCKWAY, Baron
Archibald Fenner Brockway (1888–   )

M.P. (Lab.) Leyton East, 1929–31; Eton and Slough, 1950–64.
General Secretary, Independent Labour·Party, 1928, 1933–9; Political Secretary, 1939–46.

Lord Brockway states that many of his papers were destroyed when the ILP office was bombed during World War II. The remaining papers are limited in number, and at present unsorted. Records of the Independent Labour Party are described in *Sources*, Vol. 1, pp. 109–11. Correspondence of Brockway's is available in the Helene Stoecker papers at Swarthmore College Peace Collection. Other relevant material can be found in the Labour Party archive (LP/JLP/32/1–9).

BRODIE, Henry Cunningham (1875–1956)

M.P. (Lib.) Reigate, 1906–Jan 1910.

Messrs Murray, Hutchins & Co., solicitors of London, retain contact with a son. No information on papers was available.

BRODRICK, (William) St John Fremantle, see MIDLETON, 1st E of

BROMFIELD, William (1868–1950)

M.P. (Lab.) Leek, 1918–31, 1935–45.

BROMLEY, John (1876–1945)

M.P. (Lab.) Barrow-in-Furness, 1924–31.
General Secretary, Associated Society of Locomotive Engineers and Firemen, 1914–36.

Efforts to trace Bromley's heirs proved unsuccessful. Few records of ASLEF appear to have survived: see *Sources*, Vol. 1, p. 12.

BROOK, Sir Dryden (1884–1972)

M.P. (Lab.) Halifax, 1945–55.

A niece resides in Elland, West Yorks, but no information on papers was available.

BROOKE OF CUMNOR, Baron
Henry Brooke (1903–   )

M.P. (Con.) Lewisham West, 1938–45; Hampstead, 1950–66.
Financial Secretary to the Treasury, 1954–7. Minister of Housing and Local Government, and Minister for Welsh Affairs, 1957–61. Chief Secretary to the Treasury and Paymaster-General, 1961–2. Home Secretary, 1962–4.

Lord Brooke states that he has not discovered any papers which would be of interest.

BROOKE, Brigadier-General Christopher Robert Ingham (1869–1948)

M.P. (Con.) Pontefract, 1924–9.

Lt-Col. R. A. Ingham Brooke (son), Pinsley Gate, Church Harborough, Oxford OX7 2AA, states that when his father returned to South Africa he left behind no papers apart from an album of press cuttings, which he has.

BROOKE, Stopford William Wentworth (1859–1938)

M.P. (Lib.) Bow and Bromley, 1906–Jan 1910.

Lord Brooke of Cumnor (nephew) believes that Stopford Brooke would not have retained papers. His daughter is now resident in the U.S.A.

BROOKE, Willie (1896–1939)

M.P. (Lab.) Dunbartonshire, 1929–31; Batley and Morley, 1935–9.

No heirs were traced. Brooke was an official of the Amalgamated Society of Dyers (which in 1936 became part of the National Union of Dyers, Bleachers and Textile Workers). Its records are now deposited in Bradford Central Library, and are briefly described in *Sources*, Vol. 1, pp. 192–3.

BROOKES, Warwick (d. 1935)

M.P. (Con.) Mile End, 1916–18.

Messrs Coutts & Co., bankers, acted in the estate. No information was available.

BROOKFIELD, Arthur Montagu (1853–1940)

M.P. (Con.) Rye, 1885–1903.
H.M. Consul, Danzig, 1903–10; Savannah, 1910–23.

No contacts could be established. Records of the Rye Conservative Association dating from 1885 survive with the Association.

BROOKS, Thomas Judson (1880–1958)

M.P. (Lab) Rothwell, 1942–50; Normanton, 1950–1.

BROTHERS, Michael (b. 1870)

M.P. (Lab.) Bolton, 1929–31.

BROTHERTON, 1st B
Sir Edward Allen Brotherton, 1st Bt (1856–1930)

Lord Mayor of Leeds, 1913–14.
M.P. (Con.) Wakefield, 1902–Dec 1910, 1918–22.

The Librarian of the Brotherton Library, University of Leeds, discovered that Brotherton's family know of no papers. The Brotherton Collection at the University consists of a library of books, with no Mss.

BROTHERTON, John (1867–1941)

M.P. (Lab.) Gateshead, 1922–3.

BROUGHSHANE, 1st B
Sir William Henry Davison (1872–1953)

M.P. (Con.) Kensington South, 1918–45.

Papers are deposited in the Royal Borough of Kensington and Chelsea Central Library, and consist of twenty volumes of press cuttings and other material covering the years 1899–1919, 1931–49. The volumes cover the whole range of Broughshane's interests, including educational administration and local government affairs; Ulster and Unionism; his work during World War I; and his parliamentary career.

BROUGHTON, Sir Alfred Davies Devonsher (1902–   )

M.P. (Lab.) Batley and Morley, 1949–

BROUGHTON, Urban Hanlon (1857–1929) [1]

M.P. (Con.) Preston, 1915–18.

The present (3rd) Baron Fairhaven (grandson) has a few press cuttings only relating to his grandfather's career, and knows of no other papers.

1 Broughton died on 30 Jan 1929, before his intended elevation to the peerage.

BROWN, Sir Alexander Hargreaves, 1st Bt (1844–1922)

M.P. (Lib.) Wenlock, 1868–85; (Lib.Un.) Wellington, 1885–1906.

Records relating to Liberal Unionism are described in *Sources*, Vol. 1, pp. 151–2. Sir William

Pigott-Brown, Bt, is a great-grandson, but no information on personal papers was available.

BROWN, (Alfred) Ernest (1881–1962)

M.P. (Lib., later Lib.Nat.) Rugby, 1923–4; Leith, 1927–45.
Parliamentary Secretary, Ministry of Health, 1931–2. Parliamentary Secretary, Board of Trade, Mines Department, 1932–5. Minister of Labour, 1935–9; Labour and National Service, 1939–40. Secretary of State for Scotland, 1940–1. Minister of Health, 1941–3. Chancellor of the Duchy of Lancaster, 1943–5. Minister of Aircraft Production, 1945.

Hazlehurst and Woodland, p. 20, found no papers.

BROWN, Charles (1884–1940)

M.P. (Lab.) Mansfield, 1929–40.

No family contact was established. Brown was a long-time lecturer for the National Council of Labour Colleges. Its records in the National Library of Scotland are described in *Sources*, Vol. 1, pp. 174–5.

BROWN, Douglas Clifton-, see RUFFSIDE, 1st Vt

BROWN, Lieutenant-Colonel Geoffrey Benedict Clifton- (1899–   )

M.P. (Con.) Bury St Edmunds, 1945–50.

BROWN, George Alfred, see GEORGE-BROWN, Baron

BROWN, George Mackenzie (1869–1946)

M.P. (Lib.) Edinburgh Central, 1900–6.

BROWN, Howard Clifton (1868–1946)

M.P. (Con.) Newbury, 1922–3, 1924–45.

A book of press cuttings covering the period 1876 to 1946 is in the possession of Brig.-Gen. H. C. Brown's daughter, Mrs Elizabeth Clifton-Calvert, Kilnwood, Faygate, Horsham, Sussex. This includes cuttings relating to Brig.-Gen. Brown's father, James Clifton Brown, M.P., as well as to his own parliamentary career.

BROWN, James (1862–1939)

Secretary, Ayrshire Miners' Union, 1908–18; Scottish Miners', 1917–36.
M.P. (Lab.) Ayrshire South, 1918–31, 1935–9.

No papers are known to survive. The *Dictionary of Labour Biography*, Vol. 1, pp. 54–5, makes no mention of Mss. The papers of the Scottish Miners' organisations, deposited in the National Library of Scotland, are described in *Sources*, Vol. 1, p. 197.

BROWN, John.Wesley (1873–1944)

M.P. (Con.) Middlesbrough East, 1922–3.

The Middlesbrough Conservative Association has retained many records for the relevant period. No personal papers have come to light.

BROWN, Thomas James (1886–1970)

M.P. (Lab.) Ince-in-Makerfield, 1942–64.

BROWN, Thomas Watters (1879–1944)*

M.P. (Con.) North Down, 1918–22.
Solicitor-General for Ireland, 1921. Attorney General for Ireland, Sep 1921. Judge of the High Court of Northern Ireland, 1922–44.

His Hon. Judge J. A. Brown (son), Glenlough, Stoneyford, Lisburn, Co.Antrim, has three large volumes of press cuttings which span his father's life. The Northern Ireland Public Record Office has a microfilm of this material.

BROWN, William John (1894–1960)

M.P. (Lab.) Wolverhampton West, 1929–31; (Ind.) Rugby, 1942–50.
General Secretary, Civil Service Clerical Association, 1919–42. Parliamentary General Secretary, 1942–9.

Brown's family was not traced. The Barclays Bank Trust Company Ltd, who acted in the estate, had no information. The Civil and Public Services Association (formerly Civil Service Clerical Association), 215 Balham High Road, London SW17 7BQ, has a large quantity of papers relating to Brown's period as General Secretary. These are unsorted, but it would appear that these are all 'official'. They do, however, include circulars drafted by Brown, policy files which include correspondence, etc. Brown's autobiography *So Far* is a useful source.

BROWN, Sir William Robson (1900–75)

M.P. (Con.) Esher, 1950–70.

It is believed that no papers were retained by Sir William Robson Brown.

BROWNE, Alexander Crawford (1888–1942)*

M.P. (Ulster Un.) Belfast West, 1931–42.

BROWNE, Jack Nixon, see CRAIGTON, Baron.

BRUCE, Baron
Donald William Trevor Bruce (1912–   )

M.P. (Lab.) Portsmouth North, 1945–50.

Lord Bruce states that he has retained various papers, including material relating to the Parliament of 1945–50.

BRUCE, Sir Alexander Hugh, see BALFOUR OF BURLEIGH, 6th B

BRUFORD, Robert (1868–1939)

M.P. (Con.) Wells, 1922–3.

Robert Bruford's family know of no surviving papers.

BRUGHA, Cathal.*[1]

M.P. (Sinn Fein) Waterford, 1918–22.

Mr Ruari Brugha, T. D. (son) says that his father left few documents. Two biographies (in Irish) have been written, the more recent by T. O'Doherty.

1 Formerly known as Cathal Burgess.

BRUNNER, Sir John Fowler, 2nd Bt (1865–1929)

M.P. (Lib.) Leigh, 1906–Jan 1910; Northwich, Dec 1910–18; Southport, 1923–4.

See below.

BRUNNER, Sir John Tomlinson, 1st Bt (1842–1919)

M.P. (Lib.) Northwich, 1885–6, 1887–Dec 1910.

An extensive collection of Brunner family papers has been deposited in Liverpool University Library. Among the papers are 8 boxes of correspondence (c. 2260 items), mostly letters on business and political topics, miscellaneous pamphlets, leaflets, election literature and press cuttings, together with pocket diaries for the years 1886, 1889–90 and 1892–1919. There is also material relating to Thomas Edward Ellis and his position as secretary to Sir John Brunner. A detailed list is available (NRA 19105).

BRUNSKILL, Gerald Fitzgibbon (1866–1918)*

M.P. (Con.) Mid-Tyrone, Jan–Dec 1910.

BRUNTISFIELD, 1st B
Sir Victor Alexander George Anthony Warrender, 8th Bt (1899–   )

M.P. (Con.) Grantham, 1923–42.
Junior Lord of the Treasury, 1931–2. Vice Chamberlain, H.M. Household, 1932–5. Comptroller, H.M. Household, 1935. Parliamentary and Financial Secretary, War Office, 1935–40; Admiralty, 1940–2. Parliamentary Secretary, Admiralty, 1942–5.

According to information supplied to the Imperial War Museum, Lord Bruntisfield retained no papers.

BRUTON, Sir James (1848–1933)

M.P. (Con.) Gloucester, 1918–23.

Mr C. T. Bruton (great-nephew), c/o Bruton, Knowles & Co., chartered surveyors of Gloucester, knows of no relevant political papers, though he has a collection of family material.

BRYCE, 1st Vt
James Bryce (1838–1922)

M.P. (Lib.) Tower Hamlets, 1880–5; Aberdeen South, 1885–1906.
Parliamentary Under-Secretary, Foreign Affairs, 1886. Chancellor of the Duchy of Lancaster, 1892–4. President, Board of Trade, 1894–5. Chief Secretary, Ireland, 1905–7. Ambassador, United States, 1907–13.

Lord Bryce left a mass of papers relating to his career. The Bodleian Library, Oxford, has acquired certain parts of the collection. They have been listed, but are not fully catalogued and they remain in separate series. The American material is divided from the general English papers, and includes correspondence relating to the United States, and embassy papers. The other material covers political papers, records collected while Bryce was in government office, pamphlets, photographs, and a mass of correspondence arranged in different series. Other papers and correspondence (1904–21) are available at the Public Record Office (FO 800/331–335), and papers relating to Irish affairs are held by the National Library of Ireland. For further details, readers should consult Hazlehurst and Woodland: pp. 21–2.

BRYCE, John Annan (1841–1923)

M.P. (Lib.) Inverness, 1906–18.

It is believed that a number of papers owned by John Bryce's daughter were destroyed after her death; and John Bryce's other child is also now deceased. The papers of his brother, Viscount Bryce, located in the National Library of Ireland and the Bodleian Library, Oxford, include papers relating to John Annan Bryce. The Bodleian Library particularly has letters between John and his brother.

BRYMER, William Ernest (1840–1909)

M.P. (Con.) Dorchester, 1874–1885; Dorset South, 1891–1906.

Records of the Dorset Conservative Association, 1884–1907, are deposited in Dorset Record Office. Personal papers were not located.

BUCCLEUCH, 7th D of
John Charles Montagu-Douglas-Scott, E of Dalkeith (1864–1935)

M.P. (Con.) Roxburghshire, 1895–1906.

See below.

BUCCLEUCH, 8th D of
Walter John Montagu-Douglas-Scott, E of Dalkeith (1894–1973)

M.P. (Con.) Roxburgh and Selkirk, 1931–45.

Some papers of both the 7th and 8th Dukes of Buccleuch are with the present (9th) Duke of Buccleuch at Drumlanrig Castle, Thornhill, Dumfriesshire. They are not generally available, but requests for specific information might be considered.

BUCHAN, Sir John, see TWEEDSMUIR, 1st B

BUCHANAN, Arthur Louis Hamilton (1866–1925)

M.P. (Con.) Coatbridge, 1918–22.

BUCHANAN, George (1890–1955)

M.P. (Lab.) Glasgow Gorbals, 1922–48.
Joint Parliamentary Under-Secretary, Scotland, 1945–7. Minister of Pensions, 1947–8. Chairman, National Assistance Board, 1948–53.

Hazlehurst and Woodland, p. 22, were unable to find any surviving papers.

BUCHANAN, Thomas Ryburn (1846–1911)

M.P. (Lib.) Edinburgh, 1881–5; Edinburgh West, 1885–92; Aberdeenshire East, 1892–1900; Perthshire East, 1903–11.
Financial Secretary, War Office, 1906–8. Parliamentary Under-Secretary, India Office, 1908–9.

Miss E. H. Bolitho, (whose great-aunt married T. R. Buchanan), Pentre, Lelant, St Ives, Cornwall, was left over 30 trunks of material, containing a great deal of papers. These papers are largely unsorted and only a brief description can be given. Buchanan wrote to his wife every day, and the letters give full accounts of his parliamentary career. In addition, there are letters between Buchanan and prominent politicians, and fragments of a diary. A further section of Buchanan's diary can be found in the Campbell-Bannerman collection at the British Library (Add. Ms 52520).

BUCKINGHAM, Sir Henry Cecil (1867–1931)

M.P. (Con.) Guildford, 1922–31.

Mrs Pauline Aylmer, Flat 5, 27 Onslow Square, London SW7 (daughter) has no papers, but states that four volumes of press cuttings have survived with Mrs Philip Buckingham (daughter-in-law). These largely relate to family matters, and were kept by Sir Henry's brother. They contain occasional references only to political affairs. Mrs Aylmer knows of no other relevant papers.

BUCKLE, John (1867–1925)

M.P. (Lab.) Eccles, 1922–4.

BUCKLEY, Albert (1877–1965)

M.P. (Con.) Waterloo, 1918–23.
Junior Lord of the Treasury, 1922–3. Parliamentary Secretary, Department of Overseas Trade, 1923.

Mr R. E. Buckley (son), c/o Edmund Buckley & Co., 30A Hamilton Street, Hamilton Square, Birkenhead, Merseyside L41 5AD, has a few papers and press cuttings relating to his father's career. As a rule, however, Mr Buckley did not make a habit of retaining large numbers of papers.

BUCKMASTER, 1st Vt
Sir Stanley Owen Buckmaster (1861–1934)

M.P. (Lib.) Cambridge, 1906–Jan 1910; Keighley, 1911–15.
Solicitor-General, 1913–15. Lord Chancellor, 1915–16.

Mr H. D. Miller, 22 Milner Street, London SW7, Viscount Buckmaster's grandson, has a collection of papers, mainly letters, relating to his grandfather's career. Details are given in Hazlehurst and Woodland, pp. 22–3.

BUCKTON, Baron
Sir Samuel Storey, 1st Bt (1896–   )

M.P. (Con.) Sunderland, 1931–45; Stretford, 1950–66.

Lord Buckton states that he has retained few papers relating to his career.

BUDSLEY, Donald*

M.P. (Sinn Fein) Kildare North, 1918–22.

BULL, Bartle Brennan (1902–50)

M.P. (Con.) Enfield, 1935–45.

BULL, Sir William James, 1st Bt (1863–1931)

M.P. (Con.) Hammersmith, 1900–18; Hammersmith South, 1918–29.
Chairman, London Unionist M.P.s, 1910–29.

Sir George Bull (son), 3 Hammersmith Terrace, London W6, retained a collection of his father's papers. Certain other papers have been deposited in the House of Lords Record Office, while a collection of press cuttings is preserved by Hammersmith Public Libraries.

BULLARD, Sir Harry (1841–1903)

M.P. (Con.) Norwich, 1885–6, 1895–1903.

A scrapbook is preserved in Norwich Local History Library. It appears that no papers survive in the family.

BULLER, Sir Mervyn Edward Manningham-, 3rd Bt (1876–1956)

M.P. (Con.) Kettering, 1924–9.

Viscount Dilhorne (son) was unable to provide any information.

BULLER, Sir Reginald Edward Manningham-, 4th Bt, see DILHORNE, 1st Vt

BULLOCK, Sir (Harold) Malcolm, 1st Bt (1890–1966)

M.P. (Con.) Waterloo, 1923–50; Crosby, 1950–3.

Mrs Peter Hastings (daughter), Well's Head House, Kingsclere, nr Newbury, Berks RG15 8PZ, states that her father left no diaries or correspondence. She does, however, have some press cuttings retained in a book.

BULLUS, Sir Eric Edward (1906–   )

M.P. (Con.) Wembley North, 1950–Feb 1974.

Sir Eric has certain papers and pamphlets, at present unsorted. Amongst the papers are constituency correspondence and copies of ministerial answers. Earlier papers, covering the 1950s, have been destroyed.

BURDEN, 1st B
Thomas William Burden (1885–1970)

M.P. (Lab.) Sheffield Park, 1942–50.
Lord-in-Waiting, 1950–1.

The 2nd Lord Burden says that none of his father's papers has survived.

BURDEN, Frederick Frank Arthur (1905–   )

M.P. (Con.) Gillingham, 1950–

Mr Burden states that he has no papers that he considers of value to future historians.

BURDON, Rowland (1857–1944)

M.P. (Con.) Sedgefield, 1918–22.

There are two large boxes of documents relating to the late Rowland Burdon in the custody of Messrs Wilkinson Marshall Clayton & Gibson, 27 Grainger Street, Newcastle-upon-Tyne NE1 5JY, who are prepared to arrange for an inspection of them in suitable cases.

BURGESS, Cathal, see BRUGHA, Cathal

BURGESS, Frederick George (d. 1951)

M.P. (Lab.) York, 1929–31.

The records of York Labour Party have been placed in the City Library.

BURGESS, J. Stanley (b. 1889)

M.P. (Lab.) Rochdale, 1922–3.

BURGHLEY, Lord, see EXETER, 6th M of

BURGIN, Edward Leslie (1887–1945)

M.P. (Lib.) Luton, 1929–45.
Parliamentary Secretary, Board of Trade, 1932–7. Minister of Transport, 1937–9. Minister of Supply, 1939–40.

Mrs D. Burgin, 20 Amenbury Lane, Harpenden, Herts, has a very small collection of papers relating to her late husband. Hazlehurst and Woodland, p. 23, give brief details of the material. Private Office papers (AVIA 11) can be found at the Public Record Office.

BURGOYNE, Sir Alan Hughes (1880–1929)

M.P. (Con.) Kensington North, Jan 1910–22; Aylesbury, 1924–9.

Burgoyne left his library to Kelly College, Tavistock, Devon. No papers have, however, come to light.

BURKE, Edmund Haviland (1864–1914)*

M.P. (Irish Nat.) Tullamore, 1900–14.

BURKE, James Aloysius*

M.P. (Sinn Fein) Mid-Tipperary, 1918–22.

BURKE, Wilfred Andrew (1890–1968)

M.P. (Lab.) Burnley, 1935–59.
Assistant Postmaster-General, 1945–7.

No family contact was established. Certain records of the Burnley Labour movement are in Burnley Public Library.

BURMAN, Sir John Bedford (1867–1941)

M.P. (Con.) Birmingham Duddeston, 1923–9.

Sir John's son, Sir Charles Burman, J.P., D.L., Packwood Hall, Hockley Heath, Solihull, Warwickshire, has retained eight volumes of press cuttings, covering the period from 1886 to 1941.

BURN, Sir Charles Rosdew, see FORBES-LEITH, Sir Charles Rosdew, 1st Bt

BURN, T. H. (b. 1875)*

M.P. (Con.) Belfast St Anne's, 1918–22.

BURNETT, John George (1876–1962)

M.P. (Con.) Aberdeen North, 1931–5.

BURNEY, Sir (Charles) Dennistoun, 2nd Bt (1888–1968)

M.P. (Con.) Uxbridge, 1922–9.

Sir Cecil Burney, Bt (son), 5 Lyall Street, London SW1, has certain material, and so does his mother who lives in Bermuda. The papers are so far unsorted.

BURNHAM, 1st Vt
Hon. Harry Lawson Webster Lawson (1862–1933)

M.P. (Lib.) St Pancras West, 1885–92; Gloucestershire East, 1893–5; (Con.) Mile End, 1905–6 and Jan 1910–16.

Lt-Colonel the Lord Burnham, Hall Barn, Beaconsfield, Bucks, states that most of the family papers which are unsorted are at present in store. Details are not available, and the papers are not readily available. Other records of the Lawson family are believed to survive amongst the archives of the *Daily Telegraph*, which was owned by the family. Mr Gerald Coke, C.B.E., Jenkyn Place, Bentley, Hants, has a number of papers of a more personal nature relating to his grandfather, the Viscount Burnham. This material consists of a voluminous correspondence between the 1st Viscount and his wife in the period of their engagement; letters relating to the Gallipoli campaign; an assortment of letters written to Viscount Burnham at various dates on a variety of subjects; copies of drafts of speeches; and some other personal papers. Other letters held by Mr Coke were passed to Frederick, Lord Burnham, when he was writing his history of the *Daily Telegraph*.

BURNIE, James (1882–1975)

M.P. (Lib.) Bootle, 1922–4.

Mr Burnie stated that he retained no papers concerning his parliamentary activities.

BURNS, John Elliot (1858–1943)

M.P. (Ind.Lab.) Battersea, 1892–5; (Lib.) Battersea, 1895–1918.
President of the Local Government Board, 1905–14. President of the Board of Trade, 1914.

A large collection of papers survives in the British Library (Add. Mss 46281–46345). Another small collection of papers can be found in Battersea District Library, whilst the Library of the California State University at Northridge has a further series of Burns letters. Books from Burns' library (with some papers) are held in the headquarters of the Trades Union Congress, and books and other material on London collected by Burns survive with the Greater London Record Office. Details of these collections appear in Hazlehurst and Woodland, pp. 23–5.

BURNTWOOD, Baron
Julian Ward Snow (1910–   )

M.P. (Lab.) Portsmouth Central, 1945–50; Tamworth and Lichfield, 1950–70.
Vice-Chamberlain, H.M. Household, 1945–6. Junior Lord of the Treasury, 1946–50. Parliamentary Secretary, Ministry of Aviation, 1966–7. Parliamentary Secretary, Ministry of Health, 1967–8. Parliamentary Under-Secretary, Department of Health and Social Security, 1968–9.

Lord Burntwood states 'that he has retained no papers of public interest.

BURNYEAT, William John Dalzell (1874–1916)

M.P. (Lib.) Whitehaven, 1906–Jan 1910.

BURT, Thomas (1837–1922)

M.P. (Lib.) Morpeth, 1874–1918.

The *Dictionary of Labour Biography*, Vol. 1, pp. 51–63, describes his career.

BURTON OF COVENTRY, Baroness
Elaine Frances Burton (1904–   )

M.P. (Lab.) Coventry South, 1950–9.

Extensive files of correspondence with constituents, with members of the local Labour Party and with other Coventry M.P.s are held in the Coventry Borough Labour Party Archive in the Modern Records Centre, University of Warwick Library. Also included are records of the campaigns fought by Baroness Burton and of her activities in the House of Commons.

BURTON, Henry Walter (1876–1947)

M.P. (Con.) Sudbury, 1924–45.

BURY, Vt, see ALBEMARLE, 8th E of

BURY, (Charles Kenneth) Howard (1883–1963)

M.P. (Con.) Bilston, 1922–4; Chelmsford, 1926–31.

A collection of Bury family papers (c. 200 items) covering the period 1800–1919 has been photocopied by the Northern Ireland Public Record Office and deposited at the Longford/Westmeath Library, Mullingar. Certain documents in this collection relate to Howard Bury. A full catalogue of the collection may be consulted at the Northern Ireland Public Record Office, (reference T.3069).

BUTCHER, Sir Herbert Walter, 1st Bt (1901–66)

M.P. (Lib.Nat.) Holland with Boston, 1937–50; (Nat.Lib. and Con.) 1950–66.
Junior Lord of the Treasury, 1951–3. Chairman of National Liberal Organisation, 1962–6.

The surviving records of the National Liberal Party are described in *Sources*, Vol. 1, pp. 183–4. No personal papers are known.

BUTCHER, Sir John George, 1st Bt, see DANESFORT, 1st B

BUTCHER, Samuel Henry (1850–1910)

M.P. (Con.) Cambridge University, 1906–Dec 1910.

BUTLER OF SAFFRON WALDEN, Baron
Richard Austen Butler (1902–   )

M.P. (Con.) Saffron Walden, 1929–65.
Parliamentary Under-Secretary, India Office, 1932–7. Parliamentary Secretary, Ministry of Labour, 1937–8. Parliamentary Under-Secretary of State, Foreign Office, 1938–41. President of the Board (later Minister) of Education, 1941–5. Minister of Labour, 1945. Chancellor of the Exchequer, 1951–5. Lord Privy Seal, 1955–9. Secretary of State for Home Affairs, 1957–62. 1st Secretary of State and Deputy Prime Minister, 1962–3. Secretary of State for Foreign Affairs, 1963–4.

Hazlehurst and Woodland, p. 25, found that Lord Butler intends that his papers should be placed in due course in the Wren Library at Trinity College, Cambridge.

BUTLER, Sir Geoffrey G. G. (1887–1929)

M.P. (Con.) Cambridge University, 1923–9.

The Library of Corpus Christi College, Cambridge, has in its care a large bundle of personal papers. This collection of papers was given to the Library after Sir Geoffrey's death. Some two-thirds of the papers, consisting of personal letters to his wife, were destroyed. The remainder are not made available for public inspection, and there are no current plans to do so.

BUTLER, Herbert William (1897–1971)

M.P. (Lab.) Hackney South, 1945–55; Hackney Central, 1955–70.

Butler made a practice of destroying much of his correspondence once it had been completed. There survives, however, a small but useful collection consisting of approximately eight files of correspondence and pamphlets. The correspondence is mainly constituency correspondence relating to the years 1960–8. There is also some earlier material relating to Butler's period as a borough councillor, and also to his dealings with the Hackney Labour Party. One exchange of letters dated October 1936 is of particular interest, dealing with the question of allowing the Fascists to use the Kings Hall, Hackney. These papers have been deposited in the Greater London Record Office.

BUTLER, Hugh Myddleton (1857–1943)

M.P. (Con.) Leeds North, 1922–3.

Enquiries should be directed to Mrs Harries (daughter), Knoll Hill, Prestbury, Cheltenham, Glos. Kirkstall Forge Engineering Ltd, of Leeds, the former firm of H. M. Butler, know of no personal papers, but have certain company records. Certain records of the Leeds Conservatives are deposited with Leeds City Libraries.

BUTLER, Sir James Ramsay Montagu (1889–1975)

M.P. (Ind.) Cambridge University, 1922–3.

The papers are housed in the Library of Trinity College, Cambridge, but have not yet been catalogued.

BUTT, Sir Alfred, 1st Bt (1878–1962)

Director of Rationing, Ministry of Food, 1917–18.
M.P. (Con.) Balham and Tooting, 1922–36.

Sir Kenneth Butt, Bt (son), states that his father left instructions to his executors to destroy all correspondence and files, and his wishes were carried out.

BUTTON, Sir Howard Stransom (1873–1943)

M.P. (Con.) The Wrekin, 1922–3.

Mr F. H. D. Button (son) had no relevant information regarding papers.

BUXTON, 1st E
Sir Sydney Charles Buxton (1853–1934)

M.P. (Lib.) Peterborough, 1883–5; Poplar, 1886–1914.
Under-Secretary of State, Colonial Office, 1892–5. Postmaster General, 1905–10. President,

Board of Trade, 1910–14. High Commissioner and Governor General, South Africa, 1914–20.

A collection of papers survives in the care of Lord Buxton's granddaughter, Mrs E. Clay, Newtimber Place, Hassocks, Sussex. A full description of these papers, including those relating to Buxton's term in South Africa, is given by Hazlehurst and Woodland, pp. 26–7.

BUXTON, Charles Roden (1875–1942)

M.P. (Lib.) Ashburton, Jan–Dec 1910; (Lab.) Accrington, 1922–3; Elland, 1929–31.

The papers formerly in the care of Mr David Buxton (son) have been deposited in Rhodes House Library, Oxford (ref. Mss. Brit. Emp. s. 405). The collection, contained in seven boxes, covers the years 1908–44, with a few printed additions of a later date. There is very little material before 1914. The papers fall into two categories. The first (Boxes 1–4) is concerned with European politics, chiefly with unofficial peace efforts in both World Wars. Box 4 holds pamphlets and books, many by Buxton, which are closely related to the papers in Boxes 1–3. The second part of the collection (Boxes 5–7) is classified as 'Colonial papers', and these are concerned almost entirely with Africa. Amongst topics covered are South Africa and the Protectorates, including letters and memoranda of Mr and Mrs W. G. Ballinger, 1930–5; correspondence with Tshekedi Khama, 1931–3; memoranda and other papers of the Labour Party International Department, dealing with problems of labour and land; and the Joint Select Committee on Closer Union in East Africa. Permission to quote from the papers in Boxes 1–3 must be obtained from Mr David Buxton, Old Ellwoods, 55 Bridleway, Grantchester, Cambridge CB3 9NY. A few bundles of newscuttings are retained at BLPES, but these are of ephemeral interest.

BUXTON, Lucy Edith Noel-, see NOEL-BUXTON, Lady

BUXTON, Noel Edward Noel-, see NOEL-BUXTON, 1st B

BYERS, Baron
(Charles) Frank Byers (1915-   )

M.P. (Lib.) Dorset North, 1945–50.
Liberal Leader, House of Lords, since 1967.

BYLES, Sir William Pollard (1839–1917)

M.P. (Lib.) Shipley, 1892–5; Salford North, 1906–17.

Dr J. B. Byles, 56 Southborough Road, Bickley, Kent, knows of no relevant surviving papers, and other members of the family whom he contacted similarly had no relevant material.

BYRNE, Alfred (b. 1882)*

M.P. (Irish Nat.) Dublin Harbour, 1915–18.

CADOGAN, 5th E
George Henry Cadogan, Vt Chelsea (1840–1915)

M.P. (Con.) Bath, 1873.
Parliamentary Under Secretary of State, War Office, 1875–8; Colonial Office, 1878–80. Lord Privy Seal, 1886–92. Lord Lieutenant of Ireland, 1895–1902.

The present (7th) Earl Cadogan, 28A Cadogan Square, London SW1, has a large collection of his grandfather's letters. Details are in Hazlehurst and Woodland, p. 27.

CADOGAN, Hon. Sir Edward Cecil George (1880–1962)

M.P. (Con.) Reading, 1922–3; Finchley, 1924–35; Bolton, 1940–5.

The present Earl Cadogan is a nephew. No information was forthcoming. Bolton Conservatives have retained various constituency papers dating from the 1890s, and enquiries should be directed to them.

CAIN, Hon. Arthur Ronald Nall Nall-, see BROCKET, 2nd B

CAINE, Sir Derwent Hall, 1st Bt (1891–1971)

M.P. (Lab.) Liverpool Everton, 1929–31.

The Isle of Man Bank Ltd (Trustee Department), which administered the estate, stated that it was unable to assist in the survey. The Hall Caine literary manuscripts which are in the Manx Museum include none of Sir Derwent's papers.

CAINE, Gordon Ralph Hall (1884–1962)

M.P. (Con.) Dorset East, 1922–9 and 1931–45.

Hall Caine's son, who lives in the United States, could not be contacted.

CAINE, William Sproston (1842–1903)

M.P. (Lib.) Scarborough, 1880–5; Barrow-in-Furness, 1886–9; Bradford, 1892–5; Camborne, 1900–3.
Civil Lord of the Admiralty, 1884–5.

Certain correspondence (1886–92) can be found in the Joseph Chamberlain papers at Birmingham University Library. The present (2nd) Lord Clwyd is a grandson, but no information was forthcoming. Bradford Liberals have retained certain papers prior to 1914. Caine was President of the British Temperance League and of the National Temperance Federation, and Vice-President of the United Kingdom Alliance. Records of the Temperance organisations are described in *Sources,* Vol. 1, pp. 253–7.

CAIRNS, John (1859–1923)

Miners' Leader in Northumberland.
M.P. (Lab.) Morpeth, 1918–23.

Messrs Watson Burton, solicitors of Newcastle upon Tyne, acted in the estate. They suggested that Captain R. D. Cairns should be contacted. He, however, had no information. A note on Cairns's career can be found in *Dictionary of Labour Biography,* Vol. II, pp. 79–80. Records of the Northumberland Miners in the Northumberland Record Office are described in *Sources,* Vol. 1, p. 196.

CAIRNS, Thomas (1854–1908)

M.P. (Lib.) Newcastle-upon-Tyne, 1906–8.

Captain R. D. Cairns (grandson), Ozier Hill, Taghmon, Co. Wexford, has a small collection of his grandfather's papers. This includes a book of correspondence, some of it with constituents, some with fellow M.P.s, and some letters dealing with his business, Cairns Noble & Co. The letters cover the period June 1906–Aug 1908. In addition Captain Cairns has a newspaper cuttings book, covering the period July 1903–Jan 1906.

CALDECOTE, 1st Vt
Sir Thomas Walker Hobart Inskip (1876–1947)

M.P. (Con.) Bristol Central, 1918–29; Fareham, 1931–9.
Solicitor-General, 1922–4; 1924–8 and 1931–2. Attorney-General, 1928–9 and 1932–6.
Minister for Co-ordination of Defence, 1936–9. Secretary of State for Dominion Affairs, 1939
and 1940. Lord Chancellor, 1939–40. Lord Chief Justice, 1940–6.

The papers, copies of which are held under special conditions of access at Churchill College,
Cambridge, are described by Hazlehurst and Woodland, p. 80.

CALDWELL, James (1839–1925)

M.P. (Lib.) Glasgow St Rollox, 1886–92; Mid-Lanarkshire, 1894–Jan 1910.

CALLAGHAN, (Leonard) James (1912–   )

M.P. (Lab.) Cardiff South, 1945–50; Cardiff S.E., 1950–
Parliamentary Secretary, Ministry of Transport, 1947–50. Parliamentary and Financial
Secretary, Admiralty, 1950–1. Chancellor of the Exchequer, 1964–7. Secretary of State for
Home Affairs, 1967–70. Secretary of State for Foreign and Commonwealth Affairs, 1974–6.
Prime Minister, 1976–

CALLEY, Thomas Charles Pleydell (1856–1932)

M.P. (Con.) Cricklade, Jan–Dec 1910.

Calley was survived by a daughter, now believed deceased. No other contacts were established.

CALVERLEY, 1st B
George Muff (1877–1955)

M.P. (Lab.) Hull East, 1929–31 and 1935–45.

There was no contact with the present Lord Calverley.

CAMERON, Alexander Gordon (1886–1944)

M.P. (Lab.) Widnes, 1929–31.

Messrs Vivash Robinson Hunt & Co., solicitors who acted in Cameron's estate, knew of no
papers.

CAMERON, Robert (1825–1913)

M.P. (Lib.) Houghton-le-Spring, 1895–1913.

The beneficiaries of Cameron's will were his widow and his step-daughter. The latter was not
traced. Cameron was one-time curator of Sunderland Museum, but the Sunderland Central
Library know of no papers.

CAMPBELL, Duncan Frederick (1876–1916)

M.P. (Con.) Ayrshire North, 1911–16.

Group-Captain A. P. Campbell C.B.E. (son), Perrot Farm, Graffham, Petworth, Sussex, has a
collection of material relating to his father's career. This consists largely of press cuttings

relating to various election campaigns; little material relates to D. F. Campbell's work as an M.P.

CAMPBELL, Sir Edward Taswell, 1st Bt (1879–1945)

M.P. (Con.) Camberwell N.W., 1924–9; Bromley, 1930–45.

Mrs Frances Campbell-Walter, F.S.A. (daughter), 19A Princes Gate Mews, London SW7, has a substantial collection of her father's press cuttings.

CAMPBELL, Vice-Admiral Gordon (1886–1953)

M.P. (Con.) Burnley, 1931–5.

The Rev. David Gordon Campbell (son), The Society of St John the Evangelist, 22 Great College Street, London SW1, states that his father never kept a diary, and believes that press cuttings and other papers have mostly been destroyed. Reference may be made to the Keyes papers at Churchill College, Cambridge.

CAMPBELL, James Alexander (1825–1908)

M.P. (Con.) Universities of Glasgow and Aberdeen, 1880–1906.

Mrs Hugh Campbell, 22 Carlyle Square, SW3 6EY, states that to her knowledge, no papers have survived. She believes that one of his daughters destroyed them after his death.

CAMPBELL, Sir James Henry Mussen, 1st Bt, see GLENAVY, 1st B

CAMPBELL, John*

M.P. (Irish Nat.) Armagh South, 1900–6.

CAMPBELL, John Dermot (1898–1945)*

M.P. (Con.) Antrim, 1943–5.

CAMPBELL, John Gordon Drummond (1864–1935)

M.P. (Con.) Kingston-on-Thames, 1918–22.

CAMPION, Lieutenant-Colonel Sir William Robert (1870–1951)

M.P. (Con.) Lewes, Dec 1910–24.
Governor, Western Australia, 1924–31.

Papers of Campion's when he was Governor of Western Australia are included in the Danny Mss at the East Sussex Record Office (ref. 2191–6). These consist of five volumes of Journals (1924–31).

CAMROSE, 2nd Vt
Hon. John Seymour Berry (1909–   )

M.P. (Con.) Hitchin, 1941–5.
Deputy Chairman (past Chairman), The Daily Telegraph Ltd.

Hitchin Conservatives have retained many of their records.

CAPE, Thomas (1868–1947)

M.P. (Lab.) Workington, 1918–45.

It appears that Thomas Cape kept no systematic records, and that none of his papers has survived. His daughter, Mrs Eleanor Cain, knows of no surviving papers, and though he was a miners' agent for some years, no papers appear to have survived with the local offices of the National Union of Mineworkers. The Cumbria Western Divisional Librarian at Workington Library similarly knew of no surviving records. A biography of Cape appears in *Dictionary of Labour Biography*, Vol. III, pp. 31–2.

CAPORN, Arthur Cecil
His Honour Judge Caporn (1884–1953)

M.P. (Con.) Nottingham West, 1931–5.

Mr Derek Caporn (son), c/o Caporn Campbell Clare & Clare, solicitors, 62 Victoria Road, Surbiton, Surrey KT6 4NW, has compiled a scrapbook covering various aspects of his father's career. The scrapbook contains photographs, press cuttings, and some correspondence. No other relevant papers appear to survive.

CAREW, Charles Robert Sydenham (1853–1939)

M.P. (Con.) Tiverton, 1915–22.

Attempts to contact Carew's daughter-in-law proved unsuccessful.

CAREW, James Laurence (1853–1903) *

M.P. (Irish Nat.) Kildare South, 1885–92; Dublin College Green, 1896–1900; (Ind. Nat.) Meath South, 1900–3.

CAREW, Lieutenant-General Sir Reginald Pole (1849–1924)

M.P. (Con.) Bodmin, Dec 1910–16.

Sir John Carew Pole, 12th Bt, son of Sir Reginald Pole Carew, has at his home, Antony House, Torpoint, Cornwall, a small collection of his father's political papers. Almost all of this consists of correspondence relating to the Ulster Crisis, 1914, while some deals with the South African War, 1899–1901.

CARINGTON, Neville Woodford Smith- (1878–1933)

M.P. (Con.) Rutland and Stamford, 1923–33.

Some papers relating to the parliamentary career of Neville Smith-Carington are with his nephew, Philip Smith-Carington, 53 Elystan Street, London SW3.

CARLILE, Sir (Edward) Hildred, 1st Bt (1852–1942)

M.P. (Con.) St Albans, 1906–19.

Such papers as survive are with Mr Ronald C. Buxton, M.A., F.I.Struct.E. (grandson), 67 Ashley Gardens, London SW1. Carlile's speeches and comments in the House of Commons were published in *Parliamentary Comments 1906–1919* by Sir Hildred Carlile (1924).

CARLILE, Sir (William) Walter, 1st Bt (1862–1950)

M.P. (Con.) Buckingham, 1895–1906.

Sir Walter Carlile's widow believes that no relevant papers have survived.

CARLISLE, 10th E of
Charles James Stanley Howard, Vt Morpeth (1867–1912)

M.P. (Lib.Un.) Birmingham South, 1904–11.

Mr George Howard, Castle Howard, York, has in his Muniment Room some correspondence of a family and personal nature relating to his uncle, the 10th Earl of Carlisle. Any other papers which survive would be known to the present (12th) Earl of Carlisle, Naworth Castle, Brampton, Cumbria.

CARMICHAEL, James (1894–1966)

M.P. (I.L.P., later Lab.) Glasgow Bridgeton, 1946–61.

The majority of James Carmichael's papers have not survived. However, his son, Mr N. G. Carmichael, M.P., 53 Partick Hill Road, Glasgow W1, has retained a small collection of congratulatory letters, a manuscript minute book of the Blackfriars Branch of the Independent Labour Party, 1895–6; election addresses, and pamphlets.

CARNEGIE, Lieutenant-Colonel Hon. Douglas George (1870–1937)

M.P. (Con.) Winchester, 1916–18.

The Lord Rosehill (grandson), Fair Oak, Rogate, Petersfield, knows of no papers relating to Hon. D. G. Carnegie. A certain number of family papers do survive in his care, however, including an eye-witness account of the siege of Ladysmith, and items relating to elections in Sussex.

CARPENTER, Sir Archibald Boyd Boyd- (1873–1937)

M.P. (Con.) Bradford North, 1918–23; Coventry, 1924–9; Chertsey, 1931–7.
Parliamentary Secretary, Ministry of Labour, 1922–3. Financial Secretary, Treasury, 1923. Paymaster-General, 1923–4. Financial Secretary, Admiralty, 1923–4.

Hazlehurst and Woodland, p. 27, found no papers.

CARPENTER, John Archibald Boyd-, see BOYD-CARPENTER, Baron

CARR, Sir Arthur Strettell Comyns, see COMYNS CARR

CARR OF HADLEY, Baron
(Leonard) Robert Carr (1916–   )

M.P. (Con.) Mitcham, 1950–Feb 1974; Carshalton, Feb 1974–6
Parliamentary Secretary, Ministry of Labour and National Service, 1955–8. Secretary for Technical Co-operation, 1963–4. Secretary of State for Employment, 1970–2. Lord President of the Council and Leader of the House of Commons, 1972. Secretary of State for Home Affairs, 1972–4.

Lord Carr states that he has kept no substantial collection of papers. He has never kept a diary, nor written private memoranda about his political work. He has, however, retained copies of speech notes and articles, together with a certain amount of personal correspondence.

CARR, (William) Theodore (1866–1931)

M.P. (Co.Lib.) Carlisle, 1918–22.

Carr was a former Chairman of Carr's of Carlisle Ltd, biscuit manufacturers.

CARRINGTON, 1st E, see LINCOLNSHIRE, 1st M of

CARSON, Baron[1]*
Sir Edward Henry Carson (1854–1935)

M.P. (Con.) Dublin University, 1892–1918; Belfast Duncairn, 1918–21.
Irish Solicitor-General, 1892. Solicitor-General, 1900–5. Attorney-General, 1915. 1st Lord of the Admiralty, 1916–17. Minister without Portfolio, 1917–18.

The Public Record Office of Northern Ireland holds Lord Carson's surviving papers. Hazlehurst and Woodland, p. 29, provide details of the collection.

1 A judicial life peerage.

CARSON, Hon. Edward (1920–)

M.P. (Con.) Isle of Thanet, 1945–53.

CARTER, Rei Alfred Deakin (1856–1938)

M.P. (Con.) Manchester Withington, 1918–22.

CARTER, William (1862–1932)

Miners' leader.
M.P. (Lab.) Mansfield, 1918–22.

Messrs Berryman & Co., solicitors to the executors, know of no papers. A biography of Carter appears in *Dictionary of Labour Biography* Vol. 1, pp. 69–70, but refers to no Mss.

CARTER, William (1867–1940)

M.P. (Lab.) St Pancras S.W., 1929–31.

CARTLAND, (J.) Ronald H. (1907–40)

M.P. (Con.) Birmingham King's Norton, 1935–40.

CARVER, William Henton (1868–1961)

M.P. (Con.) Howdenshire, 1926–45.

Mr P. W. J. Carver (grandson), The Croft, North Cave, Brough, North Humberside, has a scrapbook of material relating to his grandfather's parliamentary career.

CARVILL, Patrick George Hamilton (1839–1924)*

M.P. (Irish Nat.) Newry, 1892–1906.

CARY, Sir Robert Archibald, 1st Bt (1898–)

M.P. (Con.) Eccles, 1935–45; Manchester Withington, 1951–Feb 1974.
Junior Lord of the Treasury, 1935–45.

Records of the Eccles Conservative Association are now deposited in Lancashire Record Office. Enquiries as to his personal papers should be directed to Sir Robert Cary.

CASEY, 1st B
Sir Richard Gardiner Casey (1890–1976)

Australian Diplomat and Cabinet Minister.

Minister of State Resident, Middle East, and Member of War Cabinet, 1942–3. Governor, Bengal, 1944–6. Governor-General, Australia, 1965–9.

Lord Casey had retained a large number of papers relating to his career. Copies of his diaries 1944–6 are housed at the India Office Library. Further details are given by Hazlehurst and Woodland, pp. 29–30.

CASEY, Thomas Worrall (1869–1949)

M.P. (Lib.) Sheffield Attercliffe, 1918–22.

Mrs Gladys Casey (widow) believes the papers were disposed of before their marriage. Records of Sheffield Liberals may be found in Sheffield City Library, and of the Yorkshire Liberal Federation in Leeds City Library (Archives Department).

CASSEL, Sir Felix, 1st Bt (1869–1953)

M.P. (Con.) St Pancras West, Dec 1910–16.
Judge Advocate General, 1916–34.

No contact was established with Sir Felix's son, the present baronet.

CASSELLS, Thomas (1902–44)

M.P. (Lab.) Dumbarton, 1936–41.

CASSELS, Sir James Dale (1877–1972)

M.P. (Con.) Leyton West, 1922–9; Camberwell N.W., 1931–5.

CASTLE, Barbara Anne (1911–   )

M.P. (Lab.) Blackburn, 1945–50; Blackburn East, 1950–5; Blackburn, 1955–
Minister of Overseas Development, 1964–5; Transport, 1965–8. First Secretary of State and Secretary of State for Employment and Productivity, 1968–70. Secretary of State for Social Services, 1974–6.

CASTLEREAGH, Vt, see LONDONDERRY

CASTLE STEWART, 7th E
Arthur Stuart (1889–1961)

M.P. (Con.) Harborough, 1929–33.

The present (8th) Earl Castle Stewart (son) believes that no papers survive in the family. Records of the Harborough Conservative Association, covering the period when Castle Stewart was M.P. for the constituency, are desposited in Leicestershire Record Office (see *Sources*, Vol. I, p. 67).

CATOR, John (1862–1944)

M.P. (Con.) Huntingdon, Jan 1910–18.

Mr John Cator (grandson) stated that he was unable to contribute information.

CAUSTON, Richard Knight, see SOUTHWARK, 1st B

CAUTLEY, 1st B
Sir Henry Strother Cautley, 1st Bt (1863–1946)

M.P. (Con.) Leeds East, 1900–6; East Grinstead, Jan 1910–36.

Cautley died without heir. Messrs. Lee & Pemberton, solicitors who acted in the estate, knew of no papers. It was not possible to trace the executors.

CAVE, 1st Vt
Sir George Cave (1856–1928)

M.P. (Con.) Kingston, 1906–18.
Solicitor-General, 1915–16. Secretary of State for Home Affairs, 1916–19. Lord Chancellor, 1922–4 and 1924–8.

Hazlehurst and Woodland, p. 30, found some papers (closed at present) in the British Library.

CAVENDISH, Lord Richard Frederick (1871–1946)

M.P. (Lib.Un.) Lonsdale North, 1895–1906.

Lord Richard Cavendish appears to have kept no relevant papers. The correspondence of his wife has survived, however, though this is largely of a social nature. This collection is now in the care of Lord Richard Cavendish's grandson, Mr R. H. Cavendish, Holker Hall, Cark-in-Cartmel, Grange-over-Sands, Lancs.

CAVENDISH, Sir Victor Christian William, see DEVONSHIRE, 9th D of

CAVENDISH-BENTINCK, Lord Henry (1863–1931)

M.P. (Con.) Nottingham South, 1895–1906, 1918–29.

Attempts to contact a niece were not successful. The Nottingham South Conservative Association records in Nottinghamshire Record Office appear to postdate Cavendish-Bentinck's period as M.P.

CAWDOR, 3rd E
Frederick Archibald Vaughan Campbell, Vt Emlyn (1847–1911)

M.P. (Con.) Carmarthenshire, 1874–85.
1st Lord of the Admiralty, 1905.

The Dyfed Record Office at Carmarthen has a large collection of Cawdor family papers, including some material on the 3rd Earl's political career. A volume of Cawdor's Admiralty papers is held in the Ministry of Defence Library (Navy). Details are given in Hazlehurst and Woodland, p. 27.

CAWLEY, 1st B
Sir Frederick Cawley, 1st Bt (1850–1937)

M.P. (Lib.) Prestwich, 1895–1918.
Chancellor of the Duchy of Lancaster, 1916–18.

A small collection, in the care of the present (3rd) Baron Cawley, Bircher Hall, Leominster, Herefordshire, is described by Hazlehurst and Woodland, p. 31.

CAWLEY, Harold Thomas (1878–1915)

M.P. (Lib.) Heywood, Jan 1910–15.

The present (3rd) Baron Cawley (nephew) states that a considerable number of press cuttings relating to H. T. Cawley's career have survived. These are at present housed at Berrington Hall, Leominster.

CAWLEY, Hon. Oswald (1882–1918)

M.P. (Lib.) Prestwich Feb–Aug 1918.

Baron Cawley (nephew) believes that little has survived regarding Oswald Cawley's parliamentary career, which was very brief.

CAYZER, Sir Charles William, 1st Bt (1843–1916)

M.P. (Con.) Barrow-in-Furness, 1892–1906.

Sir 'Nicholas Cayzer, Bt, Cayzer House, 2 and 4 St Mary Axe, London EC3, states that a book on Sir Charles Cayzer has been commissioned to mark the centenary of Clan Line Steamers Ltd, which he founded. Enquiries regarding papers should be directed to Mr E. R. Duggan at the above address.

CAYZER, Sir Charles William, 3rd Bt (1896–1940)

M.P. (Con.) Chester, 1922–40.

Sir Charles' son, Sir James Cayzer, Bt, believes that few records have survived. However, he has in his care at Kinpurnie Castle, Newtyle, Angus, a tin trunk of unsorted material and this is believed to contain copies of Sir Charles' speeches, etc.

CAYZER, Sir Herbert Robin, 1st Bt, see ROTHERWICK, 1st B

CAZALET, Thelma, see KEIR, Thelma Cazalet-

CAZALET, Lieutenant-Colonel Victor Alexander (1896–1943)

M.P. (Con.) Chippenham, 1924–43.
Political liaison officer to General Sikorski, 1940–3.

Enquiries concerning surviving papers should be directed to his sister, Mrs Thelma Cazalet-Keir.

CECIL, Sir Evelyn, see ROCKLEY, 1st B

CECIL OF CHELWOOD, 1st Vt
Lord (Edgar Algernon) Robert Gascoyne-Cecil (1864–1958)

M.P. (Con.) Marylebone East, 1906–Jan 1910; Hitchin, 1911–23.
Parliamentary Under-Secretary, Foreign Affairs, 1916–19. Minister of Blockade, 1916–18. Lord Privy Seal, 1923–4. Chancellor of the Duchy of Lancaster, 1924–7.

Papers in the British Library (Add. Mss 51071–51204), the Public Record Office (F.O. 800/195–198) and with Lord Salisbury, are described in Hazlehurst and Woodland, p. 32.

CECIL OF ESSENDON, 1st B, see SALISBURY, 5th M of

CECIL, Lord Hugh Richard Heathcote Gascoyne-, see QUICKSWOOD, 1st B

CECIL, Lord John (Pakenham) Joicey- (1867–1942)

M.P. (Con.) Stamford, 1906–Jan 1910.

A son, Mr E. W. G. Joicey-Cecil, is believed to be living in Sevenoaks, Kent.

CECIL-WRIGHT, John Allan Cecil (1886–   )

M.P. (Con.) Birmingham Erdington, 1936–45.

Air Commodore John Cecil-Wright has retained a collection of papers relating to his career. Subjects include the Air Committee and Family Allowances.

CHADWICK, Sir Robert Burton-, 1st Bt (1869–1951)

M.P. (Con.) Barrow-in-Furness, 1918–22; Wallasey, 1922–31.
Parliamentary Secretary, Board of Trade, 1924–8.

CHALLEN, Charles (1894–1960)

M.P. (Con.) Hampstead, 1941–50.

Mr Challen died unmarried. The solicitors who acted in the estate had no papers apart from private financial material, and advised us that there was no relevant family contact to be made. The Hampstead Conservative Association has retained records which cover the period when Challen was member.

CHALMERS, John Rutherford, see RUTHERFORD, John Rutherford

CHALONER, Richard Adolphin Walmesley, see GISBOROUGH, 1st B

CHAMBERLAIN, (Arthur) Neville (1869–1940)

M.P. (Con.) Birmingham Ladywood, 1918–29; Birmingham Edgbaston, 1929–40.
Postmaster General, 1922–3. Paymaster-General, Feb–Mar 1923. Minister of Health, Mar–Aug 1923, 1924–9, 1931. Chancellor of the Exchequer, 1923–4, 1931–7. Prime Minister, 1937–40. Lord President of the Council, 1940.

Information regarding Chamberlain's papers at Birmingham University Library can be found in Hazlehurst and Woodland, pp. 34–5.

CHAMBERLAIN, Joseph (1836–1914)

M.P. (Lib.) Birmingham, 1876–86; (Lib.Un.) Birmingham West, 1886–1914.
President of the Board of Trade, 1880–5. President of the Local Government Board, Feb–Mar 1886. Secretary of State for the Colonies, 1895–1903.

The large collection in Birmingham University Library and the Private Office papers in the Public Record Office (C.O. 529 and C.O. 638) are described in Hazlehurst and Woodland, p. 36.

CHAMBERLAIN, Sir (Joseph) Austen (1863–1937)

M.P. (Lib.Un.) Worcestershire East, 1892–1914; (Con.) Birmingham West, 1914–37.
Civil Lord of the Admiralty, 1895–1900. Financial Secretary to the Treasury, 1900–2. Postmaster General, 1902–3. Chancellor of the Exchequer, 1903–5, 1919–21. Secretary of State for India, 1915–17. Minister without Portfolio, 1918–19. Lord Privy Seal, 1921–2. Secretary of State for Foreign Affairs, 1924–9. 1st Lord of the Admiralty, 1931.

Chamberlain's papers, in Birmingham University Library and at the Public Record Office (FO 800/256–263) are described in Hazlehurst and Woodland, p. 36–7.

CHAMBERLAIN, Ronald A. (1901–   )

M.P. (Lab.) Norwood, 1945–50.

Mr Chamberlain has retained no relevant records.

CHAMBERLAYNE, Tankerville (1843–1924)

M.P. (Con.) Southampton, 1892–6, 1900–6.

Major N. Chamberlayne-Macdonald, M.V.O., D.L., a member of Chamberlayne's family, knows of no relevant papers.

CHAMBERS, James (1867–1917)*

M.P. (Con.) Belfast South, Jan 1910–17.

CHAMPION, Baron
Arthur Joseph Champion (1897–   )

M.P. (Lab.) Derbyshire South, 1945–50; Derbyshire S.E., 1950–9.
Joint Parliamentary Secretary, Agriculture and Fisheries, 1951. Minister without Portfolio, 1964–7.

Lord Champion states that he has retained no papers.

CHANCE, Sir Frederick William (1852–1932)

M.P. (Lib.) Carlisle, 1905–Jan 1910.

Mr K. M. Chance (son), The Glebe House, Wreay, Carlisle, believes that no papers relating to his father's parliamentary career survive. Miss M. E. Chance (granddaughter), Hallfield, Dalston, Carlisle CA5 7QH, has a collection of family papers, but only a few cuttings relating to Sir Frederick's career.

CHANCELLOR, Henry George (1863–1945)

M.P. (Lib.) Haggerston, Jan 1910–18.

Henry Chancellor had five children: three daughters and two sons. Both sons and one daughter died unmarried, another married but died childless. It proved impossible to contact the surviving daughter. Messrs Male & Wagland, solicitors, who acted in the estate, knew of no papers. Chancellor was one-time President of the English League for the Taxation of Land Values. Its surviving records are described in *Sources*, Vol. 1, pp. 272–3.

CHANDOS, 1st Vt
Oliver Lyttleton (1893–1972)

M.P. (Con.) Aldershot, 1940–54.
President of the Board of Trade, 1940–1 and 1945. Minister of State, 1941–2. Minister of State Resident in the Middle East, 1942. Minister of Production, 1942–5. Secretary of State for the Colonies, 1951–4.

The papers at Churchill College, Cambridge, and at the Public Record Office (BT 87) are described by Hazlehurst and Woodland, p. 95.

CHANNING OF WELLINGBOROUGH, 1st B
Sir Francis Allston Channing, 1st Bt (1841–1926)

M.P. (Lib.) Northamptonshire East, 1885–Dec 1910.

Correspondence with Sir Horace Plunkett can be found in the Plunkett papers (NRA list 16228). Family contacts were not established. Channing published *Memoirs of Midland Politics 1885–1910* in 1918. A few letters can also be found in the Courtney papers in BLPES.

CHANNON, Sir Henry (1897–1958)

M.P. (Con.) Southend-on-Sea, 1935–50; Southend-on-Sea West, 1950–8.

Channon's diaries have been published as *Chips: the Diaries of Sir Henry Channon*, edited by Robert Rhodes James (1967). The originals remain with the trustees of the estate.

CHAPLIN, 1st Vt
Henry Chaplin (1840–1923)

M.P. (Con.) Mid Lincolnshire, 1868–85; Sleaford, 1885–1906; Wimbledon, 1907–16. Chancellor of the Duchy of Lancaster, 1885–6. President of the Board of Agriculture, 1889–92. President of the Local Government Board, 1895–1900.

A description of papers with the family, in the Durham Record Office (D/LO/F/626–632) and in the Lincolnshire Record Office can be found in Hazlehurst and Woodland, pp. 37–8.

CHAPMAN, Allan (1897–1966)

M.P. (Con.) Rutherglen, 1935–45.
Assistant Postmaster General, 1941–2. Parliamentary Under-Secretary, Scotland, 1942–5.

Allan Chapman's widow says that no papers survive.

CHAPMAN, Edward (1839–1906)

M.P. (Con.) Hyde, 1900–6.

Attempts to contact a great-nephew residing in Suffolk produced no information.

CHAPMAN, Colonel Sir Robert, 1st Bt (1880–1963)

M.P. (Con.) Houghton-le-Spring, 1931–5.

Sir Robert's son, Sir Robin Chapman, Bt, believes that a substantial collection of press cuttings was destroyed after his mother's death. All that remains are two press-cuttings albums covering the period after 1958. No other records appear to have survived.

CHAPMAN, Sir Samuel (d. 1947)

M.P. (Con.) Edinburgh South, 1922–45.

Messrs Bennett Brooke-Taylor & Wright, solicitors of Buxton, Derbyshire, who acted in the estate, had no relevant papers. They tried in vain to contact Sir Samuel's son, Major A. R. C. Chapman.

CHAPPLE, William Allan (1864–1936)

M.P. (Lib.) Stirlingshire, Jan 1910–18; Dumfriesshire, 1922–4.
Former M.P. for Tirapeka, New Zealand Parliament.

CHARLETON, Henry Charles (1870–1959)

M.P. (Lab.) Leeds South, 1922–31, 1935–45.

Junior Lord of the Treasury, 1931.

No family contact was established. Certain records of the Leeds Labour movement in Leeds City Library may be relevant.

CHARRINGTON, Spencer (1818–1904)

M.P. (Con.) Mile End, 1885–1904.

Mr Gerald Charrington (great-grandson), Lower Marney Tower, Colchester, Essex, retained certain papers, though these do not appear to relate to political matters.

CHARTERIS, Brigadier-General John (1877–1946)

M.P. (Con.) Dumfriesshire, 1924–9.
Military career from 1896; served European War, 1914–18; India, 1920–2.

Certain papers are in the care of the Intelligence Corps Museum. These include five books of newspaper cuttings, copies of letters written by the General to the press (1920–41), assorted notes and commentaries on military subjects, photographs and published material.

CHATER, Daniel (1870–1959)

M.P. (Lab.) Hammersmith South, 1929–31; Bethnal Green N.E., 1935–50.

Daniel Chater's son, Mr Eric Chater, 45 Chaffers Mead, Ashtead, Surrey, has in his possession a copy of his father's unpublished autobiography. A further copy has been given to Hull University Library. No other papers appear to have survived.

CHATFIELD, 1st B
Admiral of the Fleet Sir (Alfred) Ernle Montacute Chatfield (1873–1967)

Naval Career from 1886; served World War I. 4th Sea Lord, 1919–20. Assistant Chief of Naval Staff, 1920–2. 3rd Sea Lord and Controller of the Navy, 1925–8. C.-in-C. Atlantic Fleet, 1929–30. C.-in-C. Mediterranean, 1930–2. 1st Sea Lord and Chief of Naval Staff, 1933–9. Minister for Co-ordination of Defence, 1939–40.

The bulk of Chatfield's papers are deposited in the National Maritime Museum. These cover, in seven groups, all aspects of Chatfield's career, from his early naval career, his Atlantic and Mediterranean commands, to his tenure of office as 1st Sea Lord and as a Minister. For further details see Hazlehurst and Woodland, p. 38.

CHEETHAM, John Frederick (1835–1916)

M.P. (Lib.) Derbyshire North, 1880–5; Stalybridge, 1905–9.

It did not prove possible to contact persons mentioned in the will and probate act.

CHELMSFORD, 1st Vt
Frederic John Napier Thesiger (1868–1933)

Viceroy of India, 1916–21. 1st Lord of the Admiralty, 1924.

Only a few private papers are known to survive in private hands, but Chelmsford's papers as Viceroy of India are held in the India Office Library. These materials are described by Hazlehurst and Woodland, p. 143.

CHELSEA, Vt, see CADOGAN, 5th E

CHELWOOD, Baron
Sir Tufton Victor Hamilton Beamish (1917–   )

M.P. (Con.) Lewes, 1945–Feb 1974.

At the time of writing Lord Chelwood has had no opportunity to sort and assess his papers. He did not keep a diary but has retained other records, including press cuttings.

CHERRY, Richard Robert (1859–1923)

M.P. (Lib.) Liverpool Exchange, 1906–9.
Attorney-General for Ireland, 1905–9. Lord Chief Justice of Ireland, 1914–16.

Certain papers, c. 1904–13, are deposited in the Northern Ireland Public Record Office. Other papers remain with the family.

CHERWELL, 1st Vt
Frederick Alexander Lindemann (1886–1957)

Personal Assistant to Prime Minister, 1940–2. Paymaster-General, 1942–5 and 1951–3.

The papers are deposited in the Library of Nuffield College, Oxford. They are described by Hazlehurst and Woodland, pp. 90–1.

CHESHAM, 3rd B
Hon. Charles Compton William Cavendish (1850–1907)

Master, Royal Buckhounds, 1900–1.

A small collection of papers survives in the care of Chesham's grandson, the present (5th) Lord Chesham, P.C., South Hall, Preston Candover, nr Basingstoke, Hampshire RG25 2EN. The most interesting single item appears to be a personal war diary kept by Lord Chesham during his service in the South African War in 1900. Other items include family photograph albums for the years 1878 and 1896, and for the period of the South African War; and addresses of appreciation from inhabitants of Buckinghamshire. A book of telegrams from noteworthy people to Lord Chesham's family on his death in 1907 also survives.

CHESTERFIELD, 10th E of
Edwyn Francis Scudamore-Stanhope (1854–1933)

Treasurer, H.M. Household, 1892–4. Captain, Gentlemen at Arms, 1894–5. Lord Steward, H.M. Household, 1910–15. Master of the Horse, 1915–22.

Members of the family know of no surviving records.

CHESTERFIELD, 13th E of
James Richard Stanhope, Vt Mahon, 7th E Stanhope (1880–1967)

Parliamentary Secretary, War Office, 1918–19. Civil Lord of the Admiralty, 1924–9. Parliamentary and Financial Secretary, Admiralty, 1931. Parliamentary Under-Secretary, War Office, 1931–4; Foreign Office, 1934–6. 1st Commissioner of Works, 1936–7. President of the Board of Education, 1937–8. 1st Lord of the Admiralty, 1938–9. Lord President of the Council, 1939–40.

The Stanhope family archives, known as the Chevening papers, are in the Kent Archives Office. Hazlehurst and Woodland, pp. 137–8, describe the papers of the Earl of Chesterfield.

CHETWYND, George Roland (1916–)

M.P. (Lab.) Stockton-on-Tees, 1945–62.

Mr Chetwynd says he has kept few relevant papers.

CHEYNE, Sir (William) Watson, 1st Bt (1852–1932)

M.P. (Con.) Universities of Edinburgh and St Andrews, 1917–18; Scottish Universities, 1918–22.
President of the Royal College of Surgeons, 1914–17.

CHILCOTT, Lieutenant-Commander Sir Warden Stanley (1871–1942)

M.P. (Con.) Liverpool Walton, 1918–29.

Mr Stuart Wyatt, of Messrs Richard Austin & Wyatt, Chartered Surveyors, was co-executor of the estate. He knew of no papers, and informed us that his co-executor (who had been Chilcott's secretary) was now deceased.

CHILD, Brigadier-General Sir (Smith) Hill, 2nd Bt (1880–1958)

M.P. (Con.) Stone, 1918–22.

Mrs H. C. Whitbread (daughter) knows of no papers.

CHILSTON, 1st Vt
Aretas Akers-Douglas (1851–1926)

M.P. (Con.) Kent East, 1880–5; St Augustine's, 1885–1911.
Parliamentary Secretary to the Treasury, 1885–6, 1886–92, 1895. 1st Commissioner of Works, 1895–1902. Secretary of State for Home Affairs, 1902–5.

A large collection is deposited in the Kent Archives Office. See Hazlehurst and Woodland, p. 47.

CHORLEY, 1st B
Robert Samuel Theodore Chorley (1895–)

Sir Ernest Cassel Professor of Commercial and Industrial Law, University of London, 1930–46. Lord in Waiting, 1946–50.

Lord Chorley has deposited four box files of material in BLPES. These contain largely printed material relating to governmental committees of which he was a member. He is currently preparing a memoir of his period in public life.

CHORLTON, Alan Ernest Leofric (1874–1946)

M.P. (Con.) Manchester Platting, 1930–5; Bury, 1935–45.

The Public Trustee forwarded a letter to surviving heirs, but no information was forthcoming.

CHOTZNER, Alfred James (1873–1958)

M.P. (Con.) Upton, 1931–4.

Attempts to contact Chotzner's step-daughter produced no information.

CHRISTIE, James Archibald (1873–1958)

M.P. (Con.) Norfolk South, 1924–45.

J. A. Christie's son, Mr James Christie, says that no relevant papers have survived.

CHURCH, Major Archibald George (1886–1954)

M.P. (Lab.)'Leyton East, 1923–4; Wandsworth Central, 1929–31.
General Secretary, Association of Scientific Workers, 1920–31.

Records of the A.Sc.W. are deposited with the History and Social Studies of Science Division, University of Sussex (*Sources*, Vol. 1, p. 17). No information was made available by the surviving family.

CHURCHILL, 1st Vt
Victor Albert Francis Charles Spencer Churchill, 3rd B Churchill (1864–1934)

Lord in Waiting, 1889–92, 1901–5. Master of the Buckhounds, 1900–1.

The present (3rd) Viscount Churchill has a small number of letters, press cuttings and photographs.

CHURCHILL, Hon. Randolph Frederick Edward Spencer (1911–68)

Author and journalist.
M.P. (Con.) Preston, 1940–5.

Randolph Churchill's papers have been retained by his family. It is expected that they will be used for a biography.

CHURCHILL, Sir Winston Leonard Spencer- (1874–1965)

M.P. (Con.) Oldham, 1900–4; (Lib.) 1904–6; (Lib.) Manchester N.W., 1906–8; Dundee, 1908–22; (Con.) Epping, 1924–45; Woodford, 1945–64.
Parliamentary Under-Secretary, Colonial Office, 1905–8. President of the Board of Trade, 1908–10. Secretary of State for Home Affairs, 1910–11. 1st Lord of the Admiralty, 1911–15, 1939–40. Chancellor of the Duchy of Lancaster, 1915. Minister of Munitions, 1917–19. Secretary of State'for War and Air, 1919–21. Secretary of State for the Colonies, 1921–2. Chancellor of the Exchequer, 1924–9. Minister of Defence, 1940–5. Prime Minister, 1940–5, 1951–5.

Churchill's papers, not currently made available, are discussed in Hazlehurst and Woodland, pp. 38–9. They are deposited at Churchill College, Cambridge.

CHURCHMAN, Sir Arthur Charles, 1st Bt, see WOODBRIDGE, 1st B

CHUTER-EDE, Baron
James Chuter Ede (1882–1965)

M.P. (Lab.) Mitcham, 1923; South Shields, 1929–31, 1935–64.
Parliamentary Secretary, Ministry of Education, 1940–5. Secretary of State for Home Affairs, 1945–51.

Material in Epsom Borough Library, diaries in the British Library (Add Mss 59690–703), Private Office papers in the Public Record Office (Ed. 36), and papers in the Surrey Record Office are described in Hazlehurst and Woodland, p. 49.

CILCENNIN, 1st Vt
James Purdon Lewes Thomas (1903–60)

M.P. (Con.) Hereford, 1931–55.

Junior Lord of the Treasury, 1940–3. Financial Secretary to the Admiralty, 1943–5. 1st Lord of the Admiralty, 1951–6.

Surviving records of the Hereford Conservatives can be found in the Hereford Record Office. No personal papers were discovered.

CLANCY, John Joseph (1847–1928)*

M.P. (Irish Nat.) Dublin County North, 1885–1918.

Some 34 documents, mainly covering the period 1900–9, can be found in the John Redmond papers, National Library of Ireland.

CLANCY, J. J. *

M.P. (Sinn Fein) Sligo North, 1918–22.

CLARE, Octavius Leigh- (1841–1912)

M.P. (Con.) Eccles, 1895–1906.

The Lancashire Record Office has a collection of constituency records. The family, once living in Stoke-on-Trent, could not be traced.

CLARENDON, 5th E of
Edward Hyde Villiers, Baron Hyde (1846–1915)

M.P. (Lib.) Brecon, 1869–70.
Lord in Waiting, 1895–1900. Lord Chamberlain, 1900–5.

The Clarendon family papers are in the care of the present (7th) Earl of Clarendon, 8 Chelsea Square, London SW3. No records of interest have been found relating to the public life of the 5th Earl.

CLARENDON, 6th E of
George Herbert Hyde Villiers (1877–1955)

Captain, Gentlemen at Arms, 1922–5. Parliamentary Under-Secretary, Dominion Affairs, and Chairman of Overseas Settlement Committee, 1925–7. Governor-General, Union of South Africa, 1931–7. Lord Chamberlain, 1938–52.

The surviving papers of the 6th Earl are in the care of his grandson, the present (7th) Earl, at 8 Chelsea Square, London SW3. No detailed list of contents is at present available, but it appears that the bulk of the papers consists of material of a largely social nature, particularly relating to the Earl's activities as Governor-General in South Africa.

CLARKE, Andrew Bathgate (1868–1940)

Miners' leader.
M.P. (Lab.) Midlothian North, 1923–4, 1929.

No heirs were traced. The *Dictionary of Labour Biography*, Vol. 1, pp. 74–5, describes his career but mentions no Mss. Clarke was President of the Scottish Miners, 1932–40, and its records are described in *Sources*, Vol. 1, p. 197.

CLARKE, Charles Goddard (1849–1908)

M.P. (Lib.) Peckham, 1906–8.

CLARKE, Sir Edgar Chatfeild- (1863–1925)

M.P. (Lib.) Isle of Wight, 1922–3.

Mr H. Chatfeild-Clarke (great-nephew), Puddenhole Copse, Betchworth, Surrey, has a considerable amount of letters, documents and press cuttings relating to Sir Edgar's career.

CLARKE, Sir Edward George (1841–1931)

M.P. (Con.) Southwark, 1880; Plymouth, 1880–1900; City of London, Jan-Jun 1906. Solicitor-General, 1886–92.

His Honour Judge Clarke (grandson), c/o Central Criminal Court, London EC4, has a collection of papers. These were used in the biography of Sir Edward Clarke by Judge Clarke and Sir Derek Walker-Smith, published in 1939. The papers include some political correspondence and material relating to the major legal cases in which Sir Edward was involved, e.g. the trial of Oscar Wilde.

CLARKE, Frank Edward (1886–1938)

M.P. (Industrial Conservative) Dartford, 1931–8.

Clarke's widow, Mrs H. M. Clarke, Clarefield, College Lane, Hurstpierpoint, Hassocks, Sussex, has in her care a small collection of press cuttings relating to her husband's work, especially among Boy Scouts. No other papers appear to have survived.

CLARKE, John Smith (1885–1959)

M.P. (Lab.) Glasgow Maryhill, 1929–31.

CLARKE, Sir Ralph Stephenson (1892–1970)

M.P. (Con.) East Grinstead, 1936–55.

The surviving papers of Sir Ralph Clarke are in the care of his son, R. N. Stephenson Clarke, Borde Hill, Haywards Heath, Sussex. Sir Ralph made a habit of destroying his constituency correspondence files when each case was closed, and his other parliamentary files were destroyed before his death. The remaining material consists mainly of press cuttings, some notes made by Sir Ralph on a visit to Russia and some papers relating to his release from the Army in 1944 to return to political life.

CLARKE, Brigadier Terence Hugh (1904–   )

M.P. (Con.) Portsmouth, 1950–66.

CLARRY, Sir Reginald G. (1882–1945)

M.P. (Con.) Newport, 1922–9, 1931–45.

CLAY, Lieutenant-Colonel Herbert Henry Spender- (1875–1937)

M.P. (Con.) Tonbridge, Jan 1910–18.

A filing cabinet of papers survives with Mr Francis Nichols (grandson), Lawford Hall, Manningtree, Essex. It contains a collection of letters, most of them being correspondence of Mrs Spender-Clay.

CLAYTON, Sir (George) Christopher (1869–1945)

M.P. (Con.) Widnes, 1922–9; The Wirral, 1931–5.

Mrs M. G. Squarey, daughter of Sir Christopher Clayton, has no papers relating to her father's Parliamentary career.

CLEARY, Sir Joseph Jackson (1902–)

M.P. (Lab.) Liverpool Wavertree, Feb-Oct 1935.

Sir Joseph Cleary has deposited with Liverpool Record Office a small collection of material relating to his period as Lord Mayor of Liverpool, 1949–50. This includes the Lord Mayor's Engagement Diary, the Lady Mayoress's Engagement Diary, and the Lord Mayor's Accounts, 1949–50. Other surviving papers are still in Sir Joseph's care, but it is possible that these will eventually join his other papers.

CLELAND, James William (1874–1914)

M.P. (Lib.) Glasgow Bridgeton, 1906–Dec 1910.

Cleland died unmarried. It was not possible to trace relatives.

CLIFDEN, 7th Vt
Francis Gerald Agar-Robartes (1883–1966)

Diplomatic career.
Lord in Waiting, 1940–5.

CLIMIE, Robert (1868–1929)

M.P. (Lab.) Kilmarnock, 1923–4.

No information on heirs was available. Climie was an organiser of the Workers' Union. Some of its records are described in *Sources*, Vol. 1, p. 264, and others are available at the Modern Records Centre, University of Warwick Library.

CLINTON, 21st B
Charles John Robert Hepburn-Stuart-Forbes-Trefusis (1863–1957)

Parliamentary Secretary, Agriculture and Fisheries, 1918. Chairman, Forestry Commission, 1927–32.

The present Lord Clinton knows of no papers retained in the family.

CLITHEROE, 1st B
Ralph Assheton (1901–)

M.P. (Con.) Rushcliffe, 1934–45; City of London, 1945–50; Blackburn, 1950–5.
Parliamentary Secretary, Ministry of Labour and National Service, 1939–42; Ministry of Supply, 1942–3. Financial Secretary to the Treasury, 1943–4. Chairman, Conservative Party Organisation, 1944–6.

Lord Clitheroe has retained some of his papers. He does not make these available for research purposes. At the Public Record Office, the series AVIA 11 contains Private Office papers relating to his work.

CLITHEROW, Richard (1902–47)

M.P. (Lab.) Liverpool Edge Hill, 1945–7.

CLIVE, George Windsor-, see WINDSOR-CLIVE, George

CLIVE, Captain Percy Archer (1873–1918)

M.P. (Lib.Un.) Herefordshire South, 1900–6, 1908–18.

A substantial collection of papers has survived, largely concerned with Clive's military career. This includes a diary of the West African Campaign of 1898, a diary for the South African War, and letters to his wife from France, 1914–18. The only item of directly political relevance is a scrapbook relating to the by-election in South Herefordshire in 1908 and to the General Elections of 1910. The papers are retained by Mr G. M. Clive (grandson), Whitfield, Allensmore, Hereford. Certain military papers have been promised to the Liddell Hart Centre for Military Archives.

CLOUGH, Sir Robert (1873–1965)

M.P. (Con.) Keighley, 1918–22.

Mr H. P. Silverwood, Sir Robert Clough's executor, states that no papers survive relating to Sir Robert's Parliamentary career. At the request of his widow all his diaries and papers were destroyed.

CLOUGH, William (1862–1937)

M.P. (Lib.) Skipton, 1906–18.

No family contact was established. Clough directed in his will that his memoir, *My Parliamentary Experiences 1906–18*, was to be given to the Skipton Liberal Club or to the local library. It was not possible to trace the former, and the Public Library and Museum, Skipton, know of no papers.

CLOWES, Samuel (1864–1928)

M.P. (Lab.) Hanley, 1924–8.

Samuel Clowes' daughter, Mrs Doris Robinson, C.B.E., 570 Lightwood Road, Longton, Stoke-on-Trent, has a small collection of material. This largely consists of obituary notices, congratulatory letters, and letters of sympathy during his last illness.

CLUNIE, James (1889–)

M.P. (Lab.) Dunfermline, 1950–9.

Mr Clunie has retained few papers in his possession. However, a collection of letters to him from the Scottish revolutionary, John Maclean, 1921–3, with notes by Clunie, has been deposited in the National Library of Scotland, together with a quantity of printed socialist pamphlets (Acc. 4334).

CLUSE, William Sampson (1875–1955)

M.P. (Lab.) Islington South, 1923–31, 1935–50.

William Cluse's son, Mr M. D. Cluse, 78 The Walk, Potters Bar, Herts, has a small collection of material, including certain press cuttings, election addresses, and personal momentoes. No other papers appear to have survived. A biography appears in the *Dictionary of Labour Biography*, Vol. III pp. 32–4.

CLWYD, 1st B
Sir John Herbert Roberts, 1st Bt (1863–1955)

M.P. (Lib.) Denbighshire West, 1892–1918.

It was not possible to contact the present (2nd) Lord Clwyd (son).

CLYDE, Lord
James Avon Clyde (1863–1944)

M.P. (Lib.Un., later Con.) Edinburgh West, 1909–20.
Solicitor-General, Scotland, 1905–6. Lord Advocate, Scotland, 1916–20.

Lord Clyde's son, the Lord Clyde below, knew of no papers. There are 23 letters to Bonar Law in the House of Lords Record Office.

CLYDE, Lord
James Latham McDiarmid Clyde (1898–1975)

M.P. (Con.) Edinburgh North, 1950–4.
Lord Justice-General of Scotland and Lord President of the Court of Session, 1954–72.

Lord Clyde retained no papers of relevance.

CLYDESMUIR, 1st B
Sir David John Colville (1894–1954)

M.P. (Con.) Midlothian North, 1929–43.
Parliamentary Secretary, Department of Overseas Trade, 1931–5. Parliamentary Under-Secretary, Scotland, 1935–6. Financial Secretary, Treasury, 1936–8. Secretary of State, Scotland, 1938–40. Governor, Bombay, 1943–8. Viceroy and Governor-General (Acting), India, 1945, 1946 and 1947.

The present (2nd) Lord Clydesmuir retains no papers relating to his father's political career. Further information is given in Hazlehurst and Woodland, pp. 40–1.

CLYNES, John Robert (1869–1949)

M.P. (Lab.) Manchester N.E., 1906–18; Manchester Platting, 1918–31, 1935–45.
Parliamentary Secretary, Ministry of Food, 1917–18. Food Controller, 1918–19. Lord Privy Seal, 1924. Secretary of State for Home Affairs, 1929–31.

Only a few papers survive with Clynes' daughter-in-law, and are not made available (Hazlehurst and Woodland, p. 40). A variety of material can be found in the archives of the Labour Party, while papers relating to the Inter-Allied Food Council, 1918, are housed in the Hoover Institute, Stanford University.

COATES, Major Sir Edward Feetham, 1st Bt (1853–1921)

M.P. (Con.) Lewisham, 1903–21.

A number of papers have survived in the care of various members of the family. These are at present largely unsorted. It is possible that they may eventually be deposited in a suitable library. Further information may be obtained from Sir Robert Milnes Coates, Bt, Moor House Farm, Helperby, York YO6 2RG.

COATES, Lieutenant-Colonel Norman (1890–   )

M.P. (Con.) Isle of Ely, 1922–3.

COATS, Sir Stuart Auchincloss, 2nd Bt (1868–1959)

M.P. (Con.) Wimbledon, 1916–18; Surrey East, 1918–22.

The present baronet did not provide information.

COATS, Sir Thomas Glen Glen-, see GLEN-COATS

COBB, Sir Cyril Stephen (1861–1938)

M.P. (Con.) Fulham West, 1918–29; 1930–8.

Sir Cyril Cobb left his library to Lancing College, Sussex. No manuscript material was included in the bequest, and no such private papers have been located.

COBB, Edward Charles (1891–1957)

M.P. (Con.) Preston, 1936–45.

No material, apart from a small collection of press cuttings, survives with Cobb's widow, Mrs Gladys Cobb, Mother Hill, Stedham, Midhurst, Sussex GU29 0PA.

COBB, Frederick Arthur (1901–50)

M.P. (Lab.) Elland, 1945–50; Brighouse and Spenborough, 1950.

Messrs Allen & Overy, solicitors in the estate, were unable to supply relevant information. Attempts to contact a relative were not successful.

COBBOLD, Felix Thornley (1841–1909)

M.P. (Lib.) Stowmarket, 1885–6, Ipswich, 1906–9.

An attempt to contact a relative proved unsuccessful.

COBHAM, 9th Vt
Hon. John Cavendish Lyttelton (1881–1949)

M.P. (Con.) Droitwich, Jan 1910–16.
Parliamentary Under-Secretary, War, 1939–40.

The surviving papers of Viscount Cobham are in the care of his son, the present (10th) Viscount, Hagley Hall, Stourbridge, Worcs. These are, however, few in number, and are at present unsorted and uncatalogued.

COCHRANE OF CULTS, 1st B
Thomas Horatio Arthur Ernest Cochrane (1857–1951)

M.P. (Con.) Ayrshire North, 1892–Jan 1910.
Parliamentary Under-Secretary, Home Office, 1902–5.

The Hon. R. H. V. Cochrane (grandson), Cults, Cupar, Fife, states that the papers of his grandfather are not available for research purposes during the lifetime of his children (two were living at the time of writing) and this decision will not be reconsidered in that period. Mr Cochrane was unable to say what would happen after this.

COCHRANE, Captain Hon. Sir Archibald Douglas (1885–1958)

M.P. (Con.) Fife East, 1924–9; Dunbartonshire, 1932–6.
Governor of Burma, 1936–41.

Mr D. F. Cochrane (son), 22 Wilfred Street, London SW1, has retained his father's papers.

COCHRANE, Sir Cecil Agernon (1869–1960)

M.P. (Lib.) South Shields, 1916–18.

Sir Cecil's cousin and chief executor, Mr G. D. Cochrane, believes that no relevant papers have survived.

COCKERILL, Brigadier-General Sir George Kynaston (1867–1957)

M.P. (Con.) Reigate, 1918–31.

Mrs Trefor Jones, Grey Harlings, Montrose, Angus, Scotland DD10 8SW, has certain items in her care relating to Sir George's career, including a typescript description of his early life. She does not regard these as of major historical relevance.

COCKS, Frederick Seymour (1882–1953)

M.P. (Lab.) Broxtowe, 1929–53.

No direct contact was established. Cocks published a study of E. D. Morel in 1920; the latter's papers may be consulted at BLPES.

CODDINGTON, Sir William, 1st Bt (1830–1918)

M.P. (Con.) Blackburn, 1880–1906.

No contact with heirs could be established.

COGAN, Denis J. (b. 1859)*

M.P. (Irish Nat.) Wicklow East, 1900–7.

COGHILL, Douglas Harry (1855–1928)

M.P. (Con.) Newcastle-under-Lyme, 1886–92; Stoke-on-Trent, 1895–1906.

Mr Coghill's nephew, who resides near Battle in Sussex, provided no information.

COHEN, Sir Benjamin Louis, 1st Bt (1844–1909)

M.P. (Con.) Islington East, 1892–1906.

Neither Lord Cohen, nor Mr Harry Cohen, nor Sir Bernard Waley-Cohen, nor Mrs Richard Cohen, all members of the family who were contacted, knew of any surviving papers.

COHEN, Sir (Jack Benn) Brunel (1886–1965)

M.P. (Con.) Liverpool Fairfield, 1918–31.

Mr G. Brunel-Cohen (son), 3 Hollies End, Mill Hill Village, London NW7 2RY, has a small collection of his father's papers. This consists of a small group of correspondence and press cuttings.

COLDRICK, William (1896–   )

M.P. (Lab. and Co-op) Bristol North, 1945–50; Bristol N.E., 1950–9.

Since his retirement Mr Coldrick has destroyed the papers he had previously retained. A transcript of a taped interview with Mr Coldrick is available at the South Wales Miners' Library, University College, Swansea.

COLE, Thomas Loftus (1877–1961)*

M.P. (Con.) Belfast East, 1945–50.

COLEBROOKE, 1st B
Sir Edward Arthur Colebrooke, 5th Bt (1861–1939)

Lord in Waiting, 1906–11. Captain, Gentlemen at Arms, 1911–22.

Lord Colebrooke's daughters know of no surviving papers.

COLEFAX, Sir (Henry) Arthur (d. 1936)

M.P. (Lib.Un.) Manchester S.W., Jan–Dec 1910.

Records of the Liberal Unionists are described in *Sources*, Vol. 1, pp. 151–2. There are 20 letters to Bonar Law in the House of Lords Record Office.

COLEGATE, Sir (William) Arthur (1883–1956)

M.P. (Con.) The Wrekin, 1941–5; Burton, 1950–5.

Sir Arthur Colegate's daughters have retained certain material relating to his political career. The Hon Mrs A. Pomeroy, Rockfield House, Nunney, nr Frome, Somerset, has a collection of her father's diaries; and Mrs R. Whalley, 11 Johnstone Street, Bath, Somerset, has a book of press cuttings, covering the period Sep 1941 to Feb 1950.

COLERAINE, 1st B
Richard Kidston Law (1901–   )

M.P. (Con.) Hull South West, 1931–45; Kensington South, 1945–50; Haltemprice, 1950–4. Financial Secretary, War Office, 1940–1. Parliamentary Under-Secretary, Foreign Office, 1941–3. Minister of State, Foreign Office, 1943–5. Minister of Education, 1945.

Lord Coleraine has kept some papers (Hazlehurst and Woodland, p. 88). Private Office papers for 1942 are to be placed in the Public Record Office (FO 800/430).

COLFOX, Sir (William) Philip, 1st Bt (1888–1966)

M.P. (Con.) Dorset North, 1918–22; Dorset West, 1922–41.

Sir W. J. Colfox, Bt (son), Symondsbury Manor, Bridport, Dorset, retains certain papers relating to his father. These are not generally made available.

COLIVET, Michael Patrick (1884–1955)*

M.P. (Sinn Fein) Limerick City, 1918–22.
Member, Dail Eireann,
Chairman, Irish Housing Board, 1932–45.

COLLICK, Percy Henry (1897–   )

Assistant General Secretary, Associated Society of Locomotive Engineers and Firemen, 1940–57.
M.P. (Lab.) Birkenhead West, 1945–50; Birkenhead, 1950–64.
Joint Parliamentary Secretary, Ministry of Agriculture, 1945–7.

Mr Collick has retained a considerable collection of papers. It is possible that these will be deposited in BLPES. His pamphlet collection has been given to the International Institute of Social History, Amsterdam. The few surviving records of ASLEF are described in *Sources*, Vol. 1, p. 12.

COLLIE, Sir (R.) John (1860–1935)

M.P. (Nat.Lib.) Glasgow Partick, 1922–3.

COLLINDRIDGE, Frank (1890–1951)

M.P. (Lab.) Barnsley, 1938–51.
Junior Lord of the Treasury, 1945–6. Comptroller, H.M. Household, 1946–51.

COLLINGS, Jesse (1831–1920)

M.P. (Lib.) Ipswich, 1880–6; (Lib.Un.) Birmingham Bordesley, 1886–1918.
Parliamentary Secretary, Local Government Board, 1886. Parliamentary Under-Secretary of State, Home Office, 1895–1902.

There appears to be no central collection of Collings papers, though a number of papers relating to Jesse Collings can be found among the Chamberlain Archives at Birmingham University Library and also among other collections there. Mr H. G. Matheson, a great-nephew of Collings , has asked surviving members of his family, and states that no papers can be traced. Some correspondence with Balfour can be found in the Bodleian Library (Ms.Eng. hist. c. 737 fol. 9–15).

COLLINS, Cornelius*

M.P. (Sinn Fein) Limerick West, 1918–22.

COLLINS, Sir Godfrey Pattison (1875–1936)

M.P. (Lib. later Lib.Nat.) Greenock, Jan 1910–36.
Secretary of State for Scotland, 1932–6.

For information regarding papers which existed in 1967, but cannot now be traced, see Hazlehurst and Woodland, p. 40.

COLLINS, Michael (1890–1922)

Irish republican leader.
M.P. (Sinn Fein) Cork South, 1918–22.

The National Library of Ireland has relevant papers. Ms 13329 includes photocopies of reports and minutes of the Geraldine Gaelic Athletic Club, London, 1905–15, of which Collins was Secretary; three letters to Collins; and ten essays written by Collins. Ms 15374 includes three letters from Collins to Conor Maguire, 1920.

COLLINS, Patrick (1859–1943)

M.P. (Lib.) Walsall, 1922–4.

COLLINS, Sir Stephen (1847–1925)

M.P. (Lib.) Kennington, 1906–18.

The Public Trustee, who acted in the estate, was unable to supply relevant information.

COLLINS, Victor John, see STONHAM, Baron

COLLINS, Sir William Job (1859–1946)

M.P. (Lib.) St Pancras West, 1906–Dec 1910;·Derby, 1917–18.

Papers are deposited in the University of London Library, Senate House, Malet Street, London WC1, and include material collected by Sir William in preparation for his autobiography; correspondence relating to the London County Council, 1893–1905, and to the University of London, 1889–1912; Parliamentary memoirs and cuttings, 1917–18; texts of papers by Sir William, 1909–38; and his collected pamphlets from 1883.

COLLISON, Levi (1875–1971)

M.P. (Lib.) Penrith and Cockermouth, 1922–3.

COLMAN, Grace Mary (1892–1971)

M.P. (Lab.) Tynemouth, 1945–50.

A biography appears in *Dictionary of Labour Biography*, Vol. III, pp. 34–8.

COLMAN, Sir Nigel Claudian Dalziel, 1st Bt (1886–1966)

M.P. (Con.) Brixton, 1927–45.

Sir Nigel's widow, Lady Colman, Middleton Manor, Winterslow, nr Salisbury, Wilts, has a small collection of press cuttings, election addresses and a few formal letters from important political leaders. All other papers have been destroyed.

COLOMB, Sir John Charles Ready (1838–1909)

M.P. (Con.) Bow and Bromley, 1886–92; Great Yarmouth, 1895–1906.

Sir John's grandson, Mr T. G. M. Snagge, Test Lodge, Longstock, nr Stockbridge, Hants, has a number of letters and papers relating to his grandfather's career, including correspondence from notable contemporaries such as A. J. Balfour, Lord Lansdowne, etc. Mrs T. M. Gardner (granddaughter), Bramcote, Bramdean Common, Alresford, Hants SO24 OJG, has a large collection of press cuttings, and offprints of articles and speeches relating to Colomb's career. Photostats of certain papers are deposited in the National Maritime Museum.

COLSTON, Charles Edward Hungerford Athol, see ROUNDWAY, 1st B

COLVILLE, Sir David John, see CLYDESMUIR, 1st B

COLVILLE, John (1852–1901)

M.P (Lib.) Lanarkshire N.E., 1895–1901.

COLVIN, Brigadier-General Sir Richard Beale (1856–1936)

Military career: Commander, 20th Battalion, Imperial Yeomanry, South Africa, 1900–1; Essex Yeomanry, 1901–9, etc.
M.P. (Con.) Epping,. 1917–23.

A collection of papers (1900–2) at the Public Record Office (W.O. 136) includes reports of operations, patrols, orders and a diary. Eight volumes of scrapbooks have been deposited by the Brigadier-General's son at the Essex Record Office. All volumes contain photographs, cartoons and Christmas cards, newspaper cuttings, etc., as well as correspondence, from military and political colleagues, election literature, and formal notices of appointments. The volumes cover the years 1877–1936.

COLYTON, 1st B
Sir Henry Lennox d'Aubigné Hopkinson (1902–   )

Diplomatic service from 1924. Diplomatic Assistant to Minister of State, Cairo, 1941–3. Minister, Lisbon, 1943–4. Deputy High Commissioner, Italy, 1944–6.
Head, Conservative Party Parliamentary Secretariat, and Joint Director, Conservative Research Department, 1946–9.
M.P. (Con.) Taunton, 1950–6.
Parliamentary Secretary, Overseas Trade, 1951–2. Minister of State, Colonial Affairs, 1952–5.

Lord Colyton states that he has very little left in the way of papers since most papers which he had during the war and afterwards at the Conservative Research Department were destroyed in error. Certain surviving papers on the Middle East have been promised to the Middle East Centre at St Antony's College, Oxford.

COMPTON, Lord Alwyne Frederick (1855–1911)

M.P. (Lib.Un.) Biggleswade, 1895–1906; Brentford, Jan 1910–11.

Mr Robin Compton (grandson), Copt Hewick Hall, Ripon, North Yorkshire, knows of no papers.

COMPTON, Joseph (1881–1937)

M.P. (Lab.) Manchester Gorton, 1923–31, 1935–7.

Administration was granted to F. G. Compton, who was not traced. Compton was an official of the National Union of Vehicle Builders, now part of the Transport and General Workers' Union. Its records are described in *Sources*, Vol. 1, pp. 263–6.

COMYNS, Louis (1904–62)

M.P. (Lab.) Silvertown, 1945–50.

COMYNS CARR, Sir Arthur Strettell (1882–1965)

M.P. (Lib.) Islington East, 1923–4.

CONANT, Sir Roger John Edward, 1st Bt (1899–1973)

M.P. (Con.) Chesterfield, 1931–5; Bewdley, 1937–50; Rutland and Stamford, 1950–9. Comptroller, H.M. Household, 1951–4.

Sir John Conant, Bt (son), Lyndon Hall, Oakham, Leicestershire, has a collection of his father's papers. These have been sorted by Leicestershire Record Office, but no decision has been made as to their eventual destination.

CONDON, Thomas Joseph (b. 1850)*

M.P. (Irish Nat.) Tipperary East, 1885–1918.

CONESFORD, 1st B
Henry George Strauss (1892–1974)

M.P. (Con.) Norwich, 1935–45; Combined English Universities, 1946–50; Norwich South, 1950–55.
Joint Parliamentary Secretary, Ministry of Works and Planning, 1942–3. Parliamentary Secretary, Ministry of Town and Country Planning, 1943–5; Board of Trade, 1951–5.

Such political papers as survive are in the care of Lady Conesford, Old Wharf, Shillingford, Oxfordshire.

CONNOLLY, Martin H. (1874–1945)

M.P. (Lab.) Newcastle upon Tyne East, 1924–9.

Connolly was Assistant General Secretary of the Boilermakers and Iron Shipbuilders Society. Records of the Boilermakers are described in *Sources*, Vol. 1, pp. 4–6. No family contact was established.

CONSTABLE, Hon. Lord
Andrew Henderson Briggs Constable (1865–1928)

Solicitor General for Scotland, 1922.

Mr Kenneth B. Constable (son), Arlary, Bowstridge Lane, Chalfont St Giles, Bucks, reports that his father never kept a diary and such papers as survived after his death were given to the Advocates Library, Edinburgh. However, the National Library of Scotland (the successor to the Advocates Library) was unable to trace any relevant deposit.

CONWAY OF ALLINGTON, 1st B
Sir (William) Martin Conway (1856–1937)

M.P. (Con.) English Universities, 1918–31.

A collection of Conway family papers, 1822–1950, was deposited in Cambridge University Library by Dr Joan Evans, literary executor of Lord Conway's daughter, Mrs Agnes Horsfield, in 1966. The collection is centred on Lord Conway's career and contains some 4300 letters, of which the great majority are between Conway and various relatives, particularly his parents, his first wife, and his daughter and her husband. Of correspondents outside the family, only letters to and from Henry Bradshaw and Karl Pearson survive in any number. Also in this collection are 64 volumes of Conway's diaries, and miscellaneous writings, including lecture notes, drafts of books, articles, and speeches, scrapbooks, travel notes, etc. A war diary (July 1917) can be found at the Imperial War Museum.

COOK, Sir Frederick Lucas, 2nd Bt (1844–1920)

M.P. (Con.) Kennington, 1895–1906.

Sir Francis Cook, Bt (grandson), Le Coin, La Haule, St Aubin, Jersey, C.I., has some material relating to his great-grandfather's career, but knows of no relevant papers of Sir Frederick's.

COOK, Thomas Fotheringham (1908–52)

M.P. (Lab.) Dundee, 1945–50; Dundee East, 1950–2.
Parliamentary Under-Secretary, Colonial Office, 1950–1.

COOK, Lieutenant-Colonel Sir Thomas Russell Albert Mason (1907–70)

M.P. (Con.) Norfolk North, 1931–45.

Lady Cook (widow), Guist Hall, Guist, Dereham, Norfolk, has a substantial collection of her husband's papers.

COOKE, Sir Clement Kinloch-, 1st Bt (1854–1944)

M.P. (Con.) Devonport, Jan 1910–23; Cardiff East, 1924–9.
Newspaper editor, *Empire Review*, and author.

COOKE, Sir (James) Douglas (1879–1949)

M.P. (Con.) Hammersmith South, 1931–45.

Attempts to contact Lady Cooke were not successful.

COOPER OF CULROSS, 1st B
Thomas Mackay Cooper (1892–1955)

M.P. (Nat.Un.) Edinburgh West, 1935–41.
Solicitor-General, Scotland, 1935. Lord Advocate, 1935–41.

Lord Cooper appears to have left no papers. His brother, the sole beneficiary of Lord Cooper's estate, apparently retained none; and Lord Cooper's former law firm was unable to trace any surviving papers.

COOPER OF STOCKTON HEATH, Baron
John Cooper (1908–   )

M.P. (Lab.) Deptford, 1950–1.
General Secretary, National Union of General and Municipal Workers, 1962–73.

Lord Cooper states that he has retained no papers relating to his brief period in Parliament. The records of the General and Municipal Workers' Union are described in *Sources*, Vol. 1, pp. 193–4.

COOPER, Squadron Leader Albert Edward (1910–   )

M.P. (Con.) Ilford South, 1950–66, 1970–Feb 1974.

COOPER, Sir Alfred Duff, see NORWICH, 1st Vt

COOPER, Captain Bryan Ricco (1844–1930)*

M.P. (Con.) Dublin South, Jan–Dec 1910.
Member of Irish Free State Parliament from 1923.

COOPER, Wing Commander Geoffrey (1907–   )

M.P. (Lab.) Middlesbrough West, 1945–51.

It proved impossible to contact Wing Commander Cooper, who now lives in the Bahamas.

COOPER, Dr G. J. (1844–1909)

M.P. (Lib.) Bermondsey, 1906–9.

COOPER, Sir Richard Ashmole, 2nd Bt (1874–1946)

M.P. (Independent Unionist) Walsall, Jan 1910–22.

Sir Richard's son, Sir Francis Cooper, Bt, has been unable to trace any surviving papers and believes that any papers retained by Sir Richard were destroyed after his death.

COOTE, Sir Colin Reith (1893–   )

M.P. (Co.Lib.) Wisbech, 1917–18; Isle of Ely, 1918–22.
Managing Editor, *Daily Telegraph and Morning Post*, 1950–64.

Sir Colin has retained certain papers. He has incorporated information from these into his books: *Editorial* (1965) and *The Other Club* (1971).

COOTE, William (1863–1924)*

M.P. (Con.) Tyrone South, 1916–22.

COPE, 1st B
Sir William Cope, 1st Bt (1870–1946)

M.P. (Con.) Llandaff and Barry, 1919–29.
Junior Lord of the Treasury, 1923–4, 1924–8. Comptroller, H.M. Household, 1928–9.

Hon. Mrs H. M. L. Simpson (daughter), Spitchwick Manor, Poundsgate, Newton Abbot, Devon TQ13 7PB, states that no diaries or correspondence survive.

COPELAND, Ida
Ida Fenzi (1876–1964)

M.P. (Con.) Stoke, 1931–5.

Mr R. Spencer C. Copeland (son), Trelissick, Feock, Truro, Cornwall, states that following his mother's death a large number of important letters and other records were destroyed. Some material survives, however, including unsorted correspondence (mostly postmarked 1936), six press-cuttings albums, 1930–40; two albums of family photographs, 1890–3, and a visitors' book, 1923–4.

CORBET, Freda (Kunzlen)
Mrs Ian McIvor Campbell (1900–)

M.P. (Lab.) Camberwell N.W., 1945–50; Peckham, 1950–Feb 1974.

Mrs Corbet states that she has no relevant papers.

CORBETT, Archibald Cameron, see ROWALLAN, 1st B

CORBETT, Charles Henry Joseph (1853–1935)

M.P. (Lib.) East Grinstead, 1906–Jan 1910.

Dame Margery Corbett Ashby (daughter), Wickens, Horsted Keynes, Sussex RH17 7BT, states that her father left no large collection of papers but references to his career can be found in personal and family papers which she retains. Amongst these are letters from her father to herself, relating to family affairs, with references to Dame Margery's activities in the Suffrage Movement.

CORBETT, Thomas Lorimer (1854–1910)*

M.P. (Con.) Down North, 1900–Apr 1910.

Enquiries may be directed to the present (2nd) Lord Rowallan (nephew).

CORBETT, Lieutenant-Colonel Uvedale (1909–)

M.P. (Con.) Ludlow, 1945–51.

Colonel Corbett stated that he had no papers which would be of relevance to this survey.

CORLETT, Dr John (1884–1968)

M.P. (Lab.) York, 1945–50.

The National Union of Teachers, of which John Corlett was a Divisional Organiser, has copies of articles by and about Corlett, a file of which is now in BLPES. Mrs L. Roberts, (whose husband was a close friend of Corlett), 320 Burton Stone Lane, York YO3 6HA, has some personal items.

CORNWALL, Sir Edwin A., 1st Bt (1863–1953)

M.P. (Lib.) Bethnal Green N.E., 1906–18; (Co.Lib.) 1918–22.
Comptroller, H.M. Household (and Minister for National Health Insurance), 1916–19.

CORVEDALE, Vt, see BALDWIN OF BEWDLEY, 2nd B

CORY, Sir Clifford John, 1st Bt (1859–1941)

M.P. (Lib.) St Ives, 1906–22, 1923–4.
President of the Monmouthshire and South Wales Coal Owners' Association, 1906.

Records of the Coal Owners' Association, in the National Library of Wales, are described in *Sources*, Vol. 1, p. 45. Attempts to contact the family were not successful.

CORY, Sir (James) Herbert, 1st Bt (1857–1933)

M.P. (Con.) Cardiff, 1915–18; Cardiff South, 1918–22.

Attempts to contact the present baronet produced no information.

COSGRAVE, James*

M.P. (Irish Nat.) Galway East, 1914–18.

COSGRAVE, William Thomas (1880–1965)*

M.P. (Sinn Fein) Kilkenny City, 1917–18; Kilkenny North, 1918–22.
Chairman of Provisional Government, Aug 1922. Member of Dail Eireann, Carlow and Kilkenny, 1922–7; Cork, 1927–44. Offices in Government of Irish Free State: Finance, 1922–3, Defence 1924. President of the Executive Council of Irish Free State, 1922–32.

Certain letters can be found in the Alice Stopford Green papers in the National Library of Ireland (Ms 15131). Mr Liam Cosgrave (son) was unable to supply any information.

COSTELLO, Sir Leonard Wilfred James (1881–1972)

M.P. (Lib.) Huntingdonshire, 1923–4.
Judge, High Court, Calcutta, 1926–40. Acting Chief Justice of Bengal, 1937, 1939.

The papers of Sir Leonard Costello were bequeathed to his daughter, Mrs Robert Kent, Mill Lawn, Wray Common Road, Reigate, Surrey.

COTTON, Sir Harry Evan Auguste (1868–1939)

M.P. (Lib.) East Finsbury, Jul–Nov 1918.
Member, London County Council. Journalist in India. President, Bengal Legislative Council, 1922–5.

A collection of papers is in the care of Col. H. E. M. Cotton, 2 Grotes Place, Blackheath, London SE3 OQH. Many of the papers have been microfilmed for the India Office Library. The microfilm covers a series of letters from Lord Lytton (1922–9), and Lord Curzon (1924–5); letters to Sir Evan Cotton (1878–1932), and a collection of newspaper cuttings (1906–34) on Cotton's career in India. A further collection of papers relating to Cotton's historical research, and in particular a proposed book on Thomas and William Daniel, has been deposited at the India Office Library.

COTTON, Sir Henry John Stedman (1845–1915)

Chief Secretary, Government of Bengal, 1891–6. Acting Home Secretary, Government of India, 1896. Chief Commissioner, Assam, 1896–1902.
M.P. (Lib.) Nottingham East, 1906–Jan 1910.

Col. H. E. M. Cotton's collection (above) includes letters to Sir Henry Cotton (1889–1915), correspondence (1899–1902) with prominent figures including Lord Curzon, press cuttings and copies of articles on India written by Sir Henry and by Sir Evan Cotton.

COTTON, William Francis (1847–1917)*

M.P. (Irish Nat.) Dublin County South, Dec 1910–17.

COTTS, Sir William Dingwall Mitchell, 1st Bt (1871–1932)

M.P. (Nat.Lib.) Western Isles, 1922–3.

Sir William's son, Sir Crichton Cotts, Bt, believes that no papers survive.

COUPER, James Brown (1866–1946)

M.P. (Con.) Glasgow Maryhill, 1924–9.

COURTAULD, Major John Sewell (1880–1942)

M.P. (Con.) Chichester, 1924–42.

Miss J. B. Courtauld (daughter), Cooke's House, West Burton, Pulborough, Sussex, believes that no relevant papers have survived. A good collection of records relating to the Chichester Conservative Association has been deposited in West Sussex Record Office (see *Sources*, Vol. 1, p. 66),

COURTHOPE, 1st B
Sir George Loyd Courthope, 1st Bt (1877–1955)

M.P. (Con.) Rye, 1906–45.

Hon. Miss Daphne Courthope (daughter), Whiligh, Wadhurst, Sussex, states that family papers are deposited with the Sussex Archaeological Society, Barbican House, Lewes, but these contain little of recent date. She knows of no relevant papers relating to her father's career. Records of the Rye Conservative Association from 1885 survive with the Association.

COUTTS, William Lehman Ashmead Bartlett-Burdett- (1851–1921)

M.P. (Con.) Westminster, 1885–1918; Westminster Abbey, 1918–21.

Westminster Public Library (Archives Department) has a collection of papers relating to the Westminster Conservatives. Letters and papers (1846–1880) of Burdett-Coutts wife, Angela, Baroness Burdett-Coutts, are in Lambeth Palace Library. Her correspondence with the Harrowby family, relating to Coutts Bank and other business affairs, can be found with the Harrowby Manuscripts Trust, Sandon Hall, nr Stafford. The British Library also has relevant material (e.g. Add. Mss 46402–46408). Two letters from Burdett-Coutts to his wife, 1883–4, can be found in the Escott papers (NRA List 16926).

COVE, William George (1888–1963)

M.P. (Lab.) Wellingborough, 1923–4; Aberavon, 1929–59.

No family contact was established. The National Union of Teachers, of which Cove was

Parliamentary Secretary, was able to supply copies of articles by Cove published in N.U.T. journals, and these are now filed at BLPES. Records of the National Union of Teachers are briefly described in *Sources,* Vol. 1, p. 202.

COVENTRY, 9th E of
George William Coventry (1838–1930)

Captain, Gentlemen at Arms, 1877–80, 1885–6; Master of the Buckhounds, 1886–92, 1895–Nov 1900.

COWAN, Dugald McCoig (1865–1933)

M.P. (Lib.) Scottish Universities, 1918–33.

Cowan died unmarried. Family and friends mentioned in his will were not traced.

COWAN, Sir (William) Henry (1862–1932)

M.P. (Lib.) Guildford, 1906–Jan 1910; Aberdeenshire East, Jan 1910–22; (Con.) Islington North, 1923–9.

An enquiry was sent to Sir Henry's firm, Sir Parkinson Cowan Ltd of Manchester. No information came to light.

COWDRAY, 1st Vt
Sir Weetman Dickinson Pearson, 1st Bt (1856–1927)

President of the Air Board, 1917.

The Science Museum Library has a small collection of Cowdray's papers. These are described by Hazlehurst and Woodland, pp. 115–16.

COWDRAY, 2nd Vt
Hon. Weetman Harold Miller Pearson (1882–1933)

M.P. (Lib.) Eye, 1906–18.

A volume of obituary notices of both the 1st and the 2nd Viscounts Cowdray has been deposited at the Science Museum, London (see above). The present (3rd) Viscount knows of no other surviving papers relating to the 2nd Viscount's career.

COX, Harold (1859–1936)

M.P. (Lib.) Preston, 1906–Jan 1910.
Editor, *Edinburgh Review,* 1912–29.

Cox was Secretary of the Cobden Club, 1899–1904. Its records, now in the West Sussex Record Office, are described in *Sources,* Vol. 1, pp. 43–4. Some early letters can be found in the Edward Carpenter Collection in Sheffield Central Library.

COX, Irwin Edward Bainbridge (1838–1922)

M.P. (Con.) Harrow, 1899–1906.

It did not prove possible to contact heirs mentioned in the will and probate act.

COX, Sir Thomas Skewes (1849–1913)

M.P. (Con.) Kingston, Surrey, 1895–1906.

Col. M. Skewes-Cox (grandson), 62 Hyde Vale, London SE10, states that all papers were destroyed on his grandfather's death. All he has are some obituary notices.

COZENS-HARDY, 2nd B
Hon. William Hepburn Cozens-Hardy (1868–1924)

M.P. (Lib.) Norfolk South, 1918–20.

Hon. Mrs Eric Bailey, Warborough House, Stiffkey, Wells-next-the-Sea, Norfolk, has letters and press cuttings relating to her grandfather, the 1st Baron, and to her father, the 2nd Baron Cozens-Hardy.

CRADDOCK, George (1897–1974)

M.P. (Lab.) Bradford South, 1949–70.

The Bradford Labour Party has retained records. No family contact produced information.

CRADDOCK, Sir (George) Beresford (1898–1976)

Assistant Director, Ministry of Supply, World War II.
M.P. (Con.) Spelthorne, 1950–70.

CRADDOCK, Sir Reginald Henry (1864–1937)

Indian Civil Service from 1884. Lieutenant-Governor, Burma, 1917–22.
M.P. (Con.) Combined English Universities, 1931–7.

Correspondence (1910–16) can be found in the Hardinge Papers in Cambridge University Library.

CRAIG, Charles Curtis (1869–1960)*

M.P. (Con.) Antrim South, 1903–22; Co. Antrim, 1922–9.
Parliamentary Secretary, Ministry of Pensions, 1923–4.

Messrs Macfarlanes, solicitors of London, acted in the estate. They were in contact with a nephew who died in 1969. No papers have so far come to light.

CRAIG, Sir Ernest, 1st Bt (1859–1934)

M.P. (Con.) Crewe, 1912–18, 1924–9.

Under the terms of Craig's will, his property passed to his wife, then his daughter. Contact was not established with them or any heirs.

CRAIG, Herbert James (1869–1934)

M.P. (Lib.) Tynemouth, 1906–18.

Mr F. L. M. Rundall (nephew), Dove House, Stutton, nr Ipswich, Suffolk, has a small collection of press cuttings. He knows of no substantial collection of papers.

CRAIG, Sir James, 1st Bt, see CRAIGAVON, 1st Vt

CRAIG, Norman Carlyle (1868–1919)

M.P. (Con.) Isle of Thanet, Jan 1910–19.

Craig's widow and his brother were named as executors. No contact could be established with their heirs.

CRAIG, Robert Hunter (1839–1913)

M.P. (Lib.) Govan, 1900–6.

CRAIGAVON, 1st Vt
Sir James Craig, 1st Bt (1871–1940)*

M.P. (Con.) Co. Down East, 1906–18; Mid-Down, 1918–21.
Treasurer, H.M. Household, 1916–18. Parliamentary Secretary, Pensions, 1919–20. Parliamentary and Financial Secretary, Admiralty, 1920–1. Prime Minister, Northern Ireland, 1921–40.

A substantial collection is housed in the Northern Ireland Public Record Office, including diaries and correspondence dating from the Boer War period and covering events leading up to the establishment of the Parliament of Northern Ireland, together with a large collection of press cuttings. However, most of Craigavon's political papers do not appear to have survived.

CRAIGMYLE, 1st B
Thomas Shaw, Baron Shaw of Dunfermline (1850–1937)

M.P. (Lib.) Hawick, 1892–1909.
Solicitor-General, Scotland, 1894–5. Lord Advocate for Scotland, 1905–9. Lord of Appeal, 1909–29.

Certain papers relating to the Lord Advocate's Office have been deposited in the Scottish Record Office. Other papers remain with his grandson, the present (3rd) Baron Craigmyle (see below).

CRAIGMYLE, 2nd B
Hon. Alexander Shaw (1883–1944)

M.P. (Lib.) Kilmarnock, 1915–23.

The papers of the 2nd Lord Craigmyle, together with material relating to the 1st Baron, and covering the period 1902–24, are in the possession of the present (3rd) Lord Craigmyle, 18 The Boltons, London SW10. They are contained in two tin trunks and are arranged in bundles with an outline of the subject matter on each. A part of the material consists of correspondence between the 2nd Lord Craigmyle and his family, which includes matters of political interest, mainly concerned with constituency affairs. There is, in addition, a bundle of material relating to the 1st Lord Craigmyle's involvement with the Royal Commission on the Docks, 1920–4, and the Dock Strike of 1924. However, most of the collection deals with the 2nd Lord Craigmyle's career. Much of it concerns constituency affairs and election campaigns. Other papers deal with national affairs including letters and reports on gun-running in 1914, eye-witness accounts of the Sinn Fein rising in 1916, letters on conscientious objection (mainly connected with Craigmyle's immediate family), and the rates of pay of female munitions workers. There is a large folder of correspondence concerning the attempt to reunite the Liberal Party in 1918. Other material deals with aspects of Craigmyle's career both in law and in business. In addition to the bundles of letters, there are several loose letters covering a variety of topics from various correspondents. There are two indexed volumes of press cuttings, 1914–23, as well as speech notes and correspondence arising from speeches made by Craigmyle.

CRAIGTON, Baron
Jack Nixon Browne (1904–)

M.P. (Con.) Govan, 1950–5; Glasgow Craigton, 1955–9.
Parliamentary Under-Secretary, Scottish Office, 1955–9; Minister of State, Scottish Office, 1959–64.

CRAIK, Sir Henry, 1st Bt (1846–1927)

Secretary, Scottish Education Department, 1885–1904.
M.P. (Con.) Glasgow and Aberdeen Universities, 1906–18; Scottish Universities, 1918–27.

The National Library of Scotland has a large collection of correspondence to Craik, including letters from prominent statesmen, ecclesiastics and men of letters, and a few drafts of letters by Craik.

CRANBORNE, Vt, see SALISBURY

CRATHORNE, 1st B
Sir Thomas Lionel Dugdale, 1st Bt (1897–   )

M.P. (Con.) Richmond, Yorks, 1929–59.
Junior Lord of the Treasury, 1937–42. Minister of Agriculture and Fisheries, 1951–4. Chairman, Conservative Party Organisation, 1942–4.

Baron Crathorne states that he has no papers available for research purposes.

CRAVEN, 4th E
William George Robert Craven (1868–1921)

Captain, Yeomen of the Guard, 1911–15.

The Craven Estate Office knows of no relevant papers.

CRAWFORD (27th) AND BALCARRES (10th), E of
David Alexander Edward Lindsay, Lord Balcarres (1871–1940)

M.P. (Con.) Chorley, 1895–1913.
President of the Board of Agriculture and Fisheries, 1916. Lord Privy Seal, 1916–19. Chancellor of the Duchy of Lancaster, 1919–21. 1st Commissioner of Works, 1921–2.

Hazlehurst and Woodland, p. 91, state that papers survive with the family.

CRAWFORD (28th) AND BALCARRES (11th), E of
David Robert Alexander Lindsay, Lord Balniel (1900–76).

M.P. (Con.) Lonsdale, 1924–40.

The Earl of Crawford and Balcarres stated that he retained no papers of public importance relating to his parliamentary career.

CRAWFORD, Robert Gordon Sharman- (1853–1934)*

M.P. (Con.) Belfast East, 1914–18; Mid Down, 1921–2.
Senator in the Northern Ireland Parliament.

CRAWFURD, Horace Evelyn (1882–1958)

M.P. (Lib.) Walthamstow West, 1924–9.

Messrs Cardew-Smith & Holland, solicitors who acted for the executors (Crawfurd's wife and sister) were unable to help.

CRAWLEY, Aidan Merivale (1908–   )

M.P. (Lab.) Buckingham, 1945–51; (Con.) Derbyshire West, 1962–7.
Parliamentary Under Secretary, Air, 1950–1.

Chairman, later President, London Weekend Television, 1967–73.

Certain correspondence can be found in the Creech-Jones papers at Rhodes House Library, Oxford.

CREAN, Eugene (1856–1939)*

M.P. (Irish Nat.) Queen's County Ossory, 1892–1900; Cork County S.E., 1900–Jan 1910; (Ind.Nat.) Jan 1910–18.

CREMER, Sir William Randal (1838–1908)

M.P. (Lib.) Haggerston, 1885–95, 1900–8.

Some correspondence may be found in the Samuel papers in the House of Lords Record Office. Records relating to the International Arbitration League are with the Mondcivitan Republic, 27 Delancey St, London NW1.

CREWE, 1st M of
Robert Offley Ashburton Crewe-Milnes, 2nd B Houghton (1858–1945)

Lord President of the Council, 1905–8 and 1915–16. Secretary of State, Colonies, 1908–10. Lord Privy Seal, 1908–11 and 1912–15. President, Board of Education, 1916. Ambassador, France, 1922–8. Secretary of State, War, 1931.

Although many of Crewe's papers were destroyed during his lifetime, a large collection survives at Cambridge University Library. The papers comprise general correspondence, personal papers, copies of speeches (c. 1908–39), miscellaneous papers, India Office papers and printed material. At the Public Record Office, a volume of reports to Crewe (1926) from the Press Attache in France is included in the Foreign Office Private Office series (FO 800/330). For further details, readers should consult Hazlehurst and Woodland, pp. 106–7.

CRIPPS, Sir Charles Alfred, see PARMOOR, 1st B

CRIPPS, Sir (Richard) Stafford (1889–1952)

M.P. (Lab.) Bristol East, 1931–50; Bristol South East, Feb–Oct 1950.
Solicitor-General, 1930–1. Ambassador, Union of Soviet Socialist Republics, 1940–2. Lord Privy Seal and Leader of the House of Commons, 1942. Minister, Aircraft Production, 1942–5. President, Board of Trade, 1945–7. Minister, Economic Affairs, 1947. Chancellor of the Exchequer, 1947–50.

Many of Cripps's papers remain with his widow, Dame Isobel Cripps, but these are not available for research. However, other material has been deposited in the Library of Nuffield College, Oxford. These papers cover the period 1930–50 and are divided into speech files and special subject files, which include constituency and Labour Party papers. For further details, readers should see Hazlehurst and Woodland, p. 42. Private Office papers (AVIA 9) can be found at the Public Record Office.

CRITCHLEY, Alexander (1893–1974)

M.P. (Con.) Liverpool Edgehill, 1935–45.

Attempts to contact heirs were not successful.

CRITCHLEY, Alfred Cecil (1890–1963)

M.P. (Con.) Twickenham, 1934–5.
Director-General of B.O.A.C., 1943–6.

Messrs Fladgate & Co., solicitors, have correspondence relating to Critchley's estate but know of no political papers. A member of his family whom they contacted believed that political papers had probably been destroyed.

CRITTALL, Sir Valentine George, see BRAINTREE, 1st B

CROFT, 1st B
Sir Henry Page Croft, 1st Bt (1881–1947)

M.P. (Con.) Christchurch, Jan 1910–18; Bournemouth, 1918–40.
Parliamentary Under-Secretary, War, 1940–5.

The papers of Lord Croft are housed in the Library of Churchill College, Cambridge. They consist of some 20 files of correspondence, covering his career from his entry into Parliament to 1945, and illustrating his involvement in the Tariff Reform League, the Empire Industries Association, the National Party, and his attitudes to India, the Spanish Civil War, and World Wars I and II. The permission of the present Lord Croft is necessary before access is granted to these papers. Enquiries should be directed to the archivist at Churchill College.

CROMBIE, John William (1858–1908)

M.P. (Lib.) Kincardineshire, 1892–1908.

Mrs Fiona Adams-Cairns (granddaughter), Arrat's Mill, Brechin, Angus, has a scrapbook of obituary notices only, and knows of no other papers. Mrs Anne Maclean, another member of the family, knew of no papers. J. & J. Crombie Ltd., of Aberdeen, a firm of which Crombie was director, knew of no papers, nor did the archivist at Aberdeen University Library, of which Crombie was a benefactor.

CROMER, 2nd E of
Rowland Thomas Baring, Vt Errington (1877–1953)

Lord Chamberlain, 1922–38.

The present (3rd) Earl of Cromer (son) says his father left very few papers of public interest. Correspondence with Hardinge can be found in the Hardinge of Penshurst papers at Cambridge University Library.

CROOK, Charles Williamson (1862–1926)

M.P. (Con.) East Ham North, 1922–3, 1924–6.
President, National Union of Teachers, 1916–17.

Letters of Administration were granted to the widow. She and her heirs were not traced. Records of the National Union of Teachers and of the Conservative Teachers' Advisory Committee (of which Crook was Hon. Secretary) are described in *Sources*, Vol. 1, pp. 202 and 71–2 respectively.

CROOKE, Sir (John) Smedley- (d. 1951)

M.P. (Con.) Birmingham Deritend, 1922–9, 1931–45.

It is believed that Miss Bronwen Smedley-Crooke (daughter) knows of no political papers and has very few of his personal papers.

CROOKS, William (1852–1921)

M.P. (Lab.) Woolwich, 1903–Jan 1910; Dec 1910–21.

Material relating to Crooks can be found in the Labour Party archive (papers of the Labour Representation Committee). The *Dictionary of Labour Biography*, Vol. II, pp. 107–12, has an account of his career which made use of printed sources. The Woolwich Labour Party has retained an important collection of records, which should be consulted.

CROOKSHANK, 1st Vt
Harry Frederick Comfort Crookshank (1893–1961)

M.P. (Con.) Gainsborough, 1924–56.
Parliamentary Under-Secretary, Home Office, 1934–5. Parliamentary Secretary, Mines, 1935–9. Financial Secretary to the Treasury, 1939–43. Postmaster General, 1943–5. Minister of Health, 1951–2. Lord Privy Seal, 1952–5. Leader of the House of Commons, 1951–5.

A small collection of papers in the Bodleian Library (ref. Mss Eng. Hist. b. 223; c. 596–605; d. 359–61) and press cuttings in the Lincolnshire Record Office are described in Hazlehurst and Woodland, pp. 42–3.

CROOKSHANK, Chichester de Windt (1868–1958)

M.P. (Con.) Berwick and Haddington, 1924–9; Bootle, 1931–5.

Enquiries directed to a son produced no information.

CROOM-JOHNSON, Hon. Sir Reginald Powell (1879–1957)

M.P. (Con.) Bridgwater, 1929–38.
Judge, High Court of Justice, King's Bench Division, 1938–54.

Mr H. P. Croom-Johnson, 3a Ravenscourt Square, London W6, states that his father destroyed many of his papers shortly before his death. However, he has retained certain of Sir Reginald's papers. These include press-cuttings books, covering Sir Reginald's early writings and politcal work up to 1938; files of letters including letters of congratulation, letters written by Sir Reginald in the 1940s and 1950s; and letters of condolence to his family in 1957; his circuit diaries as a Judge, 1938–54 (mainly legal in character and at present in the custody of Sir Reginald's youngest son, Hon. Sir David Croom-Johnson); letters written by one of Sir Reginald's sons, Oliver, during the early 1930s; packets of unsorted papers dealing with the history of the family; and a box file of Lady Croom-Johnson's labelled 'My Political Work 1929–1938'. Few of the letters in the collection seem to be of directly political import. It is intended that certain of these papers will be deposited in Somerset Record Office.

CROSFIELD, Sir Arthur Henry, 1st Bt (1865–1938)

M.P. (Lib.) Warrington, 1906–Dec 1910.

Messrs Kenneth Brown Baker Baker, solicitors in the estate, had no relevant information. Sixty-four letters to Lloyd George can be found in the latter's papers at the House of Lords Record Office.

CROSLAND, (Charles) Anthony Raven (1918–   )

M.P. (Lab.) Gloucestershire South, 1950–5; Grimsby, 1959– .
Minister of State, Economic Affairs, 1964–5. Secretary of State for Education and Science, 1965–7. President of the Board of Trade, 1967–9. Secretary of State for Local Government and Regional Planning, 1969–70. Secretary of State for the Environment, 1974–6. Foreign Secretary, 1976–,

CROSS, 1st Vt
Sir Richard Assheton Cross (1823–1914)

M.P. (Con.) Preston, 1857–62; Lancashire S.W., 1868–85, Newton, 1885–6.
Secretary of State for Home Affairs, 1874–80, 1885–6. Secretary of State, India, 1886–92.
Chancellor of the Duchy of Lancaster, 1895. Lord Privy Seal, 1895–1900.

Papers at the India Office Library (Mss Eur. E. 243), the British Library (Add. Mss 51263–89) and the Lancashire Record Office (DDX 841) are described in Hazlehurst and Woodland, p. 43.

CROSS, Sir Alexander, 1st Bt (1847–1914)

M.P. (Lib.Un.) Glasgow Camlachie, 1892–Jan 1910.

The baronetcy became extinct in 1963. The last known address of the widow of the 2nd baronet was in Australia. No contacts could be established.

CROSS, Herbert Shepherd- (1847–1916)

M.P. (Con.) Bolton, 1885–1906.

It was not possible to make contact with members of the family. Reference should be made to the records of the Bolton Conservative Association (see *Sources*, Vol. 1, p. 65).

CROSS, Sir Ronald Hibbert, 1st Bt (1896–1968)

M.P. (Con.) Rossendale, 1931–45; Ormskirk, 1950–1.
Parliamentary Secretary, Board of Trade, 1938–9. Minister of Economic Warfare, 1939–40.
Minister of Shipping, 1940–1.

No papers have been traced (Hazlehurst and Woodland, p. 44).

CROSSLEY, Anthony Crommelin (1903–39)

M.P. (Con.) Oldham, 1931–5, Stretford, 1935–9.

Attempts to contact the family were not successful.

CROSSLEY, Sir Saville Brinton, 2nd Bt, see SOMERLEYTON, 1st B

CROSSLEY, Sir William John, 1st Bt (1844–1911)

M.P. (Lib.) Altrincham, 1906–Dec 1910.

CROSSMAN, Richard Howard Stafford (1907–74)

M.P. (Lab.) Coventry East, 1945–Feb 1974.
Minister of Housing and Local Government, 1964–6. Lord President of the Council and Leader of the House of Lords, 1966–8. Secretary of State for Social Services, 1968–70. Editor, *New Statesman*, 1970–2.

Richard Crossman kept little correspondence. From 1950 he kept a regular diary relating to his political work. The first volume of this was published in 1975. A transcript of the (recorded) diary will be placed in the Modern Records Centre, University of Warwick Library together with some of the original tapes. Records of Crossman's work as a local M.P. can be found in the papers of the Coventry Borough Labour Party at the Modern Records Centre.

CROUCH, Robert Fisher (1904–57)

M.P. (Con.) Dorset North, 1950–7.

Certain records of the Dorset Conservatives are deposited in Dorset Record Office. No family contact was established.

CROWDER, (Frederick) Petre (1919–)

M.P. (Con.) Ruislip-Northwood, 1950–

Mr Crowder states that he has no papers which he considers of relevance.

CROWDER, Sir John Ellenborough (1890–1961)

M.P. (Con.) Finchley, 1935–59.

Mr F. Petre Crowder, M.P. (son), states that there are no relevant papers.

CROWLEY, Dr John (d. 1934)*

M.P. (Sinn Fein) Mayo North, 1918–22.

CROWLEY, N. James (d. 1946)*

M.P. (Sinn Fein) Kerry North, 1918–22.

CRUDDAS, Colonel Bernard (1882–1959)

M.P. (Con.) Wansbeck, 1931–40.

A daughter, Miss D. Cruddas, resides in Middleton Hall, Morpeth. No information was made available.

CRUMLEY, Patrick*

M.P. (Irish Nat.) Fermanagh South, Dec 1910–18.

CUBITT, Hon. Henry, see ASHCOMBE, 2nd B

CULLEN, Alice
Mrs William Reynolds (1892–1969)

M.P. (Lab.) Glasgow Gorbals, 1948–69.

Messrs Geddes & Cameron, solicitors of Glasgow, are in touch with a son-in-law, Mr T. J. Cairns.

CULLINAN, J. (b. 1857)*

M.P. (Irish Nat.) Tipperary South, 1900–18.

CULVERWELL, Cyril Tom (1895–1963)

M.P. (Con.) Bristol West, 1928–45.

The papers are retained by Mr A. H. Culverwell (son), Woodex House, Limpley Stoke, Bath, Somerset, and include a political diary kept during World War II and a number of albums containing mainly press cuttings, extracts from Hansard and some correspondence from the period of his parliamentary career. Mr A. H. Culverwell grants access to these papers to *bona fide* scholars who apply in writing.

CUNDIFF, Major Frederick William (1895–)

M.P. (Con.) Manchester Rusholme, 1944–5; Manchester Withington, 1950–1.

CUNLIFFE, Sir (Joseph) Herbert (1867–1963)

M.P. (Con.) Bolton, 1923–9.

Mrs Dorothy Cunliffe (daughter) 23 Old Square, Lincoln's Inn, London WC2, believes that no papers have survived in the family. Sir Herbert made a point of destroying correspondence when he had dealt with it. Bolton Conservative Association has retained records dating from the 1890s.

CUNNINGHAM, Patrick (b. 1878)*

M.P. (Nat.) Fermanagh and Tyrone, 1935–50.

CURRAN, Peter F. (1860–1910)

M.P. (Lab.) Jarrow, 1907–Jan 1910.

Material relating to Curran can be found in the Labour Party archive (Labour Representation Committee and General Correspondence files). The records of Jarrow Labour Party in Durham Record Office date only from c. 1923 (*Sources*, Vol. 1, p. 138). An account of Curran's career will appear in the *Dictionary of Labour Biography*, Vol. IV.

CURRIE, George Welsh (1870–1950)

M.P. (Con.) Leith Burghs, 1914–18.
Member (Lab.) London County Council, 1935–40.

Dr A. S. Silver of Edinburgh, Currie's executor, knows of no papers. Mrs A. M. Leigh (niece), 11 Kings Close, Henley-on-Thames, Oxfordshire RG9 2DS, stated that the only papers she has refer to incomplete research into family history, in which Currie was interested in the later years of his life. The contents of his desk and study were left to Currie's nephew, Dr Gordon Lyall Parrer of Johannesburg, with whom the family has lost contact.

CURRY, Aaron Charlton (1887–1957)

M.P. (Lib.Nat.) Bishop Auckland, 1931–5.

Messrs Lee, Curry & Company, chartered accountants of Newcastle-upon-Tyne, know of no relevant personal papers.

CURZON, Vt, see HOWE, 4th and 5th Es

CURZON, 1st M
George Nathaniel Curzon, 5th Baron Scarsdale (1859–1925)

M.P. (Con.) Southport, 1886–98.
Under-Secretary of State, India, 1891–2, and Foreign Affairs, 1895–8. Viceroy and Governor General of India, 1898–1905. Lord Privy Seal, 1915–16. President, Air Board, 1916. Lord President of the Council, 1916–19 and 1924–5. Member, War Cabinet, 1916–19. Secretary of State, Foreign Affairs, 1919–24.

The India Office Library holds a large collection of Curzon's papers, covering his Indian activities and also the rest of his private and public life. Other papers, relating to Curzon's work at the Foreign Office, are included in the Private Office series (FO 800/28, 147–58) at the Public Record Office. A few electoral and political papers are retained by Southport Public Library. All these collections are described in further detail by Hazlehurst and Woodland, pp. 44–5.

CUSACK, Dr P.*

M.P. (Sinn Fein) Galway North, 1918–22.

CUSHENDUN, 1st B
Ronald John McNeill (1861–1934)

M.P. (Con.) St Augustine's (Kent), 1911–18; Canterbury, 1918–27.
Parliamentary Under-Secretary, Foreign Office, 1922–4 and 1924–5. Financial Secretary, Treasury, 1925–7. Chancellor of the Duchy of Lancaster, 1927–9.

Copies of many of Cushendun's papers are available at the Public Record Office of Northern Ireland (T. 1829 and Mic 63). Private Office papers can be found at the Public Record Office (FO 800/227–8). Details appear in Hazlehurst and Woodland, p. 100.

CUST, Henry John Cockayne (1861–1917)

M.P. (Con.) Stamford, 1890–5; Bermondsey, 1900–6.
Editor, *Pall Mall Gazette*, 1902–6.

Henry Cust's nephew, the present (6th) Lord Brownlow, says that no papers survive. A collection of papers had been retained by Cust's widow, but this material was inadvertently destroyed after her death.

CUTHBERT, William Nicolson (d. 1960)

M.P. (Con.) Rye, 1945–50; Arundel and Shoreham, 1950–4.

Rye Conservatives have retained constituency records dating from 1885.

D'ABERNON, 1st Vt
Sir Edgar Vincent (1857–1941)

M.P. (Con.) Exeter, 1899–1906.
Ambassador, Germany, 1920–6.

Forty-one volumes of papers are deposited in the British Library (Add. Mss 48922–62). These include papers relating to D'Abernon's Special Mission to Warsaw, 1920; to his period as Ambassador in Berlin, 1920–6; letters to Lady D'Abernon; general correspondence; diaries, 1876–98; Berlin diaries, 1920–3; and a manuscript of a proposed book on Egypt.

DAGGAR, George (1880–1950)

M.P. (Lab.) Abertillery, 1929–50.

The secretary of the Constituency Labour Party suggested that enquiries should be directed to Mr A. Smith (nephew), 12a Park Avenue, Hounslow, Middlesex. A note on Daggar's career appears in the *Dictionary of Labour Biography* Vol. III, pp. 54–5.

DAINES, Percy (1902–57)

M.P. (Lab. Co-op.) East Ham North, 1945–57.

Efforts to contact his widow, now Mrs M. Knight, proved unsuccessful.

DALHOUSIE, 16th E of
Hon. Simon Ramsay (1914–   )

M.P. (Con.) Angus, 1945–50.
Governor-General, Federation of Rhodesia and Nyasaland, 1957–63.

The Earl of Dalhousie states that he no longer has any papers.

DALKEITH, E of, see BUCCLEUCH

DALLAS, George (1878–1961)

M.P. (Lab.) Wellingborough, 1929–3'1

Mr K. G. Dallas (son), 23 Pamela Gardens, Eastcote, Pinner, Middlesex HA5 2QV, has a limited collection of press cuttings, reports and other documents. He is at present engaged in writing a biographical study of his father, which will be available for reference. A large collection of George Dallas's pamphlets on agriculture has been presented to the Department of Agricultural Economics of the Nottingham University School of Agriculture.

DALMENY, Lord, see ROSEBERY, 6th E of

DALRYMPLE, Vt, see STAIR, 12th E of

DALRYMPLE, Sir Charles, 1st Bt (1839–1916)

M.P. (Con.) Bute, 1868–85; Ipswich, 1886–1906.

The Newhailes House Mss, which have been catalogued by the NRA (Scotland), contain a number of papers relating to Sir Charles Dalrymple's political career. Amongst these is a file of letters on parliamentary and social affairs, 1885–1910, including correspondence from A. J. Balfour, Lord Bute, Lord Randolph Churchill, Austen and Joseph Chamberlain, W. E. Gladstone, etc.; letters from Sir James Fergusson in Bombay, describing administrative and social life in India (early 1880s), and life in Australia and New Zealand, where he was Governor-General (1849–74); letters to Sir Charles from friends, including politicians (c. 1865–1913); letters on ecclesiastical affairs, 1864–1910; a considerable amount of family correspondence and papers; a certain amount of Masonic correspondence, 1910–11; and a number of congratulatory letters relating to various honours he received. Enquiries concerning these records should be addressed to the NRA (Scotland).

DALRYMPLE, Hon. Sir Hew Hamilton (1857–1945)

M.P. (Con.) Wigtownshire, 1915–18.

The present (13th) Earl of Stair has given a number of family papers to the Scottish Record Office. These have been handlisted but not inventoried. However, there appear to be no papers of Sir Hew Hamilton Dalrymple.

DALTON, Baron
(Edward) Hugh (John Neale) Dalton (1887–1962)

M.P. (Lab.) Peckham, 1924–9; Bishop Auckland, 1929–31, 1935–59.
Parliamentary Under-Secretary, Foreign Affairs, 1929–31. Minister of Economic Warfare, 1940–2. President of the Board of Trade, 1942–5. Chancellor of the Exchequer, 1945–7. Chancellor of the Duchy of Lancaster, 1948–50. Minister of Town and Country Planning, 1950–1. Minister of Local Government and Planning, 1951.

The Dalton papers, including diaries, are deposited in BLPES. For details, see Hazlehurst and Woodland, pp. 45–6.

DALTON, Baroness
Mrs F. Ruth Dalton (d. 1966)

M.P. (Lab.) Bishop Auckland, Feb–May 1929.

It is believed that the only relevant papers are amongst those of her husband, Hugh Dalton, at BLPES.

DALY, James (b. 1852)*

M.P. (Irish Nat.) Monaghan South, 1895–1902.

DALZIEL, 1st B
Sir Davison Alexander Dalziel, 1st Bt (1854–1928)

M.P. (Con.) Brixton, Jan 1910–23, 1924–7.

Dalziel died without heir. Sir Peter Crisp, Bt, of Messrs Ashurst, Morris, Crisp, solicitors who acted in the estate, stated that no pre-war records of the firm survived. Lady Colman stated that the only person who might have assisted is now dead. Three letters only can be found in the Blumenfeld papers, now in the House of Lords Record Office.

DALZIEL, 1st B
Sir James Henry Dalziel, 1st Bt (1868–1935)

M.P. (Lib.) Kirkcaldy Burghs, 1892–1921.

No heirs were traced. Messrs Wilson, Chalmers and Hendry, solicitors who acted in the estate, had no information and it did not prove possible to contact an executor. Correspondence with H. H. Asquith about the *Westminster Gazette* is contained in the Asquith Papers at the Bodleian Library, Oxford.

DANESFORT, 1st B
Sir John George Butcher, 1st Bt (1853–1935)

M.P. (Con.) City of York, 1892–1906, Jan 1910–23.

DARBISHIRE, Charles William (1875–1925)

M.P. (Lib.) Westbury, 1922–4.

Mr David Darbishire (nephew), The Manor, Wormleighton, nr Leamington Spa, Warwickshire, knew of no papers. Mr C. W. Darbishire's adopted son died during World War II.

DARLING OF HILLSBOROUGH, Baron
George Darling (1905–)

M.P. (Lab. Co-op.) Sheffield Hillsborough, 1950–Feb 1974.
Minister of State, Board of Trade, 1964–8.

Lord Darling stated that he would be unable to help.

DARLING, Sir William Young (1885–1962)

Lord Provost of Edinburgh, 1941–4.
M.P. (Con.) Edinburgh South, 1945–57.

No family contacts were established. Single letters are available in the National Library of Scotland.

DARTMOUTH, 7th E
William Legge, Vt Lewisham (1881–1958)

M.P. (Con.) West Bromwich, Jan 1910–18.

The William Salt Library, Stafford, has some Dartmouth estate papers, but these contain very few references to the career of the 7th Earl of Dartmouth. Three items of a congratulatory nature refer to the January 1910 election campaign in West Bromwich. Neither the 7th Earl's daughter, Lady Mary Findlay, nor his nephew, the present (9th) Earl of Dartmouth, knows of any surviving papers.

DARWEN, 1st B
John Percival Davies (1885–1950)

Lord in Waiting, 1949–50.

DARYNGTON, 1st B
Herbert Pike Pease (1867–1949)

M.P. (Con.) Darlington, 1893–1923.
Assistant Postmaster-General, 1915–22.

Enquiries should be directed to the present Baron.

DAVENPORT, Sir Walter Henry Bromley (1903–)

M.P. (Con.) Knutsford, 1945–70.

Sir Walter Bromley Davenport has deposited a number of his family papers, including those of several nineteenth-century M.P.s, in the John Rylands University Library of Manchester. His own papers have been deposited with these.

DAVENPORT, Brigadier-General Sir William Bromley (1862–1949)

M.P. (Con.) Macclesfield, 1886–1906.
Financial Secretary, War Office, 1903–5.

A collection of papers is preserved at the John Rylands University Library of Manchester. Most of the material dates from the 1890s, and includes correspondence and papers relating to Bromley Davenport's constituency work, c. 1890–1910 (one box and sixteen volumes of press cuttings); papers (typescript and printed), relating to the period when he was at the War Office, 1903–5 (one box); and papers and a few letters relating to the Penrhyn Quarry Dispute, 1897–1911 (one box and one volume of press cuttings).

DAVIDSON, 1st Vt
Sir John Colin Campbell Davidson (1889–1970)

M.P. (Con.) Hemel Hempstead, 1920–3, 1924–37.
Chancellor of the Duchy of Lancaster, 1923–4, 1931–7. Parliamentary and Financial Secretary to the Admiralty, 1924–6.

Davidson's papers, formerly in the Beaverbrook Library, are now housed in the House of Lords Record Office. For a brief description of the papers, see Hazlehurst and Woodland, pp. 46–7.

DAVIDSON, Viscountess
Frances Joan Davidson, Baroness Northchurch (1894–   )

M.P. (Con.) Hemel Hempstead, 1937–59.

Viscountess Davidson has retained scrapbooks going back to 1913, and these cover the career of the 1st Viscount Davidson and her own. The 1st Viscount's papers are now in the House of Lords Record Office.

DAVIDSON, Major-General Sir John Humphrey (1876–1954)

General Staff, European War, 1914–18, and Director of Military Operations in France. M.P. (Con.) Fareham, 1918–31.

A slim file of papers has been given to the National Library of Scotland (Acc 3679). The papers include copies of articles, pamphlets and maps relating to World War I, a speech by Sir Archibald Sinclair on Earl Haig, and certain notes and reviews relating to Davidson's book and other books on Haig.

DAVIDSON, John James (1899–   )

M.P. (Lab.) Glasgow Maryhill, 1935–45.

Neither Mr Jim Craigen, M.P., nor Mr William Hannan, both of whom have sat for the constituency, were able to help.

DAVIES OF LEEK, Baron
Harold Davies (1904–   )

M.P. (Lab.) Leek, 1945–70.
Joint Parliamentary Secretary, Ministry of Pensions and National Insurance, 1965–6; Social Security, 1966–7.

It is believed that Lord Davies has retained his papers.

DAVIES OF LLANDINAM, 1st B
David Davies (1880–1944)

M.P. (Lib.) Montgomeryshire, 1906–29.

Lord Davies' papers are deposited in the National Library of Wales. Comparatively few of these relate to his work as an M.P., but there is a substantial series of records relating to his work as Chairman of the Welsh Council of the League of Nations Union, and to the activities of the New Commonwealth Society, which he founded.

DAVIES, (Albert) Edward (1900–53)

M.P. (Lab.) Burslem, 1945–50; Stoke-on-Trent North, 1950–3.

A small collection of Edward Davies' papers was retained by his widow, Mrs Margaret Davies, 69 Woodhouse, Biddulph, Stoke-on-Trent. The material includes a number of press cuttings, from the local and national press, dating from c. 1945; papers and photographs relating to the 1945 election campaign, and a number of letters between Edward Davies and his wife. These papers are to be deposited in Hanley Public Library.

DAVIES, Alfred (1848–1907)

M.P. (Lib.) Carmarthen, 1900–6.

It is believed that scrapbooks of press cuttings have survived with various members of the family, including a son, Mr William Davies, now resident in Greenwich, Connecticut, Mass., U.S.A. Enquiries should be directed to Mr Urban Stephenson, c/o Davies Turner & Co. Ltd, Spedition House, 326 Queenstown Road, London SW8 4NG.

DAVIES, Alfred (b. 1871).

M.P. (Lab.) Clitheroe, 1918–22.

DAVIES, Sir Alfred Thomas (1881–1941)

M.P. (Con.) Lincoln, 1918–24.

Mr A. L. Davies (son), c/o J. T. Davies & Sons Ltd, 7 Aberdeen Road, Croydon, Surrey CRO 1EQ, has files of press cuttings relating to his father's political work.

DAVIES, Dr Arthur Vernon (d. 1942)

M.P. (Con.) Royton, 1924–31.

Messrs Guillaume & Sons, solicitors who acted in the estate, know of no papers. Dr J. C. Hodgson, son-in-law, stated that Davies had no surviving relatives and he similarly knew of no papers. Dr Davies left a large part of his estate to the parish of Holy Trinity Shaw, Oldham, but it did not prove possible to ascertain whether any papers were included in this bequest.

DAVIES, (Claude) Nigel Byam (1920–   )

M.P. (Con.) Epping, 1950–1.

Mr Davies now resides in Mexico; no information was forthcoming.

DAVIES, David Lewis (d. 1937)

M.P. (Lab.) Pontypridd, 1931–7.

DAVIES, Professor David Richard Seaborne (1904–   )

M.P. (Lib.) Caernarvon Boroughs, Apr–Jul, 1945.
Professor of the Common Law, University of Liverpool, 1946–71.

DAVIES, Sir David Sanders (1852–1934)

M.P. (Co.Lib.) Denbigh, 1918–22.

Sir David was Governing Director of Pugh Davies and Co. Ltd, of Manchester, who knew of no papers.

DAVIES, (Edward) Clement (1884–1962)

M.P. (Lib.) Montgomeryshire, 1929–62.
Leader, Liberal Party, 1945–56.

The papers of Clement Davies have been deposited in the National Library of Wales, to whom enquiries should be directed.

DAVIES, Ellis William (1871–1939)

M.P. (Lib.) Caernarvonshire South, 1906–18; Denbigh, 1923–9.

Ellis Davies's papers have been deposited in the National Library of Wales.

DAVIES, Ernest Albert John (1902–   )

M.P. (Lab.) Enfield, 1945–50; Enfield East, 1950–9.
Parliamentary Under-Secretary, Foreign Office, 1950–1.

Mr Davies states that he intends to sort through his papers after his retirement.

DAVIES, Evan (1875–1960)

M.P. (Lab.) Ebbw Vale, 1920–9.

Evan Davies' daughter, Mrs Elsie Noyes, states that the family has no papers. A biography will appear in a forthcoming volume of the *Dictionary of Labour Biography*.

DAVIES, Sir George Frederick (1875–1950)

M.P. (Con.) Yeovil, 1923–45.
Junior Lord of the Treasury, 1932–5. Vice Chamberlain, H.M. Household, 1935–7. Comptroller, H.M. Household, 1937–8.

Neither Sir G. F. Davies' son, Brig. A. B. Davies, C.B.E., nor his daughter, Mrs P. G. Gambier, know of any surviving papers.

DAVIES, George Maitland Lloyd (1880–1949)

M.P. (Christian Pacifist) University of Wales, 1923–4.

Papers of Davies are housed in the National Library of Wales. They contain a considerable amount of material - letters, reports, bulletins and memoranda, 1916–47 - relating to the Fellowship of Reconciliation, for which he was a long-serving worker. The bulk of the Fellowship's records are deposited in BLPES and are described in *Sources*, Vol. 1, pp. 99–100.

DAVIES, Haydn (1905–   )

M.P. (Lab.) St Pancras S.W., 1945–50.

DAVIES, Sir Horatio David (1842–1912)

M.P. (Con.) Rochester, Jul–Dec 1892; Chatham, 1895–1906.
Lord Mayor of London, 1897–8.

DAVIES, James Henry Wootton- (1884–1964)

M.P. (Con.) Heywood and Radcliffe, 1940–5.

Letters addressed to Mr J. W. Wootton-Davies (son) were returned by the Post Office. Efforts to contact Mrs Shirley Wootton-Davies (widow) of Folkestone, were not successful.

DAVIES, John Cledwyn (1870–1952)

M.P. (Nat.Lib.) Denbigh, 1922–3.

DAVIES, John Percival, see DARWEN, 1st B

DAVIES, Sir Joseph (1866–1954)

M.P. (Co.Lib.) Crewe, 1918–22.

A collection of papers at the National Library of Wales covers Davies's work during World War I for the Cabinet Committee on the prevention and relief of distress. It also includes reports on the trade prospects of South Wales 1913–14; papers relating to conditions in the North Wales Slate Quarries, 1914–18; and papers relating to Cambrian Railways, 1865–1927.

DAVIES, Matthew Lewis Vaughan-, see YSTWYTH, 1st B

DAVIES, Rhys John (1877–1954)

M.P. (Lab.) Westhoughton, 1921–51.
Parliamentary Under-Secretary, Home Office, 1924.

Letters of Administration were granted to Davies's sons. These were not traced.

DAVIES, Stephen Owen (1886–1972)

South Wales miners' leader.
M.P. (Lab.) Merthyr Tydfil, 1934–70; (Ind.Lab.), 1970–2.

An extensive collection of papers has been deposited in the Library of University College, Swansea. It contains correspondence, documents, notebooks, personal papers and miscellaneous other material relating to S. O. Davies's trade union and political career.

DAVIES, Sir Thomas (1865–1939)

M.P. (Con.) Cirencester and Tewkesbury, 1918–29.

Neither Sir Thomas Davies's daughter, Miss E. M. Davies, nor the Cirencester Benefit Society, of which Sir Thomas was the first Chief Secretary, know of any surviving papers.

DAVIES, Thomas Hart- (1849–1920)

Indian Civil Service, traveller.
M.P. (Lib.) Hackney North, 1906–Jan 1910.

DAVIES, Timothy (1857–1951)

M.P. (Lib.) Fulham, 1906–Jan 1910; Louth, Dec 1910–20.

Mr J. O. Davies, who wound up the estate of Timothy Davies's only surviving son, knows of no papers relating to Davies's parliamentary career.

DAVIES, Sir (William) Howell (1851–1932)

M.P. (Lib.) Bristol South, 1906–22.

Mr O. D. F. Gardner (grandson), 40 Over Lane, Almondsbury, Bristol has scrapbooks covering Davies's business, local government and parliamentary work.

DAVISON, John Emanuel (1870–1927)

M.P. (Lab.) Smethwick, 1918–27.
Vice Chamberlain, H.M. Household, 1924.

Davison was survived by a widow. She and her heirs were not traced.

DAVISON, Sir William Henry, see BROUGHSHANE, 1st B

DAWES, James Arthur (1866–1921)

M.P. (Lib.) Walworth, Jan 1910–18; Southwark S.E., 1918–21.

DAWSON, Sir Philip (1898–1938)

M.P. (Con.) Lewisham West, 1921–38.

DAY, Harry (1880–1939)

M.P. (Lab.) Southwark Central, 1924–31, 1935–9.

Colonel Harry Day's son, Mr H. D. Day, believes that no papers have survived.

DEAN, Arthur Wellesley (1857–1929)

M.P. (Con.) Holland with Boston, 1924–9.

DEAN, P. T. (b. 1878)

M.P. (Con.) Blackburn, 1918–22.

DEANS, Richard Storry (1868–1938)

M.P. (Con.) Sheffield Park, 1923–9.

R. S. Deans's son, Mr R. Storry Deans, c/o Cripps, Harries, Willis & Carter, 1 New Square, Lincoln's Inn, London WC2A 3SB, has a newspaper cuttings book containing references to his father's career. Almost all other family papers were destroyed during World War II.

DE BENDERN, Count [1]
Arnold Maurice, Baron de Forest (1879–1968)

M.P. (Lib.) West Ham North, 1911–18.

Mr Lawrence B. Brody, c/o Coudert Brothers, Plantation House, 31–5 Fenchurch St, London EC3M 3DX, who acted in the estate, states that a great deal of documentation survived but this relates almost entirely to financial and personal affairs. The papers are stored in Biarritz, France, and are not made available.

[1] Hereditary Count of the Principality of Liechtenstein. He was naturalised in the Principality in 1932.

DE CHAIR, Somerset (1911–   )

M.P. (Con.) Norfolk S.W., 1935–45; Paddington South, 1950–1.

Mr de Chair has retained a number of papers relating to his parliamentary activities.

DEEDES, William Francis (1913–   )

M.P. (Con.) Ashford, 1950–Oct 1974.
Parliamentary Secretary, Ministry of Housing and Local Government, 1954–5. Parliamentary Under-Secretary, Home Office, 1955–7. Minister without Portfolio, 1962–4.
Editor, *Daily Telegraph,* from Dec 1974.

Mr Deedes believes that he has retained no papers which would be of relevance.

DEELEY, Sir Harry Mallaby Mallaby-, 1st Bt (1863–1937)

M.P. (Con.) Harrow, Jan 1910–18; Willesden East, 1918–22.

DEER, George (1890–1974)

M.P. (Lab.) Lincoln, 1945–50; Newark, 1950–64.

Approaches from the Modern Records Centre, University of Warwick Library, and from Hull University after Deer's death resulted in a number of books being donated to these two institutions, but elicited no papers. Richard Hyman's research papers for his study of the Workers' Union (1971) in the Modern Records Centre include a file of correspondence with Deer, 1964–5.

DE FOREST, Baron, see DE BENDERN, Count

DE FRECE, Sir Walter (1870–1935)

M.P. (Con.) Ashton-under-Lyne, 1920–4; Blackpool, 1924–31.

Records of Blackpool Conservatives have been deposited in Lancashire Record Office. No personal papers were discovered.

DE FREITAS, Sir Geoffrey Stanley (1913–   )

M.P. (Lab.) Nottingham Central, 1945–50; Lincoln, 1950–61; Kettering, 1964–
Parliamentary Under-Secretary, Air, 1946–50; Home Office, 1950–1. High Commissioner, Ghana, 1961–3; Kenya, 1963–4.

Sir Geoffrey has retained a number of records.

DE LA BÈRE, Sir Rupert, 1st Bt (1893–   )

M.P. (Con.) Evesham, 1935–50; Worcestershire South, 1950–5.
Lord Mayor of London, 1952–3.

Sir Rupert has retained many files and press cuttings. Marguerite de la Bère's *Reminiscences of a Lady Mayoress* (1954) contain many references to Sir Rupert's career.

DELACOURT-SMITH, Baron
Charles Percy George Smith (1917–72)

M.P. (Lab.) Colchester, 1945–50.
General Secretary, Post Office Engineering Union, 1953–72. Minister of State, Ministry of Technology, 1969–70.

Lady Delacourt-Smith, 56 Aberdare Gardens, London NW6, widow of Lord Delacourt-Smith, states that her husband kept only a little unpublished material. This consists of some formal letters and a diary which he kept while Minister of State. The diary is mainly composed of notes which Delacourt-Smith had intended for later use in a book. The records of the Post Office Engineering Union are described in *Sources*, Vol. 1, p. 214.

DELANY, William (1855–1916)*

M.P. (Irish Nat.) Queen's County Ossory, 1900–16.

DELARGY, Captain Hugh James (1908–76)

M.P. (Lab.) Manchester Platting, 1945–50; Thurrock, 1950–76.

DE LA WARR, 9th E
Herbrand Edward Dundonald Brassey Sackville, Lord Buckhurst (1900–76)

Parliamentary Under-Secretary, War Office, 1929–30. Parliamentary Secretary, Ministry of Agriculture and Fisheries, 1930–5. Parliamentary Under-Secretary, Board of Education, 1935–6; Colonial Office, 1936–7. Lord Privy Seal, 1937–8. President of the Board of Education, 1938–40. 1st Commissioner of Works, 1940. Postmaster General, 1951–5.

Hazlehurst and Woodland, p. 125, state that Earl de la Warr kept no papers.

DE L'ISLE, 1st Vt
Hon. William Philip Sidney, 6th B De L'Isle and Dudley (1909–   )

M.P. (Con.) Chelsea, 1944–5.
Parliamentary Secretary, Ministry of Pensions, 1945. Secretary of State for Air, 1951–5.
Governor-General, Australia, 1961–5.

No information was available with regard to Viscount De L'Isle's papers.

DENBIGH, 9th E of
Rudolph Robert Basil Aloysius Augustine Fielding (1859–1939)

Lord in Waiting, 1897–1906.

Family papers have been listed by the Warwickshire County Record Office.

DENHAM, 1st B
Sir George Edward Wentworth Bowyer, 1st Bt (1886–1948)

M.P. (Con.) Buckingham, 1918–37.
Junior Lord of the Treasury, 1927–9. Comptroller, H.M. Household, 1935. Parliamentary Secretary, Agriculture and Fisheries, 1939–40.

The 2nd Lord Denham says he has no political papers relating to his father's career. Press cuttings relating to Denham's career, Oct 1921–Jul 1929, are deposited in Buckinghamshire Record Office.

DENISON, Ernest William, see GRIMTHORPE, 2nd B

DENMAN, 3rd B
Sir Thomas Denman (1874–1954)

Lord in Waiting, 1905–7. Captain, Gentlemen at Arms, 1907–11.
Governor-General, Australia, 1911–14.

The National Library of Australia, Canberra, holds a small collection of letters, telegrams and other documents (1909–14). Family papers are in the care of the present Lord Denman.

DENMAN, Hon. Sir Richard Douglas, 1st Bt (1876–1957)

M.P. (Lib.) Carlisle, Jan 1910–18; (Lab.) Leeds Central, 1929–31; (Nat.Lab.) 1931–45.

Some 13 boxes of papers have been deposited in the Bodleian Library, Oxford. In addition to printed material, the collection includes some correspondence on election campaigns, a few letters concerning National Labour politics in the 1930s, and other miscellaneous material.

DENNIS, John William (1865–1949)

M.P. (Con.) Birmingham Deritend, 1918–22.

Mr Peter K. Dennis (nephew), Stenigot House, nr Louth, Lincolnshire, says his uncle left few papers, having moved house at the beginning of World War II. Dennis was a member of the Tariff Commission, 1904–20. Its records are housed at BLPES. See *Sources*, Vol. 1, p. 252.

DENNISON, Robert (1879–1951)

M.P. (Lab.) Birmingham, King's Norton, 1924–9.

Mr R. Dennison (son) states that most of his father's papers were probably inadvertently destroyed; he knows of none. Robert Dennison was Assistant Secretary of the Iron and Steel Confederation. Its records, many of which are now in the Modern Records Centre, University of Warwick Library, are described in *Sources*, Vol. 1, pp. 120–1.

DENNISS, Sir Edmund Robert Bartley Bartley- (1854–1931)

M.P. (Con.) Oldham, 1911–22.

Bird & Lovibond, solicitors who acted in Sir Edmund's estate, had no information.

DENNY, John McAusland (1858–1921)

M.P. (Con.) Kilmarnock, 1895–1906.

Neither Denny's grandson, Mr W. A. K. Marshall, nor Sir Alistair Denny, Bt, his great-nephew, knows of any surviving papers.

DENVILLE, Alfred (1876–1955)

M.P. (Con.) Newcastle on Tyne Central, 1931–45.

Many of Alfred Denville's papers were destroyed by vandals shortly after his death. However his grandson, Mr Terence Denville-Faulkner, has preserved eight albums, containing press cuttings, photographs and letters. Five of these concern Denville's theatrical career, while the remaining three relate to his political career. These political albums contain material relating to Denville's election campaigns, 1928–32 and drafts of speeches and newspaper cuttings covering the period up to 1945. Alfred Denville's daughter, Mrs Marguerite Faulkner, Northgate, Tower Road, Jersey, C.I., has certain material relating to her father's theatrical activities.

DERBY, 17th E of
Edward George Villiers Stanley, Baron Stanley (1865–1948)

M.P. (Con.) Westhoughton, 1892–1906.
Financial Secretary, War Office, 1900–3. Postmaster-General, 1903–5. Under-Secretary of State, War, 1916, and Secretary of State, War, 1916–18 and 1922–4.
Ambassador, Paris, 1918–20.

The Derby family papers at Liverpool Record Office include a very large collection of papers relating to the 17th Earl. The material is divided into five main series, relating to Liverpool, Lancashire, Government Offices, public life and domestic life. A mass of correspondence up to 1947, and papers connected with each of Derby's public offices have survived, and a good number of subject files, memoranda and minutes, and correspondence files relate to the period at the Paris embassy. Further details are given in Hazlehurst and Woodland, pp. 138–9.

DE ROTHSCHILD, see ROTHSCHILD

DESBOROUGH, 1st B
William Henry Grenfell (1855–1945)

M.P. (Con.) Salisbury, 1880–6; Hereford, 1892–3; Wycombe, 1900–5.
Captain, Yeomen of the Guard, 1925–9.

DE VALERA, Eamon (1882–1975)

M.P. (Sinn Fein) Clare East, 1917–22.
President, Sinn Fein, 1917–26.

Prime Minister and Minister of External Affairs, Irish Free State and Republic of Ireland. President of Ireland, 1959–73.

De Valera's papers are preserved at the Franciscan House of Studies, Dun Mhuire, Killiney, Co. Dublin.

DEVLIN, C. R. (b. 1858)*

M.P. (Irish Nat.) Galway Town, 1903–6.

DEVLIN, Joseph (1872–1934)*

M.P. (Irish Nat.) Kilkenny North, 1902–6; Belfast, 1906–18; Belfast Falls, 1918–22; (Nat.) Fermanagh and Tyrone, 1929–34.

Various papers relating to Devlin's political activities can be found in the Northern Ireland Public Record Office, including papers, 1910–23 (D 1919, T 2307); newspaper cuttings; a typescript biography, 1919 (T 2505/2); correspondence concerning him and Matthew Keating, c. 1933 (T. 2307); and letters to Henry Maloney, 1915–34 (T. 2257).

DEVONPORT, 1st Vt
Sir Hudson Ewbanke Kearley, 1st Bt (1856–1934)

M.P. (Lib.) Devonport, 1892–Jan 1910.
Parliamentary Secretary, Board of Trade 1905–9. Food Controller, 1916–17.

Hazlehurst and Woodland, p. 83, located no papers.

DEVONSHIRE, 8th D of
Spencer Compton Cavendish, Lord Cavendish and Marquess of Hartington (1833–1908)

M.P. (Lib., later Lib. Un.) Lancashire North, 1857–68; Radnor, 1869–80; Lancashire N.E., 1880–5; Rossendale, 1885–92.
Parliamentary Under-Secretary, War Office, 1863–6. Secretary of State for War, 1866 and 1882–5. Postmaster General, 1868–71. Chief Secretary for Ireland, 1871–4. Secretary of State for India, 1880–2. Lord President of the Council, 1895–1903.

Papers remain with the present (11th) Duke of Devonshire, and enquiries should be addressed to the Keeper of the Devonshire Collections, Chatsworth, Bakewell, Derbyshire DE4 1PN. Details appear in Hazlehurst and Woodland, pp. 30–1.

DEVONSHIRE, 9th D of
Sir Victor Christian William Cavendish, Marquess of Hartington (1868–1938)

M.P. (Lib.Un.) Derbyshire West, 1891–1908.
Financial Secretary, Treasury, 1903–5. Civil Lord of the Admiralty, 1915–16. Governor-General, Canada, 1916–21. Secretary of State, Colonies, 1922–4.

A small collection of papers, mainly relating to the period in Canada, survives with the present (11th) Duke of Devonshire, at Chatsworth House, Bakewell, Derbyshire DE4 1PN (Hazlehurst and Woodland, p. 31).

DEVONSHIRE, 10th D of
Edward William Spencer Cavendish, Marquess of Hartington (1895–1950)

M.P. (Con.) Derbyshire West, 1923–38.

Parliamentary Under-Secretary, Dominion Affairs, 1936–40; India and Burma, 1940–2; Colonies, 1943–5.

It is believed that few relevant papers survive at Chatsworth House.

DEWAR, Lord
Arthur Dewar (1860–1917)

M.P. (Lib.) Edinburgh South, 1899–1900, 1906–Apr 1910.
Solicitor-General for Scotland, 1909–10.

DEWAR, 1st B
Sir Thomas Robert Dewar, 1st Bt (1864–1930)

M.P. (Con.) St George's, 1900–6.

Messrs Freshfields, solicitors of London, have acted in the estate, but no papers have come to light. It was suggested that enquiries should be directed to the Hon. J. J. Dewar.

DEWAR, Sir John Alexander Dewar, 1st Bt, see FORTEVIOT, 1st B

DEWHURST, Harry (1866–1931)

M.P. (Con.) Northwich, 1918–22.

Mr T. L. Dewhurst (grandson) knows of no papers and believes none have survived.

DIAMOND, Baron
John Diamond (1907–   )

M.P. (Lab.) Manchester Blackley, 1945–51; Gloucester, 1957–70.
Chief Secretary to the Treasury, 1964–70.

Lord Diamond was unable to be of assistance.

DICKIE, J. P. (b. 1874)

M.P. (Lib.) Gateshead, 1923–4; (Lib.Nat.) Consett, 1931–5.

DICKINSON, 1st B
Sir Willoughby Hyett Dickinson (1859–1943)

M.P. (Lib.) St Pancras North, 1906–18.

It is believed that Lord Dickinson destroyed many of his papers in the 1930s. However, at the Bodleian Library there is a collection of papers concerning Dickinson's work for the League of Nations movement in England, 1914–44 (Mss Eng. Hist. c. 402 - c. 407). This includes papers relating to the proposals of Dickinson and others for a League of Nations; correspondence concerning the foundation of the League; papers of the League of Nations Union; and papers relating to the International Union of League of Nations Societies. At the Greater London Record Office there are four bundles of papers relating to Dickinson's political activities, 1886–1939, together with a file on his work for Women's Suffrage and Electoral Reform, 1916–43.

DICKINSON, Robert Edmund (1862–1949)

M.P. (Con.) Wells, 1899–1906.

According to information supplied by Dickinson's executors, the Standard Bank Ltd, Trustee and Taxation Branch, any surviving papers were destroyed by the sole residuary beneficiary of the estate.

DICKSON, Lord
Scott Dickson (1850–1922)

M.P. (Con.) Glasgow Bridgeton, 1900–6; Glasgow Central, 1909–15.
Solicitor-General, Scotland, 1896–1903. Lord Advocate, 1903–6.

According to information received by the NRA (Scotland), Lord Dickson's family know of no records.

DICKSON, Thomas S. (1885–1935)

M.P. (Lab.) Lanark, 1923–4, 1929–31.

No contacts were established. Dickson was President of the National Union of Journalists, 1925–6, and its records are described in *Sources*, Vol. 1, pp. 194–5.

DIGBY, John Kenelm Digby Wingfield (1859–1904)

M.P. (Con.) Mid-Somerset, 1885; Dorset North, 1892–1904.

Mr Simon Wingfield Digby (grandson), Sherborne Castle, Sherborne, Dorset, believes that few papers have survived. One exception is a diary recording his grandfather's attendance at political functions in the late nineteenth century.

DIGBY, (K) Simon Wingfield (1910–   )

M.P. (Con.) Dorset West, 1941–Feb 1974.
Civil Lord of the Admiralty, 1951–7.

Mr Wingfield Digby has retained a number of papers at present unsorted.

DILHORNE, 1st Vt
Sir Reginald Edward Manningham-Buller, 4th Bt (1905–   )

M.P. (Con.) Daventry, 1943–50; Northamptonshire South, 1950–62.
Parliamentary Secretary, Ministry of Works, 1945. Solicitor-General, 1951–4. Attorney-General, 1954–62. Lord Chancellor, 1962–4.

Viscount Dilhorne was unable to provide information.

DILKE, Sir Charles Wentworth, 2nd Bt (1843–1911)

M.P. (Lib.) Chelsea, 1868–86; Forest of Dean, 1892–1911.
Parliamentary Under-Secretary, Foreign Affairs, 1880–2. President of the Local Government Board, 1882–5.

A collection of Dilke's papers is housed in the British Library (Add. Mss 43874–967, 49385–455). His diaries, dating from the 1880s, are housed in Birmingham University Library. Twenty-eight letters from Dilke are in the Boston Public Library (Mass.), while some 25 letters have been sold to the Library of Texas University. Other collections contain a great deal of important correspondence. Some 294 letters can be found in the Morel papers at BLPES, and other relevant material can be found in the Sir Stafford Northcote, Asquith, Joseph Chamberlain and Balfour collections. Some correspondence may also be found at Churchill College Cambridge.

DILLON, John (1851–1927) *

M.P. (Irish Nat.) Co. Tipperary, 1880–3; Mayo East, 1885—1918.

Chairman, Irish Nationalist Party, 1918.

A collection of papers, 1876–1927, has been deposited in the Library of Trinity College, Dublin. It contains a great deal of material relating to the Irish Nationalist Party, and a considerable quantity of correspondence with its members. Dillon's correspondence with William O'Brien can be found in the National Library of Ireland (see *Sources*, Vol. 1, p. 296).

DIMSDALE, Sir Joseph Cockfield, 1st Bt (1849–1912)

M.P. (Con.) City of London, 1900–6.
Lord Mayor of London, 1901–2

Sir Joseph's grandson, Sir John Dimsdale, Bt, 16 Willis Road, Swaythling, Southampton SO2 2NT, has a small collection of autograph letters, largely of a formal nature, dated from 1902. No other papers seem to have survived.

DINGWALL, 11th B, see LUCAS, 8th B, and DINGWALL, 11th B

DISRAELI, Coningsby Ralph (1867–1936)

M.P. (Con.) Altrincham, 1892–1906.

The Hughenden Papers, Hughenden Manor, High Wycombe, Bucks, contain some material. Miss Calverley (niece), Corner House, Fittleworth, Pulborough, Sussex, has some press cuttings retained in albums. It is believed that further volumes of cuttings survive with Mr Simon Bradley-Williams, 7 Field End, Waldegrave Park, Twickenham, London.

DIXEY, Arthur Carlyne Niven (1889–1954)

M.P. (Con.) Penrith and Cockermouth, 1923–5.

DIXON, Charles Harvey (1862–1923)

M.P. (Con.) Boston, Jan 1910–18; Rutland and Stamford, 1922–3.

DIXON, Sir Daniel, 1st Bt (1844–1907)*

M.P. (Con.) Belfast North, 1906–7.

The present (2nd) Lord Glentoran, Drumadarragh House, Ballyclare, Co. Antrim BT39 OTA, has a book of obituary notices only.

DIXON, Herbert, see GLENTORAN, 1st B

DOBBIE, William (1878–1950)

M.P. (Lab.) Rotherham, 1933–50.
President, National Union of Railwaymen, 1925–8, 1930–3.

No contact with Dobbie's family was established. Records of the National Union of Railwaymen are described in *Sources*, Vol. 1, p. 199.

DOBBS, Alfred James (d. 1945)

M.P. (Lab.) Smethwick, 1945.

DOBSON, Thomas William (1853–1935)

M.P. (Lib.) Plymouth, 1906–Jan 1910.

No contacts were established with persons mentioned in the will and Probate Act.

DOCKRELL, Sir Maurice Edward (1850–1929)*

M.P. (Con.) Rathmines, 1918–22.

DODD, Sir John Samuel (1904–73)

M.P. (Lib.Nat.) Oldham, 1935–45.

Lady Dodd (widow), Les Fraises, Fort Lane, Rozel, Trinity, Jersey, C.I., states that her husband kept a very full record of his parliamentary career. The papers are now in her care.

DODD, William Huston (1844–1930)*

M.P. (Lib.) Tyrone North, 1906–7.

DODDS, Norman Noel (1903–65)

M.P. (Lab. and Co-op.) Dartford, 1945–55; Erith and Crayford, 1955–65.

All surviving material is with Mr Dodds (son), 11 Pinecroft Wood, New Barn, Kent. This does not appear to contain any relevant political material. Mrs Eva Toogood (widow of Norman Dodds) believes private papers were destroyed after his death.

DODDS, Stephen Roxby (1881–1943)

M.P. (Lib.) The Wirral, 1923–4.

Mr G. Percival Harris, LL.B., who was a partner of S. R. Dodds, and who acted as executor to both Dodds and his wife, knows of no papers and believes that none survived.

DOLAN, C. J. (b. 1882)*

M.P. (Irish Nat.) Leitrim North, 1906–8.

DOLAND, George Frederick (1872–1946)

M.P. (Con.) Balham and Tooting, 1936–45.

Neither Doland's only surviving son, Mr F. H. Doland, nor his former company, George Doland Ltd, know of any surviving papers.

DOLAN, J. N. *

M.P. (Sinn Fein) Leitrim, 1918–22.

DONALD, Thompson *

M.P. (Lab. Un.) Belfast Victoria, 1918–22.

DONELAN, Captain Anthony J. (1846–1924)*

M.P. (Irish Nat.) Cork County East, 1892–1911, (unseated on petition). Wicklow, 1911–18.

DONNELLY, Desmond Louis (1920–74)

M.P. (Lab.) Pembroke, 1950–68; (Ind.) 1968–70.

Before his death Mr Donnelly stated that he had kept a copy of every letter he had written from his first entry into the House of Commons. It was his intention to deposit these in the National Library of Wales.

DONNELLY, P. J. *

M.P. (Irish Nat.) Armagh South, 1918–22.

DONNER, Sir Patrick William (1904–   )

M.P. (Con.) Islington West, 1931–5; Basingstoke, 1935–55.

Sir Patrick states that most of his papers were destroyed during World War II, though some letters and press cuttings survived. He retains records of constituency speeches and one memorandum to Churchill on India.

DONOUGHMORE, 6th E of
Richard Walter John Hely-Hutchinson (1875–1948)

Parliamentary Under-Secretary, War, 1903–5.

The present (7th) Earl knows of no relevant papers in his care. Letters from Donoughmore to Sir John Sprigg (1898–1904) are in the Cory Library, Rhodes University, Grahamstown, South Africa. Correspondence (1916) can also be found in the Hardinge papers at Cambridge University Library.

DONOUGHMORE, 7th E of
John Michael Henry Hely-Hutchinson, Vt Suirdale (1902–   )

M.P. (Con.) Peterborough, 1943–5.

Lord Donoughmore knows of no relevant papers.

DONOVAN, Baron
Terence Norbert Donovan (1898–1971)

M.P. (Lab.) Leicester East, 1945–50; Leicester N.E., 1950.
Lord Justice of Appeal, 1960–3. Chairman, Royal Commission on Trade Unions and Employers' Associations, 1965–8.

Some papers of the Donovan Committee on Trade Unions and Employers' Associations, 1965–8, are housed in Nuffield College, Oxford.

DONOVAN, James Thomas (1878–1922)*

M.P. (Irish Nat.) Wicklow West, 1914–18.

DOOGAN, P. C. (1841–1906)*

M.P. (Irish Nat.) Tyrone East, 1895–1906.

DORAN, Edward (1892–1945)

M.P. (Con.) Tottenham North, 1931–5.

DORINGTON, Sir John Edward, 1st Bt (1832–1911)

M.P. (Con.) Tewkesbury, 1886–1906.

DORIS, William (1860–1926)*

M.P. (Irish Nat.) Mayo West, Jan–Dec 1910.
Secretary, United Irish League.

Records of the United Irish League are described in *Sources*, Vol. 1, pp. 295–6.

DOUGHERTY, Sir James Brown (1844–1934)*

M.P. (Lib.) Londonderry, 1914–18.
Under-Secretary to the Lord Lieutenant, Ireland, 1908–14.

The solicitors who acted in the estate, Messrs Wells & Hind of Nottingham, retain no contact with the family. A son and daughter, John Gerald Dougherty and Miss Mary Dougherty, were named in the will, but they were not traced.

DOUGHTY, Sir George (1854–1914)

M.P. (Lib., later Lib. Un.) Great Grimsby, 1895–Jan 1910; Dec 1910–14.

DOUGLAS OF BARLOCH, 1st B
Sir Francis Campbell Ross Douglas (1889–   )

M.P. (Lab.) Battersea North, 1940–6.
Governor, Malta, 1946–9.

Lord Douglas has retained few records relating to his membership of the House of Commons. Most of his correspondence of this period dealt with constituency matters and was subsequently destroyed. He has retained a few papers relating to his Governorship of Malta, but no official correspondence. A collection of material relating to the period that Lord Douglas was Deputy Chairman of the Corby Development Corporation, 1950–62, is to be deposited in the Northamptonshire Record Office.

DOUGLAS, Aretas Akers-, see CHILSTON, 1st Vt

DOUGLAS, Charles Mackinnon (1865–1924)

M.P. (Lib.) Lanarkshire N.W., 1899–1906.

DOUGLAS-HOME, Sir Alec, see HOME OF THE HIRSEL, Baron

DOVERCOURT, 1st B
Sir (Joseph) Stanley Holmes (1878–1961)

M.P. (Lib.) Derbyshire North East, 1918–22; (Lib.Nat. and Con.) Harwich, 1935–54.

A collection of constituency records survives with the Harwich Conservative Association. The material includes minutes of the National Liberal Executive Committee, 1931–8; press cuttings; A.G.M. minutes and E.C. minutes. Messrs Farrer & Co, solicitors, and Coutts Bank acted in the estate of Eva Lady Dovercourt.

DOVERDALE, 2nd B
Oswald Partington (1872–1935)

M.P. (Lib.) High Peak, 1900–Dec 1910; Shipley, 1915–18.
Junior Lord of the Treasury, 1909–11.

DOWER, Alan Vincent Gandar (1898–   )

M.P. (Con.) Stockport, 1931–5; Penrith and Cockermouth, 1935–50.

DOWNHAM, 1st B
William Hayes Fisher (1853–1920)

M.P. (Con.) Fulham, 1885–1906 and Jan 1910–18.
Financial Secretary, Treasury, 1902–3. Parliamentary Secretary, Local Government Board,

1915–17. President of the Local Government Board, 1917–18. Chancellor of the Duchy of Lancaster, 1918–19.

Hazlehurst and Woodland, p. 54, describe the papers which survive in the possession of Downham's grandson, Mr Peter Hayes Fisher, Cock Farm, Stonegate, Wadhurst, Sussex.

DOXFORD, Sir William Theodore (1841–1916)

M.P. (Con.) Sunderland, 1895–1906.

Messrs Hedleys, solicitors of Sunderland, acted in the estate but were unable to supply information regarding papers.

DOYLE, Sir Nicholas Grattan- (1862–1941)

Deputy Director, Education and Propaganda, Ministry of Food, 1918.
M.P. (Con.) Newcastle-on-Tyne North, 1918–40.

DRAYSON, George Burnaby (1913–)

M.P. (Con.) Skipton, 1945–

Records of Skipton Conservatives since 1900 have been retained by the Constituency Association.

DREWE, Sir Cedric (1896–1971)

M.P. (Con.) South Molton, 1924–9; Honiton, 1931–55.
Junior Lord of the Treasury, 1944–5.

DRIBERG, Thomas Edward Neil, see BRADWELL, Baron

DRUMALBYN, 1st B
Niall Malcolm Stewart Macpherson (1908–)

M.P. (Nat.Lib., later Nat.Lib. and Con.) Dumfriesshire, 1945–63.
Joint Parliamentary Under-Secretary, Scottish Office, 1955–60. Parliamentary Secretary, Board of Trade, 1960–2. Minister of Pensions and National Insurance, 1962–3. Minister of State, Board of Trade, 1963–4. Minister without Portfolio, 1970–4.

Lord Drumalbyn has kept his papers, which are largely unsorted. The material is mentioned in *Sources*, Vol. 1, pp. 183–4.

DUCKWORTH, (George) Arthur Victor (1901–)

M.P. (Con.) Shrewsbury, 1929–45.

DUCKWORTH, Sir James (1840–1915)

M.P. (Lib.) Middleton, 1897–1900; Stockport, 1906–Jan 1910.

Sir James Duckworth's grandsons know of no substantial collection of papers. Mr Alan Duckworth does however have a typed copy of some autobiographical notes which Sir James began to write in 1910. These end with the death of his first wife in 1881, and contain little of a political character.

DUCKWORTH, John (1863–1946)

M.P. (Lib.) Blackburn, 1923–9.

Duckworth's solicitors, having contacted his son and daughter and accountants, state that they have been informed by them that they have no information which could be of assistance.

DUCKWORTH, William Rostron (1879–1952)

M.P. (Con.) Manchester Moss Side, 1935–45.

Neither Mrs A. Taylor (niece) nor Mr W. R. Lawton (whose late brother-in-law, Mr I. G. Aspinall, was friend and solicitor to Duckworth) knows of any papers.

DU CROS, Alfred (1868–1946)

M.P. (Con.) Bow and Bromley, Jan–Dec 1910.

Material relating to his election can be found in the Lansbury Collection at BLPES.

DU CROS, Sir Arthur Philip, 1st Bt (1871–1955)

M.P. (Con.) Hastings, 1908–18; Clapham, 1918–22.

Records of the Hastings Conservative Association, 1859–1918, are deposited in Hastings Public Museum. A full and interesting collection of Clapham Conservative Association papers is deposited in BLPES, and covers the period when Du Cros was M.P. there (see *Sources*, Vol. 1, pp. 66–7).

DU CROS, William Harvey (1846–1918)

M.P. (Con.) Hastings, 1906–8.

Minute books of the Hastings Conservative Association, covering the period when Du Cros was M.P., can be found in Hastings Public Museum.

DUDGEON, Cecil Randolph (1885–1970)

M.P. (Lib.) Galloway, 1922–4; 1929–31.

It is believed that no papers have survived.

DUDHOPE, Vt, see DUNDEE, 11th E of

DUDLEY, 2nd E of
William Humble Ward, Vt Ednam (1867–1932)

Parliamentary Secretary, Board of Trade, 1895–1902. Lord Lieutenant, Ireland, 1902–6. Governor-General, Australia, 1908–11.

DUDLEY, 3rd E of
William Humble Eric Ward, Vt Ednam (1894–1969)

M.P. (Con.) Hornsey, 1921–4; Wednesbury, 1931–2.

DUFFERIN AND AVA, 4th M of
Basil Sheridan Hamilton-Temple-Blackwood (1909–45)

Lord in Waiting 1936–7. Parliamentary Under-Secretary, Colonial Office, 1937–40. Director of Empire Division, Ministry of Information, 1941–2.

Papers of the 4th Marquess have been deposited in the Northern Ireland Public Record Office. The bulk of the material relates to Indian affairs, and includes letters and papers relating to the Indian Franchise Committee, the 'Union of Britain and India' organisation, and general Indian matters. Other material relates to Dufferin and Ava's ministerial responsibilities in the House of Lords, e.g. for Home Office matters and the Colonies, and to his general political interests. Certain non-political papers also survive. Correspondence with W. A. Creech-Jones, 1937–9, concerning the organisation of labour in Mauritius can be found in the Creech-Jones papers at Rhodes House Library, Oxford.

DUFFY, George Gavan *

M.P. (Sinn Fein) Dublin County South, 1918–22.

Correspondence concerning the Nationalist Movement, 1906–21, can be found in the National Library of Ireland (Mss 5581–3).

DUFFY, Thomas Gavan- (1867–1932)

M.P. (Lab.) Whitehaven, 1922–4.

DUFFY, William J.*

M.P. (Irish Nat.) Galway South, 1900–18.

Duffy was one time Honorary Secretary of the United Irish League, and some of its records are in the National Library of Ireland (see *Sources*, Vol. 1, p. 295).

DUGDALE, John (1905–63)

M.P. (Lab.) West Bromwich, 1941–63.
Parliamentary and Financial Secretary, Admiralty, 1945–50. Minister of State, Colonial Office, 1950–1.

Mrs Irene Dugdale (widow), 113 Church Road, London SW13, has certain of her husband's papers.

DUGDALE, Sir Thomas Lionel, 1st Bt, see CRATHORNE, 1st B

DUGGAN, Edmund John (d. 1936)

M.P. (Sinn Fein) Meath South, 1918–22.
Member, Dail Eireann.
Minister in Government of Irish Free State. Senator, Irish Free State, 1933–6.

DUGGAN, Hubert John (1904–43)

M.P. (Con.) Acton, 1931–43.

Messrs Withers, solicitors, who acted in the estate, state that all their relevant files have been destroyed.

DUKE, Sir Henry Edward, see MERRIVALE, 1st B

DUKESTON, 1st B
Charles Dukes (1881–1948)

M.P. (Lab.) Warrington, 1923–4; 1929–31.
General Secretary, National Union of General and Municipal Workers.

Lord Cooper of Stockton Heath (son-in-law) states that he has no papers nor does he think any exist. A great deal of early material was destroyed when Dukes left Chester for London in 1934. Seven volumes of press cuttings are preserved at Warrington Public Library. Records of the GMWU are described in *Sources*, Vol. 1, pp. 193–4.

DULVERTON, 1st B
Sir Gilbert Alan Hamilton Wills, 2nd Bt (1880–1956)

M.P. (Con.) Taunton, 1912–18; Weston-super-Mare, 1918–22.

The present (2nd) Lord Dulverton knows of few papers relating to his father's parliamentary career. He has copies of two speeches made by his father, and a book of press cuttings covering the years 1912–33. Messrs W. D. & H. O. Wills, Bedminster, Bristol BS99 7UJ, have a few notes concerning Dulverton's business activities.

DUMPHREYS, J. M. T.*

M.P. (Con.) Bermondsey, 1909–Jan 1910.

DUMPLETON, Cyril Walter (1897–1966)

M.P. (Lab.) St Albans, 1945–50.

Mr John Dumpleton (son) reports that his father destroyed all relevant papers when he left politics. No papers now survive in the care of the family.

DUNCAN, Colonel Sir Alan Gomme Gomme- (1893–1963)

M.P. (Con.) Perth and East Perthshire, 1945–59.

Mr A. M. Gomme-Duncan (son), Dunbarney, Bridge of Earn, Perth PH2 9EE, has a collection of papers relating to his father's career. These include press cuttings and other papers with particular reference to Scotland, agriculture and the army, 1945–59.

DUNCAN, Sir Andrew Rae (1884–1952)

M.P. (Con.) City of London, 1940–50.
President of the Board of Trade, 1940, 1941–2. Minister of Supply, 1940–1, 1942–5.

Hazlehurst and Woodland, pp. 47–8, report that no papers of note have survived. Papers kept by Sir Andrew Duncan as Minister of Supply are included in the Private Office series AVIA 11 at the Public Record Office.

DUNCAN, Charles (1865–1933)

M.P. (Lab.) Barrow-in-Furness, 1906–18; Clay Cross, 1922–33.

It has not proved possible to trace any of Duncan's heirs. Duncan was Secretary of the Workers' Union from 1900. Some of its records are described in *Sources*, Vol. 1, p. 264. Others are now in the Modern Records Centre, University of Warwick Library.

DUNCAN, Sir James Alexander Lawson, 1st Bt (1899–1974)

M.P. (Con.) Kensington North, 1931–45; Angus South, 1950–64.

Sir James stated before his death that he had no documents relating to his parliamentary career.

DUNCAN, Sir (James) Hastings (1855–1928)

M.P. (Lib.) Otley, 1900–18.

Mr R. H. H. Duncan (grandson), c/o William Ackroyd & Co. Ltd, Otley Mills, Otley, West Yorkshire, has certain papers of his grandfather, including diaries of his youth and early manhood, and minute books and other papers of the Otley Liberal Association and Liberal Club. No relevant political papers seem to survive, however. The papers of Sir J. H. Duncan's firm, William Ackroyd & Co. Ltd, dating from 1819 are deposited in the Brotherton Library, University of Leeds.

DUNCAN, R. (b. 1850)

M.P. (Con.) Govan, 1906–Jan 1910.

DUNCANNON, Vt, see BESSBOROUGH, 9th E of

DUNCAN-SANDYS, Baron
Duncan Edwin Sandys (1908–)

M.P. (Con.) Norwood, 1935–45; Streatham, 1950–Feb 1974.
Financial Secretary, War Office, 1941–3. Parliamentary Secretary, Ministry of Supply, 1942–4.
Minister of Works, 1944–5. Minister of Supply, 1951–4. Minister of Housing and Local
Government, 1954–7. Minister of Defence, 1957–9; Aviation, 1959–60. Secretary of State for
Commonwealth Relations, 1960–4. Secretary of State for the Colonies, 1962–4.

Lord Duncan-Sandys informed Hazlehurst and Woodland (pp. 127–8) that he had a large
collection of unsorted papers which were not available for research. Private Office papers (AVIA
11) are at the Public Record Office.

DUNDAS, Hon. Lord
David Dundas (1854–1922)

Solicitor-General for Scotland, 1903–5.

Neither Lt.-Col. David Dundas Robertson nor Mr Ralph Dundas, kinsmen of Lord Dundas,
knows of any surviving papers.

DUNDAS, Lord, see ZETLAND, 2nd M of

DUNDEE, 11th E of
Henry James Scrymgeour-Wedderburn, Vt Dudhope (1902–)

M.P. (Con.) Renfrewshire West, 1931–45.
Parliamentary Under-Secretary, Scotland, 1936–9, 1941–2. Minister without Portfolio,
1958–61. Minister of State, Foreign Affairs, 1961–4. Assistant Deputy Leader, House of Lords,
1960–2; Deputy Leader, 1962–4.

DUNEDIN, 1st Vt
Andrew Graham Murray (1849–1942)

M.P. (Con.) Bute, 1891–1905.
Solicitor-General for Scotland, 1891–2 and 1895–6. Lord Advocate for Scotland, 1896–1903.
Secretary of State for Scotland, 1903–5. Lord Justice General and Lord President of the Scottish
Court of Session, 1905–13. Lord of Appeal in Ordinary, 1913–32.

Hazlehurst and Woodland, p. 111, located no papers, apart from a collection at the Public
Record Office (CO 905/17,18).

DUNGLASS, Lord, see HOME OF THE HIRSEL, Baron

DUNN, Albert Edward (1864–1937)

M.P. (Lib.) Camborne, 1906–Dec 1910.

Messrs Dunn & Baker, solicitors, of Exeter, a firm in which A. E. Dunn was a partner, have no
papers and know of no other contacts who might be of assistance.

DUNN, Edward (1880–1945)

M.P. (Lab.) Rother Valley, 1935–45.

A biography appears in the *Dictionary of Labour Biography*, Vol. III, pp. 68–9. Dunn's daughters, Mrs G. D. C. Shaw and Dr Margaret Hallinan, live in Maltby.

DUNN, John Freeman (1874–1956)

M.P. (Lib.) Hemel Hempstead, 1923–4.

DUNN, Sir William, 1st Bt (1833–1912)

M.P. (Lib.) Paisley, 1891–1906.

Attempts to contact Dunn's old firm proved inconclusive.

DUNN, Sir William Henry, 1st Bt (1856–1926)

M.P. (Con.) Southwark, Jan–Dec 1910.
Lord Mayor of London, 1916–17.

DUNNE, Edward Martin (1864–1944)

M.P. (Lib.) Walsall, 1906–Jan 1910.

See below.

DUNNE, Philip Russell Rendel (1904–65)

M.P. (Con.) Stalybridge and Hyde, 1935–7.

A collection of Dunne family papers has been deposited in the Hereford County Record Office by Captain T. Dunne. This, however, contains very little material relating to the political career of E. M. Dunne and nothing at all on that of Philip Dunne. The chief relevant item is a volume of newspaper cuttings relating to E. M. Dunne's candidature at Kingswinford, 1905, and Walsall, 1906, and a volume presented to him on his retirement from the Walsall constituency.

DUNNICO, Sir Herbert (1876–1953)

M.P. (Lab.) Consett, 1922–31.

The surviving papers of the Rev. Sir Herbert Dunnico are retained by his son, Mr Herbert Dunnico, Robert Browning Settlement (Inc.), Fellowship House, 3 Browning Street, London SE17. Mr Dunnico states that these records are, however, few in number.

DUNRAVEN AND MOUNTEARL, 5th E of
Windham Henry Wyndham-Quin (1857–1952)

M.P. (Con.) Glamorganshire South, 1895–1906.

DUNROSSIL, 1st Vt
William Shepherd Morrison (1893–1961)

M.P. (Con.) Cirencester and Tewkesbury, 1929–59.
Financial Secretary, Treasury, 1935–6. Minister of Agriculture and Fisheries, 1936–9. Chancellor of the Duchy of Lancaster, 1939–40. Minister of Food, 1939–40. Postmaster General, 1940–2. Minister of Town and Country Planning, 1942–5. Speaker of the House of Commons, 1951–9.
Governor-General, Australia, 1960–1.

Hazlehurst and Woodland, p. 111, state that the present (2nd) Viscount Dunrossil has in his care only some personal or private papers which are not available for research.

DU PRE, William Baring (1875–1946)

M.P. (Con.) Wycombe, 1914–23.

Lady Loehnis (stepdaughter) believes that papers were probably destroyed. Any surviving papers would be with Mrs Pickering (Du Pre's daughter) but it was not possible to confirm whether any papers do in fact survive.

DURBIN, Evan Frank Mottram (1906–48)

M.P. (Lab.) Edmonton, 1945–8.
Parliamentary Secretary, Ministry of Works, 1947–8.

A collection of papers has survived. Enquiries should be directed to Mrs M. Durbin (widow), 2 Eldon Grove, London NW3.

DURHAM, 4th E of
Hon. Frederick William Lambton, (1855–1929)

M.P. (Lib.) Durham South, 1880–5; (Lib.Un.) Durham S.E., 1900–Jan 1910.

The Lambton family archive, Lambton Estate Office, Lambton Park, Chester-le-Street, Co. Durham, is at present being catalogued. However, no papers relating to the parliamentary career of the 4th Earl have been found.

DUTHIE, Sir William Smith (1892–   )

M.P. (Con.) Banffshire, 1945–64.

DYE, Sidney (1900–58)

M.P. (Lab.) Norfolk S.W., 1945–51, 1955–8.

Mrs Grace Dye (widow) has retained a collection of papers relating to her husband's career. Enquiries should be directed to Mrs Dye, Norbrick House, Sporle, King's Lynn, Norfolk.

DYKE, Sir William Hart, 7th Bt (1837–1931)

M.P. (Con.) Kent West, 1865–8; Mid Kent, 1868–85; Dartford, 1885–1906.
Parliamentary Secretary to the Treasury and Government Chief Whip, 1874–80. Chief Secretary, Ireland, 1885–6. Vice President, Committee of Council on Education, 1887–92.

The present baronet resides in Canada: no information on papers was forthcoming.

DYNEVOR, 7th B
Hon. Walter Fitz-Uryan Rhys (formerly Rice) (1873–1956)

M.P. (Con.) Brighton, Jan 1910–11.
See below.

DYNEVOR, 8th B
Hon. Charles Arthur Uryan Rhys (1899–1962)

M.P. (Con.) Romford, 1923–9; Guildford, 1931–5.

The Dynevor family papers are deposited in the National Library of Wales and in the Dyfed Archives, County Hall, Carmarthen, Wales. In addition to family and estate papers, the latter collection contains 75 boxes of military and political correspondence, 1618–1960, and 35 boxes of miscellaneous material including press cuttings, 1734–1956. The present (9th) Lord Dynevor, 18 Brook Green, London W6 has retained three boxes of material, including scrapbooks relating to his father's career.

EADY, George Hathaway (d. 1941)

M.P. (Con.) Bradford Central, 1931–5.

No family contact was established, but records of the Bradford Conservatives, dating from 1870, and covering the period of Eady's term as M.P., are deposited in Bradford Public Library, and are described in *Sources,* Vol. 1, p. 65.

EALES, John Frederick (1881–1936)

M.P. (Con.) Birmingham Erdington, 1931–6.

Miss Winifred R. Eales (daughter), 14 Oakwood Drive, Iwerne Minster, Blandford, Dorset, says her father did not keep a diary or many other political papers. She does, however, have a book of press cuttings, which chiefly relates to Eales' appointment as Recorder of Coventry, to his first election as M.P., and to his death. She also has a leather-bound book recording the re-establishment of Coventry Quarter Sessions, 1928, and a Recorder's notebook of all the cases he tried between 1928 and 1934.

EASTWOOD, John Francis (1887–1952)

M.P. (Con.) Kettering, 1931–40.

The papers of the Eastwood family, dating from Elizabethan times, are deposited in the Guildford Muniment Room. Mr Hugo Eastwood, The Old Vicarage, Chobham, nr Woking, Surrey, son of John Eastwood, has a collection of his father's papers. He proposes to deposit these with the family papers in Guildford. In addition, he retains a large collection of photographs covering family affairs.

EBBISHAM, 1st B
Sir George Rowland Blades, 1st Bt (1868–1953)

M.P. (Con.) Epsom, 1918–28.
Treasurer of the Conservative Party, 1931–3.

The present Lord Ebbisham believes that his father's papers were destroyed when his office was bombed during World War II. The archives of the Conservative Party are described in *Sources,* Vol. 1, pp. 53–73.

EBRINGTON, Vt, see FORTESCUE, 5th E of

EBURY, 5th B
Robert Egerton Grosvenor (1914–57)

Lord in Waiting, 1939–40.

The present (6th) Lord Ebury lives in Australia: no contact was established.

ECCLES, 1st Vt
Sir David McAdam Eccles (1904–   )

M.P. (Con.) Chippenham, 1943–62.
Minister of Works, 1951–4. Minister of Education, 1954–7, 1959–62. President of the Board of Trade, 1957–9. Paymaster-General (with responsibility for the Arts), 1970–3.
Chairman, British Library Board, 1973–.

Viscount Eccles has retained various papers relating to his public service. He is to make provision for the preservation of these papers.

ECKERSLEY, Peter Thorp (1904–40)

M.P. (Con.) Manchester Exchange, 1935–40.

EDE, James Chuter, see CHUTER-EDE, Baron

EDELMAN, Maurice (1911–75)

M.P. (Lab.) Coventry West, 1945–50; Coventry North, 1950–Feb 1974; Coventry N.W., Feb 1974–5.

Mrs·Edelman has placed many of the surviving papers of her husband in the Modern Records Centre, University of Warwick Library. In view of the recent date of much of the deposit, it is subject to restrictions on consultation, but it includes subject files on industries and other topics directly related to Coventry, as well as subject files of general interest, constituency correspondence and files relating to five general elections. Additional correspondence relating to Edelman's work as a Coventry M.P., can be found in the archives of the Coventry Borough Labour Party, also at the Modern Records Centre.

EDEN, Sir (Robert) Anthony, see AVON, 1st E of

EDGAR, Clifford Blackburn (1857–1931)

M.P. (Con.) Richmond, Surrey, 1918–22.

EDGE, Sir William, 1st Bt (1880–1948)

M.P. (Lib.) Bolton, 1916–23; (Lib.) Bosworth, 1927–31; (Lib.Nat.) 1931–45. Junior Lord of the Treasury, 1919–22.

It is believed that no papers survive with the present (2nd) baronet. The surviving records of the Liberal National Party, are described in *Sources*, Vol. 1, pp. 183–4.

EDMONDS, Garnham (1866–1946)

M.P. (Lib.) Bethnal Green, 1922–3.

EDMONDSON, Sir Albert James, see SANDFORD, 1st B

EDMUNDS, James Ewart (1882–1962)

M.P. (Lab.) Cardiff East, 1929–31.

No information is available. It is hoped to include a biographical note in a forthcoming volume of the *Dictionary of Labour Biography*.

EDNAM, Vt, see DUDLEY

EDWARDS, Alfred (1888–1958)

M.P. (Lab.) Middlesbrough East, 1935–48; (Ind.) 1948–9; (Con.) 1949–50.

Miss S. K. Edwards (daughter), Hemble Hill, Guisborough, Cleveland, has a small collection of her father's papers. This includes appointment diaries, notes for speeches, copies of articles contributed to magazines, and the opening pages of an unfinished autobiography. It seems that other relevant papers were destroyed.

EDWARDS, (Allen) Clement (1869–1938)

M.P. (Lib.) Denbigh Borough, 1906–Jan 1910; Glamorganshire East, Dec 1910–18; East Ham South, 1918–22.

A collection of some 2000 items is deposited in the Mitchell Library, Glasgow. Of these items, some 1000 are volumes of press cuttings, 1889–1915, with annual indexes, collected by Edwards. The press cuttings cover all subjects of political interest including reports of speeches, elections, parliamentary debates, trade union activities, etc., and reveal a particular interest in education policies. The rest of the collection consists of books and pamphlets. A further collection of material is held by Clement Edwards's son, Mr J. C. G. C. Edwards, 18 Fairmount Road, Bexhill-on-Sea, Sussex, including a typescript memoir, and newspaper cuttings from 1890 to 1917. A note on Edwards's career appears in the *Dictionary of Labour Biography*, Vol. III. pp. 69–78.

EDWARDS, Sir Charles (1867–1954)

M.P. (Lab.) Bedwellty, 1918–50.
Junior Lord of the Treasury, 1929–31. Labour Chief Whip, 1931–42. Joint Parliamentary Secretary to the Treasury and Government Chief Whip, 1940–2.
Bedwellty Constituency Labour Party retains certain formal records covering the relevant period. Mr Neil Kinnock, present M.P. for Bedwellty, stated that the local Labour Party has no remaining contacts with the family.

EDWARDS, Ebenezer ('Ebby') (1884–1961)

M.P. (Lab.) Morpeth, 1929–31.

No family contact was established but Morpeth Constituency Labour Party retained certain records dating from the 1920s. Edwards was Secretary of the Miners' Federation of Great Britain, 1932–46, and its records are described in *Sources*, Vol. 1, pp. 195–8.

EDWARDS, Enoch (1852–1912)

M.P. (Lab.) Hanley, 1906–12.

Full biographical details can be found in the *Dictionary of Labour Biography*, Vol. I, pp. 109–11. Messrs Hollinshead & Moody, solicitors of Stoke-on-Trent, who acted in the estate, had no information.

EDWARDS, Sir Francis, 1st Bt (1852–1927)

M.P. (Lib.) Radnorshire, 1892–5, 1900–Jan 1910, Dec 1910–18.

EDWARDS, Sir George (1850–1933)

M.P. (Lab.) Norfolk South, 1920–2, 1923–4.

No information was available. An account of Edwards' career will appear in a forthcoming volume of the *Dictionary of Labour Biography*.

EDWARDS, John (1882–1960)

M.P. (Co.Lib.) Aberavon, 1918–22.

Mrs G. E. Edwards (widow) knows of no papers. She believes papers may have been lost in various moves her husband made.

EDWARDS, John Hugh (d. 1945)

M.P. (Lib.) Mid-Glamorgan, Dec 1910–18; Neath, 1918–22; Accrington, 1923–9.

EDWARDS, (Lewis) John (1904–59)

M.P. (Lab.) Blackburn, 1945–50; Brighouse, 1950–9.
Parliamentary Secretary, Ministry of Health, 1947–9; Board of Trade, 1949–50. Economic Secretary to the Treasury, 1950–1.

Edwards was General Secretary of the Post Office Engineering Union, 1938–47, and its records are described in *Sources*, Vol. 1, p. 214. No family contact was established.

EDWARDS, Ness (1897–1968)

M.P. (Lab.) Caerphilly, 1939–68.
Parliamentary Secretary, Ministry of Labour and National Service, 1945–50. Postmaster General, 1950–1.

Hazlehurst and Woodland, p. 50, state that the papers are not available for research.

EDWARDS, Walter James (1900–64)

M.P. (Lab.) Whitechapel, 1942–50; Stepney, 1950–64.
Civil Lord of the Admiralty, 1945–51.

Letters of administration were granted to Edwards's widow, with whom it proved impossible to establish contact.

EGAN, William Henry (1869–1943)

M.P. (Lab.) Birkenhead West, 1923–4, 1929–31.

Messrs Bremner, Sons & Corlett, of Liverpool, who acted in the estate, were unable to supply any relevant information.

EGERTON OF TATTON, 3rd B (1845–1920)
Hon. Alan de Tatton Egerton

M.P. (Con.) Mid-Cheshire, 1883–5; Knutsford, 1885–1906.

Mr T. E. S. Egerton, a kinsman of Lord Egerton, who was contacted, knew of no papers relating to the 3rd Baron and was unable to suggest any further contacts.

ELGIN (9th) AND KINCARDINE (13th), E of
Victor Alexander Bruce, Lord Bruce (1849–1917)

Viceroy of India, 1894–8.
Secretary of State for the Colonies, 1905–8.

The present (11th and 15th) Earl of Elgin and Kincardine, Broomhall, Dunfermline, Scotland, has a collection of his grandfather's papers, and a microfilm of these papers has been prepared for Queen's College, Kingston, Ontario (see Hazlehurst and Woodland, p. 21). Papers and correspondence, kept whilst Elgin was Viceroy, are housed in the India Office Library.

ELIBANK, 2nd Vt
Hon. Gideon Murray (1877–1951)

Colonial Service.
M.P. (Con.) Glasgow St Rollox, 1918–22.

The 2nd Viscount's papers comprise correspondence etc. concerning the Empire Free Trade Movement, 1929–31, including a memorandum of an interview between Elibank (acting for Beaverbrook) and Baldwin; correspondence concerning Winston Churchill's Abbey parliamentary election, 1924; miscellaneous correspondence on political and other matters, 1903–50; and press cuttings, 1895–1950. The papers have been deposited in the National Library of Scotland.

ELIBANK, 3rd Vt
Hon. Arthur Cecil Murray (1879–1962)

M.P. (Lib.) Kincardineshire, 1908–23.

The papers are to be found in the National Library of Scotland, as part of the larger Elibank archive. The collection relates to military, political and diplomatic matters, and covers service in the House of Commons and the Lords, and with the London and North Eastern Railway (1923–47).

ELIBANK, Master of, see MURRAY OF ELIBANK, 1st B

ELLICE, Edward Charles (1858–1934)

M.P. (Lib.) St Andrews Burgh, 1903–6.

Mr J. R. Maxwell-Macdonald of Glasgow, whose grandfather acted as executor to Ellice, knew of no papers and suggested we contact Strathclyde Regional Archives. They however stated that they had no relevant information. No material relating to Ellice is amongst the Maxwell-Macdonald papers in the Glasgow Archives Office.

ELLIOT, Walter Elliot (1888–1958)

M.P. (Con.) Lanark, 1918–23; Kelvingrove, 1924–45 and 1950–8; Scottish Universities, 1946–50.
Parliamentary Secretary and Minister of Health for Scotland, 1923–4 and 1924–6. Parliamentary Under-Secretary of State, Scotland, 1926–9. Financial Secretary, Treasury, 1931–2. Minister of Agriculture and Fisheries, 1932–6. Secretary of State for Scotland, 1936–8. Minister of Health, 1938–40.

The papers kept by Elliot's widow, Baroness Elliot of Harwood, are described by Hazlehurst and Woodland, p. 50. Details are available from the National Library of Scotland.

ELLIOT, Walter Travers Scott- (1895–   )

M.P. (Lab.) Accrington, 1945–50.

ELLIOTT, Arthur Ralph Douglas (1846–1923)

Editor, *Edinburgh Review*, 1895–1912.
M.P. (Lib.) Roxburghshire, 1880–6; (Lib.Un.) 1886–92; Durham City, 1898–1906.
Financial Secretary to the Treasury, Apr–Sep 1903.

An extensive collection of the papers of Arthur Elliott has been presented to the National Library of Scotland (Acc. 4246). His various activities are fully reflected in the collection. Of particular interest are the papers relating to the Free Trade controversy and his resignation in 1903. The papers have been arranged in 148 bundles, which are sorted into chronological order. A main series of Elliott's papers (1–127) is followed by a quantity of printed material (128–34) and several scrapbooks of political cartoons and extracts (135–8); and correspondence with his family (his father was 3rd Earl of Minto) (139–40). The remainder of the collection is largely of a family or personal nature.

ELLIOTT, Sir George Samuel (d. 1925)

M.P. (Con.) Islington West, 1918–22.

ELLIS, John Edward (1841–1910)

M.P. (Lib.) Rushcliffe, 1885–Dec 1910.
Parliamentary Under-Secretary, India Office, 1905–6.

It is not known whether papers now survive. Mr Roger Ellis says that family tradition believes J. E. Ellis destroyed his correspondence when it ceased to be current. This confirms a statement made by A. T. Bassett on p. 30 of his *Life* of J. E. Ellis. Bassett quotes extensively from diaries and notebooks in his biography but it is presumed that these are now lost. However, a bound volume of Ellis's speeches has come to light. Certain correspondence can be found in the Campbell-Bannerman papers at the British Library (Add. Ms 41214).

ELLIS, Sir (Robert) Geoffrey, 1st Bt (1874–1956)

M.P. (Con.) Wakefield, 1922–3, 1924–9; Winchester, 1931–5; Sheffield Ecclesall, 1935–45.

Messrs Charlesworth, Wood & Brown, solicitors of Skipton, North Yorkshire, who approached members of Sir Geoffrey's family, believe that there are no political papers available, and only his private and confidential mail survives.

ELLIS, William Craven- (1882–1959)

M.P. (Con.) Southampton, 1931–45.

Mrs D. Campbell (daughter), Cotterell House, Ewhurst Road, Shere, Surrey, who acted as her father's private secretary, has many unsorted press cuttings in her care.

ELLISTON, Sir George Sampson (1875–1954)

M.P. (Con.) Blackburn, 1931–45.

Mr G. L. C. Elliston (son), Tinker's Wood, 15 St Catherine's Drive, Guildford, Surrey, states that carbon copies of letters written by Sir George were destroyed when the magazine he edited moved offices. Mr Elliston believes, however, that other papers may survive with the family.

ELMLEY, Vt, see BEAUCHAMP, 8th E

ELTISLEY, 1st B
Sir George Douglas Cochrane Newton (1879–1942)

M.P. (Con.) Cambridge, 1922–34.
Agricultural Adviser, Imperial Economic Conference (Ottawa), 1932, and World Monetary Economic Conference (London), 1933.

Family papers are held by the Hon Lady Fox at Croxton Park, Croxton, Cambs. The unsorted material would include papers of Lady Fox's father, Lord Eltisley, but details are not available. Enquiries may be addressed to Miss D. Bowie, 12 Crossways Gardens, Anstey Way, Trumpington, Cambridge CB2 2JT.

ELVEDEN, Vt, see IVEAGH, 2nd E of

ELVERSTON, Sir Harold (1866–1941)

M.P. (Lib.) Gateshead, Jan 1910–18.

Mr W. M. Elverston-Trickett (son) knows of no papers relating to his father's career, and his enquiries of his brother and of other members of his family similarly proved negative.

ELWYN-JONES, Baron
Sir (Frederick) Elwyn Jones (1909–)

M.P. (Lab.) Plaistow, 1945–50; West Ham South, 1950–Mar 1974.
Attorney-General, 1964–70. Lord Chancellor, 1974–

Lord Elwyn-Jones has retained his papers.

EMERY, Sir (James) Frederick (1886–)

M.P. (Con.) Salford West, 1935–45.

EMMOTT, 1st B
Alfred Emmott (1858–1926)

M.P. (Lib.) Oldham, 1899–1911.

Parliamentary Under-Secretary of State, Colonial Office, 1911–14. 1st Commissioner of Works, 1914–15.

Papers held at Nuffield College, Oxford, the House of Lords Record Office, and at the Fawcett Library, are described by Hazlehurst and Woodland, p. 50.

EMMOTT, Charles Ernest George Campbell (1898–1953)

M.P. (Con.) Glasgow Springburn, 1931–5; Surrey East, 1935–45.

Letters of Administration were granted to Emmott's sister. No contact with her or her heirs was established.

ENGLAND, Abraham (1867–1949)

M.P. (Lib.) Heywood and Radcliffe, 1922–31.

Mr A. L. Beckett, of England, Poole & Co. Ltd, knew of no papers. No other information was available.

ENTWISTLE, Sir Cyril Fullard (1887–1974)

M.P. (Lib.) Hull S.W., 1918–24; (Con.) Bolton, 1931–45.

Lady Entwistle (widow) states that her husband kept neither diaries nor correspondence.

ERNE, 5th E of
John Henry George Crichton (1907–40)

Lord in Waiting, 1936–9.

The family and estate papers of the Earls of Erne are deposited in the Northern Ireland Public Record Office.

ERNLE, 1st B
Rowland Edmund Prothero (1851–1937)

M.P. (Con.) Oxford University, 1914–19.
President of the Board of Agriculture and Fisheries, 1916–19.

Hazlehurst and Woodland, p. 120, found that only a very few papers have survived. These are with Lord Ernle's grandson, Mr T. E. Gilpin.

ERRINGTON, Sir Eric, 1st Bt (1900–73)

M.P. (Con.) Bootle, 1935–45; Aldershot, 1954–70.

ERROLL, 20th E of.[1]
Charles Gordon Hay (1852–1927)

Lord in Waiting, 1903–5.

The Erroll and Crimonmogate papers have been surveyed by the National Register of Archives (Scotland). It would seem from the survey that no papers of the 20th Earl have survived.

[1] Described in his *Who's Who* entry as the 19th Earl, but according to *Burke's Peerage* (1970 ed., p. 951) he was the 20th holder of the title.

ERROLL OF HALE, 1st B
Frederick James Erroll (1914–)

M.P. (Con.) Altrincham and Sale, 1945–64.
Parliamentary Secretary, Ministry of Supply, 1955–6; Board of Trade, 1956–8. Economic Secretary to the Treasury, 1958–9. Minister of State, Board of Trade, 1959–61. President of the Board of Trade, 1961–3. Minister of Power, 1963–4.

Lord Erroll has retained his personal papers and has made arrangements for their safe keeping.

ERSKINE, Lord
John Francis Ashley Erskine (1895–1953)

M.P. (Con.) Weston-super-Mare, 1922–3 and 1924–34; Brighton, 1940–1.
Governor, Madras, 1934–40.

Papers kept by Lord Erskine while Governor of Madras are deposited at the India Office Library. The collection includes official and personal correspondence with the Viceroy of India, and files on specific problems. Mr David Erskine knows of no further papers.

ERSKINE, David C. (1866–1922)

M.P. (Lib.) Perthshire West, 1906–Jan 1910.

The present (16th) Earl of Buchan knew of no papers.

ERSKINE, Sir James Malcolm Monteith (1863–1944)

M.P. (Ind.Con., subsequently Con.) Westminster St George's, 1921–9.

A small collection of material has survived, chiefly consisting of press cuttings and photographs, but also including a little political correspondence concerning election campaigns and a subsequent libel case. The papers are at present with the granddaughter, Mrs J. Delaney, of Hooklands, Scaynes Hill, Haywards Heath, Sussex.

ESMONDE, Sir John Lymbrick, 14th Bt (1893–1958)*

M.P. (Irish Nat.) Tipperary North, 1915–18.

See below.

ESMONDE, John Joseph (1862–1915)*

M.P. (Irish Nat.) Dec 1910–15.

See below.

ESMONDE, Sir Thomas Henry Grattan, 13th Bt (1862–1935)*

M.P. (Irish Nat.) Dublin South, 1885–92; Kerry West, 1892–1900; Wexford North, 1900–18.

Sir Anthony Esmonde, Bt, reported that the family papers were lost when the ancestral home was destroyed by fire in 1922. Sir John Ainsworth, Bt, of the National Library of Ireland confirmed that to his knowledge no political papers survived. For general information on archives in Ireland, see Appendix I. R. J. Hayes, *Manuscript Sources for the History of Irish Civilisation* (Boston, 1965) mentions copies of correspondence of members of the Esmonde family, 1900–15, in the National Library of Ireland (Ms 8520).

ESSENHIGH, Reginald Clare (1890–1955)

M.P. (Con.) Newton, 1931–5.

Messrs Neals & Shelley Barker, solicitors in the estate, knew of no papers.

ESSEX, Sir (Richard) Walter (1857–1941)

M.P. (Lib.) Cirencester, 1906–Jan 1910; Stafford, Dec 1910–18.

It seems that the bulk of Sir Walter's papers have been destroyed. However, Mr D. E. Wright (grandson), Woldingham Dene, Woldingham Road, Woldingham, Caterham, Surrey CR3 7LA, has a number of volumes relating to his grandfather's travels abroad, 1900–25. These do not appear to contain much of political note, although the volume for 1917 details his activities as a British delegate to an Inter-Parliamentary Congress in Rome. The British group visited various sectors of the Somme battle-front during the latter days of May 1917, and the volume contains details of this.

ESSLEMONT, George Birnie (1860–1917)

M.P. (Lib.) Aberdeen South, 1907–17.

Attempts to contact Miss Mary Esslemont (daughter), who lives in Aberdeen, were not successful.

ESTCOURT, Thomas Edmund Sotheron (1881–1958)

M.P. (Con.) Pontefract, 1931–5.

Mrs E. Morris-Keating (daughter), Newnton Priory, Long Newnton, Tetbury, Glos., GL8 8RR, has certain press cuttings relating to her father.

ETCHINGHAM, John R.*

M.P. (Sinn Fein) Wicklow East, 1918–22.

ETHERTON, Ralph H. (1904–   )

M.P. (Con.) Stretford, 1939–45.

Mr Etherton states that he has retained a certain amount of personal material, particularly covering the war years. He has not kept a substantial collection of political material.

EVANS, Albert (1903–   )

M.P. (Lab.) Islington West, 1947–50; Islington S.W., 1950–70.

EVANS, Sir David Owen (1872–1945)

M.P. (Lib.) Cardiganshire, 1935–45.

EVANS, Edward (1883–1960)

M.P. (Lab.) Lowestoft, 1945–59.

Records of the Lowestoft Constituency Labour Party have survived: see *Sources*, Vol. 1, p. 139. No family contact was established. The Royal National Institute for the Deaf (of which Evans was Chairman) have a number of references to Evans's work in their records, as well as press cuttings relating to him.

EVANS, Emlyn Hugh Garner (1911–63)

M.P. (Nat.Lib.) Denbigh, 1950–9.

Certain papers can be found in the Davies of Llandinam papers at the National Library of Wales.

EVANS, Ernest (1885–1965)

Private Secretary to Prime Minister, 1918–20.
M.P. (Co.Lib.) Cardiganshire, 1921–3; (Lib.) University of Wales, 1924–42.

Mrs Constance A. Evans (widow) stated that most of her husband's papers were destroyed when his chambers were bombed during World War II. She retains only papers of a private and personal nature. Some letters can be found in the Lloyd George papers.

EVANS, Sir Francis Henry, 1st Bt (1840–1907)

M.P. (Lib.) Southampton, 1896–1900; Maidstone, 1901–6.

Mrs De Grasse Ramsay (granddaughter) stated that all of Sir F. H. Evans's papers that she had possessed were destroyed by fire during World War I.

EVANS, Sir (H.) Arthur (1898–1958)

M.P. (Con.) Leicester East, 1922–3; Cardiff South, 1924–9, 1931–45.

Attempts to contact the widow were not successful.

EVANS, Herbert (1868–1931)

M.P. (Lab.) Gateshead, Jun–Oct 1931.

The Public Trustee, who acted in the estate, had no information.

EVANS, John (1875–1961)

M.P. (Lab.) Ogmore, 1946–50.

Reference should be made to the records of the South Wales Miners, held at University College, Swansea, though these do not pertain directly to Evans. No family contact was established.

EVANS, Sir Laming Worthington-, 1st Bt (1868–1931)

M.P. (Con.) Colchester, Jan 1910–29; Westminster St George's, 1929–31.
Parliamentary Secretary, Ministry of Munitions, 1916–18. Minister of Blockade, 1918–19. Minister of Pensions, 1919–20. Minister without Portfolio, 1920–1. Secretary of State for War, 1921–2 and 1924–9. Postmaster General, 1923–4.

The papers at the Bodleian Library, and at the Public Record Office (MUN 4/396–451), are described by Hazlehurst and Woodland, pp. 51–2.

EVANS, Paul Vychan Emrys- (1894–1967)

M.P. (Con.) Derbyshire South, 1942–5.
Parliamentary Under-Secretary, Dominion Affairs, 1942–5.

The Emrys-Evans correspondence and papers have been placed by his daughter in the British Library (Add. Mss 58235–73). The collection consists of some 39 volumes, certain of which are reserved and to which no access is given. Among the correspondents are Lord Harvey of Tasburgh, J. H. Martin, M.P., Viscount Crookshank, Sir Orme Sargent, Sir H. Knatchbull-Hugessen, Lord Coleraine, Sir A. Eden (Earl of Avon), Sir Richard Cross, Baron Wakehurst, 4th Lord Harlech and 4th Marquess of Salisbury. One useful volume consists of correspondence with politicians and historians concerning Munich, its aftermath and World War II in retrospect, 1940–67; another consists of general political and official correspondence, 1935–45. Constituency correspondence (two volumes) covers the period 1934–47. Five volumes of general correspondence (58253–7) include early diplomatic letters to Emrys-Evans, and date from 1916 to 1967. Add. Mss 58258 consists of official papers, including Foreign Office material, 1918–24; and Dominion Office papers, 1942. Another volume concerns Evans's memoirs, including drafts.

EVANS, Richard Thomas (1889–1946)

M.P. (Lib.) Carmarthen, 1931–5.

EVANS, Sir Samuel Thomas (1859–1918)

M.P. (Lib.) Mid-Glamorgan, 1890–Mar 1910.
Solicitor-General, 1908–10.

Papers are deposited in the National Library of Wales (ref. NLW 2231–42). Further letters addressed to Lord Rendel may be found in the Rendel papers, also at the National Library of Wales.

EVANS, Stanley Norman (1898–1970)

M.P. (Lab.) Wednesbury, 1945–56.
Parliamentary Secretary, Ministry of Food, 1950.

Mrs M. K. Evans (widow), who resides in Birmingham, was unable to provide any information regarding the papers in the care of the family.

EVE, Sir Harry Trelawney (1856–1940)

M.P. (Lib.) Ashburton, 1904–7.

EVERARD, Sir (William) Lindsay (1891–1949)

M.P. (Con.) 'Melton, 1924–45.

Mr P. A. Everard (son) knows of no papers relating to his father's career.

EVERETT, Robert Lacey (1833–1916)

M.P. (Lib.) Woodbridge, 1885–6, 1892–5, 1906–Jan 1910.

Papers remain with the family. It is believed that they will be deposited in Suffolk Record Office (Ipswich branch).

EWART, Richard (1904–53)

M.P. (Lab.) Sunderland, 1945–50; Sunderland South, 1950–3.

Richard Ewart died unmarried. A biography of Ewart appears in *Dictionary of Labour Biography*, Vol. IV.

EWING, Sir (Charles) Ian Orr-, 1st Bt, see ORR-EWING, Baron

EWING, Charles Lindsay Orr- (1860–1903)

M.P. (Con.) Ayr Burghs, 1895–1903.

See below.

EWING, Sir Ian Leslie Orr- (1893–1958)

M.P. (Con.) Weston-super-Mare, 1934–58.

It was not possible to make contact with Lady Orr-Ewing, widow of Sir Ian and daughter-in-law of C. Orr-Ewing. The records of both the Ayr and the Weston-super-Mare Conservative Associations are described in *Sources*, Vol. 1, p. 64 and p. 70.

EXETER, 6th M of
David George Brownlow Cecil, Baron Burghley (1905–)

M.P. (Con.) Peterborough, 1931–43.
Governor and C.-in-C. Bermuda, 1943–5.

The Marquess of Exeter states that he has retained no relevant papers.

EYRE, Sir Oliver Eyre Crosthwaite- (1913–)

M.P. (Con.) New Forest and Christchurch, 1945–50; New Forest, 1950–68.

FABER, 1st B
Edmund Beckett Faber (1847–1920)

M.P. (Con.) Andover, 1901–5.

Neither Mr T. H. Faber, a distant relative, nor the present (4th) Lord Airedale, whose grandfather was a beneficiary of Faber's estate, were able to supply information on surviving papers.

FABER, George Denison, see WITTENHAM, 1st B

FABER, George Henry (1839–1910)

M.P. (Lib.) Boston, 1906–Apr 1910.

FABER, Walter Vavasour (1857–1928)

M.P. (Con.) Andover, 1906–18.

FAHY, Francis Patrick (1880–1953)*

M.P. (Sinn Fein) Galway South, 1918–22.
Ceann Comhairle (Speaker) of Dail Eireann, 1932–51.

The National Library of Ireland has only two Fahy Mss: a copy of a circular about a meeting of the Dail, with associated items, 1918–19 (Ms 8385 (2)), and a typescript of an address to the Irish Literary Society on 'Ireland in London', 1921 (Ms 11431).

FAIRBAIRN, Richard Robert (1867–1941)

M.P. (Lib.) Worcester, 1922–3.

Fairbairn's personal press cuttings have been deposited in the County Record Office, Shirehall, Worcester. Mr R. C. H. Fairbairn (son) states that members of the family have personal mementos but these are not available for research.

FAIRFAX, James Griffyth (1886–1976)

M.P. (Con.) Norwich, 1924–9.

Records dating from 1904 have been retained by the Norwich Conservative Association. No personal papers are known to survive.

FAIRHURST, Frank (1892–1953)

M.P. (Lab.) Oldham, 1945–50; Oldham East, 1950–1.

FALCON, Michael (1888–   )

M.P. (Con.) Norfolk East, 1918–23.

FALCONER, James (1856–1931)

M.P. (Lib.) Forfarshire, 1909–18, 1922–4.

Enquiries should be directed to Mrs Margery P. Todd, whose husband was the stepson of Falconer.

FALLE, Sir Bertram Godfray, 1st Bt, see PORTSEA, 1st B

FALLS, Sir Charles F. (b. 1860)*

M.P. (Ulster Un.) Fermanagh and Tyrone, 1924–9.

FANSHAWE, Guy Dalrymple (1882–1962)

M.P. (Con.) Stirlingshire West, 1924–9.

Fanshawe's son, Captain Peter Fanshawe, lives in London. No information was forthcoming.

FARDELL, Sir (Thomas) George (1833–1917)

M.P. (Con.) Paddington South, 1895–Jan 1910.

FARINGDON, 1st B
Sir Alexander Henderson, 1st Bt (1850–1934)

M.P. (Lib.Un.) Stafford West, 1898–1906; St George's Hanover Square, 1913–16.

The present (2nd) Lord Faringdon has no papers relating to his grandfather's career. A short biographical note (10 pp.) exists in the offices of Henderson Administration Ltd, 28 Austin Friars, London EC2N 2ED.

FARQUHAR, 1st E (1844–1923)
Sir Horace Brand Farquhar, 1st Bt

M.P. (Con.) Marylebone West, 1895–8
Lord Steward, 1915–22.

Farquhar left his estate to members of the Royal Family, but the Royal Archives, Windsor, has very little relating to Farquhar's career.

FARQUHARSON, Alexander Charles (1864–1951)

M.P. (Co.Lib.) Leeds North, 1918–22.

Records of the Leeds Liberals are deposited in Leeds City Libraries. No family contact was established.

FARQUHARSON, Robert (1836–1918)

M.P. (Lib.) Aberdeenshire West, 1880–1906.

Attempts to contact a kinsman proved unsuccessful.

FARRELL, James Patrick (1865–1921)*

M.P. (Irish Nat.) Cavan West, 1895–1900; Longford North, 1900–18.

FARTHING, Walter John (1889–1954)

M.P. (Lab.) Frome, 1945–50.

FAWKES, Frederick Hawksworth (1870–1936)

M.P. (Con.) Pudsey and Otley, 1922–3.

FELL, Sir Arthur (1850–1934)

M.P. (Con.) Great Yarmouth, 1906–22.

Mr Anthony Fell, M.P. (grandson) was unable to help, while Mr A. P. Whitehead, another grandson, believes that no papers survive.

FELLOWES, Sir Ailwyn Edward, see AILWYN, 1st B

FENBY, Thomas Davis (1875–1956)

M.P. (Lib.) Bradford East, 1924–9.

Mrs P. Fell (daughter) knows of no surviving papers.

FENTON, Sir John Charles (1880–1951)

Solicitor-General for Scotland, 1924.

Attempts to contact Lady Fenton (widow) were not successful.

FENWICK, Charles (1850–1918)

M.P. (Lib.) Wansbeck, 1885–1918.

The *Dictionary of Labour Biography*, Vol. I, pp. 115–18, gives biographical details but mentions no papers.

FERENS, Thomas Robinson (1847–1930)

M.P. (Lib.) Hull East, 1906–18.

Mrs Mona Black, who has prepared a study of Ferens (on file at the Adult Education Library of Hull University) has traced various documents. Four early volumes of diaries (chiefly written in Pitman's shorthand) are deposited in the Institute of Education Library, Hull University; other volumes remain in the family. Ferens left his library to Hull University, which now has copies of his *Hansards*, but no other material. The librarian of Reckitt & Colman Ltd (Ferens's old firm),

Dansom Lane, Hull, has various details of his business career. There are frequent references to his work in B. N. Reckitt, *The History of Reckitt & Sons Ltd*. (1965).

FERGUSON, H.

M.P. (Con.) Motherwell, 1923–4.

FERGUSON, Sir John (1870–1932)

M.P. (Con.) Twickenham, 1929–32.

Mr. I. Ferguson (son), Spriggs Holly House, Chinnor Hill, Oxon OX9 4BY, has a collection of letters to his father from various political personalities of the 1920s; and a large collection of press cuttings, covering his Government Committee work during and after World War I, and his brief parliamentary career. The latter are particularly numerous, explained by the support given to his parliamentary campaigns by Beaverbrook newspapers.

FERGUSON, Sir Ronald Crauford Munro-, see NOVAR, 1st Vt

FERGUSSON, Sir James, 6th Bt (1832–1907)

M.P. (Con.) Ayrshire, 1854–68; Manchester N.E., 1885–1906.
Parliamentary Under-Secretary, India, 1860–7; Home Affairs, 1867–8; Foreign Office, 1886–91. Postmaster General, 1891–2.
Governor and C.-in-C., South Australia, 1868–73; New Zealand, 1873–5. Governor, Bombay, 1880–5.

Family papers survive with the present (9th) baronet, Sir Charles Fergusson, Kilkerran, by Maybole, Ayrshire KA19 7SJ. A great quantity of papers relating to Sir James was destroyed after his death, and the relevant papers that survive relate chiefly to the latter part of the nineteenth century. Fergusson's letter-books as Governor of Bombay are in the India Office Library. One box of letters from Fergusson can be found in the Cranbrook papers (NRA 1182).

FERMOY, 4th B
Edmund Maurice Roche (1885–1955)

M.P. (Con.) King's Lynn, 1924–35, 1943–5.

The present (5th) Lord Fermoy knows of no papers.

FERNYHOUGH, Ernest (1908–)

M.P. (Lab.) Jarrow, 1947-
Joint Parliamentary Under-Secretary, Department of Employment and Productivity, 1967–9.

Durham Record Office has a number of records of the Jarrow Labour Party. No information on Mr Fernyhough's papers was available.

FERRIS, Sir Robert Grant Grant-, see HARVINGTON, Baron

FETHERSTONHAUGH, Godfrey (1859–1928)*

M.P. (Con.) Fermanagh North, 1906–16.

FEVERSHAM, 2nd E of
Charles William Reginald Duncombe, Vt Helmsley (1879–1916)

M.P. (Con.) Thirsk and Malton, 1906–15.

The agent for the Duncombe Park Estate made enquiries among various members of the Feversham family, but was unable to locate papers relating to the 2nd Earl. The family records at the North Yorkshire Record Office include none of his papers.

FEVERSHAM, 3rd E of
Charles William Slingsby Duncombe, Vt Helmsley (1906–64)

Lord in Waiting, 1934–6. Parliamentary Secretary, Minister of Agriculture and Fisheries, 1936–9.

See above. It appears that relevant papers survive at the Duncombe Park Estate. Family papers at the North Yorkshire Record Office should be consulted.

FFRENCH, Peter (1844–1929)*

M.P. (Irish Nat.) Wexford South, 1893–1918.

FIELD, William (1848–1935)*

M.P. (Irish Nat.) Dublin St Patrick's, 1892–1918.

FIELD, William James (1909–)

M.P. (Lab.) Paddington North, 1946–53.

FIELDEN, Edward Brocklehurst (1857–1942)

M.P. (Con.) Middleton, 1900–6; Manchester Exchange, 1924–35.

Mr John Fielden, 29 Lonsdale Road, London SW13 9JP, who retains a collection of family papers says that none relate to E. B. Fielden. He does, however, hold papers of Joshua, John and Thomas Fielden, all M.P.s in the nineteenth century. Mr J. A. Fielden, Court of Hill, Ludlow, Salop SY8 3AL, has diaries of E. B. Fielden, but the entries are brief and generally personal. He also retains an album of press cuttings, some of which relate to constituency affairs.

FIENNES, Hon. Sir Eustace Edward Twisleton-Wykeham-, 1st Bt (1864–1943)

M.P. (Lib.) Banbury, 1906–Jan 1910; Dec 1910–18.
Governor, Seychelles, 1918–21; Leeward Isles, 1921–9.

Audrey, Lady Fiennes, Sir Eustace's daughter-in-law, knows of no corpus of papers, but has certain press cuttings, mainly obituary notices.

FILDES, Sir Henry (1870–1948)

M.P. (Co.Lib.) Stockport, 1920–3; (Lib.Nat.) Dumfries, 1935–45.

FINBURGH, Samuel (1867–1935)

M.P. (Con.) Salford North, 1924–9.

His son knows of no surviving papers.

FINCH, George Henry (1835–1907)

M.P. (Con.) Rutland, 1867–1907.

The Rutland and Stamford Conservative Association have kept certain formal records dating from 1883. No family contact was established.

FINCH, Harold Josiah (1898–   )

M.P. (Lab.) Bedwellty 1950–70.
Parliamentary Under-Secretary, Welsh Office, 1964–6.

Harold Finch retained a few papers. These are now deposited in the Library of University College, Swansea. His autobiography, *Memoirs of a Bedwellty M.P.* (Risca, Mon, 1972) was based largely on memory. A transcript of a taped interview with him is held by the South Wales Miners' Library, University College, Swansea.

FINDLAY, Alexander (b. 1844)

M.P. (Lib.) Lanarkshire N.E., 1904–Jan 1910.

FINDLAY, Sir (John) Edmund Ritchie, 2nd Bt (1902–62)

M.P. (Con.) Banffshire, 1935–45.

Mrs J. N. Brockbank (daughter) knows of no surviving papers.

FINLAY, 1st Vt
Sir Robert Bannatyne Finlay (1842–1929)

M.P. (Lib., later Lib.Un.) Inverness Burghs, 1885–92 and 1895–1906; (Con.) Edinburgh and St Andrews Universities, Jan 1910–16.
Solicitor-General, 1895–1900. Attorney-General, 1900–5. Lord Chancellor, 1916–19.

Hazlehurst and Woodland, p. 53, gives details of papers which survive with Viscount Finlay's granddaughter, Hon. Lady Hayes, Arabella House, by Tain, Nigg, Ross-shire.

FINNEY, Samuel (1857–1935)

M.P. (Lab.) Staffordshire N.W., 1916–18; Burslem, 1918–22.

Messrs Hollinshead & Moody, solicitors to Samuel Finney's executors, know of no papers. A biography of Finney appears in the *Dictionary of Labour Biography*, Vol. I, pp. 120–1.

FINNEY, Victor Harold (1897–1970)

M.P. (Lib.) Hexham, 1923–4.

The Rank Organisation (Finney's former firm) referred us to Mr Jarlath Finney (son), who lives in London.

FIRBANK, Sir Joseph Thomas (1850–1910)

M.P. (Con.) Hull East, 1895–1906.

Attempts to contact heirs proved unsuccessful.

FISHER, Herbert Albert Laurens (1865–1940)

M.P. (Lib.) Sheffield Hallam, 1916–18; English Universities, 1918–26.
President of the Board of Education, 1916–22.

The papers at the Bodleian Library are described in Hazlehurst and Woodland, p. 53. Fisher's personal and household accounts are available at the Institute of Economics and Statistics, Oxford, and his correspondence during the 1926 General Strike is housed in New College, Oxford.

FISHER, Sir Nigel Thomas Loveridge (1913–   )

M.P. (Con.) Hitchin, 1950–5; Surbiton, 1955–

Parliamentary Under-Secretary, Colonies, 1962–3; Commonwealth Relations and the Colonies, 1963–4.

Sir Nigel states that he has retained no papers of historical significance.

FISHER, William Hayes, see DOWNHAM, 1st B

FISON, Sir (Frank Guy) Clavering (1892–   )

M.P. (Con.) Woodbridge, 1929–31.

Sir Clavering states that he has retained no papers relating to his political career.

FISON, Sir Frederick William, 1st Bt (1847–1927)

M.P. (Con.) Doncaster, 1895–1906.

A small collection of letters to Sir Frederick, 1890–1918, is available at the Bodleian Library, Oxford. Sir Richard Fison, Bt (grandson) knows of no other surviving papers.

FITZALAN OF DERWENT, 1st Vt
Edmund Bernard Fitzalan-Howard, Lord Edmund Talbot.[1] (1855–1947)

M.P. (Con.) Chichester, 1894–1921.
Junior Lord of the Treasury, 1905. Joint Parliamentary Secretary to the Treasury and Government Chief Whip, 1915–21.
Viceroy of Ireland, 1921–2.

According to information supplied to Dr Cameron Hazlehurst, neither of Fitzalan's granddaughters nor the family solicitor know of any papers. Correspondence regarding the ownership of the *Morning Post* can be found in the Balfour papers.

1 He assumed the surname of Talbot in 1876.

FITZGERALD, Thomas Desmond*

M.P. (Sinn Fein) Dublin Pembroke, 1918–22.

FITZGERALD, Sir Robert Uniacke-Penrose-, 1st Bt (1839–1919)

M.P. (Con.) Cambridge, 1885–1906.

Sir Robert requested in his will that all his diaries were to be destroyed after his death. It was not possible to confirm whether this was done.

FITZGIBBON, John (1849–1919)*

M.P. (Irish Nat.) Mayo South, Dec 1910–18.

FITZMAURICE, 1st B
Edmond George Petty-Fitzmaurice, Lord Edmond Fitzmaurice, (1846–1935)

M.P. (Lib.) Calne, 1868–85; Cricklade, 1898–1905.
Parliamentary Under-Secretary of State, Foreign Office, 1883–5 and 1905–8. Chancellor of the Duchy of Lancaster, 1908–9.

The present (8th) Marquess of Lansdowne, Bowood Estate Office, Bowood, Calne, Wilts, has possession of his great-uncle's papers. These are described in Hazlehurst and Woodland, pp. 54–5.

FITZPATRICK, John Lalor*

M.P. (Irish Nat.) Queen's Co., Ossory 1916–18.

FITZROY, Hon. Edward Algernon (1869–1943)

M.P. (Con.) Northamptonshire South, 1900–6 and Jan 1910–18; Daventry, 1918–43. Speaker of the House of Commons, 1928–43.

Fitzroy's son is the present Lord Daventry.

FITZWILLIAM, 7th E
William Charles de Meuron Wentworth-Fitzwilliam, Vt Milton (1872–1943)

M.P. (Lib.Un.) Wakefield, 1895–1902.

The present Earl Fitzwilliam states that the bulk of the papers from Wentworth Woodhouse is deposited with Sheffield Central Library, and other family papers remain with Earl Fitzwilliam's agent at Fitzwilliam (Wentworth) Estates, Estate Office, Wentworth, Rotherham S62 7TD. The 7th Earl's papers at Sheffield relate chiefly to estate and personal matters, apart from a few letters from leading politicians.

FLANAGAN, William Henry (1871–1944)

M.P. (Con.) Manchester Clayton, 1922–3, 1931–5.

FLANNERY, Sir James Fortescue, 1st Bt (1851–1943)

M.P. (Con.) Shipley, 1895–1906; Maldon, Jan 1910–22.

Neither Sir James's daughter, Mrs E. F. Lindsay, nor his daughter-in-law, Lady Fortescue-Flannery, know of any papers.

FLAVIN, Michael Joseph (1866–1944)*

M.P. (Irish Nat.) Kerry North, 1896–1918.

FLEMINGN Lord
David Pinkerton Fleming (1877–1944)

M.P. (Con.) Dunbartonshire, 1924–6.
Solicitor-General, Scotland, 1922–3, 1924–5.

Lord Fleming's nephew, Mr I. D. Barber Fleming who lives in Glasgow, has retained personal papers only. He knows of no records of political note.

FLEMING, Edward Lascelles (1890–1950)

M.P. (Con.) Manchester Withington, 1931–50.

Enquiries should be directed to Mr M. Landy, solicitor, Rembrandt House, 100 Great Portland Street, London W1N 5PD.

FLEMING, Sir John (1847–1925)

M.P. (Lib.) Aberdeen South, 1917–18.

Sir John Fleming's grandson, Mr R. J. C. Fleming of Aberdeen, believes that no relevant papers survive. All that he has in his possession are papers relating to the formation of Sir John's business, and he knows of no other members of the Fleming family with whom papers may have survived. Certain records of the Aberdeen Liberals are deposited in Aberdeen University

Library.

FLEMING, Major Valentine (1882–1917)

M.P. (Con.) Henley, Jan 1910–17.

Mr Richard Fleming (son), Leygore Manor, Northleach, Glos, has a small collection of material relating to his father.

FLETCHER, Baron
Sir Eric George Molyneux Fletcher (1903–   )

M.P. (Lab.) Islington East, 1945–70.
Minister without Portfolio, 1964–6.

The surviving papers of Lord Fletcher, including constituency correspondence and correspondence relating to his public offices, have been placed in the BLPES.

FLETCHER, Sir Henry Aubrey-, 4th Bt (1835–1910)

M.P. (Con.) Horsham, 1880–5; Lewes, 1885–May 1910.
Groom in Waiting, 1885–6.

Sir John Aubrey-Fletcher, Bt (greatnephew) knows of no papers. Papers of the Aubrey branch of the family have been deposited in the Buckinghamshire Record Office, but these relate to the nineteenth century and earlier.

FLETCHER, Sir John Samuel, 1st Bt (1841–1924)

M.P. (Con.) Hampstead, 1905–18.

Sir John died without a direct heir, and the baronetcy lapsed. No direct contact could be established. Hampstead Conservative Association has retained certain formal records dating from 1888.

FLETCHER, J. R. Kebty- (1849–1918)

M.P. (Con.) Altrincham, Dec 1910–13.

FLETCHER, Reginald Thomas Herbert, see WINSTER, 1st B

FLETCHER, Sir Walter (1892–1956)

M.P. (Con.) Bury, 1945–50; Bury and Radcliffe, 1950–5.

Messrs Trower, Still & Keeling, solicitors of London, who acted in the estate, knew of private and business papers only.

FLINT, His Honour Judge Abraham John (1903–71)

M.P. (Nat.Lab.) Ilkeston, 1931–5.

It is believed that Flint's daughter knows of no papers.

FLOWER, Sir Ernest Francis Swan (1865–1926)

M.P. (Con.) Bradford West, 1895–1906.

Messrs Sole, Sawbridge & Co, solicitors to Sir Ernest Flower, were unable to provide any information. Bradford Central Library has Conservative Association records covering the relevant period.

FLYNN, James Christopher (b. 1852)*

M.P. (Irish Nat.) Cork County, 1885–Jan 1910.

FOLLICK, Mont (1887–1958)

M.P. (Lab.) Loughborough, 1945–55.

Mr S. W. Sillem, Dr Follick's executor, believes that no papers have survived.

FOOT, Sir Dingle Mackintosh (1905–   )

M.P. (Lib.) Dundee, 1931–45; (Lab.) Ipswich, 1957–70.
Parliamentary Secretary, Ministry of Economic Warfare, 1940–5. Solicitor-General, 1964–7.

Sir Dingle Foot never kept a diary. Such papers as he has retained relate mainly to the period 1940–5. He also has notes relating to his meetings with political leaders in various parts of the world.

FOOT, Isaac (1880–1960)

M.P. (Lib.) Bodmin, 1922–4, 1929–35.
Parliamentary Secretary, Mines Department, 1931–2.

Some of the surviving papers are in the care of Rt Hon. Michael Foot, M.P. Mr Isaac Foot's extensive library was transferred to America.

FOOT, Michael M. (1913–   )

M.P. (Lab.) Plymouth Devonport, 1945–55; Ebbw Vale, 1960–
Secretary of State for Employment, 1974–6. Lord President of the Council and Leader of the House of Commons, 1976–

FORBES-LEITH of FYVIE,[1] Sir Charles Rosdew, 1st Bt (1859–1930)

M.P. (Con.) Torquay, Dec 1910–23.

Sir Andrew Forbes-Leith, Bt (grandson) believes that few papers have survived. Many were accidentally destroyed some years ago, and it is believed that little of interest survives.

[1] Formerly Charles Rosdew Burn.

FORD, Sir Patrick Johnstone, 1st Bt (1880–1945)

M.P. (Con.) Edinburgh North, 1920–3, 1924–35.
Junior Lord of the Treasury, 1923.

His sons know of no surviving papers.

FOREMAN, Sir Henry (1852–1924)

M.P. (Con.) Hammersmith North, 1918–24.

Messrs Watson Sons & Room, solicitors to the executors, know of no papers.

FORESTIER-WALKER, Sir (Charles) Leolin, 1st Bt (1866–1934)

M.P. (Con.) Monmouth, 1918–34.

Mrs Daphne Young (daughter), 34 Cadogan Square, London SW1, has press cuttings only relating to her father's career. The Monmouth Conservative Association retains in its care records relating to its work during this period.

FORGAN, Robert (1891–1976)

M.P. (Lab.) Renfrewshire West, 1929–31.

FORMAN, John Calder (b. 1884)

M.P. (Lab. Co-op.) Glasgow Springburn, 1945–64.

Mrs Barbara Forman (widow), 168 Knightswood Road, Glasgow G13 2XH, retains certain of her husband's papers.

FORRES, 1st B
Sir Archibald Williamson, 1st Bt (1860–1931)

M.P. (Lib., later Co.Lib.) Moray and Nairn, 1906–22.
Financial and Parliamentary Secretary, War Office, 1919–21.

Papers of the 1st Baron are retained by the present Baron Forres at Auchnacree House, Glen Ogil, by Forfar, Angus. The papers cover the period 1860–1920s, and consist largely of records of a family and formal nature, together with political letters. These cover Williamson's parliamentary candidatures, letters from prime ministers, letters concerning appointments, etc., and privately printed accounts of Lord Forres's business activities. A full list is available at the NRA (Scotland), (list 0658).

FORREST, Sir Walter (1869–1939)

M.P. (Co.Lib.) Pontefract, 1919–22; (Lib.) Batley and Morley, 1924–9.

Messrs Allen & Overy, solicitors to the executors, know of no papers.

FORSTER, 1st B
Sir Henry William Forster (1866–1936)

M.P. (Con.) Sevenoaks, 1892–1919.
Financial Secretary, War Office, 1915–19.
Governor-General, Australia, 1920–5.
Member of Army Council.

The Rt Hon. Dorothy Lady Wardington (daughter), Lepe House, Exbury, Southampton SO4 1AD, states that her family has very few records or personal papers of her father. Lepe House suffered bomb damage during the war, and many of its contents were put in store. Also Lady Forster has destroyed many old papers. It may be that two or three boxes of old letters have survived.

FORSTER, Hugh Oakeley Arnold- (1855–1909)*

M.P. (Lib.Un.) Belfast West, 1892–1906; (Con.) Croydon, 1906–9.
Parliamentary Secretary, Admiralty, 1900–3.

The papers and diaries at the British Library (Add. Mss 50275–357) are described by Hazlehurst and Woodland, p. 56. Family correspondence, 1859–1921, is in Trinity College, Dublin.

FORT, Richard (1907–59)

M.P. (Con.) Clitheroe, 1950–9.

Mrs Jean Fort (widow), Ruscombe House, Twyford, Reading, Berks, has a collection of material including a series of letters that Richard Fort wrote regularly to friends in America to keep them informed of the progress of affairs in Britain. Fort kept no diaries, but Mrs Fort has a fairly comprehensive collection of press cuttings relating to his political career.

FORTESCUE, 5th E of
Hugh William Fortescue, Vt Ebrington (1888–1958)

Lord in Waiting, 1937–45. Vice Chamberlain, H.M. Household, 1945. Captain, Gentlemen at Arms, 1945, 1951–8.

The present Earl of Fortescue believes that most family papers were destroyed in two serious fires. The surviving papers have been deposited in Devon Record Office. This collection contains no large corpus of material directly concerned with the career of the 5th Earl.

FORTEVIOT, 1st B
Sir John Alexander Dewar, 1st Bt (1856–1929)

M.P. (Lib.) Inverness-shire, 1900–16.

The present (2nd) Lord Forteviot believes that no papers now survive.

FOSTER, Sir (Balthazar) Walter, see ILKESTON, 1st B

FOSTER, Sir Harry Braustyn Hylton Hylton- (1905–65)

M.P. (Con.) York, 1950–9; Cities of London and Westminster, 1959–65.
Solicitor-General, 1954–9.
Speaker of the House of Commons, 1959–65.

Enquiries should be directed to Lady Hylton-Foster.

FOSTER, Sir Harry Seymour (1855–1938)

M.P. (Con.) Lowestoft, 1892–1900; Suffolk North, Jan–Dec 1910; Portsmouth Central, 1924–9.

Messrs Stafford Clark & Co., solicitors to the executors, know of no papers.

FOSTER, Sir John Galway (1904–   )

M.P. (Con.) Northwich, 1945–74.
Parliamentary Under-Secretary, Commonwealth Relations Office, 1951–4.

Sir John Foster did not retain any papers relating to his parliamentary career and kept no diary or memoranda.

FOSTER, (John) Kenneth (1866–1930)

M.P. (Con.) Coventry, Jan–Dec 1910.

FOSTER, Sir Michael (1836–1907)

Fellow of the Royal Society.
M.P. (Lib.Un.) London University, 1900–6.

His correspondence with T. H. Huxley (c. 200 items) is in the Huxley papers (NRA 8194) in the Imperial College Archives, London. Notes (by J. G. Adami) on his lectures on physiology in 1881 are in the Wellcome Institute. Some 50 letters to various persons are with the Royal Society.

FOSTER, Philip Staveley (1865–1933)

M.P. (Con.) Stratford-on-Avon, 1901–6, 1909–18.

FOSTER, William (1887–1947)

M.P. (Lab.) Wigan, 1942–7.
Parliamentary Secretary, Ministry of Fuel and Power, 1945–6.

FOWLER, Sir Henry Hartley, see WOLVERHAMPTON, 1st Vt

FOX, George Richard Lane- see BINGLEY 1st B

FOX, Sir Gifford Wheaton Grey, 2nd Bt (1903–59)

M.P. (Con.) Henley, 1932–50.

Mrs P. Telfer-Smollet (daughter) Cameron House, Alexandria, Dunbartonshire G83 8QZ, has press-cuttings books relating to her father's candidature for Huntingdon, 1929–31, and others dealing with his membership of the House of Commons, 1932–49.

FOX, Henry Wilson- (1863–1921)

M.P. (Con.) Tamworth, 1917–21.

It was not possible to make contact with Mr G. H. Wilson-Fox (son) of Robertsbridge, Sussex.

FOXCROFT, Charles Talbot (1868–1929)

M.P. (Con.) Bath, 1918–23, 1924–9.

A collection of papers was retained by Mr Robin Robertson-Glasgow (greatnephew), Hinton House, Hinton Charterhouse, Bath BA3 6AZ. These are likely to be deposited in the Bath City Office, which also has the records of the local Conservative Association.

FRANCE, Gerald Ashburner (1870–1935)

M.P. (Lib.) Morley, Jan 1910–18; Batley and Morley, 1918–22.

Mr B. A. France, one of G. A. France's sons, knows of no surviving papers.

FRANKEL, Dan (1900–)

M.P. (Lab.) Mile End, 1935–45.

Mr Frankel believes he has mislaid his surviving papers.

FRANKLIN, Sir Leonard Benjamin (1862–1944)

M.P. (Lib.) Hackney Central, 1923–4.

Mr A. W. L. Franklin (son), Upper Lawn, Goudhurst, Kent, has papers of a personal nature only. Mrs Helene B. Bromnick, 5 Solent Road, London NW6, has only a few items relating to her grandfather's career, including three letters to his daughter Jeanette and some election literature.

FRASER OF LONSDALE, Baron
Sir William Jocelyn Ian Fraser (1897–1974)

M.P. (Con.) St Pancras North, 1922–9 and 1931–6; Lonsdale, 1940–50; Morecambe and Lonsdale, 1950–8.

Lord Fraser of Lonsdale retained a substantial collection of papers covering the various aspects of his career, including political correspondence and material relating to his constituencies, to St Dunstan's, and to his business affairs. It is expected that these will be deposited in the House of Lords Record Office.

FRASER, Hugh Charles Patrick Joseph (1918–)

M.P. (Con.) Stone, 1945–50; Stafford and Stone, 1950–
Parliamentary Under-Secretary and Financial Secretary, War Office, 1958–60; Parliamentary Under-Secretary, 1960–2. Secretary of State for Air, 1962–4.

FRASER, James Alexander Lovat- (1868–1938)

M.P. (Lab.) Lichfield, 1929–31; (Nat.Lab.) 1931–8.

Messrs J. D. Langton & Passmore, solicitors to the executors, were unable to supply any information that would indicate the location of any surviving papers.

FRASER, Major Sir Keith Alexander, 5th Bt (1867–1935)

M.P. (Con.) Harborough, 1918–23.

It is believed that the widow destroyed all relevant papers before her death. Records of the Harborough Conservative Association covering the period of Sir Keith's tenure are deposited in Leicestershire Record Office. See *Sources*, Vol. 1, p. 67.

FRASER, Thomas (1911–)

M.P. (Lab.) Hamilton, 1943–67.
Joint Parliamentary Under-Secretary, Scottish Office, 1945–57. Minister of Transport, 1964–5.

Mr Fraser states that he has retained none of his papers.

FREEMAN, John (1915–)

M.P. (Lab.) Watford, 1945–55.
Parliamentary Secretary, Ministry of Supply, 1947–51.
Editor, *New Statesman*, 1961–5.
High Commissioner, India, 1965–8.
Ambassador, United States, 1969–71.
Chairman and Chief Executive, London Weekend Television, 1971–

Mr Freeman states that he has tended not to keep papers and therefore has few in his care, apart from certain packages of personal papers dating back to the 1940s.

FREEMAN, Peter (1888–1956)

M.P. (Lab.) Brecon and Radnor, 1929–31; Newport, 1945–56.

FREMANTLE, Sir Francis Edward (1872–1943)

M.P. (Con.) St Albans, 1919–43.

St Albans Conservative Association has retained many of its records dating from 1900. No family contact was established.

FRENCH, Sir John Denton Pinkstone, see YPRES, 1st E of

FREWEN, Moreton (1853–1924)*

M.P. (Irish Nat.) Cork N.E., Dec 1910–Jul 1911.

Frewen's papers (1871–1920) are deposited in the Library of Congress, Washington D.C. Correspondence relating to the Irish Question can be found in the Plunkett papers and there are 35 letters (1912–21) to Bonar Law in the House of Lords Record Office.

FULLER, Albert George Hubert (1894–1969)

M.P. (Con.) Manchester Ardwick, 1931–5.

FULLER, Sir John Michael Fleetwood, 1st Bt (1864–1915)

M.P. (Lib.) Westbury, 1900–11.
Junior Lord of the Treasury, 1906–7. Vice Chamberlain, H.M. Household, 1907–11.
Governor of Victoria, 1911–14.

A useful collection of papers has been deposited in Wiltshire Record Office. It consists of several boxes of political material, largely covering the period 1900–11, and dealing mainly with the elections between those dates. The papers are predominantly local in character, and although there is some correspondence with prominent Liberal politicians, this consists largely of letters from Fuller with regard to constituency matters. There are no papers relating to his period as Governor of Victoria.

FULLERTON, Hugh (1851–1922)

M.P. (Lib.) Egremont West, 1906–Jan 1910.

FURNESS, 1st B
Sir Christopher Furness (1852–1912)

M.P. (Lib.) The Hartlepools, 1891–5, 1900–Jan 1910.

The 2nd Viscount Furness (grandson), 60 St James's Street, London SW1A 1LE, states that when his father's house was burnt down during World War II almost everything of interest was destroyed. It appears that all that survives are two bound volumes of letters and telegrams received on Christopher Furness's elevation to the peerage, together with a bound volume of press cuttings on the 1891 election campaign; and a volume of obituary notices.

FURNESS, George James (1868–1936)

M.P. (Con.) Willesden West, 1922–3.

FURNESS, Stephen Noel (1902–74)

M.P. (Lib.Nat.) Sunderland, 1935–45.
Junior Lord of the Treasury, 1938–40.

Enquiries should be directed to Mr F. W. Furness (brother), Knowle House, Kirby Knowle, Thirsk, YO7 2JB, who retains a number of family papers. Sir Stephen Furness, Bt (nephew), Milbanke Farm, Bedburn, Hamsterley, nr Bishop Auckland, Co. Durham DL13 3NN, has a volume of his uncle's selected speeches, which were privately printed in a small edition.

FURNESS, Sir Stephen Wilson, 1st Bt (1872–1914)

M.P. (Lib.) The Hartlepools, June 1910–14.

Mr F. W. Furness (son), Knowle House, Kirby Knowle, Thirsk, YO7 2JB, has a number of family papers, which are not generally made available. The present holder of the baronetcy, Sir Stephen Furness (grandson), knows of no relevant papers.

FYFE, Sir David Patrick Maxwell-, see KILMUIR, 1st E of

FYLER, J. A.

M.P. (Con.) Chertsey, 1903–4.

GADIE, Sir Anthony (1868–1948)

M.P. (Con.) Bradford Central, 1924–9.

Sir Anthony's family knows of no extant papers.

GAGE, 6th Vt
Henry Rainald Gage (1895–   )

Lord in Waiting, 1924–9; 1931–9.

The Gage family papers, from the 12th century to the present, are deposited with the Sussex Archaeological Society, Barbican House, Lewes, Sussex. These contain a few papers relating to the political career of the 6th Viscount. He has also retained, for the present, his own personal papers.

GAGE, Conolly Hugh
His Honour Judge Gage (1905–   )*

M.P. (Ulster Un.) Belfast South, 1945–52.

Judge Gage has retained certain letters and press cuttings, as well as certain family papers.

GAINFORD, 1st B
Joseph Albert Pease (1860–1943)

M.P. (Lib.) Tyneside, 1892–1900; Saffron Walden, 1901–Jan 1910; Rotherham, Mar 1910–16.
Chancellor of the Duchy of Lancaster, 1910–11. President of the Board of Education, 1911–15. Postmaster General, 1916.

Hazlehurst and Woodland, pp. 116–17, describe the large collection of papers and diaries which are housed in the Library of Nuffield College, Oxford.

GAITSKELL, Hugh Todd Naylor (1906–63)

M.P. (Lab.) Leeds South, 1945–63.
Parliamentary Under-Secretary, Ministry of Fuel and Power, 1946–7. Minister of Fuel and Power, 1947–50. Minister of State for Economic Affairs, 1950. Chancellor of the Exchequer, 1950–1.

Hazlehurst and Woodland, p. 58, describe the papers which are owned by Lady Gaitskell and which are held temporarily by Mr Philip Williams, Nuffield College, Oxford, who is compiling a biography.

GALBRAITH, James Francis Wallace (1872–1945)

M.P. (Con.) Surrey East, 1922–35.

Messrs Dawson & Co., solicitors to the executors, know of no papers. They had no knowledge of the whereabouts of Mrs A. Pattinson (sister), sole beneficiary of the estate.

GALBRAITH, Samuel (1853–1936)

M.P. (Lib.) Mid Durham, 1915–18; Spennymoor, 1918–22.

No direct contact with heirs was established. The *Dictionary of Labour Biography*, Vol. 1, pp. 126–8, describes Galbraith's career but makes no mention of Mss. Galbraith was a miners' leader in the Durham coalfield and the records of the Durham Miners are described in *Sources*, Vol. 1, p. 196.

GALBRAITH, Thomas Dunlop, see STRATHCLYDE, 1st B

GALBRAITH, Hon. Thomas Galloway Dunlop (1917–)

M.P. (Con.) Glasgow Hillhead, 1948–
Junior Lord of the Treasury, 1951–4. Comptroller, H.M. Household, 1954–5. Treasurer, H.M. Household, 1955–7. Civil Lord of the Admiralty, 1957–9. Joint Parliamentary Under-Secretary, Scottish Office, 1959–62; Transport, 1963–4.

Mr Galbraith has retained an almost complete record of constituency correspondence dating back to 1948, and press cuttings covering the same period, together with papers relating to the Vassall affair.

GALLACHER, William (1881–1965)

Chairman, Clyde Workers' Committee, 1914–18.
M.P. (Comm.) Fife West, 1935–50.
President, Communist Party, 1956–63.

According to information supplied to Mr Ian Macdougall of the Scottish Labour History Society, no papers remain with the family. Some eleven files of letters and documents concerning unemployment benefit cases which Gallacher raised in the House of Commons are deposited in the Marx Memorial Library. The surviving records of the Communist Party are described in *Sources*, Vol. 1, pp. 49–50.

GALLIGAN, Peter Paul*

M.P. (Sinn Fein) Cavan West, 1918–22.

GALLOWAY, William Johnson (1866–1931)

M.P. (Con.) Manchester S.W., 1895–1906.

Galloway died unmarried. It did not prove possible to establish contact with any surviving heirs.

GAMMANS, Sir (Leonard) David, 1st Bt (1895–1957)

Director and Secretary, Land Settlement Association, 1934–9.
M.P. (Con.) Hornsey, 1941–57.
Assistant Postmaster General, 1951–5.

The surviving papers of Sir David Gammans have been deposited in the Greater London Record Office (ref. Ac.71.101) and consist of fourteen large parcels, which include scrapbooks and newspaper cuttings. At the time of writing these had not been catalogued in detail. The records of the Land Settlement Association, and the conditions relating to access, are described in *Sources*, Vol. 1, pp. 142–3.

GANDAR DOWER, Eric Leslie (1895–)

M.P. (Con.) Caithness and Sutherland, 1945–50.

GANGE, Edwin Stanley (1871–1944)

M.P. (Co.Lib.) Bristol North, 1918–22.

GANLEY, Caroline Selina (1879–1966)

M.P. (Lab. Co-op.) Battersea South, 1945–51.

GANZONI, Sir Francis John Childs, 1st Bt, see BELSTEAD, 1st B

GARDINER, James (1860–1924)

M.P. (Co.Lib.) Kinross and Perthshire West, 1918–23.

GARDNER, Alan Coulstoun (1846–1907)

M.P. (Lib.) Ross, 1906–8.

GARDNER, Benjamin Walter (1865–1948)

M.P. (Lab.) Upton, 1923–4, 1929–31, 1934–45.

It proved impossible to trace Gardner's heirs.

GARDNER, Sir Ernest (1846–1925)

M.P. (Con.) Wokingham, 1901–18; Windsor, 1918–22.

GARDNER, James Patrick (1883–1937)

M.P. (Lab.) Hammersmith North, 1923–4, 1926–31.

GARDNER, Sir James Tynte Agg- (1846–1928)

M.P. (Con.) Cheltenham, 1874–80, 1885–95, 1900–6, Dec 1910–28.

Messrs Hancock & Willis, solicitors to Agg-Gardner, had no knowledge of papers, and it is believed that a relative who lives in Gloucester knows of no papers.

GARFIT, William (1840–1920)

M.P. (Con.) Boston, 1895–1906.

Attempts to contact a kinsman, who lives in Sandgate, Kent, were unsuccessful.

GARLAND, Charles Samuel (1887–1960)

M.P. (Con.) Islington South, 1922–3.

Mr G. Flower, who was an executor of the estate, knew of no papers. Mr J. A. Rye, also mentioned in the Probate Act, could not be contacted.

GASTRELL, Sir William Houghton- (1852–1935)

M.P. (Con.) Lambeth North, Jan 1910–18.

GATES, Ernest Everard (1903–   )

M.P. (Con.) Middleton and Prestwich, 1940–51.

Records of the local Conservative Association are deposited in the Lancashire Record Office.

GATES, Percy George (1863–1940)

M.P. (Con.) Kensington North, 1922–9.

No family contact could be established. Charrington & Co. Ltd, brewers, of which Gates had been a director, knew of no papers.

GAULT, (Andrew) Hamilton (1882–1958)

M.P. (Con.) Taunton, 1924–35.

GAUNT, Admiral Sir Guy Reginald Archer (1870–1953)

M.P. (Con.) Buckrose, 1922–6.

Attempts to contact Lady Gaunt (widow) were not successful.

GEDDES, 1st B
Sir Auckland Campbell Geddes (1879–1954)

M.P. (Con.) Basingstoke, 1917–20.
Minister, National Service, 1917–19. President, Local Government Board, 1918–19. Minister, Reconstruction, 1919. President, Board of Trade, 1919–20.
Ambassador, United States, 1920–4.

The late (2nd) Baron Geddes, who died in 1975, had stated that none of his father's papers had survived (Hazlehurst and Woodland, p. 58).

GEDDES, Sir Eric Campbell (1875–1937)

M.P. (Con.) Cambridge, 1917–22.
1st Lord of the Admiralty, 1917–19. Minister without Portfolio, 1919. Minister of Transport, 1919–21.

Hazlehurst and Woodland, p. 59, located only the Private Office collections of papers at the Public Record Office (Adm. 116/1804–10; M.T. 49; MUN 4/1733–6; and MUN 5/26/262.1/49).

GEE, Robert (1876–1960)

M.P. (Con.) Woolwich East, 1921–2; Bosworth, 1924–7.
Commissioner of Declarations, Western Australia, 1953–60.

Records of the Bosworth Conservatives are deposited in Leicestershire Record Office.

GELDER, Sir William Alfred (1855–1941)

M.P. (Lib.) Brigg, Jan 1910–18.

Sir William Gelder's family believe that many papers were destroyed during World War II. There are, however, some press cuttings in the possession of Mr A. D'Orton Gelder, Dolphin Cottage, 12 Manor Road, Wallington, Surrey. Further enquiries should be directed to Mrs E. Kingswell, 24 Elsworthy, East Molesey, Surrey.

GEOFFREY-LLOYD, Baron
Geoffrey William Lloyd (1902–   )

M.P. (Con.) Birmingham Ladywood, 1931–45; Birmingham King's Norton, 1950–5; Sutton Coldfield, 1955–Feb 1974.
Parliamentary Under-Secretary, Home Office, 1935–9. Parliamentary Secretary (Mines), Board of Trade, 1939–40. Parliamentary Secretary (Petroleum), Board of Trade, 1940–2. Parliamentary Secretary (Petroleum), Ministry of Fuel, Light and Power, 1942–5. Minister of Information, 1945. Minister of Fuel and Power, 1951–5. Minister of Education, 1957–9.

Lord Geoffrey-Lloyd did not keep a diary, nor did he make a habit of retaining official correspondence. Shortly after he retired from Parliament, Lord Geoffrey-Lloyd had all his constituency correspondence destroyed.

GEORGE, David Lloyd, see LLOYD GEORGE OF DWYFOR, 1st E

GEORGE, Gwilym Lloyd, see TENBY, 1st Vt

GEORGE, Lady Megan Lloyd, see LLOYD GEORGE, Lady Megan

GEORGE-BROWN, Baron
George Alfred Brown (1914–   )

M.P. (Lab.) Belper, 1945–70.
Joint Parliamentary Secretary, Ministry of Agriculture and Fisheries, 1947–51. Minister of Works, 1951. First Secretary of State and Secretary of State for Economic Affairs, 1964–6. Secretary of State for Foreign Affairs, 1966–8.

Hazlehurst and Woodland, p. 21, provide no details of Lord George-Brown's private papers, which are not available for research.

GIBB, James (1844–1910)

M.P. (Lib.) Harrow, 1906–Jun 1910.

GIBBINS, Frederick William (1861–1937)

M.P. (Lib.) Mid-Glamorgan, Jan–Dec 1910.

GIBBINS, Joseph (1888–1965)

M.P. (Lab.) Liverpool Toxteth West, 1924–31, 1935–50.

GIBBONS, Colonel William Ernest (1898–1976)

M.P. (Nat. Con.) Bilston, 1944–5.

GIBBS, Hon. Alban George Henry, see ALDENHAM, 2nd B

GIBBS, George Abraham, see WRAXALL, 1st B

GIBBS, Hon. Vicary (1853–1932)

M.P. (Con.) St Albans, 1892–1904.

Relevant papers relating to the 2nd Baron Aldenham and Vicary Gibbs may be found in the archives of Anthony Gibbs and Sons Ltd deposited in the Guildhall Library, London. Amongst these are various 'family' letters, 1883–1905 (ref. Ms 11021/29 and 30); a file of 'private' letters by Vicary Gibbs from Australian branches of the firm, mainly relating to business matters, 1883–4. Vicary Gibbs's activities are also recorded in the substantial business archive itself e.g. directors' general copy out-letter books, 'private', 1907–35 (ref. Ms 11041/1–6); and directors' special copy out-letter books, 'private', 1881–1922 (ref. Ms 11041/1 and 2).

GIBSON, Hon. Lord
Robert Gibson (1886–1965)

M.P. (Lab.) Greenock, 1936–41.
Chairman, Scottish Land Court, 1941–65.

GIBSON, Sir Charles Granville (1880–1948)

M.P. (Con.) Pudsey and Otley, 1929–45.

Mrs M. Aylwin (daughter), Clos Nicolle, Le Couvent, St Lawrence, Jersey, Channel Islands, has none of her father's papers. She does, however, have two large scrapbooks of press cuttings relating to her father's career as Lord Mayor of Leeds, 1924–5.

GIBSON, Charles William (1889–   )

M.P. (Lab.) Kennington, 1945–50; Clapham, 1950–9.
Member of London County Council from 1928.

Mr Gibson has retained a substantial collection of papers, including an unpublished autobiography, consisting of some 126 typescript pages. Other papers include miscellaneous letters, notes, etc., and scrapbooks of press cuttings dealing with trade union and socialist themes, dating from 1911. He has also kept a large collection of pamphlets dating back to the World War I period.

GIBSON, Edward, see ASHBOURNE, 1st B

GIBSON, Herbert Mellor (1896–1954)

M.P. (Lab.) Mossley, 1929–31.
Director, Colonial Development Corporation, 1948–54.

Gibson was Director of the Co-operative Wholesale Society; enquiries should be directed to its Librarian.

GIBSON, Sir James Puckering, 1st Bt (1849–1912)

M.P. (Lib.) Edinburgh East, 1909–12.

Gibson died without direct heir. No contact could be established.

GIFFARD, Sir Hardinge Stanley, see HALSBURY, 1st E of

GILBERT, James Daniel (1864–1941)

M.P. (Lib.) Newington West, 1916–18; Southwark Central, 1918–24.

Messrs Lee & Pembertons, solicitors to the executors of J. D. Gilbert, know of no papers.

GILHOOLY, James (1845–1916)*

M.P. (Independent Nat.) Cork West, 1885–1916.

GILL, Alfred Henry (1856–1914)

M.P. (Lab.) Bolton, 1906–14.
Secretary, Bolton Operative Spinners' Association.

The *Dictionary of Labour Biography*, Vol. II, pp. 137–9, describes Gill's career but mentions no Mss.

GILL, Sir Thomas Harry (1885–1955)

M.P. (Lab.) Blackburn, 1929–31.

Mr W. A. Shawdon, solicitor to the executors, knows of no papers. Gill's papers passed to his wife, and on her death to their daughter. She could not be contacted.

GILLETT, Sir George Masterman (1870–1939)

M.P. (Lab.) Finsbury, 1923–31; (Nat.Lab.) 1931–5.
Parliamentary Secretary, Overseas Trade, 1929–31; Transport, 1931.
Commissioner for the Special Areas (England and Wales), 1936–9.

Mr E. S. Gillett (son), Marsh Lock House, Wargrave Road, Henley-on-Thames, Oxon, has retained a collection of papers relating to his father's career. This includes the following: family and personal letters, including those written by Gillett at school, in the early 1880s; political letters, 1924–39, including some from J. R. MacDonald and others; copies of speeches, 1929–39; a case of press cuttings, 1929–39; letters received by Sir George after his resignation from the Government in 1931 and after his retirement as Commissioner for the Special Areas in 1939; and letters of condolence following his death in 1939.

GILLIS, William (1859–1929)

M.P. (Lab.) Penistone, 1921–2.

Enquiries should be directed to Mr Alfred Gillis (son), 31 Steadfield Road, Hayland Common, Barnsley, South Yorks. A great granddaughter, Mrs D. Birch, who lives in Silkstone, nr Barnsley, South Yorkshire, knows of no papers. A note on Gillis's career appears in the *Dictionary of Labour Biography*, Vol. III, pp. 86–7.

GILMOUR, Sir John, 2nd Bt (1876–1940)

M.P. (Con.) Renfrewshire East, Jan 1910–18; Glasgow Pollok, 1918–40.
Secretary of State for Scotland, 1924–9. Minister of Agriculture and Fisheries, 1931–2. Secretary of State for Home Affairs, 1932–5. Minister of Shipping, 1939–40.

Hazlehurst and Woodland, p. 61, state that the papers are held by Gilmour's son, Rt Hon. Col. Sir John Gilmour, Bt, D.S.O., M.P.

GILZEAN, Andrew (1877–1957)

M.P. (Lab.) Edinburgh Central, 1945–51.

Mr Harry Gilzean (greatnephew) knows of no papers.

GINNELL, Laurence (1854–1923)*

M.P. (Irish Nat.) West Meath North, 1906–22.

The National Library of Ireland has copies of documents relating to Ginnell covering the period 1896–1923.

GISBOROUGH, 1st B
Richard Adolphin Walmesley Chaloner (1856–1938)

M.P. (Con.) Westbury, 1895–1900; Liverpool Abercromby, Jan 1910–17.

Neither Lord Gisborough's daughter, Hon. Miss Ursula Chaloner, nor the present holder of the title, the 3rd Lord Gisborough, have any knowledge of relevant political records. The Chaloner family records are housed in the County Record Office, Northallerton, but these contain no political papers.

GLADSTONE, 1st Vt
Sir Herbert John Gladstone (1854–1930)

M.P. (Lib.) Leeds, 1880–5; Leeds West, 1885–Jan 1910.
Financial Secretary, War Office, 1886. Under-Secretary of State, Home Affairs, 1892–4. 1st Commissioner of Works, 1894–5. Secretary of State for Home Affairs, 1905–10. Governor-General, South Africa, 1910–14.

Hazlehurst and Woodland, pp. 61–2, describe the Herbert Gladstone papers in the British Library (Add. Mss 45985–6118 and 46474–86), and the family collection at St Deiniol's Library, Hawarden, Clwyd.

GLADSTONE, William Glynne Charles (1885–1915)

M.P. (Lib.) Kilmarnock, 1911–15.

A few papers relating to W. G. C. Gladstone have survived among the Glynne-Gladstone Mss at the Clwyd County Record Office, The Old Rectory, Hawarden, Deeside, Clwyd. A number of letters are quoted in H. Gladstone, *William G. C. Gladstone: A Memoir* (1918).

GLANVILLE, Harold James (1854–1930)

M.P. (Lib.) Bermondsey, Jan 1910–18; Bermondsey West, 1918–22.

GLANVILLE, James Edward (1891–1958)

M.P. (Lab.) Consett, 1943–55.

GLASSEY, Alec Ewart (1887–1970)

M.P. (Lib.) Dorset East, 1929–31.
Junior Lord of the Treasury, 1931.

Mrs M. E. Glassey (widow), The Homestead, Penn Hill Avenue, Parkstone, Poole, Dorset, has retained press cuttings only.

GLAZEBROOK, Philip Kirkland (1880–1918)

M.P. (Con.) Manchester South, 1912–18.

Glazebrook died unmarried, and it proved impossible to trace any contacts.

GLEDHILL, Gilbert (1889–1946)

M.P. (Con.) Halifax, 1931–45.

Messrs Clarkson, Thomas & Hanson, solicitors to the executors, know of no papers.

GLENAVY, 1st B
Sir James Henry Mussen Campbell, 1st Bt (1851–1931)

M.P. (Con.) Dublin St Stephen's Green, 1898–1900; Dublin University, 1903–16. Solicitor-General for Ireland, 1901–5. Attorney-General for Ireland, 1905, 1916. Lord Chief Justice of Ireland, 1916–18. Lord Chancellor of Ireland, 1918–21.

Relevant material can be found in the Carson papers in the Public Record Office of Northern Ireland. Two letters can be found in the Blumenfeld papers, now at the House of Lords Record Office. Lord Glenavy's grandson is Patrick Campbell, the journalist. Press cuttings concerning his career can be found in the Local History Library, Belfast Public Library.

GLEN-COATS, Sir Thomas Glen, 1st Bt (1846–1922)

M.P. (Lib.) Renfrewshire West, 1906–Jan 1910.

Efforts to contact a granddaughter produced no relevant information.

GLENCONNER, 1st B
Sir Edward Priaulx Tennant, 2nd Bt (1859–1920)

M.P. (Lib.) Salisbury, 1906–Jan 1910.

The papers of Lord Glenconner are with his grandson, Hon. Colin Tennant, Glen, Innerleithan, Peebles-shire. The collection spans approximately 40 years and includes diaries, correspondence and press cuttings. At the time of writing the material was being listed by the NRA (Scotland).

GLENDEVON, 1st B
Lord John Adrian Hope (1912–   )

M.P. (Con.) Midlothian North and Peebles-shire, 1945–50; Edinburgh Pentlands, 1950–64. Joint Parliamentary Under-Secretary, Foreign Office, 1954–6; Scottish Office, 1957–9. Parliamentary Under-Secretary, Commonwealth Relations Office, 1956–7. Minister of Works, 1959–62.

Lord Glendevon states that he has kept only a series of scrapbooks relating to his political career. He has never kept a diary.

GLENDINNING, Robert Graham (1844–1928)*

M.P. (Lib.) Antrim North, 1906–Jan 1910.

GLENRAVEL, 1st B
Sir Arthur Shirley Benn, 1st Bt (1858–1937)

M.P. (Con.) Plymouth, Dec 1910–18; Plymouth Drake, 1918–29; Sheffield Park, 1931–5.

Records of the Sheffield Conservative Federation and other Sheffield Conservative records survive in the care of the Sheffield Conservative Association (see *Sources*, Vol. 1, pp. 69–70).

GLENTORAN, 1st B
Herbert Dixon (1880–1950)*

M.P. (Con.) Belfast Pottinger, 1918–22; Belfast East, 1922–39.
Minister in Government of Northern Ireland.

The present (2nd) Lord Glentoran, Drumadarragh House, Ballyclare, Co. Antrim BT39 OTA, has a volume of obituary notices only.

GLOSSOP, Clifford William Hudson (1901–75)

M.P. (Con.) Penistone, 1931–5; Howdenshire, 1945–7.

Glossop spent the latter years of his life in South Africa. No contact could be established.

GLOVER, Thomas (1852–1913)

M.P. (Lab.) St Helens, 1906–Dec 1910.

A note on Glover's career appears in the *Dictionary of Labour Biography* Vol. I, pp. 130–1. No family contact was established, though it appears that relatives survive in the Norwich area.

GLUCKSTEIN, Sir Louis Halle (1897–   )

M.P. (Con.) Nottingham East, 1931–45.

Sir Louis, 199 Piccadilly, London W1V 9LE, has retained some papers, including box files of correspondence, two short diaries relating to his active service during World War II, and press-cutting books from 1928. These may be consulted by bona fide scholars with the written permission of Sir Louis.

GLYN, 1st B
Ralph George Campbell Glyn (1885–1960)

M.P. (Con.) Stirlingshire East and Clackmannan, 1918–22; Abingdon, 1924–53.

The bulk of Lord Glyn's papers has been deposited at the Berkshire Record Office. These papers are as yet uncatalogued, but include personal papers and correspondence; material on his war service; and also material relating to Lord Glyn's business affairs. There are restrictions on access to the papers for a number of years. In addition, the Hon. Lady Meade-Fetherstonhaugh (sister), Lassams, Selborne, nr Alton, Hants GU34 3LG, has in her possession several dozen letters written by her brother to his parents during World War I. This collection includes letters on the military situation written from Egypt, the Dardanelles and Russia. Photocopies of this correspondence are now available at the Imperial War Museum.

GLYN-JONES, Sir William Samuel (1869–1927)

M.P. (Lib.) Stepney, Dec 1910–18.
Secretary, Pharmaceutical Society of Great Britain, 1918–26.

Sir Hildreth Glyn-Jones (son) stated that he knew of no papers. The records of the Pharmaceutical Society are described in *Sources,* Vol. 1, pp. 211–12.

GODDARD, Sir Daniel Ford (1850–1922)

M.P. (Lib.) Ipswich, 1895–1918.

No papers are known to survive.

GODSON, Sir Augustus Frederick (1835–1906)

M.P. (Con.) Kidderminster, 1886–1906.

Attempts to contact a grandson proved unsuccessful.

GOFF, Sir Park, 1st Bt (1871–1939)

M.P. (Con.) Cleveland, 1918–23, 1924–9; Chatham, 1931–5.

Goff bequeathed to his trustees all his diaries and correspondence. A granddaughter, Mrs Veronica Fenwick-Clennell, lives near Morpeth in Northumberland.

GOLDIE, Sir Noel Barré (1882–1964)

M.P. (Con.) Warrington, 1931–45.

Messrs Arkle & Darbishire, solicitors of Liverpool, acted for both Sir Noel and Lady Goldie. However, they knew of no surviving papers.

GOLDMAN, Charles Sydney (1868–1958)

M.P. (Con.) Penryn and Falmouth, Jan 1910–18.

It is believed that surviving papers are with Mr John Monck (son), Aldern Bridge House, Newbury, Berks.

GOLDNEY, Francis Bennett- (1865–1918)

M.P. (Con.) Canterbury, Dec 1910–18.

Administration of Bennett-Goldney's estate was granted to Sir J. R. Twisden, Bt, who died without heirs in 1937. No contact could be established with any other relevant person. It seems that most of the early records of the Canterbury Conservatives have been destroyed.

GOLDSMITH, Francis Benedict Hayun (1878–1967)

M.P. (Con.) Stowmarket, Jan 1910–18.

Mr Edward Goldsmith, Catesby, Molesworth Street, Wadebridge, Cornwall, one of F. B. H. Goldsmith's sons, has several press-cutting books relating to both his father's local government and parliamentary career.

GOLDSTONE, Sir Frank Walter (1870–1955)

M.P. (Lab.) Sunderland, Dec 1910–18.
General Secretary, National Union of Teachers, 1924–31.

The records of the National Union of Teachers are described in *Sources,* Vol. 1, p. 202. No personal papers are known to survive.

GOMM, Hubert William Culling Carr- (1877–1939)

M.P. (Lib.) Rotherhithe, 1906–18.

The bulk of the papers have not survived. All that remains, apart from some family scrapbooks for an earlier period, are three letters from Winston Churchill to Carr-Gomm and a typescript reminiscence (13 pages) of Carr-Gomm's period in Parliament. Photocopies of these have been lodged in BLPES through the good offices of Mr Antony Carr-Gomm, Hubert Carr-Gomm's nephew.

GOOCH, Edwin George (1889–1964)

M.P. (Lab.) Norfolk North, 1945–64.
President, National Union of Agricultural Workers, 1928–64.

The records of the National Union of Agricultural Workers, mainly deposited in the Institute of Agricultural History, University of Reading, are described in *Sources,* Vol. 1, p. 191. No contact with the family was established.

GOOCH, George Peabody (1873–1968)

M.P. (Lib.) Bath, 1906–Jan 1910.
Historian; editor, *Contemporary Review,* 1911–50.

Professor U. F. J. Eyck, c/o History Department, University of Calgary, 2920 24th Avenue N.W., Calgary, Alberta, Canada, has care of a collection of Gooch's papers. Certain press cuttings may be found in Bath City Library, and some 66 letters (1903–36) can be found in the papers of W. H. Dawson (NRA 14020) at the University of Birmingham.

GOOCH, Sir Henry Cubitt (1871–1959)

M.P. (Con.) Peckham, 1908–Dec 1910.
Member of London County Council, 1907–10, 1914–34. Chairman, L.C.C., 1923–4.

Mr G. H. Gooch, (son), 28 Brook Street, Woodbridge, Suffolk, has a collection of his father's papers, which are at present unsorted.

GOODMAN, Albert William (1880–1937)

M.P. (Con.) Islington North, 1931–7.

Mr A. C. Goodman (son), The Pantiles, Boyle Farm, Thames Ditton, Surrey, knows of no papers. Further enquiries may be directed to Mrs H. Gotein (daughter), Top Farm, Broadway, Worcs, who acted as her father's private secretary.

GOODRICH, Henry Edwin (1887–1961)

M.P. (Lab.) Hackney North, 1945–50.

GORDON, A. T. (1881–1919)

M.P. (Con.) Aberdeenshire and Kincardineshire Central, 1918–19.

GORDON, John
Hon. Mr Justice Gordon (1849–1922)*

M.P. (Lib.Un.) Londonderry South, 1900–16.
Attorney-General for Ireland, 1915–16.

Gordon's son inherited all his father's books and the contents of his study. It proved impossible however to trace the son or his heirs.

GORDON, Hon. John Edward (1850–1915)

M.P. (Con.) Elgin and Nairn, 1895–1906; Brighton, 1911–15.

Enquiries should be directed to Mr J. M. Askew (grandson), Ladykirk, Norham, Berwick-on-Tweed.

GORDON, Major Sir William Eden Evans (1857–1913)

M.P. (Con.) Stepney, 1900–7.

No family contact was established. Gordon was a member of the British Brothers' League. No papers of this body seem to have survived (see *Sources*, Vol. 1, p. 219).

GORDON-WALKER, Baron
Patrick Chrestien Gordon Walker (1907–   )

M.P. (Lab.) Smethwick, 1945–64; Leyton, 1966–Feb 1974.
Parliamentary Under-Secretary, Commonwealth Relations Office, 1947–50. Secretary of State for Commonwealth Relations, 1950–1. Secretary of State for Foreign Affairs, 1964–5. Minister without Portfolio, 1966–7. Secretary of State for Education and Science, 1967–8.

Hazlehurst and Woodland, p. 146, found that Baron Gordon Walker's papers are not available for research. Private Office papers (1950–1) will be placed in the Public Record Office.

GORE, Hon. George Ralph Charles Ormsby-, see HARLECH, 3rd B

GORE, Hon. Seymour Fitzroy Ormsby- (1863–1950)

M.P. (Con.) Gainsborough, 1900–6.

It was not possible to establish contact with his greatnephew, the present (5th) Lord Harlech.

GORE, William George Arthur Ormsby-, see HARLECH, 4th B

GORE, Hon. William David Ormsby-, see HARLECH, 5th B

GORELL, 3rd B
Ronald Gorell Barnes (1884–1963)

Parliamentary Under-Secretary, War and Air, 1921–2.

Papers are deposited in the Bodleian Library, Oxford and include: literary manuscripts, drafts, etc.; an unpublished chapter of autobiography concerned with the offer of the Viceroyalty of India, 1930; Gorell's literary and family correspondence; correspondence relating to his service in World War I; 58 volumes of his diary, 1901–13, 1915, 1918–63; and certain of Lady Gorell's papers, including correspondence and diaries.

GORMAN, Sir William
Hon. Mr Justice Gorman (1891–1964)

M.P. (Lib.) Royton, 1923–4

Some routine correspondence of Gorman's, in the care of Heywood and Royton Divisional Liberal Association, is described in *Sources*, Vol. 1, p. 150.

GORONWY-ROBERTS, Baron
Goronwy Owen Roberts (1913–   )

M.P. (Lab.) Caernarvonshire, 1945–50; Caernarvon, 1950–Feb 1974.
Minister of State, Welsh Office, 1964–6; Department of Education and Science, 1966–7; Foreign and Commonwealth Office, 1967–9; Board of Trade, 1969–70. Parliamentary Under-Secretary, Foreign and Commonwealth Office, 1974–

Lord Goronwy-Roberts has in his own possession such papers as survive. These are unsorted.

GORST, Sir John Eldon (1835–1916)

M.P. (Lib.) Cambridge, 1866–8; Chatham, 1875–92; Cambridge University, 1892–1906.
Solicitor-General, 1885–6. Parliamentary Under-Secretary, India, 1886–91. Financial Secretary to the Treasury, 1891–2. Vice-President of Committee of Council on Education, 1895–1902.

Efforts to trace papers have proved unsuccessful. Neither Sir R. Sykes, Bt (whose mother was Gorst's daughter) nor another grandson, John Gorst, M.P., know of any papers. Relevant papers may be found in other collections. The Northcote Mss at the British Library contains correspondence with Lord Iddesleigh, 1880–2. Letters on Gorst's parliamentary candidature for Cambridge University (1891) are available at Cambridge University Library.

GOSCHEN, 1st Vt
George Joachim Goschen (1831–1907)

M.P. (Lib.) City of London, 1863–80; Ripon, 1880–5; Edinburgh East, 1885–6; (Lib.Un.) St George's, Hanover Square, 1887–1900.
Paymaster-General, 1865–6. Chancellor of the Duchy of Lancaster, 1866. President of the Poor Law Board, 1868–71. 1st Lord of the Admiralty, 1871–4 and 1895–Nov 1900. Chancellor of the Exchequer, 1887–92.

The papers at the Bodleian Library, Oxford, and in the care of Goschen's greatnephew, Mr D. C. Goschen, P.O. Box 49, Rusape, Rhodesia, are described by Hazlehurst and Woodland, pp. 63 and 167.

GOSCHEN, 2nd Vt
George Joachim Goschen (1866–1952)

M.P. (Con.) East Grinstead, 1895–1906.
Joint Parliamentary Secretary, Agriculture and Fisheries, 1918.
Governor, Madras, 1924–9. Acting Viceroy and Governor-General, India, 1929.

Papers relating to Goschen's career in India have been deposited in the India Office Library, by Hon. Mrs F. Balfour. The principal correspondents include successive Viceroys and Secretaries of State for India (1921–31), and the collection consists of correspondence, speeches and lectures. Hon. Mrs Balfour knows of no further papers remaining with the family.

GOSLING, Harry (1861–1930)

M.P. (Lab.) Whitechapel and St George's, 1923–30.
Minister of Transport and Paymaster-General, 1924.

Hazlehurst and Woodland, p. 63, found no private papers. A note on his career will be found in the *Dictionary of Labour Biography*, Vol. IV.

GOSSLING, Archibald George (1878–1950)

M.P. (Lab.) Birmingham Yardley 1929–31.

Gossling's nephew knew of no surviving papers. References to his work can be found in the archives of the Amalgamated Society of Woodworkers at the Modern Records Centre, University of Warwick Library.

GOULD, Barbara Ayrton (d. 1950)

M.P. (Lab.) Hendon North, 1945–50.

Michael Ayrton, Barbara Gould's son, knows of no papers. Some correspondence can be found in the Lansbury Collection at BLPES.

GOULD, Frederick (1879–1971)

M.P. (Lab.) Frome, 1923–4, 1929–31.

Sir Ronald Gould (son) says that his father left few papers, and these were destroyed at his death.

GOULD, James Childs (1870–1942)

M.P. (Con.) Cardiff Central, 1918–24.

GOULDING, Sir Edward Alfred, 1st Bt, see WARGRAVE, 1st B

GOWER, Frederick Neville Sutherland Leveson (1874–1959)

M.P. (Lib.Un.) Sutherland, 1900–6.

F. N. S. Leveson-Gower was resident in France. The Royal Bank of Scotland acted as executors to his estate. No information regarding papers was forthcoming.

GOWER, Sir Robert Vaughan (1880–1953)

M.P. (Con.) Hackney Central, 1924–9; (Con.) Gillingham, 1929–45.

Lady Gower (widow) stated that she gave all surviving papers to the Central Library, Mount Pleasant, Tunbridge Wells, TN1 1NS. The Library holds a collection of scrapbooks covering the life of Sir R. V. Gower, 1918–45, containing news cuttings and reporting speeches and events Sir Robert attended or was connected with; and letters, programmes, souvenirs, documenting major events in his life.

GRACE, John (1887–   )

M.P. (Con.) The Wirral, 1924–31.

GRAEME, Philip Lloyd-, see SWINTON, 1st E of

GRAHAM, Alan Crosland (1896–1964)

M.P. (Con.) The Wirral, 1935–45.

Mrs M. Graham (widow), 14 Lansdowne Road, Wimbledon, London SW20 8AN, retained a small collection of papers relating to her husband's career and interests. Most of the material relates to Captain Graham's involvement with various Continental bodies, 1940–6, and also with certain British anti-German organisations. Of particular interest is a file containing correspondence and minutes of the *Never Again Association,* and also correspondence with *Allies inside Germany.* Another file, in French, relates to calls for the restoration of the French Monarchy, 1940. A number of smaller files contain material on Austria, Cyprus, Greece and Spain, 1936–60. Another file contains details of Polish anti-Communist propaganda, 1946, and also a draft history of Poland. Only a little material relating to Captain Graham's parliamentary career is contained in the collection; it includes two volumes of press cuttings relating to his candidatures for Stirling, 1926–7; Denbigh, 1929; Darwen, 1931; and the Wirral, 1935. Many of these papers have been deposited in BLPES.

GRAHAM, Duncan MacGregor (1867–1942)

M.P. (Lab.) Hamilton, 1918–42.

A note on Graham's career appears in *Dictionary of Labour Biography,* Vol. I, pp. 133–4, but this makes no mention of Mss. Graham was secretary to the Lanarkshire Miners, 1918–30. Records of the Scottish Miners, largely in the National Library of Scotland, are described in *Sources,* Vol. 1, p. 197.

GRAHAM, Edward John (d. 1918)*

M.P. (Irish Nat.) Tullamore, 1914–Mar 1918.

GRAHAM, Sir (Frederick) Fergus, 5th Bt (1893–   )

M.P. (Con.) Cumberland North, 1926–35; Darlington, 1951–9.

No information was made available.

GRAHAM, Harry Robert (1850–1933)

M.P. (Con.) St Pancras West, 1892–1906.

H. R. Graham's niece, Miss M. L. Graham, knows of no papers.

GRAHAM, Robinson (b. 1878)

M.P. (Lab.) Nelson and Colne, 1920–2.

The Nelson and Colne Labour Party retained records dating from c. 1919 (*Sources,* Vol. 1, p. 139).

GRAHAM, William (1887–1932)

M.P. (Lab.) Edinburgh Central, 1918–31.
Financial Secretary, Treasury, 1924. President of the Board of Trade, 1929–31.

Hazlehurst and Woodland, p. 64, located no papers.

GRANARD, 8th E of
Bernard Arthur William Patrick Hastings Forbes (1874–1948)

Lord in Waiting, 1905–7. Master of the Horse, 1907–15, 1924–36. Assistant Postmaster General, 1906–9.

The present Earl of Granard states that his father's papers are preserved at Castle Forbes, Longford. They are not catalogued and cannot be examined until this is done.

GRANT, Sir James Augustus, 1st Bt (1867–1932)

M.P. (Con.) Egremont, Jan 1910–18; Whitehaven, 1918–22; Derbyshire South, 1924–9.

It is believed that no papers survive.

GRANT, J. Corrie (1850–1924)

M.P. (Lib.) Rugby, 1900–Jan 1910.

Neither Lady Slesser nor Miss Kathleen Grant (daughters), knew of any relevant surviving papers. Certain correspondence can be found in the Lansbury Collection at BLPES.

GRANT OF MONIMUSK, Lady, see TWEEDSMUIR OF BELHELVIE, Baroness

GRANVILLE, 3rd E
Granville George Leveson Gower (1872–1939)

Lord in Waiting, 1905–15.
Counsellor, Berlin, 1911–13; Paris, 1913–17. Diplomatic Agent, Salonika, 1917. Minister, Greece, 1917–21; Denmark, 1921–6; Netherlands, 1926–8. Ambassador, Belgium, 1928–33.

No information about papers was secured from the family. A little correspondence (c. 1916–19) can be found in the Hardinge papers at Cambridge University Library.

GRANVILLE OF EYE, Baron
Edgar Louis Granville (1899–   )

M.P. (Lib.) Eye, 1929–51.

GRANVILLE-WEST, Baron
Daniel Granville-West (1904–   )

M.P. (Lab.) Pontypool, 1946–58.

Lord Granville-West was unable to supply any information regarding his papers.

GRAVES, (Frances) Marjorie (1884–1961)

M.P. (Con.) Hackney South, 1931–5.

Mrs Ann Hutchison (cousin), Kildary House, Kildary, Ross-shire, has a substantial collection of papers covering the whole range of Miss Graves's varied interests.

GRAY, Sir Ernest (1857–1932)

M.P. (Con.) West Ham North, 1895–1906; Accrington, 1918–22.

Sir Ronald Gould, former General Secretary of the National Union of Teachers, of which Gray was a prominent member, knew of no papers. Reference should be made to the N.U.T., whose records are described in *Sources*, Vol. 1, p. 202.

GRAY, Frank (1880–1935)

M.P. (Lib.) Oxford City, 1922–4.

One box of typed and manuscript drafts of autobiographical works by Gray, drawn on by Charles Fenby for his book *The Other Oxford* (1971) is deposited in the Modern Records Centre, University of Warwick Library (ref. Mss 92). Gray's daughter, Mrs R. Chamberlayne of Jersey, knows of no other papers.

GRAY, Sir Harold William Stannus (1867–1951)

M.P. (Con.) Cambridgeshire, 1922–3.

Records of the Eastern Region Conservatives (an area which covers Cambridgeshire) are described in *Sources*, Vol. 1, p. 61. No family contact was established.

GRAY, Milner (1871–1943)

M.P. (Lib.) Mid Bedfordshire, 1929–31.
Parliamentary Secretary, Ministry of Labour, 1931.

GRAY, Sir William John St Clair Anstruther-, 1st Bt, see KILMANY, Baron

GRAY, William Anstruther- (1859–1938)

M.P. (Lib.Un. later Con.) St Andrews Burghs, 1906–Jan 1910; Dec 1910–18.

Lord Kilmany (son), has retained a collection of papers, including diaries and correspondence.

GRAYSON, (A.) Victor (b. 1882)

M.P. (Soc.) Colne Valley, 1907–Jan 1910.

Grayson disappeared in mysterious circumstances in the early 1920s. His daughter, Mrs Elaine Watkins, Shepherds Cross, 12 Meadow Close, Hove, Sussex, is preparing a biography of him. No single collection of papers is known to survive. Records of the Colne Valley Labour Party covering the period when Grayson was M.P. are described briefly in *Sources*, Vol. 1, p. 136. Two files of material relating to Grayson can be found in the archives of the Labour Party at Transport House (ref. LP/Lan/06/2/31–159). A poetic tribute is available at Wigan Public Library. A letter from Grayson (c. 1913) can be found in the George Lansbury collection at BLPES. Further biographical details are available in Reg Grove's biography of Grayson (1975), and in a forthcoming note in the *Dictionary of Labour Biography*.

GRAYSON, Sir Henry Mulleneux, 1st Bt (1865–1951)

M.P. (Con.) Birkenhead West, 1918–22.

Attempts to contact a son proved unsuccessful.

GREAVES-LORD, Sir Walter (1878–1942)

M.P. (Con.) Norwood, 1922–35.

Efforts to contact members of the family were not successful.

GREEN, Albert (1874–1941)

M.P. (Con.) Derby Borough, 1918–22.

GREEN, Joseph Frederick (1855–1932)

M.P. (Nat.Dem.) Leicester West, 1918–22.
Secretary, International Arbitration and Peace Association, 1886–1917.

Certain correspondence relating to international affairs can be found in the Labour Party archive at Transport House (refs. LRC; LP/GC). Records of the International Arbitration League are housed in the office of the Mondcivitan Republic, 27 Delancey Street, London NW1. Certain records relating to the National Democratic Party are described in *Sources*, Vol. 1. pp. 31–2.

Records of the English Positivist Committee, of which he was Chairman, 1923–31, are deposited in BLPES (*Sources*, Vol. 1. p. 157).

GREEN, Walford Davis (1869–1941)

M.P. (Con.) Wednesbury, 1895–1906.

Mrs Eleanor Salisbury (daughter), 47 Shelvers Way, Tadworth, Surrey, has an album of press cuttings relating to her father's campaign in the 1900 General Election. Neither Mrs Salisbury nor her sister, Mrs Morris, know of other surviving material.

GREEN, Walter Henry (1878–1958)

M.P. (Lab.) Deptford, 1935–45.

GREENALL, Thomas (1857–1937)

Miners' leader.
M.P. (Lab.) Farnworth, 1922–9.

The *Dictionary of Labour Biography*, Vol. 1, p. 136, describes Greenall's career but makes no mention of Mss.

GREENE, Sir (Edward) Walter, 1st Bt (1842–1920)

M.P. (Con.) Bury St Edmunds, 1900–6.

Dr Raymond Greene, 10 Cheltenham Terrace, London SW3 4RD, retained certain papers but none related to Sir Walter Greene nor Sir Raymond Greene, 2nd Bt. Mr Edward Greene, 63F High Street, Oxford OX1 4BA, has certain family papers, but again it is doubted whether any relevant material survives amongst them.

GREENE, Henry David (1843–1915)

M.P. (Con.) Shrewsbury, 1892–1906.

Dr Raymond Greéne (nephew) knows of no papers; and the solicitors who acted in the estate and in the estate of H. D. Greene's widow, Messrs Peacock & Goddard and Messrs Macfarlanes, were unable to help.

GREENE, Sir (Walter) Raymond, 2nd Bt (1869–1947)

M.P. (Con.) Chesterton, 1895–1906; Hackney North, Jan 1910–23.

Neither Dr Raymond Greene nor Mr Edward Greene know of papers relating to Sir Raymond, nor to Sir Edward Walter Greene, 1st Bt (see above).

GREENE, William Pomeroy Crawford (1885–1959)

M.P. (Con.) Worcester, 1923–45.

The Viscountess St Vincent (niece), Les Charrières, St Ouen, Jersey, C.I., has certain papers in store. She was unable to provide any details as to the extent and nature of this material.

GREENWELL, Colonel Thomas George (1894–1967)

M.P. (Con.) The Hartlepools, 1943–5.

A collection of records of the Hartlepool Conservative Association dating from the 1940s is deposited in Durham Record Office. Greenwell's son, Mr T. A. Greenwell, Witton House, Cleadon, nr Sunderland knows of no relevant political records.

GREENWOOD, 1st Vt
Sir (Thomas) Hamar Greenwood, 1st Bt (1870–1948)

M.P. (Lib.) York, 1906–Jan 1910; Sunderland, Dec 1910–22; (Con.) Walthamstow East, 1924–9.
Parliamentary Under-Secretary of State, Home Office, 1919. Secretary for Overseas Trade, 1919–20. Chief Secretary for Ireland, 1920–2.

Hazlehurst and Woodland, p. 64, found no papers.

GREENWOOD OF ROSSENDALE, Baron
Arthur William James Greenwood (Anthony Greenwood) (1911–)

M.P. (Lab.) Heywood and Radcliffe, 1946–50; Rossendale, 1950–70.
Secretary of State for Colonial Affairs, 1964–5. Minister of Overseas Development, 1965–6. Minister of Housing and Local Government, 1966–70.

Lord Greenwood retains family papers.

GREENWOOD, Arthur (1880–1954)

M.P. (Lab.) Nelson and Colne, 1922–31; Wakefield, 1932–54.
Parliamentary Secretary, Ministry of Health, 1924. Minister of Health, 1929–31. Minister without Portfolio, 1940–2. Lord Privy Seal, 1945–7. Paymaster-General, 1946–7.

Hazlehurst and Woodland, p. 64, state that the papers are owned by Greenwood's son, Lord Greenwood of Rossendale, 38 Downshire Hill, London NW3. The papers are not open for research.

GREENWOOD, Sir (Granville) George (1850–1928)

M.P. (Lib.) Peterborough, 1906–18.

Papers relating to the Eighty Club, of which Greenwood was a founder member, are described in *Sources*, Vol. 1, pp. 86–7. No family contact could be established. His correspondence with Harrington Putnam is in the Library of Congress.

GREENWOOD, William (1875–1925)

M.P. (Con.) Stockport, 1920–5.

GREER, Sir Harry (1876–1947)

M.P. (Con.) Clapham, 1918; Wells, 1918–22.

Greer's daughter, Mrs Sheila Pritchett, lives in Brockenhurst, Kent. It is not known if papers survive.

GREGORY, Sir Holman H. (1864–1947)

M.P. (Lib.) Derbyshire South, 1918–22.
Chairman, Royal Commission on Unemployment Insurance, 1930–2.

GREIG, Sir James William (1859–1934)

M.P. (Lib.) Renfrewshire West, Jan 1910–22.

Mr Charles Greig states that there is no relevant material amongst family papers.

GRENFELL, Cecil Alfred (1864–1924)

M.P. (Lib.) Bodmin, Jan–Dec 1910.

GRENFELL, David Rhys (1881–1968)

M.P. (Lab.) Gower, 1922–59.
Parliamentary Secretary, Department of Mines, 1940–2.

Grenfell's papers, at present in the care of his family, have been promised to the South Wales Miners' Library, University College, Swansea.

GRENFELL, Edward Charles, see ST JUST, 1st B

GRENFELL, William Henry, see DESBOROUGH, 1st B

GRETTON, 1st B
John Gretton (1867–1947)

M.P. (Con.) Derbyshire South, 1895–1906; Rutland, 1907–18; Burton, 1918–43.

The present (2nd) Lord Gretton states that his father made a special point of destroying all his correspondence and private papers during the last two years of his life. A few letters can be found in the Croft papers at Churchill College, Cambridge.

GRETTON, 2nd B
Hon. John Frederic Gretton (1902–   )

M.P. (Con.) Burton, 1943–5.

Lord Gretton states that he has nothing of outstanding interest relating to his own career.

GREVILLE, Hon. Ronald Henry Fulke (1864–1908)

M.P. (Con.) Bradford East, 1896–1906.

The present (4th) Baron Greville (greatnephew) knows of no papers.

GREY OF FALLODON, 1st Vt
Sir Edward Grey, 3rd Bt (1862–1933)

M.P. (Lib.) Berwick-on-Tweed, 1885–1916.
Parliamentary Under-Secretary, Foreign Affairs, 1892–5. Secretary of State for Foreign Affairs, 1905–16.
Ambassador, United States, 1919–20.

The Private Office collection of correspondence and papers (1892–5, 1905–16) is available at the Public Record Office (F.O. 800/35–113), and no further private papers have been found. Details are given in Hazlehurst and Woodland, pp. 64–5. Some ornithological letters can be found at the Edward Grey Institute, Oxford.

GREY, Charles Frederick (1903–   )

M.P. (Lab.) Durham, 1945–70.
Comptroller, H.M. Household, 1964–6; Treasurer, 1966–9.

GREY, George Charles (1918–44)

M.P. (Lib.) Berwick-on-Tweed, 1941–4.

Enquiries should be directed to Messrs Bird & Bird, solicitors, who are in contact with Grey's sole executrix.

GRIDLEY, 1st B
Sir Arnold Babb Gridley (1878–1965)

M.P. (Con.) Stockport, 1935–50; Stockport South, 1950–5.

The present (2nd) Lord Gridley has certain of his father's papers, which are at present unsorted. These are not generally made available.

GRIERSON, Edgar (1884–1959)

M.P. (Lab.) Carlisle, 1945–50.

Grierson's son was his executor but no contact with him could be established.

GRIFFITH, Arthur (1872–1922)*

M.P. (Sinn Fein) East Cavan and Tyrone N.W., 1918–22.
Founder and first editor of *Sinn Fein*, 1906–15.

A few letters about the 1918 election are in the Northern Ireland Public Record Office (ref. T. 1635). There is also relevant material in the National Library of Ireland.

GRIFFITH, Sir Ellis Jones Ellis-, 1st Bt (1857–1920)

M.P. (Lib.) Anglesey, 1895–1918; Carmarthen, 1923–4.
Parliamentary Under-Secretary, Home Office, 1912–15.

A collection of papers is deposited in the National Library of Wales, and includes a number of personal papers, and a draft of a biography of Sir Ellis; press cuttings, both personal and political; copies of lectures, talks and speeches; election addresses; and correspondence of a political nature to a wide variety of correspondents, 1890s - 1920s.

GRIFFITH, Frank Kingsley (1889–1962)

M.P. (Lib.) Middlesbrough West, 1928–40.

Mrs A. Bullock (daughter) knows of no papers.

GRIFFITHS, David (1896–   )

M.P. (Lab.) Rother Valley, 1945–70.

GRIFFITHS, George Arthur (1880–1945)

M.P. (Lab.) Hemsworth, 1934–45.

Messrs Raley & Pratt, solicitors to the executors, know of no papers. A note on his career appears in the *Dictionary of Labour Biography* Vol. III, pp. 87–9.

GRIFFITHS, James (1890–1975)

M.P. (Lab.) Llanelli, 1936–70.
Minister of National Insurance, 1945–50. Secretary of State for the Colonies, 1950–1. Secretary of State for Wales, 1964–6.

Hazlehurst and Woodland, p. 65, describe the papers at Coleg Harlech. A transcript of an interview with Griffiths is available at the South Wales Miners' Library, University College, Swansea. Mrs W. Griffiths (widow), retained the remainder of the papers, including manuscripts and typescripts of articles, scripts of broadcasts, and unpublished writings. Among the latter is a manuscript entitled 'Welsh Politics in my Lifetime'. These papers have now been deposited in the National Library of Wales.

GRIFFITHS, Lt.-Col. Sir John Norton-, 1st Bt (1871–1930)

Military career.
M.P. (Con.) Wednesbury, Jan 1910–18; Wandsworth Central, 1918–24.

Sir Peter Norton-Griffiths Bt., (son), confirmed that no political papers have survived.

GRIFFITHS, Thomas (1867–1955)

M.P. (Lab.) Pontypool, 1918–35.
Treasurer, H.M. Household, 1924.

GRIFFITHS, William (1912–73)

M.P. (Lab.) Manchester Moss Side, 1945–50; Manchester Exchange, 1950–73.

GRIGG, Sir Edward William Maclean, see ALTRINCHAM, 1st B

GRIGG, Sir Percy James (1890–1964)

Principal Private Secretary to successive Chancellors of the Exchequer, 1921–30. Chairman, Board of Customs and Excise, 1930; Board of Inland Revenue, 1930–4. Finance Member, Council of the Viceroy of India, 1934–9. Permanent Under-Secretary, War Office, 1939–42.
M.P. (Nat.) Cardiff East, 1942–5.
Secretary of State for War, 1942–5.

A collection of papers is held at Churchill College, Cambridge. Most of the papers relate to Grigg's period in India; with a few papers from the early 1940s when Grigg was in the government and a good deal of material relating to the publication of the autobiography *Prejudice and Judgement* (1948). Details are given by Hazlehurst and Woodland, p. 67.

GRIGGS, Sir (William) Peter (1854–1920)

M.P. (Con.) Ilford, 1918–20.

Griggs's heirs were not traced. The South Essex Recorders Ltd, a company of which Griggs was Governing Director, were unable to trace any material relating to him.

GRIMOND, Joseph (1913–   )

M.P. (Lib.) Orkney and Shetland, 1950–
Leader of the Parliamentary Liberal Party, 1956–67.

GRIMSTON OF WESTBURY, 1st B
Sir Robert Villiers Grimston, 1st Bt (1897–   )

M.P. (Con.) Westbury, 1931–64.
Junior Lord of the Treasury, 1937. Vice Chamberlain, H.M. Household, 1938–9; Treasurer, 1939–42. Assistant Postmaster General, 1942–5. Parliamentary Secretary, Ministry of Supply, 1945. Deputy Chairman of Ways and Means, 1962–4.

Private Office papers (AVIA 11) can be found at the Public Record Office.

GRIMSTON, Hon. John, see VERULAM, 6th E of

GRIMTHORPE, 2nd B
Ernest William Beckett (formerly Denison) (1856–1917)

M.P. (Con.) Whitby, 1885–1905.

The present (4th) Lord Grimthorpe believes that none of his grandfather's papers have survived.

GRITTEN, William George Howard (1870–1943)

M.P. (Con.) The Hartlepools, 1918–22, 1929–43.

Gritten bequeathed his library to West Hartlepool Public Library. Attempts to ascertain whether this bequest contained papers were not successful. Records of Hartlepool Conservative Association dating from the 1940s are deposited in Durham Record Office.

GROTRIAN, Sir Herbert Brent, 1st Bt (1886–1951)

M.P. (Con.) Hull S.W., 1924–9.

Sir J. A. B. Grotrian, Bt (son) has deposited in the Hull University Library three small albums of press cuttings relating to the election campaign of 1922, together with a file of press cuttings on his grandfather's election campaign in Hull East, 1892. No other records appear to survive.

GROVE (Thomas Newcomen) Archibald (1855–1920)

M.P. (Lib.) West Ham North, 1892–5; Northamptonshire South, 1906–Jan 1910.

GROVES, James Grimble (1854–1914)

M.P. (Con.) Salford South, 1900–6.

The family has retained only obituary notices, and these are not available.

GROVES, Thomas Edward (1884–1958)

M.P. (Lab.) Stratford, 1922–45.

Enquiries should be directed to Mr T. E. Groves (son), 10 Hope Road, South Benfleet, Essex.

GRUFFYDD, Professor William John (1881–1954)

Professor of Celtic, University College of South Wales and Monmouthshire.
M.P. (Lib.) University of Wales, 1943–50.

Mr Dafydd Gruffydd (son), Kewstoke, Lower Cwrt-y-Vil Road, Penarth, South Glamorgan, knows of no papers which relate to his father's brief parliamentary activities. Such papers as survive relate to Professor Gruffydd's lifelong work in the field of Celtic studies. Files relating to the University of Wales by-election in 1943 are available in a deposit of Plaid Cymru records at the National Library of Wales.

GRUNDY, Thomas Walter (1864–1942)

M.P. (Lab.) Rother Valley, 1918–35.

Mr T. W. G. Grundy (grandson), 73 Grange Road, Rotherham, South Yorkshire, has certain press cuttings relating to his grandfather's career. Neither he nor other members of the family know of other papers. A note on his career appears in the *Dictionary of Labour Biography*, Vol. III, pp. 89–90.

GUEST, Hon. (Christian) Henry Charles (1874–1957)

M.P. (Lib.) Dorset East, Jun–Dec 1910; Pembroke and Haverford West, Dec 1910–18; Bristol North, 1922–3; (Con.) Plymouth Drake, 1937–45.

Mr John S. Guest (son), 839 Weed Street, New Canaan, Conn., U.S.A., stated that he had no papers which would be of use to this project.

GUEST, Frederick Edward (1875–1937)

M.P. (Lib.) Dorset East, Jan 1910–22.[1] Stroud, 1923–4; Bristol North, 1924–9; (Con.) Plymouth Drake, 1931–7.

Secretary of State for Air, 1921–2.

Hazlehurst and Woodland, p. 68, located no papers.

1 After the January 1910 elections. Guest was unseated on petition and a by-election was held on 30 June 1910. He was re-elected in December 1910 and held the seat until 1922.

GUEST, Ivor Churchill, see WIMBORNE, 1st Vt

GUEST, Hon. Ivor Grosvenor, see WIMBORNE, 2nd Vt

GUEST, John (1867–1931)

M.P. (Lab.) Hemsworth, 1918–31.

Messrs Bury & Walkers, solicitors of Barnsley, were in contact with a member of the family, but no information on papers was made available. The *Dictionary of Labour Biography,* Vol. III, pp. 90–1 has an entry on his career.

GUEST, Leslie Haden Haden-, see HADEN-GUEST, 1st B

GUEST, Hon. Oscar Montague (1888–1958)

M.P. (Co.Lib.) Loughborough, 1918–22; (Con.) Camberwell N.W., 1935–45.

Hon. Mrs Susan Guest (widow), Cabalva House, Whitney-on-Wye, Hereford, has a collection of her husband's papers, which are at present unsorted.

GUINEY, John (b. 1868)*

M.P. (Irish Nat.) Cork North, 1913–18.

GUINEY, Patrick (1862–1913)*

M.P. (Irish Nat.) Cork North, Jan 1910–13.

GUINNESS, Thomas Loel Evelyn Bulkeley (1906–)

M.P. (Con.) Bath, 1931–45.

Mr Guinness states that he has retained none of his political papers. Records of the Bath Conservatives, a very full and important collection, are deposited in the Bath Archives and Record Office.

GUINNESS, Walter Edward, see MOYNE, 1st B

GULLAND, John William (1864–1920)

M.P. (Lib.) Dumfries Burghs, 1906–18.
Junior Lord of the Treasury, 1909–15. Joint Parliamentary Secretary to the Treasury and Government Chief Whip, 1915–16.

According to information obtained by Dr Cameron Hazlehurst, a collection of letters from Gulland to his wife and letters of condolence on his death are preserved by his nephew, Mr J. Gulland Osborne.

GULLY, William Court, see SELBY, 1st Vt

GUNSTON, Major Sir Derrick Wellesley, 1st Bt (1891–   )

M.P. (Con.) Thornbury, 1924–45.

Sir Derrick states that he has retained few papers.

GUNTER, Raymond Jones (1909–   )

M.P. (Lab.) Essex S.E., 1945–50; Doncaster, 1950–1; Southwark, 1951–72.
Minister of Labour, 1964–8. Minister of Power, Apr–Jun 1968.

Mr Gunter stated that he did not retain any private papers relating to his parliamentary career.

GUNTER, Sir Robert, 1st Bt (1831–1905)

M.P. (Con.) Barkston Ash, 1885–1905.

Records of the Barkston Ash Conservative Association, dating from 1895, are deposited with Leeds City Libraries. See *Sources*, Vol. 1, p. 46. No family contact was established.

GURDON, Sir William Brampton (1840–1910)

M.P. (Lib.) Norfolk North, 1899–Jan 1910.

Certain papers relating to the political career of Sir William Gurdon are deposited with the Cranworth Mss at the Suffolk Record Office, Ipswich branch. They span the years 1865–1908, although some years are thinly represented, covering his activities as private secretary to Gladstone, 1865–6 and 1868–74, as well as his membership of the House of Commons. These are open to use by scholars but permission to quote from the papers should be obtained from Lord Cranworth. No other papers have been traced.

GUTHRIE, Thomas Maule (d. 1943)

M.P. (Nat.Lib.) Moray and Nairn, 1922–3.

GUTHRIE, Walter Murray (1864–1911)

M.P. (Con.) Bow and Bromley, 1899–1906.

GUY, James Campbell Morrison (1894–   )

M.P. (Con.) Edinburgh Central, 1931–41.

GUY, William Henry (d. 1968)

M.P. (Lab.) Poplar South, 1942–50.

Attempts to contact the widow were not successful.

GWYNN, Stephen Lucius (1864–1950)*

Journalist and author.
M.P. (Irish Nat.) Galway North, 1906–18.

Correspondence (1919–38) can be found in the Lothian papers at the Scottish Record Office. Letters (1905–6) to Lord Aberdeen are included in the Gordon of Haddo collection (NRA list 9758); and correspondence (1914–18) relating to the Irish Convention is contained in the Plunkett papers.

GWYNNE, Rupert Sackville (1873–1924)

M.P. (Con.) Eastbourne, Jan 1910–24.
Financial Secretary, War Office, 1923–4.

Mrs Elizabeth David (daughter) has no papers. She believes that the only surviving material consists of press cuttings and scrapbooks in the care of her eldest sister, Mrs Priscilla Gwynne-Longland, Wootton Manor, Polegate, Sussex.

HACKETT, John (b. 1866)*

M.P. (Irish Nat.) Mid Tipperary, Jan 1910–18.

HACKING, 1st B
Sir Douglas Hewitt Hacking, 1st Bt (1884–1950)

M.P. (Con.) Chorley, 1918–45.
Vice Chamberlain, H.M. Household 1922–4; Nov 1924–Dec 1925. Parliamentary Under-Secretary, Home Office, 1925–7. Parliamentary Secretary, Board of Trade, 1927–9. Parliamentary Under-Secretary, Home Office, 1933–4; Financial Secretary, War Office, 1934–5. Parliamentary Under-Secretary, Dominion Office, 1935–6.

Few of Lord Hacking's papers have survived. However, there are twelve volumes of press cuttings covering his parliamentary and ministerial career with his widow, Margery, Lady Hacking, 8 Dorchester Court, Sloane Street, London SW1. In addition, there are a number of largely formal letters.

HADDOCK, George Bahr (1863–1930)

M.P. (Con.) Lonsdale North, 1906–18.

Lt.-Col. L. Rathbone (nephew), knows of no papers.

HADEN-GUEST, 1st B
Leslie Haden Haden-Guest (1877–1960)

M.P. (Lab.) Southwark North, 1923–7; Islington North, 1937–50.
Lord in Waiting, 1951.
Author, journalist and doctor.

The papers which are in private hands are not available for research. The Labour Party archives contain a number of letters and papers from or concerning Haden-Guest.

HAILES, 1st B
Patrick George Thomas Buchan-Hepburn (1901–74)

M.P. (Con.) Liverpool East Toxteth, 1931–50; Beckenham, 1950–7.
Junior Lord of the Treasury, 1939 and 1944. Parliamentary Secretary, Treasury and Government Chief Whip, 1951–5. Minister of Works, 1955–7.

Governor-General and C.-in-C., West Indies, 1958–62.

Lady Hailes, 1 Pelham Place, London SW7 2NQ, states that her husband left a great many papers which are at present unsorted.

HAILSHAM, 1st Vt
Sir Douglas McGarel Hogg (1872–1950)

M.P. (Con.) St Marylebone, 1922–8.
Attorney-General, 1922–4 and 1924–8. Lord Chancellor, 1928–9 and 1935–8. Secretary of State for War, 1931–5. Lord President of the Council, 1938.

Hazlehurst and Woodland, p. 77, found that only fee books and letters of congratulation and condolence have survived. These are in the care of Lord Hailsham of St. Marylebone. Some Hailsham correspondence is included in the 2nd Viscount Elibank collection.

HAILSHAM OF SAINT MARYLEBONE, Baron
Quintin McGarel Hogg, 2nd Vt Hailsham (1907–   )

M.P. (Con.) Oxford, 1938–50; St Marylebone, 1963–70.
Joint Parliamentary Under-Secretary, Air Ministry, 1945. 1st Lord of the Admiralty, 1956–7. Minister of Education, 1957. Deputy Leader, House of Lords, 1957–60, and Leader, 1960–3 Lord Privy Seal, 1959–60. Lord President of the Council, 1957–9 and 1960–4. Minister for Science and Technology, 1959–64. Minister with special responsibility for Sport, 1962–4; unemployment in the North East, 1963–4; Higher Education, 1963–4. Secretary of State for Education and Science, 1964. Lord Chancellor, 1970–4.

Lord Hailsham states that he has not consciously thrown away anything, and he has many papers. However, these are unsorted and unavailable for study.

HAILWOOD, Augustine (1875–1939)

M.P. (Con.) Manchester Ardwick, 1918–22.

HAIN, Sir Edward (1851–1917)

M.P. (Lib.Un.) St Ives, 1900–6.

Records of the Hain Steamship Company are at the St Ives Museum, but the papers have little bearing on Sir Edward Hain's career. The solicitors, T. J. Chellew & Son of St Ives, and other persons contacted, know of no papers.

HAIRE OF WHITEABBEY, Baron
John Edwin Haire (1908–66)

Royal Air Force career.
M.P. (Lab.) Wycombe, 1945–51.

Mr Christopher Haire (son), 49 Star Street, London W2, has a collection of papers. This includes correspondence, notes for speeches, and press cuttings.

HALDANE, 1st Vt
Richard Burdon Haldane (1856–1928)

M.P. (Lib.) Lothian East, 1885–1911.
Secretary of State for War, 1905–12. Lord Chancellor, 1912–15 and 1924.

The Haldane papers at the National Library of Scotland are described by Hazlehurst and Woodland, p. 68.

HALE, Baron
(Charles) Leslie Hale (1902–)

M.P. (Lab.) Oldham, 1945–50; Oldham West, 1950–68.

HALE, Joseph (1913–)

M.P. (Lab.) Rochdale, 1950–1.

HALES, Harold Keates (1868–1942)

M.P. (Con.) Hanley, 1931–5.

Attempts made to contact Hales Brothers (Overseas) Ltd, London, successors to the shippers, export and import merchants of which H. K. Hales was sole proprietor, were unsuccessful. No member of the family was traced.

HALIFAX, 1st E of
Edward Frederick Lindley Wood, 1st Baron Irwin (1881–1959)

M.P. (Con.) Ripon, Jan 1910–25.
Parliamentary Under-Secretary, Colonies, 1921–2. President, Board of Education, 1922–4 and 1934–5. Minister, Agriculture and Fisheries, 1924–5. Viceroy of India, 1926–31. Secretary of State, War, 1935. Lord Privy Seal, 1935–7. Lord President of the Council, 1937–8. Secretary of State, Foreign Affairs, 1938–40. Ambassador, United States, 1941–6.

The present (2nd) Earl of Halifax, of Garrowby, Yorkshire, retains many of his father's papers. A microfilm of some of the papers relating to 1938–9 and to the period in Washington is kept at Churchill College, Cambridge, and the Indian papers are deposited in the India Office Library. Foreign Office correspondence (1938–40) remains at the Public Record Office (FO 800/309–28). Researchers should consult Hazlehurst and Woodland pp. 153–4, for further details. Papers in other collections are listed in the NRA personal index. Speeches (1938–40) remain at the Foreign and Commonwealth Office.

HALIFAX, 2nd E of
Charles Ingram Courtenay Wood, Lord Irwin (1912–)

M.P. (Con.) York, 1937–45.

The Earl of Halifax states that he has no diaries, letters, etc., relating to his short period in the House of Commons .

HALL, 1st Vt
George Henry Hall (1881–1965)

M.P. (Lab.) Aberdare, 1922–46.
Civil Lord of the Admiralty, 1929–31. Parliamentary Under-Secretary, Colonial Office, 1940–2; Foreign Office, 1943–5. Financial Secretary, Admiralty, 1942–3. Secretary of State for the Colonies, 1945–6. 1st Lord of the Admiralty, 1946–51.

The present (2nd) Vt Hall, Belgrave Cottage, Upper Belgrave Street, London SW1, has a number of his father's papers. These are described by Hazlehurst and Woodland, p. 69. Copies of some of these papers are deposited in Hull University Library.

HALL, Sir Douglas Bernard, 1st Bt (1866–1922)

M.P. (Con.) Isle of Wight, Jan 1910–22.

Sir John Hall, Bt, believes that his grandfather's papers were destroyed.

HALL, Sir Edward Marshall- (1858–1927)

M.P. (Con.) Southport, 1900–6; Liverpool East Toxteth, Jan 1910–16.

Miss E. Marshall-Hall states that her father's papers were used by E. Marjoribanks in his *Life of Sir Edward Marshall-Hall* (1929) and then destroyed by Marshall-Hall's executors as instructed. All that has survived is five volumes of press cuttings (1920–7) relating to Marshall-Hall's legal career. These are in the Library of the Inner Temple, Inner Temple, London, EC4Y 7DA.

HALL, Fred (1855–1933)

M.P. (Lib-Lab., later Lab.) Normanton, 1905–33.
Junior Lord of the Treasury, 1924.

It was not possible to contact members of the family. The *Dictionary of Labour Biography*, Vol. II, pp. 144–5, refers only to published source materials.

HALL, Sir Frederick, 1st Bt (1864–1932)

M.P. (Con.) Dulwich, Dec 1910–32.

Sir John Hall, Bt, knew of no papers relating to his grandfather's career.

HALL, James Henry (1877–1942)

M.P. (Lab.) Whitechapel and St George's, 1930–1 and 1935–42.

Efforts to contact Hall's son, Mr S. W. H. Hall, of Walthamstow, London E17, were unsuccessful.

HALL, John Thomas (1896–1955)

M.P. (Lab.) Gateshead West, 1950–5.

Information available at Somerset House was insufficient to trace members of the family. Records of the General and Municipal Workers Union, of which Hall was Northern District Chairman, are described in *Sources*, Vol. 1, pp. 193–4.

HALL, Lt.-Col. Walter D'Arcy (1891–   )

M.P. (Con.) Brecon and Radnor, 1924–9, 1931–5.

Efforts to contact Lt.-Col. Hall were unsuccessful. His son, Professor E. T. Hall, states that it is unlikely that there are any papers.

HALL, William George Glenvil (1887–1962)

M.P. (Lab.) Portsmouth Central, 1929–31; Colne Valley, 1939–62.
Financial Secretary, Treasury, 1945–50.

Mr J. A. S. Hall, 2 Dr Johnson's Buildings, Temple, London EC4, has a number of papers relating to his father's career. Details are not available.

HALL, Admiral Sir (William) Reginald (1870–1943)

Director of Intelligence Division, Admiralty War Staff, 1914–18.
M.P. (Con.) Liverpool West Derby, 1919–23; Eastbourne, 1925–9.

Commander R. A. Hall has presented all his father's papers to Churchill College, Cambridge. The small collection includes memoirs and documents, 1915–33.

HALL, Sir William Stephen Richard King-, see KING-HALL, Baron

HALLAS, Eldred (1870–1926)

M.P. (Nat.Dem.) Birmingham Duddeston, 1918–22.

The will and Act of Probate were not helpful in tracing members of the family. The *Dictionary of Labour Biography*, Vol. II, pp. 152–4, refers only to published sources. Correspondence with Hallas concerning his attitude to the Council of Action (*Sources*, Vol. 1, p. 83) is included in the Labour Party archive.

HALLS, Walter (1871–1953)

M.P. (Lab.) Heywood and Radcliffe, 1921–2.

Miss E. Halls (daughter) knows of no papers, apart from a few press cuttings. The Nottingham Co-operative Society Limited, kindly provided biographical information on Halls as President of the Society.

HALPIN, James (1843–1909)*

M.P. (Irish Nat.) Clare West, 1906–9.

HALSBURY, 1st E of
Sir Hardinge Stanley Giffard (1823–1921)

M.P. (Con.) Launceston, 1877–85.
Solicitor-General, 1875–80. Lord Chancellor, 1885–6, 1886–92 and 1895–1905.

The papers at the British Library (Add. Mss 56370–7) are described by Hazlehurst and Woodland, p. 61.

HALSEY, Sir Thomas Frederick, 1st Bt (1839–1927)

M.P. (Con.) Watford, 1876–1907.

Five scrapbooks survive in the care of the Halsey family, The Golden Parsonage, Hemel Hempstead, Herts. These contain letters of congratulation to Sir Thomas, copies of speeches, particularly on the South African War, photographs, press cuttings, etc. Halsey family papers are deposited in Hertfordshire Record Office, but these contain no political papers relating to Sir Thomas.

HALSTEAD, Major David (1861–1937)

M.P. (Con.) Rossendale, 1922–3.
Author.

Mr and Mrs J. Witham, Major Halstead's son-in-law and daughter, know of no papers. Papers at his old home in Haslingden were destroyed. The Public Library, Deardengate, Haslingden, Rossendale, Lancs, has a small collection of letters written by Halstead, and copies of articles by him in the *Haslingden Observer* (28 May 1927 onwards).

HAMBLEDEN, 2nd Vt
Hon. William Frederick Danvers Smith (1868–1928)

M.P. (Con.) Strand, 1891–Jan 1910.

A number of letters and press cuttings covering the career of the 2nd Viscount Hambleden are held by W. H. Smith & Son Ltd, Strand House, 10 New Fetter Lane, London EC4. The letters are mainly personal or financial. In addition, there are a few military records relating to the 1st Devon Yeomanry and estate papers relating to land in Berkshire, Buckinghamshire, Devon and Suffolk. Letters (1894) to the 4th and 5th Earls of Harrowby are in the Harrowby collection (NRA 1561).

HAMBRO, Captain Angus Vlademar (1883–1957)

M.P. (Con.) Dorset South, Jan 1910–22; Dorset North, 1937–45.

Mrs V. Hambro (widow) has given her husband's collection of press cuttings to the Dorset North Conservative Association, Dale House, Blandford Forum, Dorset. Enquiries should be addressed to the Secretary and Agent. No diaries or correspondence of Captain Hambro are known to survive.

HAMBRO, Sir (Charles) Eric (1872–1947)

M.P. (Con.) Wimbledon, 1900–7.

Neither Mrs Diana Gibson-Watt (granddaughter) nor Hambros Bank Ltd have any papers.

HAMERSLEY, Alfred St George (1848–1929)

M.P. (Con.) Woodstock, Jan 1910–18.

Col. J. H. St G. Hamersley, O.B.E., Beechfold, Harrow Lane, Petersfield, Hants, has a number of papers relating to his grandfather's career.

HAMILTON, 14th D of
Douglas Douglas-Hamilton, M of Douglas and Clydesdale (1903–73)

M.P. (Con.) Renfrewshire East, 1930–40.
Lord Steward, 1940–60.

The Hamilton family papers are preserved at Lennoxlove, Haddington, East Lothian. Amongst these are papers relating to the 14th Duke, including press-cuttings albums.

HAMILTON, Marquess of, see ABERCORN, 3rd D of

HAMILTON OF DALZELL, 2nd B
Hon. Gavin George Hamilton (1872–1952)

Lord in Waiting, 1906–11.

A small collection of papers is retained by Lord Hamilton of Dalzell's nephew, the 3rd Baron, at Snowdenham House, Bramley, Surrey. It consists of a notebook and a small amount of correspondence concerning Lord Hamilton's career, chiefly for the period 1906–11.

HAMILTON, Hon. Charles William Baillie- (1900–39)

M.P. (Con.) Bath, 1929–31.

The present (12th) Earl of Haddington (brother) has no papers, and believes that they must have been destroyed.

HAMILTON, Lord Claud John (1843–1925)*

M.P. (Con.) Londonderry, 1865–8; King's Lynn, 1869–80; Liverpool, 1880–8; Kensington South, Jan 1910–18.
Junior Lord of the Treasury, 1868.

According to information available at the National Register of Archives, Lord Claud's papers were destroyed. The Abercorn family papers are in the Northern Ireland Public Record Office.

HAMILTON, Sir (Collingwood) George Clements, 1st Bt (1877–1947)

M.P. (Con.) Altrincham, 1913–23; Ilford, 1928–37.

Sir Patrick Hamilton, 2nd Bt, states that his father destroyed almost all his papers during his life and consequently only material of personal interest has survived.

HAMILTON, Lord George Francis (1854–1927)

M.P. (Con.) Middlesex, 1868–85; Ealing, 1885–1906.
Parliamentary Under-Secretary, India Office, 1874–8. Vice President of the Council, 1878–80. 1st Lord of the Admiralty, 1885–6, and 1886–92. Secretary of State for India, 1895–1903.

The papers at the India Office Library, and a further collection at the Bodleian Library's India Institute, are described by Hazlehurst and Woodland, p. 70. The papers of Hamilton's correspondents, including Hicks Beach, Lord Rendel, Lord Randolph Churchill, Lord Kitchener and Lord Hardinge, contain an assortment of his letters.

HAMILTON, Lord Malcolm Avendale Douglas- (1909–64)

M.P. (Con.) Inverness, 1950–4.

No relevant papers are retained at Lennoxlove, Haddington, East Lothian. Enquiries should be directed to Alasdair Douglas-Hamilton (son), Fountainhall Manse, Pencartland, East Lothian.

HAMILTON, Mary Agnes (d. 1966)

M.P. (Lab.) Blackburn, 1929–31.

All Mrs Hamilton's papers were destroyed after her death in accordance with instructions contained in her will. Some correspondence may be found in the Norman Angell collection at Ball State University.

HAMILTON, Sir Robert William (1867–1944)

M.P. (Lib.) Orkney and Shetland, 1922–35.
Parliamentary Under-Secretary, Colonial Office, 1931–2.

The Public Trustee acted as executor, but the files regarding Sir Robert have now been destroyed, and it was not possible to trace any members of the family.

HAMILTON, Lieutenant-Colonel Roland (1886–1953)

M.P. (Lab.) Sudbury, 1945–50.

Mr M. A. Stern, Critchfield, Old Bosham, nr Chichester, West Sussex, has certain papers, which include press cuttings, speeches, and the manuscript of an unpublished book, *Great Experiment*.

HAMILTON, William Winter (1917–)

M.P. (Lab.) Fife West, 1950–

Mr Hamilton has kept some records including a few constituency papers and research materials and drafts for his published works. These records have been promised to the National Library of Scotland.

HAMMERSLEY, Samuel Schofield (1892–1965)

M.P. (Con.) Stockport, 1925–35; Willesden East, 1938–45.

Approximately 53 box files and about a dozen bundles of Hammersley's papers are deposited in Manchester Public Library. The collection covers most of his activities but is mainly concerned with his business interests. The collection also contains most of Hammersley's correspondence relating to his tenure as Chairman of the Parliamentary Palestine Committee, 1943–5, and as executive Chairman of the Anglo-Israel Association, 1957–63. Two bundles of papers deal with Hammersley's work with the Ministry of Supply on tank warfare. Some of the files deal with the affairs of the Stockport Constitutional Club in the early 1920s. In addition there are five volumes of press cuttings, 1922–63.

HAMMOND, John (1842–1907)*

M.P. (Irish Nat.) Carlow, 1891–1907.

HANBURY, Sir Cecil (1871–1937)

M.P. (Con.) Dorset North, 1924–37.

Efforts to contact Sir Cecil's son, Lt.-Col. H. C. Hanbury, were unsuccessful.

HANBURY, Robert William (1845–1903)

M.P. (Con.) Tamworth, 1872–8; Staffordshire North, 1878–80; Preston, 1885–1903.
Financial Secretary, Treasury, 1895–1900. President of the Board of Agriculture and Fisheries, 1900–3.

Hazlehurst and Woodland, p. 70, located no papers.

HANCOCK, John George (1857–1940)

M.P. (Lab.) Mid-Derbyshire, 1909–18; (Co Lib.) Belper, 1918–23.

The persons and firm of solicitors mentioned in the will and Act of Probate could not be traced. The *Dictionary of Labour Biography*, Vol. II, pp. 159–61, mentions no papers, but refers to information provided by Mr E. Hancock (nephew), Lowdham, nr Nottingham. Mrs L. Walvin of Pinxton, Nottingham, provided one or two papers which refer to Hancock. Correspondence (1910, 1912–13) concerning relations with the Labour Party can be found at Transport House.

HANKEY, 1st B
Sir Maurice Pascal Alers Hankey (1877–1963)

Secretary, Committee of Imperial Defence, 1912–38; War Cabinet, 1916; Imperial War Cabinet, 1917–18; Cabinet, 1919–38; and Clerk of the Privy Council, 1923–38.
Minister without Portfolio, 1939–40. Chancellor of the Duchy of Lancaster, 1940–1. Paymaster-General, 1941–2.

A large collection of papers and diaries has been deposited with Churchill College, Cambridge. Another set of papers is available at the Public Record Office (Cab 63). Details are given by Hazlehurst and Woodland, pp. 70–1.

HANLEY, Denis Augustine (1903–   )

M.P. (Con.) Deptford, 1931–5.

HANNAH, Ian Campbell (1874–1944)

M.P. (Con.) Bilston, 1935–44.

HANNAN, William (1906–   )

M.P. (Lab.) Glasgow Maryhill, 1945–Feb 1974.
Junior Lord of the Treasury, 1946–51.

Mr Hannan regrets that he has kept no papers. Minute books of the Glasgow Maryhill C.L.P. are now with the Mitchell Library in Glasgow.

HANNON, Sir Patrick Joseph Henry (1874–1963)

M.P. (Con.) Birmingham Moseley, 1921–50.

Formerly housed in the Beaverbrook Library, the papers are now held in the House of Lords Record Office. The papers include some 118 boxes of material covering Hannon's work for the Navy League, the British Commonwealth Union, and his business activities, together with papers relating to his parliamentary career. Personal papers include diaries and notes for a book. Considerable correspondence between Lord Beaverbrook and Sir Patrick, 1930–63, may be found in the Beaverbrook papers, also at the House of Lords Record Office.

HANSON, Sir Charles Augustin, 1st Bt (1846–1922)

M.P. (Con.) Bodmin, 1916–22.

Sir John Hanson, Bt (grandson) has five volumes of press cuttings covering the period 1913–18. They are mainly reports of political speeches and newspaper comment from the local and national press.

HANWORTH, 1st Vt
Sir Ernest Murray Pollock, 1st Bt (1861–1936)

M.P. (Con.) Warwick and Leamington, Jan 1910–23.
Solicitor-General, 1919–22. Attorney-General, 1922.

The collection of papers in the Bodleian Library is described by Hazlehurst and Woodland, pp. 117–18.

HARBISON, Thomas James Stanislaus (1864–1930)*

M.P. (Irish Nat.) Tyrone East, 1918; Tyrone N.E., 1918–22; Fermanagh and Tyrone, 1922–4, 1929–30.

Mrs M. E. Donaghy (daughter) has only some interesting press cuttings relating to her father's career.

HARBORD, Sir Arthur (1865–1941)

M.P. (Lib.) Great Yarmouth, 1922–4, 1929–31; (Lib.Nat.) 1931–41.

Sir Arthur's solicitors, Chamberlain, Talbot & Bracey of Great Yarmouth, have no information regarding papers or the whereabouts of the surviving family.

HARCOURT, 1st Vt
Lewis Harcourt (1863–1922)

M.P. (Lib.) Rossendale, 1904–16.
1st Commissioner of Works, 1905–10, and 1915–16. Secretary of State for the Colonies, 1910–15.

The large collection of papers at the Bodleian Library is described by Hazlehurst and Woodland, p. 71.

HARCOURT, Robert Vernon (1878–1962)

M.P. (Lib.) Montrose Burghs, 1908–18.

Family papers are held in the Bodleian Library, Oxford. These include letters from R. V. Harcourt to his brother Lewis (c. 1887–1919), and to his father. Mrs Ian Johnston (daughter) knows of no further papers.

HARCOURT, Sir William George Granville Venables Vernon (1827–1904)

M.P. (Lib.) Oxford, 1868–80; Derby, 1880–95; Monmouthshire West, 1895–1904. Solicitor-General, 1874. Secretary of State for Home Affairs, 1880–5. Chancellor of the Exchequer, 1886 and 1892–5.

The large collection of papers (NRA 3679) is held in the Bodleian Library, Oxford. The material comprises some 35 boxes of political correspondence and Cabinet papers (c. 1864–1904). Other Harcourt papers are included in the collections of several of his correspondents.

HARDEN, Major James Richard Edwards (1916–   )*

M.P. (Ulster Un.) Armagh, 1948–54.

Major Harden says he has kept no records whatsoever relating to his parliamentary career.

HARDIE, Agnes Agnew (d. 1951)

M.P. (Lab.) Glasgow Springburn, 1937–45.

See Hardie, G.D.B.C.

HARDIE, David (d. 1939)

M.P. (Lab.) Rutherglen, May-Oct 1931.

HARDIE, George Downie Blyth Crookston (d. 1937)

M.P. (Lab.) Glasgow Springburn, 1922–31, 1935–7.

The widow of J. C. Forman, who succeeded George Hardie and his wife, Agnes, as member for Glasgow Springburn, knows of no papers.

HARDIE, James Keir (1856–1915)

M.P. (Ind.Lab.) West Ham South, 1892–5; (Lab.) Merthyr Tydfil, 1900–15.

Many papers relating to Keir Hardie have survived. The main collection is housed with the Emrys Hughes papers in the National Library of Scotland. It includes a small number of letters, cards and papers, some of minor political interest, 1884–1914; notes on a tour of India, 1907; correspondence and press cuttings on the suffragette movement; political press cuttings; photographs; and a letter-book, 1879–90. The National Library also has minutes (c. 1911), written by Keir Hardie, of the provisional committee for publication of the *Daily Herald*. Other letters from Keir Hardie can be found in the A. M. Simons collection of the Sate Historical Society of Wisconsin (NU Cat 62–2956) and in the Charlotte Gilman papers at Radcliffe College (NU Cat 73–853). The Independent Labour Party archive (*Sources*, Vol. 1, pp. 109–11) is rich in Keir Hardie material including correspondence with his agent at Merthyr.

HARDMAN, David Rennie (1901–   )

M.P. (Lab.) Darlington, 1945–51.
Parliamentary Secretary, Ministry of Education, 1945–51.

Mr Hardman states that he has kept no political papers relevant to his public career except private correspondence. He is using this material to prepare an autobiographical account.

HARDWICKE, 6th E of
Albert Edward Philip Henry Yorke, Vt Royston (1867–1904)

Parliamentary Under-Secretary, India Office, 1900–2, 1903–4; War Office, 1902–3.

HARDY, Edward Arthur (1884–1960)

M.P. (Lab.) Salford South, 1945–50; Salford East, 1950–5.

Mr E. A. Hardy (son), 30 Monkstone Crescent, Tynemouth, North Shields, Tyne and Wear NE30 2QE, states that he has in his care only a small collection of newspaper cuttings, some election addresses, and photographs. A cuttings book for 1933–4 covers the period when Mr and Mrs Hardy were Mayor and Mayoress of Salford. Mr Hardy's sister has their father's diary for 1959.

HARDY, George Alexander (1851–1920)

M.P. (Lib.) Stowmarket, 1906–Jan 1910.

Information available in the will and Act of Probate was insufficient to trace executors or members of the family.

HARDY, Laurence (1854–1933)

M.P. (Con.) Ashford, 1892–1918.

There is a diary in the possession of Major Arthur Hardy (son). This is not available for inspection.

HARDY, Hon. William Hepburn Cozens-, see COZENS-HARDY, 2nd B

HARE, Hon. John Hugh, see BLAKENHAM, 1st Vt

HARE, Sir Thomas Leigh, 1st Bt (1859–1941)

M.P. (Con.) Norfolk South West, 1892–1906.

Major G. C. Howard (grandson) and Major Sir Ralph L. Hare, Bt (nephew) have no papers of Sir Thomas Hare. The Hare family papers at the Norfolk Record Office include only one or two formal documents relating to Sir Thomas.

HARGREAVES, Alfred (1899–   )

M.P. (Lab.) Carlisle, 1950–5.

Mr Hargreaves says he has kept no personal papers relating to his career in the Labour movement.

HARLAND, Albert (1869–1957)

M.P. (Con.) Sheffield Ecclesall, 1923–9.

A niece, Mrs J. E. Howard, wife of Rev. S. R. Howard, of Cheltenham, could not be contacted.

HARLAND, Henry Pierson (1876–1945)*

M.P. (Ulster Un.) Belfast East, 1939–45.

Harland & Wolfe Ltd's Public Affairs Manager could provide no information regarding H. P. Harland (at one time a director of the company) or his papers.

HARLECH, 3rd B
Hon. George Ralph Charles Ormsby-Gore (1855–1938)

M.P. (Con.) Oswestry, 1901–4.

Enquiries should be directed to the present (5th) Lord Harlech.

HARLECH, 4th B
William George Arthur Ormsby-Gore (1885–1964)

M.P. (Con.) Denbigh, Jan 1910–18; Stafford, 1918–38.
Parliamentary Under-Secretary of State, Colonial Office, 1922–4 and 1924–9. Postmaster General, 1931. 1st Commissioner of Works, 1931–6. Secretary of State for the Colonies, 1936–8.

Hazlehurst and Woodland, pp. 62–3, located no papers. Correspondence with Sir Granville Orde Browne, especially concerning African labour, is in the Orde Browne collection, and other Harlech correspondence can be found in the Creech Jones and Coryndon collections at Rhodes House Library, Oxford.

HARLECH, 5th B
Hon. William David Ormsby-Gore (1918–   )

M.P. (Con.) Oswestry, 1950–61.
Parliamentary Under-Secretary, Foreign Office, 1956–7. Minister of State, Foreign Office, 1957–61. Ambassador, United States, 1961–5.

HARMAR-NICHOLLS, Baron
Sir Harmar Nicholls, 1st Bt (1912–   )

M.P. (Con.) Peterborough, 1950–Oct 1974.
Parliamentary Secretary, Ministry of Agriculture, Fisheries and Food, 1955–7; Ministry of Works, 1957–60.

HARMSWORTH, 1st B
Cecil Bisshopp Harmsworth (1869–1948)

M.P. (Lib.) Droitwich, 1906–Jan 1910; Luton, 1911–22.
Parliamentary Under-Secretary, Home Office, 1915. Member, Prime Minister's Secretariat, 1917–19. Parliamentary Under-Secretary, Foreign Office, 1919–22; and acting Minister of Blockade, 1919.

Papers survive with the present (2nd) Lord Harmsworth, Lime Lodge, Egham, Surrey. Details are not available. One box of papers kept by Harmsworth when a member of the Superior Council of the Blockade in Paris, 1919, is available in the Public Record Office (FO 800/250). A few further Harmsworth papers survive in the Lothian collection at the National Library of Scotland and in the records of Sir Horace Plunkett.

HARMSWORTH, Hon. Esmond Cecil, see ROTHERMERE, 2nd Vt

HARMSWORTH, Sir Robert Leicester, 1st Bt (1870–1937)

M.P. (Lib.) Caithness, 1900–18; Caithness and Sutherland, 1918–22.

There are a number of typewritten copies of Sir Robert's diaries in the care of his son, Sir Geoffrey Harmsworth, Bt, White Cottage, Tealby, Lincoln.

HARNEY, Edward Augustine St Aubyn (1871–1929)

M.P. (Lib.) South Shields, 1922–9.

The project failed to trace persons mentioned in the will and Act of Probate.

HARRINGTON, Timothy Charles (1851–1910)*

M.P. (Irish Nat.) Westmeath, 1883–5; Dublin Harbour, 1885–June 1910.

There is a collection of papers in the National Library of Ireland (Mss 8576, 8577, 5385 and 8931). A large volume of letters (1881–1909) deal with political affairs, and further correspondence includes letters (1881–1910) from C. S. Parnell, J. Dillon, J. Redmond, M. Davitt and Archbishop Croke. There are also a number of telegrams to headquarters by members of the Irish Parliamentary Party (1886, 1890, 1891 and 1896), and a series of documents covering Harrington's legal work.

HARRIS, 4th B
Hon. George Robert Canning Harris (1851–1932)

Parliamentary Under-Secretary, India Office, 1885–6; War Office, 1886–9. Governor of Bombay, 1890–5. Lord in Waiting, 1895–1900.

Lord Harris's letters, when Governor of Bombay, are held in the India Office Library. Other correspondence can be found in the collections of Lord Kimberley, Lord Randolph Churchill, Viscount Wolseley and Lord Hardinge of Penshurst.

HARRIS, Frederick Leverton (1864–1926)

M.P. (Con.) Tynemouth, 1900–6; Stepney, 1907–Dec 1910; Worcestershire East, 1914–18.

Mr P. E. C. Harris (nephew), Flat 41, Kingston House North, London SW7 1LW, has only a very small file of his uncle's correspondence, etc., mostly of a private nature. There are 33 letters to Bonar Law in the House of Lords Record Office.

HARRIS, Dr Frederick Rutherford (1856–1920)

M.P. (Con.) Monmouth, 1900–1; Dulwich, 1903–6.
Career in South Africa.

There was no trace of persons mentioned in the will and Act of Probate. Letters and telegrams from Harris occur throughout the Cecil Rhodes Collection at Rhodes House Library, Oxford.

HARRIS, Frederic Walter (1915–)

M.P. (Con.) Croydon North, 1948–55; Croydon North West, 1955–70.

HARRIS, Sir Henry Percy (1856–1941)

M.P. (Con.) Paddington South, Jan 1910–22.

The family know of no papers.

HARRIS, Henry Wilson (1883–1955)

M.P. (Ind.) Cambridge University, 1945–50.

Messrs Beale & Co., solicitors to the executors, know of no papers.

HARRIS, Sir John Hobbis (1874–1940)

M.P. (Lib.) Hackney North, 1923–4.
Missionary, traveller and author.

A collection of papers, mainly relating to the Congo and the proposed reforms of 1908, and an incomplete autobiography and some press cuttings, are held in the Library of Rhodes House, Oxford.

HARRIS, Sir Percy Alfred (1876–1952)

M.P. (Lib.) Harborough, 1916–18; Bethnal Green South West, 1922–45.
Liberal Party Chief Whip, 1935–45, and Deputy Leader, 1940–5.

A collection of papers, formerly in the care of Mr T. N. R. Harris, c/o Bing, Harris & Co. Limited, Canberra House, 313 Regent Street, London W1, has been placed with the House of Lords Record Office.

HARRIS, Richard Reader (1913–)

M.P. (Con.) Heston and Isleworth, 1950–70.

HARRISON, Francis Capel (1863–1938)

Indian Civil Service.
M.P. (Con.) Kennington, 1922–3.

Harrison's brother and chief beneficiary of his estate was living out of Britain at the time of F. C. Harrison's death. The solicitors who dealt with the estate have lost contact with the family.

HARRISON, Gerald Joseph Cuthbert (1895–1954)

M.P. (Con.) Bodmin, 1924–9.

Major A. J. R. Harrison, Wreay Hall, Wreay, nr Carlisle, states that his father left a collection of papers, cuttings and other documents relating to his parliamentary career. These remain with Major Harrison's sister-in-law in Galway.

HARRISON, James (1899–1959)

M.P. (Lab.) Nottingham East, 1945–55; Nottingham North, 1955–9.

David E. Martin (*Dictionary of Labour Biography*, Vol. II, pp. 171–2) found no papers with Harrison's surviving family.

HARROWBY, 6th E of
Dudley Ryder, Vt Sandon (1892–)

M.P. (Con.) Shrewsbury, 1922–3; 1924–9.

The family papers (the Ryder Papers, some 1500 volumes) are preserved by the Harrowby Mss Trust, Sandon Hall, nr Stafford, and have largely been calendared by full-time archivists. There is no general availability of the papers beyond those calendared (i.e. after 1900), but specific queries from accredited scholars may be answered at the Trustees' discretion.

HARTINGTON, M of, see DEVONSHIRE, 10th D of

HARTLAND, Sir Frederick Dixon Dixon-, 1st Bt (1832–1909)

M.P. (Con.) Evesham, 1880–5; Uxbridge, 1885–1909.

No members of the family were traced. The greatnephew of Charles Scott-Chad, who acted as executor to Dixon-Hartland, knew of no papers. Records of the Uxbridge Conservative Association are deposited in the Greater London Record Office (Middlesex Records).

HARTLAND, George Albert (1884–1944)

M.P. (Con.) Norwich, 1931–5.

HARTSHORN, Vernon (1872–1931)

M.P. (Lab.) Ogmore, 1918–31.
Postmaster General, 1924. Lord Privy Seal, 1930–1.

According to Hazlehurst and Woodland, p. 73, no private papers survive other than a few press cuttings. The Labour Party archive includes only a few papers relating to Hartshorn. His career is outlined in the *Dictionary of Labour Biography*, Vol. I, pp. 150–2.

HARVEY OF PRESTBURY, Baron
Sir Arthur Vere Harvey (1906–)

Royal Air Force career.
M.P. (Con.) Macclesfield, 1945–71.

Lord Harvey states that he has not retained many papers during his public career, but he has kept a series of personal diaries which would not be appropriate for public use.

HARVEY, (Alexander) Gordon Cummins (1858–1922)

M.P. (Lib.) Rochdale, 1906–18.

Mr A. E. C. Harvey (nephew), c/o C. H. Hill (Market) Ltd, Fruit and Vegetable Market, Albert Crescent, Bristol, has certain papers.

HARVEY, Sir (Charles) Malcolm Barclay- (1890–1969)

M.P. (Con.) Kincardineshire and Aberdeenshire West, 1923–9, 1931–9.
Governor of South Australia, 1939–44.

Mr J. M. M. Humphrey (grandson), a trustee of the estate, believes that Sir Malcolm's papers were destroyed. Sir Malcolm's second wife knows of no surviving papers.

HARVEY, Sir George (1870–1939)

M.P. (Con.) Kennington, 1924–9 and 1931–9.

Messrs McKenna & Co., solicitors of 12 Whitehall, London SW1A 2DZ, who were the trustees of Sir George Harvey's family settlement, secured no information from Mr Michael Harvey (grandson).

HARVEY, Ian Douglas (1914–)

M.P. (Con.) Harrow East, 1950–8.
Parliamentary Secretary, Ministry of Supply, 1956–7. Joint Parliamentary Under-Secretary, Foreign Office, 1957–8.

Mr Harvey has a number of papers. Details are not available.

HARVEY, Major Sir Samuel Emile (1885–1959)

M.P. (Con.) Totnes, 1922–3, 1924–35.

No contact with Harvey's daughter, details of whom are given in *Burke's Landed Gentry*, was established.

HARVEY, Thomas Edmund (1875–1955)

M.P. (Lib.) Leeds West, Jan 1910–18, Dewsbury, 1923–4; (Ind. Progressive) Combined English Universities, 1937–45.
Author.

A collection of papers has survived. Enquiries should be directed to the Librarian at Friends House.

HARVEY, William Edwin (1852–1914)

M.P. (Lib.) Derbyshire North East, 1907–14.

The *Dictionary of Labour Biography*, Vol. I, pp. 152–3, refers to no private papers. The firm of chartered accountants mentioned in the will knows of no papers. The National Union of Mineworkers (Saltergate, Chesterfield, Derbyshire) has minutes of the Derbyshire Miners' Association, in which Harvey was heavily involved. Correspondence covering his relations with the Labour Party, and including letters from W. E. Harvey (1910–13) are included in the Labour Party archive.

HARVINGTON, Baron
Sir Robert Grant Grant-Ferris (1907–)

M.P. (Con.) St Pancras North, 1937–45; Nantwich, 1955–Feb 1974.
Chairman of Ways and Means, and Deputy Speaker, House of Commons, 1970–4.

HARWOOD, George (1845–1912)

M.P. (Lib.) Bolton, 1895–1912.

Mrs Ruth Harris (daughter) has retained a collection of papers at her home, Swerford Park, Oxfordshire. This includes several family letters, three chapters of an unpublished autobiography, press cuttings, and election addresses, 1906–10. The collection will in due course be deposited in Lancashire Record Office.

HASLAM, Sir Alfred Seale (1844–1927)

M.P. (Lib.Un.) Newcastle-under-Lyme, 1900–6.

Mrs N. H. Haslam (daughter-in-law) knows of no papers concerning his political activities. No other members of the family could be traced.

HASLAM, Henry Cobden (1870–1948)

M.P. (Con.) Horncastle, 1924–45.

Five volumes of press cuttings (1928–35) have been placed by Mrs S. L. Haslam (daughter-in-law) in the Lincolnshire Archives Office (ref. MISC. DEP. 276). No other collection appears to have survived.

HASLAM, James (1842–1913)

M.P. (Lib.-Lab., later Lab.) Chesterfield, 1906–13.

No members of the family could be traced. The *Dictionary of Labour Biography*, Vol. I, pp. 153–5, refers to no private papers but cites useful material in the minutes of the Derbyshire Miners Association (National Union of Mineworkers, Saltergate, Chesterfield).

HASLAM, Sir John (1878–1940)

M.P. (Con.) Bolton, 1931–40.

Mr J. Rigg, 11 Bleasdale Road, Smithills, Bolton, has some interesting press cuttings. Messrs Denton, Hall & Burgin, solicitors to the executors, know of no papers.

HASLAM, Lewis (1856–1922)

M.P. (Lib.) Monmouth Boroughs, 1906–18; Newport, 1918–22.

Haslam's solicitors, Halsey, Lightly & Hemsley (in amalgamation with Garrard Wolfe & Co.), know of no papers. There was no trace of persons mentioned in the will. Haslam's correspondence (1912–13) concerning agricultural co-operation survives in the papers of Sir Horace Plunkett.

HASLETT, Sir James Horner (1832–1905)*

M.P. (Con.) Belfast West, 1885–6; Belfast North, 1896–1905.

HASTINGS, Sir Patrick Gardiner (1880–1952)

M.P. (Lab.) Wallsend, 1922–6.
Attorney-General, 1924.

Hazlehurst and Woodland, p. 73, found no papers.

HASTINGS, Somerville (1878–1967)

M.P. (Lab.) Reading, 1923–4 and 1929–31; (Lab.) Barking, 1945–59.

A microtext of the papers is held in the library of Hull University. The material consists of (A) general papers, including correspondence (1929–59) and notebooks of visits to Romania and Yugoslavia (1947 and 1950); (B) biographical papers, notes, photographs and press cuttings; (C) genealogical papers, including letters from Hastings in Heidelberg and Berlin to his parents (1905–6); (D) correspondence and papers relating to the preservation of Kingwood Common, nr Henley-on-Thames. The papers of the Socialist Medical Association, with which Hastings was closely involved, are described in *Sources,* Vol. 1, pp. 240–1.

HATCH, Sir Ernest Frederic George, 1st Bt (1859–1927)

M.P. (Con.) Manchester Gorton, 1895–1906.

Messrs Hatch, Mansfield & Company, of which Sir Ernest was co-founder, know of no papers and no other contact was traced.

HAUGHTON, Col. Samuel Gilmor (1889–1959)*

M.P. (Ulster Un.) Co. Antrim, 1945–50.

Messrs Frazer & Haughton Ltd, of Ballymena, Co. Antrim (the firm of which Col. Haughton was managing director) provided no information, and no other contacts were traced.

HAVERSHAM, 1st B
Sir Arthur Divett Hayter, 1st Bt (1835–1917)

M.P. (Lib.) Wells, 1865–8; Bath, 1873–85; Walsall, 1893–5 and 1900–5.
Junior Lord of the Treasury, 1880. Financial Secretary, War Office, 1881–5.

Captain H. M. P. de Lisle, whose father was a greatnephew and executor to Lady Haversham, states that the estate passed to a Major Rickman. Captain de Lisle knows of no papers.

HAWKE, Sir John Anthony (1869–1941)

M.P. (Con.) St Ives, 1922–3 and 1924–8.

Lady Hawke (daughter-in-law) knows of no papers.

HAWKESBURY, 1st B, see LIVERPOOL

HAWORTH, Sir Arthur Adlington, 1st Bt (1865–1944)

M.P. (Lib.) Manchester South, 1906–12.
Junior Lord of the Treasury, 1912.

Dr Cameron Hazlehurst found that neither the present baronet, Sir A. G. Haworth, nor his sister have any papers relating to their father. Manchester Central Library has a few papers of the Manchester South Liberal Association, which include one or two documents relating to Haworth.

HAWORTH, James (1896–   )

M.P. (Lab.) Liverpool Walton, 1945–50.

HAY, Hon. Claude George Drummond (1862–1920)

M.P. (Con.) Hoxton, 1900–Jan 1910.

The present (15th) Earl of Kinnoull, Sir Iain Moncrieffe of that Ilk, Bt, and other members of the family knew of no papers.

HAY, John Albert (1919–   )

M.P. (Con.) Henley, 1950–Feb 1974.
Parliamentary Secretary, Ministry of Transport, 1959–63. Civil Lord of the Admiralty, 1963–4. Parliamentary Under-Secretary, Ministry of Defence (Royal Navy), 1964.

HAY, Captain John Primrose (1878–1949)

M.P. (Lab.) Glasgow Cathcart, 1922–3.

HAY, Thomas William (1882–1956)

M.P. (Con.) Norfolk South, 1922–3.

The present (21st) Earl of Morton, Hay's nephew and executor of his will, knows of no papers.

HAYCOCK, Alexander Wilkinson (1882–1970)

M.P. (Lab.) Salford West, 1923–4 and 1929–31.

The editors of the *Dictionary of Labour Biography* were unable to contact the executors. Minute books of the Salford City Labour Party (1920–61) are extant (*Sources*, Vol. 1, p. 160).

HAYDAY, Arthur (1869–1956)

M.P. (Lab.) Nottingham West, 1918–31 and 1935–45.

Sir Frederick Hayday says that shortly before his death his father destroyed papers relating to his career.

HAYDEN, John Patrick (1863–1954)*

M.P. (Irish Nat.) Roscommon South, 1897–1918.

Hayden was editor and proprietor of the *Westmeath Examiner*. No information was secured.

HAYES, John*

M.P. (Sinn Fein) Cork Co. West, 1918–22.

HAYES, John Henry (1889–1941)

M.P. (Lab.) Liverpool Edge Hill, 1923–31.
Vice Chamberlain, H.M. Household, 1929–31.

It was not possible to contact persons mentioned in the letters of administration.

HAYES, Dr Richard*

M.P. (Sinn Fein) Limerick East, 1918–22.

HAYMAN, Frank Harold (1894–1966)

M.P. (Lab.) Falmouth and Camborne, 1950–66.
Parliamentary Private Secretary to Leader of the Opposition, 1959–63.

After extensive correspondence with Hayman's solicitors, with the Midland Bank Executor & Trustee Co. (Plymouth), and with the solicitors who acted for the late Mrs A. V. Hayman, it was determined that no papers of any description relating to F. H. Hayman's parliamentary or political career have survived.

HAYNE, Charles Hayne Seale- (1833–1903)

M.P. (Lib.) Mid Devon, 1885–1903.

Sir John Seale, Bt, a distant relation of Charles Seale-Hayne, states that his effects were sold by auction after his death and that he knows of no surviving papers. Seale-Hayne's sole surviving executor, the Viscount Lambert, established an agricultural college, the Seale-Hayne Agricultural College. The Librarian knows of no surviving papers. Certain correspondence exists in the papers of Lord Rendel at the National Library of Wales.

HAYTER, Sir Arthur Divett, see HAVERSHAM, 1st B

HAYWARD, Evan (1876–1958)

M.P. (Lib.) Durham S.E., Jan 1910–18; Seaham, 1918–22.

There are no private papers relating to Evan Hayward's career in the possession of his grand-daughter, Mrs P. Craig, Pond House, Bishops Down Park Road, Tunbridge Wells, Kent. There are, however, a few election addresses and a copy of the *Ealing Liberal Magazine* (Feb 1914) and a memorandum on Army Liaison (with the munitions workers) dated 1917.

HAZEL, Alfred Ernest William (1869–1944)

M.P. (Lib.) West Bromwich, 1906–Jan 1910.

There are five scrapbooks concerning municipal elections (1908–13) at the West Bromwich public library.

HAZLETON, Richard (1880–1943)*

M.P. (Irish Nat.) Galway North, 1906–18. (Also elected for Louth North, Dec 1910, but unseated on petition, 1911.)

HEAD, 1st Vt
Antony Henry Head (1906–   )

Assistant Secretary, Committee of Imperial Defence, 1940–1.
M.P. (Con.) Carshalton, 1945–60.
Secretary of State for War, 1951–6. Minister of Defence, 1956–7.
High Commissioner, Nigeria, 1960–3; Malaysia, 1963–6.

HEADLAM, Sir Cuthbert Morley, 1st Bt (1876–1964)

M.P. (Con.) Barnard Castle, 1924–9, 1931–5; Newcastle North, 1940–52.
Parliamentary and Financial Secretary, Admiralty, 1926–9. Parliamentary Secretary, Pensions, 1931–2; Transport, 1932–4.

Papers are deposited in Durham Record Office, and include 46 volumes of diaries, 1890, 1895–7, 1899, 1902–4, 1910–15, 1919–45, 1947–51; a small amount of political correspondence, 1896–1962; and a collection of letters from Headlam to his wife, 1914–19. Access to certain groups of these papers is restricted.

HEALD, Sir Lionel Frederick (1897–   )

M.P. (Con.) Chertsey, 1950–70.
Attorney-General, 1951–4.

HEALY, Cahir (1877–1970)*

M.P. (Irish Nat.) Fermanagh and Tyrone, 1922–4, 1931–5; (Rep. and Anti-Partition) Fermanagh and Tyrone South, 1950–5.

An unsorted, uncatalogued and as yet incomplete collection of the papers (correspondence, press cuttings, speeches and articles) of Cahir Healy, 1924–1967, is deposited in the Northern Ireland Public Record Office (ref D 2991).

HEALY, Maurice (1859–1923)*

M.P. (Irish Nat.) Cork City, 1885–1900, 1909–Jan 1910, Dec 1910–18; Co. Cork N.E., Jan–Dec 1910.

There are two letters (1910) from Healy in the papers of Sir Horace Plunkett. Maurice Healy was the younger brother of T. M. Healy.

HEALY, Timothy Michael (1855–1931)*

M.P. (Irish Nat.) Wexford, 1880–3; Co. Monaghan, 1883–5; Londonderry South, 1885–6; Longford North, 1887–92; Louth North, 1892–Jan 1910; and Co. Cork N.E., 1911–18.
Governor-General, Irish Free State, 1922–8.

University College Dublin, has a few of Healy's papers. The papers contain much family correspondence, mainly of a personal nature but also referring to political issues (1875–1930); correspondence with fellow-politicians, including Gladstone and Asquith (1880–1920); and other correspondence (1922–8). Correspondence of T. M. Healy is included in the William O'Brien collection at the National Library of Ireland and in the Asquith, A. J. Balfour and Blumenfeld collections. Healy gave to Lord Beaverbrook proofs of his autobiography *Letters and Leaders of my Day*, which was published in 1928. The proofs are marked with Healy's own corrections, fill four boxes and are now deposited in the House of Lords Record Office.

HEARN, Michael Lewis (b. 1866)*

M.P. (Irish Nat.) Dublin Co. South, 1917–18.

HEATH, Colonel Arthur Howard (1856–1930)

M.P. (Con.) Hanley, 1900–6; Leek, Jan–Dec 1910.

Mr G. N. Bell (Messrs Knight & Sons, solicitors of Newcastle-under-Lyme), who was one of the trustees of Colonel Heath's will, knows of no papers.

HEATH, Edward Richard George (1916–)

M.P. (Con.) Bexley, 1950–Feb 74; Bexley Sidcup, Feb 1974–
Junior Lord of the Treasury, 1951; Joint Deputy Chief Whip, 1952; Deputy Chief Whip, 1953–5. Parliamentary Secretary, Treasury and Chief Whip, 1955–9. Minister of Labour, 1959–60. Lord Privy Seal, 1960–3. Secretary of State for Industry, Trade, Regional Development, and President of the Board of Trade, 1963–4. Prime Minister, 1970–4.

Mr Heath states that it is not his practice to indicate the nature of the papers he has kept.

HEATH, Sir James, 1st Bt (1852–1942)

M.P. (Con.) Staffordshire N.W., 1892–1906.

It was not possible to contact Lady Heath, Sir James's widow.

HEATON, Sir John Henniker, 1st Bt (1848–1914)

Postal reformer.
M.P. (Con.) Canterbury, 1885–Dec 1910.

Mrs L. Buckley (granddaughter), Sheepcote, Bartestree, Hereford, writes that her mother, Mrs Rose Porter, wrote *The Life and Letters of Sir John Henniker Heaton, Bt.* (1916). Letters to Sir John from correspondents such as Marconi, Cecil Rhodes and Lord Randolph Churchill, memoirs, and photographs, are used in the book. However, these papers have not survived, apart from an album of press cuttings and cartoons. The Samuel papers (House of Lords Record Office) include Sir John's letters (1912–14) concerning the Marconi contract and postal affairs, and personal and literary correspondence (1893–1909) is included in the papers of Douglas Sladen (NRA 14252).

HEDGES, Alfred Paget (1867–1929)

M.P. (Lib.) Tonbridge, 1906–Jan 1910.

Alfred Hedges had four sons, none of whom is still alive. Hedges's nephew knows of no papers extant among the family and believes that it is unlikely that any papers relating to his parliamentary career have survived.

HEILGERS, Frank Frederick Alexander (1892–1944)

M.P. (Con.) Bury St Edmunds, 1931–44.

HELDER, Sir Augustus (1827–1906)

M.P. (Con.) Whitehaven, 1895–1906.

Mrs K. R. Helder, The Garden Flat, 18 Tregunter Road, London SW10, has a leather-bound book of press cuttings and obituary notices.

HELME, Sir Norval Watson (1849–1932)

M.P. (Lib.) Lancaster, 1900–18.

Sir Norval left two sons, T. W. and J. Helme, whom it has not been possible to trace. Clark

Oglethorpe & Sons, solicitors of Lancaster, acted in the estate.

HELMORE, Hon. Air Commodore William (1894–1964)

Technical Adviser, Ministry of Aircraft Production, 1941–5. Member of Brabazon Committee on Civil Aviation, 1943–5, etc.
M.P. (Con.) Watford, 1943–5.

There was no contact with Mr Patrick Helmore (son), 59 Campden Hill Road, London W8.

HELMSLEY, Vt, see FEVERSHAM

HEMINGFORD, 1st B
Sir Dennis Henry Herbert (1869–1947)

M.P. (Con.) Watford, 1918–43.
Chairman of Ways and Means and Deputy Speaker, 1931–43.

The present Lord Hemingford, son of the 1st Baron, has two dozen volumes of press cuttings from the local and national press, 1917–47.

HEMMERDE, Edward George (1871–1948)

M.P. (Lib.) Denbigh East, 1906–Dec 1910; Norfolk North West, 1912–18; (Lab.) Crewe, 1922–4.

The solicitors, M. A. Jacobs & Sons, have no papers. Efforts to trace Hemmerde's daughter and chief beneficiary of his estate were unsuccessful.

HEMPHILL, 1st B
Sir Charles Hare Hemphill (1821–1908)*

M.P. (Lib.) Tyrone North, 1895–1906.
Solicitor-General for Ireland, 1892–5.

HENDERSON, 1st B
William Watson Henderson (1891–   )

M.P. (Lab.) Enfield, 1923–4 and 1929–31.
Lord in Waiting, 1945–8.
Parliamentary Under-Secretary, Foreign Office, 1948–51.

Lord Henderson states that he never kept a diary, and when leaving government office he took away no papers. He may have a very few private papers, but he has destroyed most of his records.

HENDERSON OF ARDWICK, 1st B
Joseph Henderson (1884–1950)

M.P. (Lab.) Manchester Ardwick, Jun–Oct 1931 and 1935–50.
Junior Lord of the Treasury, 1945–50.

It was not possible to contact Lord Henderson's daughter, Hon. Mrs G. T. Irwin of Coventry.

HENDERSON, Sir Alexander, see FARINGDON, 1st B

HENDERSON, Arthur, see ROWLEY, Baron

HENDERSON, Arthur (1863–1935)

M.P. (Lab.) Barnard Castle, 1903–18; Widnes, 1919–22; Newcastle East, 1923; Burnley, 1924–31; Clay Cross, 1933–5.
President of the Board of Education, 1915–16. Paymaster-General, 1916. Minister without Portfolio, 1916–17. Secretary of State for Home Affairs, 1924; Foreign Affairs, 1929–31.

Hazlehurst and Woodland, pp. 73–4, describe the Henderson papers in the Labour Party archives at Transport House, and the small Private Office collection at the Public Record Office (FO 800/280–4).

HENDERSON, Hon. Harold Greenwood (1875–1922)

M.P. (Con.) Abingdon, Jan 1910–16.

Lord Faringdon, son of Hon. H. G. Henderson, knows of no papers relating to his father's career. Henderson Administration Ltd were also unable to supply any information.

HENDERSON, Sir John (1888–   )

M.P. (Con.) Glasgow Cathcart, 1946–64.

HENDERSON, Sir John Craik (1890–1971)

M.P. (Con.) Leeds N.E., 1940–5.

Messrs Simpson Henderson & Co., the firm of solicitors in which Sir John was a partner, destroyed the parliamentary files in their possession after his death. It would appear from information supplied by Sir John before his death that these were the only papers he had retained.

HENDERSON, John McDonald (1846–1922)

M.P. (Lib.) Aberdeenshire West, 1906–18.

Information available in the will and Act of Probate was insufficient to trace papers or family.

HENDERSON, Captain Robert Ronald (1876–1932)

M.P. (Con.) Henley, 1924–32.

The executry papers of R. R. Henderson, mainly legal documents concerning the sale of estates, are in the collection of MacDonald, Jameson & Morris (NRA 14670, p. 1). Contact was not established with Henderson's son, Mr J. K. Henderson of Taunton.

HENDERSON, Thomas (1867–1960)

M.P. (Lab.-Co-op) Glasgow Tradeston, 1922–31 and 1935–45.
Comptroller of H.M. Household, 1929–31.

HENDERSON, Sir Thomas (1874–1951)

M.P. (Co.Lib.) Roxburgh and Selkirk, 1922–3.

Sir James Henderson (son), 4 Merchiston Crescent, Edinburgh EH10 5AN, had a scrapbook containing a number of cuttings and other papers connected with his father's parliamentary career. This appears to have been lost.

HENDERSON, Lieutenant-Colonel Sir Vivian Leonard (1884–1965)

M.P. (Con.) Glasgow Tradeston, 1918–22; Bootle, 1924–9; Chelmsford, 1931–5.
Parliamentary Under-Secretary, Home Office, and Representative of Office of Works in House

of Commons, 1927–9.

Messrs Fladgate & Co., solicitors and executors to Sir Vivian, have lost contact with his widow. According to the will, papers and manuscripts were left to Lady Henderson.

HENEAGE, Lieutenant-Colonel Sir Arthur Pelham (1881–1971)

M.P. (Con.) Louth, 1924–45.

The family papers at the Lincolnshire Archives Office include no papers of Sir Arthur. Enquiries should be directed to Lady Heneage, Walesby Hall, Market Rasen, Lincs.

HENN, Sir Sydney Herbert Holcroft (1861–1936)

M.P. (Con.) Blackburn, 1922–9.

A collection of correspondence and memoranda (1922–36), in three boxes, is held at Rhodes House Library Oxford. These papers relate mainly to the Joint East Africa Board and the affairs of East Africa.

HENNESSY, Sir George Richard James, 1st Bt, see WINDLESHAM, 1st B

HENRY, Sir Charles Solomon, 1st Bt (1860–1919)

M.P. (Lib.) Wellington, 1906–18; The Wrekin, 1918–19.

No papers were found by Dr Hazlehurst in connection with his research for *Politicians at War*, (1971).

HENRY, Sir Denis Stanislaus, 1st Bt (1864–1925)*

M.P. (Con.) Londonderry County South, 1916–21.
Solicitor-General, Ireland, 1918–19. Attorney-General, Ireland, 1919–21. Lord Chief Justice of Northern Ireland, 1921–5.

Sir J. H. Henry, Bt (son), states that no papers survive. His father kept no official documents in his possession, and no diary or letters.

HEPBURN, Patrick George Thomas Buchan-, see HAILES, 1st B

HEPWORTH, Joseph (d. 1945)

M.P. (Con.) Bradford East, 1931–45.

The Bradford Public Library has various records of the Bradford East Conservative Association and the Bradford Liberal National Association. The latter include a book containing questions put to Hepworth, 1937–9. Messrs Yablon Temple-Milnes & Carr, Hepworth's solicitors, have no information.

HERBERT, Sir Alan Patrick (1890–1971)

Author and barrister-at-law.
M.P. (Independent) Oxford University, 1935–50.

Lady Herbert, 12 Hammersmith Terrace, London W5, has some of her late husband's papers. Others are in the University of Texas.

HERBERT, Hon. Aubrey Nigel Henry Molyneux (1880–1923)

M.P. (Con.) Somerset South, 1911–18; Yeovil, 1918–23.

Extracts from a war diary (1914–16) can be found in *Mons, Anzac, and Kut* (1930).

HERBERT, Sir Dennis Henry, see HEMINGFORD, 1st B

HERBERT, George (1892–   )

M.P. (Con.) Rotherham, 1931–3.

Major Herbert has retained a collection of material, chiefly consisting of press cuttings for the period 1920–45.

HERBERT, Sir Ivor John Caradoc, 1st Bt, see TREOWEN, 1st B

HERBERT, Sir John Arthur (1895–1943)

M.P. (Con.) Monmouth, 1934–8.
Governor of Bengal, 1939–43.

Sir John's son, Mr Robin Herbert, of Llanover, nr Abergavenny, Gwent, possesses some private papers of his father including newspaper scrapbooks, and correspondence regarding his resignation as Governor of Bengal between Lady Herbert, the Marquess of Linlithgow and Field-Marshal Earl Wavell. These papers are not currently available.

HERBERT, Captain Sir Sidney (1890–1939)

M.P. (Con.) Scarborough and Whitby, 1922–31; Westminster Abbey, 1932–9.

The family papers of the Earls of Pembroke, c/o The Wilton Estate Office, Wilton, nr Salisbury, include a considerable volume of correspondence of Sir Sidney Herbert. These papers are sorted and collected together in chronological order. Enquiries should be directed to the agent.

HERBERT, Thomas Arnold (1863–1940)

M.P. (Lib.) Buckinghamshire South, 1906–Jan 1910.

Messrs Bird & Bird, solicitors to the estate, know of no papers. The firm have lost touch with members of the family.

HERBISON, Margaret McCrorie (1907–   )

M.P. (Lab.) Lanarkshire North, 1945–70.
Joint Parliamentary Under-Secretary, Scottish Office, 1950–1. Minister of Pensions and National Insurance, 1964–6. Minister of Social Security, 1966–7.

Miss Herbison states that she has retained no papers which relate to her political career.

HERRIOTTS, John (1874–1935)

M.P. (Lab.) Sedgefield, 1922–3, 1929–31.

The *Dictionary of Labour Biography*, Vol. III, pp, 101–2, gives an account of Herriotts's career. Messrs Hewitt, Brown-Humes & Hare of Bishop Auckland have no information regarding papers.

HERSCHELL, 2nd B
Sir Richard Farrer (1878–1929)

Lord in Waiting, 1907–19 and 1924–9.

Efforts to contact the present Lord Herschell proved unsuccessful.

HERVEY, Rear-Admiral Lord Frederick William Fane, see BRISTOL, 4th M of

HESKETH, 1st B
Sir Thomas Fermor-Hesketh, 8th Bt (1881–1944)

M.P. (Con.) Enfield, 1922–3.

Lord Hesketh, grandson of the 1st baron, states that there are none of his grandfather's papers in existence.

HEWART, 1st Vt
Sir Gordon Hewart (1870–1943)

M.P. (Lib.) Leicester, 1913–18; Leicester East, 1918–22.
Solicitor-General, 1916–19. Attorney-General, 1919–22. Lord Chief Justice, 1922–40.

Hazlehurst and Woodland, p. 75, located no papers.

HEWETT, Sir John Prescott (1854–1941)

M.P. (Con.) Luton, 1922–3.
Indian Civil Service.

Messrs Charles Russell & Co., solicitors to the executors, know of no papers. An assortment of Hewett's correspondence (1910–16) and papers on the Delhi Durbar survive in the Hardinge collection at Cambridge University Library, and Sir H. E. Richard's papers at the India Office Library include Hewett's correspondence, 1907–9.

HEWINS, William Albert Samuel (1865–1931)

Director of London School of Economics, 1895–1903.
M.P. (Con.) Hereford, 1912–18.
Under-Secretary, Colonies, 1917–19.

The papers are deposited in Sheffield University Library and consist of printed and manuscript material, particularly relating to tariff reform and Imperial Preference. The collection includes a considerable amount of correspondence with leading politicians; biographies of English politicians and economists written by Hewins; correspondence concerning the Catholic Church; and diaries, 1882, 1905–6, 1908–14, 1919–21, 1923–5, 1925–9. Papers of the Tariff Commission, of which Hewins was Secretary, 1903–17, are deposited in BLPES. The Labour Party archive holds a memorandum (1917) on the aims of the peace committee, prepared by Hewins for the War Cabinet.

HEWITSON, Captain Mark (1897–1973)

M.P. (Lab.) Hull Central, 1945–55; Hull West, 1955–64.

Efforts to contact Capt. Hewitson's heirs were unsuccessful.

HEWLETT, Thomas Henry (1882–1956)

M.P. (Con.) Manchester Exchange, 1940–5.
Industrialist.

The Rt. Hon. Lord Hewlett has possession of the family archives. These include a scrapbook kept by his father, T. H. Hewlett. Further details are not available, but enquiries may be directed to Lord Hewlett's secretary, Anchor Chemical Company Ltd, Clayton, Manchester M11 4SR.

HIBBERT, Sir Henry Flemming, 1st Bt (1850–1927)

M.P. (Con.) Chorley, 1913–18.

Information available in the will and Act of Probate was insufficient to trace members of the family.

HICKMAN, Sir Alfred, 1st Bt (1830–1910)

Ironmaster and colliery proprietor.
M.P. (Con.) Wolverhampton West, 1885–6, 1892–1906.

See below.

HICKMAN, Brigadier-General Thomas Edgecumbe (1859–1930)

Military career, Egypt, Sudan and South Africa.
M.P. (Con.) Wolverhampton South (later Bilston), Jan 1910–22.

Enquiries concerning papers remaining with the family should be directed to the NRA.

HICKS, (Ernest) George (1879–1954)

M.P. (Lab.) Woolwich East, 1931–50.
Parliamentary Secretary, Ministry of Works, 1940–5.
General Secretary, Amalgamated Union of Building Trade Workers, 1921–40.

Hicks's solicitor knows of no surviving papers. Minute books, annual reports and other papers of the Woolwich Labour party remain in the constituency offices, and the U.C.A.T.T. archives at the Modern Records Centre, Warwick University, include a quantity of records relevant to Hicks's trade union work. The records are described in *Sources*, Vol. 1, pp. 267–9.

HICKS, Sir William Joynson, 1st Bt, see BRENTFORD, 1st Vt

HIGGINBOTTOM, Samuel Wasse (d. 1902)

M.P. (Con.) Liverpool West Derby, 1900–2.

HIGGINS, Frederick Platt- (1840–1910)

M.P. (Con.) Salford North, 1895–1906.

His grand-daughter, Mrs C. P. Wight, Century Cottage, Drinkstone Green, nr Bury St Edmunds, Suffolk, believes no papers survive.

HIGGINS, T.*

M.P. (Irish Nat.) Galway North, 1906.

Higgins died on the day of his election.

HIGGS, Sir (John) Michael Clifford (1912–)

M.P. (Con.) Bromsgrove, 1950–5.

Sir Michael says he has not retained any papers.

HIGGS, Walter Frank (1886–1961)

M.P. (Con.) Birmingham West, 1937–45.

Mrs C. E. Higgs, The Little House, 253 High Street, Henley-in-Arden, Solihull, West Midlands, states that her husband left a box of newspaper cuttings and various articles, dating from 1921. These remain with her. Appointment diaries have not survived.

HIGHAM, Sir Charles Frederick (1876–1938)

Author and publicist.
M.P. (Con.) Islington South, 1918–22.

HIGHAM, John Sharp (1857–1932)

M.P. (Lib.) Sowerby, 1904–18.

Enquiries might be directed to Mr R. H. Higham (grandson), Highar-Tong Ltd, Hyde Bank Mill, New Mills, Stockport, Greater Manchester.

HILDER, Lieutenant-Colonel Frank (1864–1951)

M.P. (Con.) Essex S.E., 1918–23.

A number of papers relating to Hilder's parliamentary career, his earlier military service and his plans for 'A Senate of Civilisation' survive in the care of Major T. Hilder, Buddington House, Woolbeding, Midhurst, Sussex. The material is pasted into a number of scrapbooks. The papers will not be available until they have been deposited in the Essex Record Office.

HILEY, Sir Ernest Varvill (1868–1949)

M.P. (Con.) Birmingham Duddeston, 1922–3.
Deputy Director of National Service, 1917.

The solicitors who acted in the estate know of no papers. Sir Ernest was chairman of Glover & Main Ltd, engineers and appliance manufacturers, of London.

HILL OF LUTON, Baron
Dr Charles Hill (1904–   )

M.P. (Nat.Lib.) Luton, 1950–63.
Parliamentary Secretary, Ministry of Food, 1951–5. Postmaster General, 1955–7. Chancellor of the Duchy of Lancaster, 1957–61. Minister of Housing and Local Government and Minister for Welsh Affairs, 1961–2.
Chairman of the Independent Television Authority, 1963–7; and Chairman of the Governors of the BBC, 1967–72.

Lord Hill states that he has no important papers. Reference should be made to his published autobiography, *The Other Side of the Hill.*

HILL, Sir Alexander Galloway Erskine-, 1st Bt (1894–1947)

M.P. (Con.) Edinburgh North, 1935–45.
Chairman, Conservative Members ('1922') Committee, 1940–4.

HILL, Alfred (d. 1945)

M.P. (Lab.) Leicester West, 1922–3.

HILL, Dr Archibald Vivian (1886–   )

M.P. (Independent Con.) Cambridge University, 1940–5.
Member of War Cabinet Scientific Advisory Committee, 1940–6; etc.

Dr Hill has given a collection of his papers to the Archives Centre at Churchill College, Cambridge, but he retains in his care a good many letters and notes. Churchill College has his un-published autobiography, and a series of letters and telegrams (1915–70) relating mainly to anti-aircraft defences. Recent material is not available for research. Further papers will be transferred in due course to Churchill College.

HILL, Captain Arthur (1873–1913)*

M.P. (Con.) Down West, 1898–1905.

Family papers given by Lord Downshire to the Berkshire Record Office include no relevant material. Similarly the Downshire archive at the Northern Ireland Public Record Office contains no papers of Capt. A. Hill or Lord Arthur William Hill.

HILL, Lord Arthur William (1846–1931)*

M.P. (Con.) County Down, 1880–5; Down West, 1895–8 and 1907–8.
Comptroller of H.M. Household, 1885–6, 1886–92 and 1895–8.

See above.

HILL, Sir Clement Lloyd (1845–1913)

Diplomatic service,
Superintendent of African Protectorates, Foreign Office, 1900–5.
M.P. (Con.) Shrewsbury, 1906–13.

A collection of papers can be found at Rhodes House Library, Oxford. This consists of letters and documents concerning Hill's career and work in the East African department of the Foreign Office (1867–1905).

HILL, Eveline (1898–1973)

M.P. (Con.) Manchester Wythenshawe, 1950–64.

Mrs E. Fay Cave-Browne-Cave, Holly Cottage, 42 Acre Lane, Cheadle Hulme, Cheshire SK8 7PL, states that her mother's surviving papers are in her care. Correspondence and minutes of meetings have been destroyed, and there remain only papers relating to special functions which Mrs Hill attended during her local government and parliamentary life.

HILL, His Honour Henry Staveley Staveley- (1865–1946)

M.P. (Con.) Kingswinford, 1905–18.

Mr H. de B. Staveley-Hill (son) could not be contacted.

HILL, Sir James, 1st Bt (1849–1936)

M.P. (Lib.) Bradford Central, 1916–18.

No contact was established with Sir James Hill, Bt (grandson).

HILLARY, Albert Ernest (1868–1954)

M.P. (Lib.) Harwich, 1922–4.

Brigadier J. B. Hillary, C.B.E. (son) states that his father left no papers relating to his political career.

HILLIER, Dr Alfred Peter (1858–1911)

M.P. (Con.) Hitchin, Jan 1910–11.

The solicitors, Lithgow Pepper & Eldridge, could provide no information regarding papers or surviving members of the family.

HILLINGDON, 3rd B
Hon. Arthur Robert Mills (1891–1952)

M.P. (Con.) Uxbridge, 1915–18.

No information. Enquiries should be addressed to the present Lord Hillingdon, Messing Park, Kelvedon, Essex.

HILLMAN, George Brown (1867–1932)

M.P. (Con.) Wakefield, 1931–2.

Persons mentioned in the will could not be traced.

HILLS, Adam (1880–1941)

M.P. (Lab.) Pontefract, 1935–41.

There was no trace of persons mentioned in the letters of administration.

HILLS, John Waller (1867–1938)

M.P. (Con.) Durham, 1906–22; Ripon, 1925–38.
Financial Secretary, Treasury, 1922–3.

Lady Hills, formerly of 40 Argyll Road, London W8, has a certain amount of her late husband's correspondence and a quantity of press cuttings dating back to 1906. Some of the material relates to the campaign for equal pay for women. Other papers, including political diaries, were destroyed in air raids.

HILTON, Cecil (1884–1931)

M.P. (Con.) Bolton, 1924–9.

Minute books, etc., of the Bolton Conservative Association remain in the local offices. Hilton's brother and sisters, mentioned in the will, could not be traced.

HINCHCLIFFE, William Algernon Simpson- (1880–1963)

M.P. (Con.) Sowerby, 1922–3.

Messrs Titley, Paver-Crow & Feddon, who acted in the estate, were unable to supply any information regarding the location of any papers that Simpson-Hinchcliffe may have left.

HINCHINBROOKE, Vt, see SANDWICH, 9th E of

HINCHINBROOKE, Vt (10th E of Sandwich), see MONTAGU, Victor

HINDLE, Sir Frederick (1877–1953)

M.P. (Lib.) Darwen, 1923–4.
Lady Hindle has no papers.

HINDLE, Frederick George (1848–1925)

M.P. (Lib.) Darwen, Jan–Dec 1910.

Lady Hindle has no papers relating to the parliamentary career of her father-in-law.

HINDS, John (1862–1928)

M.P. (Lib.) Carmarthenshire West, Dec 1910–18; (Co. Lib.) Carmarthen, 1918–23.

There was no trace of persons mentioned in the will and Act of Probate.

HIRST, Geoffrey Anders Nicholson (1904–   )

M.P. (Con.) Shipley, 1950–70.

Mr Hirst destroyed his papers before emigrating to France.

HIRST, George Henry (1868–1933)

M.P. (Lab.) Wentworth, 1918–33.

Messrs Raley & Pratt, solicitors to the executors, were unable to supply any information that would lead us to the whereabouts of any papers. The *Dictionary of Labour Biography*, Vol. III, pp. 108–9, gives an account of Hirst's career.

HIRST, William (1873–1946)

M.P. (Lab. Co-op) Bradford South, 1924–31.

It was not possible to contact any of the people mentioned in the will.

HOARE, Edward Brodie (1841–1911)

M.P. (Con.) Hampstead, 1888–1902.

Captain E. M. Hoare (grandson) knows of no surviving papers.

HOARE, Sir Samuel, 1st Bt (1841–1915)

M.P. (Con.) Norwich, 1886–1906.

The Templewood papers at Cambridge University Library include four files consisting mainly of correspondence and other papers of Sir Samuel Hoare, 1st Bt, Viscount Templewood's father. Any other material could be with Mr P. E. Paget, Lord Templewood's nephew and literary executor.

HOARE, Sir Samuel John Gurney, 2nd Bt, see TEMPLEWOOD, 1st Vt

HOBART, Sir Robert Henry, 1st Bt (1836–1928)

Private Secretary to various Cabinet Ministers, etc.
M.P. (Lib.) New Forest, 1906–Jan 1910.

Cdr. Sir Robert Hampden Hobart, Bt, 4 Halkin Street, London SW1X 7DJ, states that he has very few of his grandfather's papers. Details are not available.

HOBHOUSE, Sir Arthur Lawrence (1886–1965)

M.P. (Lib.) Wells, 1923–4.

According to Mr John Hobhouse, any family papers would be kept at the family home, Hadspen House, Castle Cary, Somerset.

HOBHOUSE, Sir Charles Edward Henry, 4th Bt (1862–1941)

M.P. (Lib.) Devizes, 1892–5; Bristol East, 1900–18.
Parliamentary Under-Secretary, India Office, 1907–8. Financial Secretary, Treasury, 1908–11.
Chancellor of the Duchy of Lancaster, 1911–14. Postmaster General, 1914–15.

Hazlehurst and Woodland, p. 76, found no papers.

HOBHOUSE, Henry (1854–1937)

M.P. (Con.) Somerset East, 1885–1906.

According to Mr John Hobhouse, any family papers would be kept at the family home, Hadspen
House, Castle Cary, Somerset. It was not possible to contact other members of the family. Henry
Hobhouse was the father of Sir A. L. Hobhouse.

HOBSON, Baron
Charles Rider Hobson (1904–66)

M.P. (Lab.) Wembley North, 1945–50; Keighley, 1950–9.
Assistant Postmaster General, 1947–51. Lord in Waiting, 1964–6.

Lady Hobson, 115 Dewsbury Road, Dollis Hill, London NW10 1EN, retained a small collection of her husband's papers. She has given these to BLPES.

HODGE, Lieutenant-Colonel James Philip (1879–1946)

M.P. (Lib.) Preston, 1922–4.

HODGE, John (1855–1937)

M.P. (Lab.) Gorton, later Manchester Gorton, 1906–23.
Minister of Labour, 1916–17. Minister of Pensions, 1917–19.

Hazlehurst and Woodland, p. 76, found only a very few press cuttings in private possession.
However, the Labour Party archive at Transport House contains in its Labour Representation
Committee records a number of papers relating to Hodge's work. A note on his career appears
in the *Dictionary of Labour Biography*, Vol. III, pp. 109–15.

HODGE, Sir Robert Trotter Hermon-, 1st Bt, see WYFOLD, 1st B

HODGES, Frank (1887–1947)

M.P. (Lab.) Lichfield, 1923–4.
Civil Lord of the Admiralty, 1924.
General Secretary, Miners' Federation of Great Britain, 1918–24.

Records of the Miners' Federation of Great Britain are described in *Sources*, Vol. 1, pp. 195–8.
No member of the family was traced.

HOFFMAN, Philip Christopher (1878–1959)

M.P. (Lab.) Essex South East, 1923–4; Sheffield Central, 1929–31.

Mrs A. M. Hoffman (widow) has a scrapbook relating to her late husband's career with the
shopworkers' union. Hoffman's book *They Also Serve* was published in 1949. Enquiries may be
addressed to Mrs Hoffman, c/o Tolson, 15A De Villiers Street, Johannesburg 2001, R.S.A.
Records of the Union of Shop, Distributive and Allied Workers are described in *Sources*, Vol.
1, pp. 270–1.

HOGAN, M. H. (b. 1851)*

M.P. (Irish Nat.) Tipperary North, 1906–Dec 1910.

HOGBIN, Henry Cairn (1880–1966)

M.P. (Lib.) Battersea North, 1923–4.

It was not possible to contact Hogbin's widow, now Mrs J. Skinner of Wick, Caithness.

HOGG, David C. (1840–1914)*

M.P. (Lib.) Londonderry City, 1913–14.

HOGG, Sir Douglas McGarel, see HAILSHAM, 1st Vt

HOGG, Sir Lindsay Lindsay-, 1st Bt (1853–1923)

M.P. (Con.) Eastbourne, 1900–6.

No contact was made with Sir William Lindsay-Hogg, Bt (grandson).

HOGG, Hon. Quintin McGarel, see HAILSHAM OF SAINT MARYLEBONE, Baron

HOGGE, James Myles (1873–1928)

M.P. (Lib.) Edinburgh East, 1912–24.

There was no trace of persons mentioned in the will. Papers of the National Federation of Discharged and Demobilised Sailors and Soldiers, of which he was a founder, are described in *Sources*, Vol. 1, p. 228.

HOHLER, Sir Gerald Fitzroy (1862–1934)

M.P. (Con.) Chatham, Jan 1910–18; Gillingham, 1918–29.

There are a few papers only amongst the material collected by Sir Thomas Beaumont Hohler with Mr G. A. Hohler, Trent Manor, Sherborne, Dorset. Mr Hohler and other friends and members of the family know of no further papers.

HOLBROOK, Sir Arthur Richard (1850–1946)

M.P. (Con.) Basingstoke, 1920–3 and 1924–9.

Major-General A. W. Holbrook states that his father did not keep any diaries or correspondence, and that a collection of press cuttings was destroyed after his father's death.

HOLDEN, 3rd B
Sir Angus William Eden Holden, 4th Bt (1898–1951)

Parliamentary Under-Secretary, Commonwealth Relations Office, 1950.

No contact was established. Lord Holden died without an immediate heir, but his baronetcy passed to another branch of the family. Enquiries might be directed to Sir Edward Holden, Bt.

HOLDEN, Sir Edward Hopkinson, 1st Bt (1848–1919)

M.P. (Lib.) Heywood, 1906–Jan 1910.

Mr H. Hayes (executor) states that the business papers, etc., belonging to Sir Cassie Holden and his father, Sir Edward, which were in a metal box, were handed to the Midland Bank Trustee & Executor Co. at the time of Sir Cassie Holden's death.

HOLDSWORTH, Sir Herbert (1890–1949)

M.P. (Lib., later Lib. Nat.) Bradford South, 1931–45.
Assistant Government Whip, 1940–2.

HOLLAND, Alfred (1900–36)

M.P. (Lab.) Clay Cross, 1935–6.

HOLLAND, Lieutenant-General Sir Arthur Edward Aveling (1862–1927)

Military career.
M.P. (Con.) Northampton, 1924–7.

Only Sir Arthur's wife and daughter, Mary Hilaire Duval Holland, are mentioned in the will and Act of Probate. The Imperial War Museum knows of no papers.

HOLLAND, Sir William Henry, 1st Bt, see ROTHERHAM, 1st B

HOLLINS, Arthur (1876–1962)

M.P. (Lab.) Hanley, 1928–31 and 1935–45.
General Secretary, National Society of Pottery Workers, 1910–47.

The records of the Ceramic and Allied Trades Union, 5 Hillcrest Street, Hanley, Stoke-on-Trent ST1 2AB, contain relevant material, and the General Secretary of the Union contributed copies of certain notes, letters and press cuttings to the BLPES., relating to Arthur Hollins and to Sam Clowes. No member of Arthur Hollins's family was traced.

HOLLINS, James Henry (d. 1954)

M.P. (Lab.) West Ham Silvertown, 1940–5.

The London Borough of Newham Libraries, and the Newham Labour Parties, know of no papers. No members of the family were traced.

HOLLIS, (Maurice) Christopher (1902–   )

M.P. (Con.) Devizes, 1945–55.

Mr Hollis has not retained any of his papers.

HOLMAN, Percy (1891–   )

M.P. (Lab. Co-op.) Bethnal Green South West, 1945–50; Bethnal Green, 1950–66.

HOLMES, Daniel Turner (1863–1955)

M.P. (Lib.) Govan, 1911–18.

The Scottish Labour History project found no papers.

HOLMES, Sir Horace Edwin (1888–1971)

M.P. (Lab.) Hemsworth, 1946–59.
Parliamentary Private Secretary to Minister of Fuel and Power, 1947–51. Opposition Whip, 1951–9.
Miner and trade union official.

Shortly before his death, Sir Horace lent his private diaries (1926–60) and a number of parliamentary letters, mainly dealing with his retirement from the House of Commons, to Mr C. C. Storm-Clark of the Department of Economics at the University of York. Enquiries regarding these papers and any others which may survive should be addressed to Mr Trevor Jones, Alder Hill House, Alder Hill Avenue, Leeds 6.

HOLMES, Sir (Joseph) Stanley, see DOVERCOURT, 1st B

HOLT, Major Herbert Paton (1890–1971)

M.P. (Con.) West Ham Upton, 1924–9.

Mrs C. E. Holt, who resides in the Bahamas, knows of no papers.

HOLT, Sir John (Anthony) Langford- (1916–   )

M.P. (Con.) Shrewsbury, 1945–

Sir John has retained a scrap-book, and press cuttings from 1950 to 1970.

HOLT, Sir Richard Durning, 1st Bt (1868–1941)

M.P. (Lib.) Hexham, 1907–18.

The records of the Durning and Holt families in the Liverpool Record Office include the personal correspondence and diaries (c. 1900–41) of Sir Richard Holt, as well as a collection of news cuttings relating to his political career and public life. Some records of the shipowners Alfred Holt & Co. are held by the Ocean Steamship Co. Ltd, Liverpool.

HOMAN, Cornelius William James Andrew (1900–   )

M.P. (Con.) Ashton-under-Lyne, 1924–8.

HOME OF THE HIRSEL, Baron
Sir Alec (Alexander Frederick) Douglas-Home, Lord Dunglass, 14th E of Home (1903–   )

M.P. (Con.) Lanark South, 1931–45; Lanark, 1950–1; Kinross and West Perthshire, 1963–Oct 1974.
Joint Parliamentary Under-Secretary, Foreign Office, 1945. Minister of State, Scottish Office, 1951–5. Secretary of State for Commonwealth Relations, 1955–60. Leader of the House of Lords, and Lord President of the Council, 1957–60. Secretary of State for Foreign Affairs, 1960–3 and 1970–4. Prime Minister, 1963–4.

Lord Home states that he has kept his papers, which include diaries. These remain in his possession, and are not available for research.

HOOD, Sir A. F. Acland-, 4th Bt, see ST AUDRIES, 1st B

HOOD, Sir Joseph, 1st Bt (1863–1931)

M.P. (Con.) Wimbledon, 1918–24.

Sir Harold Hood, Bt (son) may have information regarding papers.

HOOPER, Arthur George (1857–1940)

M.P. (Lib.) Dudley, 1906–Dec 1910.

Mr K. V. Hooper, 15 Cherry Orchard Close, Chipping Campden, Glos GL55 6DH, has a number of his father's papers. These include a book of news cuttings, mainly of a personal and local (Dudley) nature. Some of the cuttings and a few letters relate to the elections of 1906 and 1910 in Dudley; to Hooper's Railway (Contracts) Bill (1907); to his visit to India; and to the Dudley Grammar School, the Electric Tramways Scheme for Dudley, etc. There are also copies of speeches made by Hooper, and some correspondence with Sir Henry Campbell-Bannerman and Sir Edward Grey.

HOPE, A. O. J., see RANKEILLOUR, 2nd B

HOPE, Sir Harry, 1st Bt (1865–1959)

M.P. (Con.) Buteshire, Jan 1910–18; Stirlingshire West and Clackmannan, 1918–22; Forfarshire, 1924–31.

Sir James Hope, Bt (son) may have information regarding papers.

HOPE, Lord John Adrian, see GLENDEVON, 1st B

HOPE, Lieutenant-Colonel Sir John Augustus, 16th Bt (1869–1924)

M.P. (Con.) Midlothian, 1912–18; Midlothian North and Peebleshire, 1918–22.

Sir Archibald Hope, Bt, Upton Grey Lodge, nr Basingstoke, Hants, has possession of the family papers. Some of this material has been listed by the NRA (Scotland). The papers of Sir John Hope, Sir Archibald's father, consist largely of school letters and records of his army career, particularly during World War I. There appear to be no papers relating to his parliamentary career. However, some four large volumes of newspaper cuttings have survived. These cover the years 1910–14 and 1919, and they cover parliamentary elections, meetings and local affairs.

HOPE, John Deans (1860–1949)

M.P. (Lib.) Fife West, 1900–Dec 1910; Haddingtonshire, 1911–18; Berwick and Haddington, 1918–22.

Contact was not established with J. D. Hope's nephew, Sir James Hope, Bt.

HOPE, J. F., see RANKEILLOUR, 1st B

HOPE, Sydney (1905–59)

M.P. (Con.) Stalybridge and Hyde, 1931–5.

Neither Mr P. Eastwood nor Mrs A. E. Taylor, M.B.E., J.P., Hope's executors, know of any papers. Mr R. M. A. Mitchell, who benefited from his estate, now lives in Canada. It is believed that he has no papers.

HOPE, William Henry Bateman (b. 1865)

M.P. (Lib.) Somerset North, 1906–Jan 1910.

HOPE SIMPSON, Sir John (1868–1961)

M.P. (Lib.) Taunton, 1922–4.

The papers of Sir John Hope Simpson are with his son, Mr J. B. Hope Simpson, Craig-y-Dorth, Mitchel Troy Common, Monmouth, NP5 4JQ. They are at present uncatalogued, but a brief list has been drawn up. The material includes papers relating to Sir John's involvement with Indian affairs, including two diaries, 1895 and 1899, and a few letters. There is a file of papers relating to the India Colonies Committee, of which Sir John was Chairman in 1924. A large part of the collection concerns Palestine and Hope Simpson's report on Palestine in 1930, including correspondence with Arnold Toynbee and Sir John Chancellor. Hope Simpson's continuing involvement in Palestinian affairs is reflected by miscellaneous correspondence of the 1940s with, among others, Sir John Campbell, Sir John Chancellor, Lord Passfield and the Jewish Agency. Another substantial part of the collection relates to the Commission of Government in New Zealand, 1934–7. The papers also include material, correspondence and press cuttings on the National Flood Relief Commission, Shanghai, 1931–3, as well as printed material and correspondence on Greek affairs, 1927–30. There is also personal correspondence, 1902–61. Mr J. B. Hope Simpson is currently writing a biography of his father and is adding family correspondence to the collection.

HOPKIN, Major Daniel (1886–1951)

M.P. (Lab.) Carmarthen, 1929–31, 1935–41.

Enquiries should be directed to Mrs Ann Boyd (daughter), 28 Canonbury Grove, London N1.

HOPKINS, Sir John Wells Wainwright, 1st Bt (1863–1946)

M.P. (Con.) St Pancras S.E., 1918–23 and 1924–9.

Cdr. and Mrs Farmer, Sir John's son-in-law and daughter, know of no papers apart from one or two press cuttings.

HOPKINSON, Sir Alfred (1851–1939)

M.P. (Con.) Cricklade, 1895–8; Combined English Universities, 1926–9.

Mr J. F. Hopkinson, Four Ways, Windermere, Cumbria, has a number of volumes of press cuttings kept by his grandfather. These papers cover the years from 1898. It appears that no further material has survived.

HOPKINSON, Austin (1879–1962)

M.P. (Lib.) Prestwich, 1918; (Ind.) Mossley, 1918–29 and 1931–45.

Mr J. F. Hopkinson, Fourweep, Windermere, Cumbria, has only books left by Austin Hopkinson. He thinks that Austin Hopkinson destroyed his papers. It was not possible to trace the beneficiaries of Hopkinson's estate.

HOPKINSON, Edward (1859–1922)

M.P. (Con.) Manchester Clayton, 1918–22.

The Lady Chorley (daughter), The Rookery, Stanmore, Middlesex, has some material relating to her father's career. However, she knows of no diaries or letters, and the records in her care cover Hopkinson's business and scientific work rather than his time in parliament. In addition, Mr B. E. Hopkinson (grandson), Redlands, Leamington Road, Kenilworth, Warwickshire, has some similar material. Correspondence (1916–17) regarding a projected journey to India is included in the papers of Sir Horace Plunkett.

HOPKINSON, Sir Henry Lennox d'Aubigné, see COLYTON, 1st B

HORABIN, Thomas Lewis (1896–1956)

M.P. (Lib.) Cornwall North, 1939–47; (Lab.) 1947–50.

HORE-BELISHA, 1st B
(Isaac) Leslie Hore-Belisha (1893–1957)

M.P. (Lib., later Lib.Nat.) Plymouth Devonport, 1923–45.
Parliamentary Secretary, Board of Trade, 1931–2. Financial Secretary, Treasury, 1932–4. Minister of Transport, 1934–7. Secretary of State for War, 1937–40. Minister of National Insurance, 1945.

Hazlehurst and Woodland, pp. 14–15, found that the papers in the care of Miss Hilda Sloane, Hore-Belisha's secretary, are not available for inspection. Some of his correspondence is included in the Lothian, Herbert Samuel, R. D. Blumenfeld, H. Page Croft and W. A. Creech Jones collections.

HORLICK, Sir James Nockells, 4th Bt (1886–   )

M.P. (Con.) Gloucester, 1923–9.

Sir James has not retained any papers relating to his time in parliament.

HORNBY, Frank (1863–1936)

M.P. (Con.) Liverpool Everton, 1931–5.

No contact was established, except with the solicitors Owen Dawson & Wynn Evans of Liverpool, who were unable to provide any information.

HORNBY, Sir (William) Henry, 1st Bt (1841–1928)

M.P. (Con.) Blackburn, 1886–Jan 1910.

Miss A. M. Hornby (daughter) doubts whether any papers have been kept, but enquiries might be addressed to the family solicitor, Mr A. Carter of Carter & Co., 2 Shear Bank Road, Blackburn BB1 8AR.

HORNE OF SLAMANNAN, 1st Vt
Sir Robert Stevenson Horne (1871–1940)

M.P. (Con.) Glasgow Hillhead, 1918–37.
Minister of Labour, 1919–20. President of the Board of Trade, 1920–1. Chancellor of the Exchequer, 1921–2.

Horne's nephew, Mr J. R. Lamberton, retains a collection of personal and family papers. This material is closed (Hazlehurst and Woodland, p. 77).

HORNE, Reverend (Charles) Silvester (1865–1914)

M.P. (Lib.) Ipswich, Jan 1910–14.

HORNE, Sir William Edgar, 1st Bt (1856–1941)

M.P. (Con.) Guildford, Jan 1910–22.

Sir A. Horne, Bt (son) believes that no relevant papers have survived. He does however possess a diary of a trip made by his father to the U.S.A. in autumn 1879. Minute books from 1906 survive in the offices of the local constituency association.

HORNER, Andrew L. (1863–1916)*

M.P. (Con.) Tyrone South, Jan 1910–16.

There is a letter (1915) by Horner to Sir Edward Carson at the Northern Ireland Public Record

Office, together with a clipping from the *Belfast Newsletter* (1915). Members of the family were not traced.

HORNER, Frederick W. (1854–1946)

M.P. (Con.) Lambeth North, 1900–6.

HORNIMAN, Emslie John (1863–1932)

M.P. (Lib.) Chelsea, 1906–Jan 1910.

See below. The Royal Anthropological Institute has papers relating to the Emslie Horniman Scholarship Fund.

HORNIMAN, Frederick John (1835–1906)

M.P. (Lib.) Falmouth and Penryn, 1895–1906.

For papers of F. J. Horniman and his son, E. J. Horniman, enquiries should be directed to the Curator of the Horniman Museum, London Road, Forest Hill, London SE23 3PQ.

HORNSBY-SMITH, Baroness
Dame (Margaret) Patricia Hornsby-Smith (1914–   )

M.P. (Con.) Chislehurst, 1950–66 and 1970–Feb 1974.
Parliamentary Secretary, Health 1951–7. Joint Parliamentary Under-Secretary, Home Office, 1957–9. Joint Parliamentary Secretary, Pensions and National Insurance, 1959–61.

Lady Hornsby-Smith has retained some of her papers. These include press-cutting books relating to eight election campaigns, transcripts of some of her more important broadcasts, speeches that she made as U.K. delegate to the United Nations, 1958. She has also retained a limited number of papers covering her wartime work in the Ministry of Economic Warfare and copies of post-war lectures on S.O.E.

HOROBIN, Sir Ian Macdonald (1899–   )

M.P. (Con.) Southwark Central, 1931–5; Oldham East, 1951–9.
Parliamentary Secretary, Ministry of Power, 1958–9.

HORRABIN, (James) Francis (1884–1962)

M.P. (Lab.) Peterborough, 1929–31:

Horrabin's widow, Mrs Margaret Horrabin, has no relevant papers. The papers of his first wife, Winifred Horrabin, are deposited in Hull University Library, and include diaries and journals, manuscript and typescript works, and correspondence. No personal papers of J. F. Horrabin survive in this collection.

HORRIDGE, Sir Thomas Gardner (1857–1938)

M.P. (Lib.) Manchester East, 1906–Jan 1910.

The solicitors who acted in the estate could provide no information which would lead to the whereabouts of Sir Thomas's papers.

HORSBRUGH, Baroness
Florence Horsbrugh (d. 1969)

M.P. (Con.) Dundee, 1931–45; Manchester Moss Side, 1950–9.
Parliamentary Secretary, Ministry of Health, 1939–45; Ministry of Food, 1945. Minister of

Education, 1951–4.

Churchill College, Cambridge, has eleven boxes of material including papers (1918–53) and newspaper cuttings (1931–9).

HOTCHKIN, Stafford Vere (1876–1953)

M.P. (Con.) Horncastle, 1920–2.

Contact with Major N. S. Hotchkin (son) was not established.

HOUFTON, Sir John Plowright (1857–1929)

M.P. (Con.) Nottingham East, 1922–3.

There was no trace of persons mentioned in the will.

HOUGHTON, Baron
(Arthur Leslie Noel) Douglas Houghton (1898–   )

Secretary, Inland Revenue Staff Federation, 1922–60.
M.P. (Lab.) Sowerby, 1949–Feb 1974.
Chancellor of the Duchy of Lancaster, 1964–6. Minister without Portfolio, 1966–7.
Chairman, Parliamentary Labour Party, 1967–74.

Lord Houghton states that he has in his care a complete set of notes (in date order) of proceedings at Parliamentary Labour Party meetings kept when he was Chairman (1967–74), and also some isolated items of correspondence and reports. The latter material is small in quantity and unsorted.

HOUGHTON, 2nd B, see CREWE, 1st M of

HOULDSWORTH, Sir William Henry, 1st Bt (1834–1917)

M.P. (Con.) Manchester North West, 1883–1906.

Sir Reginald Houldsworth, Bt, states that to the best of his knowledge no papers of the 1st Baronet have survived with the family.

HOULT, Joseph (1847–1917)

M.P. (Con.) The Wirral, 1900–6.

No member of the family was traced.

HOUSE, George (1892–1949)

M.P. (Lab.) St Pancras North, 1945–9.

No members of the family were traced. The Camden Labour Party knows of none of his papers, but has a number of unsorted C.L.P. records.

HOUSTON, Sir Robert Paterson, 1st Bt (1853–1926)

M.P. (Con.) Liverpool West Toxteth, 1892–1924.

Mrs B. De Veulle of the Société Jersiaise kindly undertook research to trace Sir Robert's heirs and associates. It would appear that no papers survive in Jersey, where Sir Robert died, and no personal collection has been located elsewhere.

HOWARD, Hon. Sir Arthur Jared Palmer (1896–1971)

M.P. (Con.) Westminster St George's, 1945–50.

Enquiries should be directed to Sir Arthur's son, Mr Alexander Howard, Wappingthorn, Steyning, West Sussex BN4 3AA.

HOWARD, Hon. Donald Sterling Palmer, see STRATHCONA AND MOUNT ROYAL, 3rd B

HOWARD, Hon. Geoffrey William Algernon (1877–1935)

M.P. (Lib.) Eskdale, 1906–Dec 1910; Westbury, 1911–18; Luton, 1923–4.
Vice Chamberlain, H.M. Household, 1911–15. Junior Lord of the Treasury, 1915–16 and 1916.

Mr George Howard (son) of Castle Howard, York, has possession of the family papers. The collection includes a certain amount of material, such as letters and press cuttings. There is no general access to these papers, although individual requests from well-known historians will be considered.

HOWARD, Hon. Greville Reginald (1909–   )

M.P. (Nat.Lib. and Con.) St Ives, 1950–66.

Mr Howard, who now lives in Luxembourg, has a number of press-cuttings books which cover most of his post-war career.

HOWARD, John (1865–1911)

M.P. (Con.) Faversham, 1900–6.

HOWARD, Joseph (1834–1923)

M.P. (Con.) Tottenham, 1885–1906.

There was no trace of persons mentioned in the will. Haringey Libraries could provide no information. ·

HOWARD, Sir (Stephen) Gerald
Hon. Mr Justice Howard (1896–1973)

M.P. (Con.) Cambridgeshire, 1950–61.

Lady Howard (widow), 4 Hamilton Road, Newmarket, Suffolk GC8 ONQ, was unable to help.

HOWARD, Major Stephen Goodwin (1867–1934)

M.P. (Lib.) Sudbury, 1918–22.

Lady Howard (daughter-in-law) was unable to help with the location of papers.

HOWARD, Tom Forest (1888–1953)

M.P. (Con.) Islington South, 1931–5.

Mr W. Shepherd, 77 George Street, Portman Square, London W1H 5PL (son-in-law), made enquiries of his mother-in-law. Unfortunately, no information regarding papers was forthcoming.

HOWE, 4th E
Richard George Penn Curzon, Vt Curzon (1861–1929)

Treasurer, H.M. Household, 1896–1900. Lord in Waiting, 1900–3.

HOWE, 5th E
Francis Richard Henry Penn Curzon, Vt Curzon (1884–1964)

M.P. (Con.) Battersea South, 1918–29.
Junior Lord of the Treasury, 1924–9.

HOWITT, Sir Alfred Bakewell (1879–1954)

M.P. (Con.) Reading, 1931–45.

A press-cuttings album relating to the Preston by-election in 1929 survives in the care of Sir Alfred's daughter, Mrs Selwyn Taylor, 5 Addisland Court, Holland Villas Road, London W14 8DA.

HOY, Baron
James Hutchison Hoy (1909–76)

M.P. (Lab.) Leith, 1945–50; Edinburgh Leith, 1950–70.
Joint Parliamentary Secretary, Ministry of Agriculture, Fisheries and Food, 1964–70.

Lord Hoy stated that he had some press cuttings of the first three elections he fought in Leith. Otherwise he had kept no diary or records.

HOZIER, Hon. James Henry Cecil, see NEWLANDS, 2nd B

HUBBARD, Thomas Frederick (1898–1961)

M.P. (Lab.) Kirkcaldy Burghs, 1944–59.

Efforts to contact Mrs J. Hubbard (widow) in Dysart, Fife, were unsuccessful.

HUDSON, 1st Vt
Robert Spear Hudson (1886–1957)

M.P. (Con.) Whitehaven, 1924–9; Southport, 1931–52.
Parliamentary Secretary, Ministry of Labour, 1931–5. Minister of Pensions, 1935–6. Parliamentary Secretary, Ministry of Health, 1936–7; Department of Overseas Trade, Board of Trade, 1937–40. Minister of Shipping, 1940. Minister of Agriculture and Fisheries, 1940–5.

Hazlehurst and Woodland, p. 78, report that some papers survive with Hudson's sister, Miss Violet Hudson, Manor Farm, Manningford Bohun, Pewsey, Wilts.

HUDSON, Sir Austin Uvedale Morgan, 1st Bt (1897–1956)

M.P. (Con.) Islington East, 1922–3; Hackney North, 1924–45; Lewisham North, 1950–6.
Junior Lord of the Treasury, 1931–5. Parliamentary Secretary, Ministry of Transport, 1935–9. Civil Lord of the Admiralty, 1939–42. Parliamentary Secretary, Ministry of Fuel and Power, 1945.

Enquiries should be directed to Mr Philip Hudson (nephew), Newbridge Mill, Coleman's Hatch, Hartfield, Sussex.

HUDSON, George Bickersteth (1845–1912)

M.P. (Con.) Hitchin, 1892–1906.

Hudson's heirs and executors have not been traced.

HUDSON, James Hindle (1881–1962)

M.P. (Lab.) Huddersfield, 1923–31; Ealing West, 1945–50; Ealing North, 1950–5.
Secretary, National Temperance Federation and Parliamentary Temperance Group.

Miss M. H. Hudson (sister) states that most of her brother's papers concerning his political and public life were taken to the office of the National Commercial Temperance League, now part of the United Kingdom Alliance, Alliance House, 12 Caxton Street, London SW1H 0QS. Records of this organisation are detailed in *Sources*, Vol. 1, pp. 255–6. Miss Hudson has only a few press cuttings and a note on her brother's career.

HUDSON, Ralph Milbanke (1849–1938)

M.P. (Con.) Sunderland, 1918–22.

It was not possible to contact Hudson's family.

HUDSON, Walter (1852–1935)

M.P. (Lab.) Newcastle-upon-Tyne, 1906–18.
President of Labour Party Congress, 1908.

It was not possible to trace surviving members of the Hudson family. The *Dictionary of Labour Biography*, Vol. II, pp. 197–200, refers only to the Labour Party archives and records of the Amalgamated Society of Railway Servants (see *Sources*, Vol. 1, p. 199). The Labour Party archive contains material by and concerning Walter Hudson.

HUDSON, Walter Richard Austen (1894–1970)

M.P. (Con.) Hull North, 1950–9.

It is understood that Hudson's widow lives in Malta. No contact could be established.

HUGHAN, Admiral Sir Arthur John Henniker-, 6th Bt (1866–1925)

M.P. (Con.) Galloway, 1924–5.

According to his daughter, Miss Henniker-Hughan, none of Sir John's parliamentary papers have survived. However, Miss Henniker-Hughan, has placed in the National Maritime Museum, London SE10, a copy of an autobiographical account of her father's naval career, 1881–1919. She has also retained a number of press cuttings relating to his election in 1924, and his obituary notices.

HUGHES, Collingwood James (1872–1963)

M.P. (Con.) Camberwell Peckham, 1922–4.

A daughter, Mrs H. L. C. Barnett, believed to be living in Tasmania, could not be contacted. The solicitors, Messrs Wolferstans, Snell & Turner of Plymouth, know of no papers.

HUGHES, Colonel Sir Edwin (1832–1904)

M.P. (Con.) Woolwich, 1885–1902.

There was no trace of persons mentioned in the will.

HUGHES, Emrys (1894–1969)

M.P. (Lab.) Ayrshire South and Bute, 1946–69.

A collection of papers is held in the National Library of Scotland. The material includes papers kept by Emrys Hughes himself and papers of his father-in-law, James Keir Hardie. Apart from correspondence and photographs, there are complete files of the *Labour Leader*, 1894–1900, 1906, 1908, and of *Forward*, 1932–51. Many of Emrys Hughes's papers are concerned with his work as editor of *Forward*. They include miscellaneous letters (1932–66), correspondence and drafts of articles from George Bernard Shaw (1937–49) and Leon Trotsky (1937–9), and papers and a draft of an article by Bertrand Russell (1945). Later material consists of manuscript and typescript drafts of various books, articles and speeches (1952–65) by Emrys Hughes. The autobiographical drafts and notes are of particular interest. Some political correspondence and papers are extant, including letters on constituency affairs, general politics, journalism and broadcasting (1950–69); election addresses (1950–66); notes on defence policy; extracts from speeches and parliamentary questions by Hughes; a personal diary (1961); a diary of the 64th Annual Conference of the Labour Party (1965); photographs; and press cuttings.

HUGHES, Hector Samuel James (1887–1970)

M.P. (Lab.) Aberdeen North, 1945–70.

A collection of Hughes's papers is currently housed at the Royal Bank of Scotland, 49 Charing Cross, London SW1A 2DX. The collection is composed of two suitcases, one of which contains largely literary material. The other case includes, as well as election addresses and press cuttings, eleven folders of autobiographical detail, 1939–69, mainly consisting of correspondence and articles. It also includes two folders marked 'autograph' which contain correspondence with ministers, ambassadors and colleagues in the House of Commons. There are also three unpublished books in typescript with research material for these books. Permission to see the papers can be obtained on application to Hughes's daughter, Mrs I. Quinn, 13 Meredith House, Boleyn Road, London N16 8LP.

HUGHES, Herbert Delauney (1914–   )

M.P. (Lab.) Wolverhampton West, 1945–50.

Mr Hughes has retained a number of box files, relating mainly to his work for the Workers' Education Association and the Fabian Society. They contain minutes and correspondence.

HUGHES, Ronw Moelwyn (1897–1955)

M.P. (Lab.) Carmarthen, 1941–5; Islington North, 1950–1.

Hon. Mrs Louise Moelwyn Hughes (widow), Rose Cottage, Wappenden Road, Helmdon, Brackley, Northants, has a number of personal letters referring to political events, a number of letters sent to her after her husband's death, and also a small collection of obituary notices.

HUGHES, Spencer Leigh (1858–1920)

M.P. (Lib.) Stockport, Dec 1910–20.
Parliamentary journalist, with the *Morning Leader* and the *Star*.

There was no trace of Hughes's daughter or legal representatives.

HULBERT, Wing-Commander Sir Norman Jack (1903–72)

British Liaison Officer, Polish Forces in Great Britain, 1943–5.
M.P. (Con.) Stockport, 1935–50; Stockport North, 1950–64.

Lady Hulbert, Sir Norman's second wife, knows of no papers.

HUME, Sir George Hopwood (1866–1946)

M.P. (Con.) Greenwich, 1922–3; 1924–9; 1931–45.
Leader of Municipal Reform Party, London County Council, 1917–25.

Records of the Municipal Reform Party are described in *Sources*, Vol. 1, pp. 156–7. Lady Hume (widow) has retained a mass of papers, including appointment diaries and correspondence, 1922–44.

HUNLOKE, Lieutenant-Colonel Henry Philip (1906–   )

M.P. (Con.) Derbyshire West, 1938–44.

HUNT, Rowland (1858–1943)

M.P. (Con.) Ludlow, 1903–18.

No contact with members of the family could be established.

HUNTER, Hon. Lord
William Hunter (1865–1957)

M.P. (Lib.) Govan, Jan 1910–11.
Solicitor-General, Scotland, 1910–11.

The Trustee Department of the Bank of Scotland, executors to Lord Hunter, were unable to supply any information.

HUNTER, General Sir Archibald (1856–1936)

Military service, Egypt and Sudan, South Africa. Governor, Omdurman, 1899. Commander, Southern Army, India, 1907–9. Governor and C.-in-C., Gibraltar, 1910–13. General Officer Commanding, 13th (Western) Division, 1914. Commander, 3rd Army, 1914.
M.P. (Con.) Lancaster, 1918–22.

Mr F. A. H. Russel of Glennie, Ramsden Road, Godalming, Surrey, acted as executor to the General's estate. Mrs M. L. Russel of that address could not be contacted. The Imperial War Museum knows of no collection of papers. A few letters (1899) to Viscount Wolseley are in the collection at the Hove Central library.

HUNTER, Sir Charles Roderick, 3rd Bt (1858–1924)

M.P. (Con.) Bath, Jan 1910–18.

Dame Agnes Lillie Hunter was Sir Charles's sole executor. Messrs Dawson & Co., solicitors of Lincolns Inn, acted in her estate. No further information was secured. An important collection of constituency association records can be found in the Archives and Record Office, Guildhall, Bath.

HUNTER, Dr Joseph (1875–1935)

M.P. (Lib.) Dumfriesshire, 1929–35.

Messrs Grierson, Moodie & Walker, solicitors of Dumfries, provided no information.

HUNTER, Michael John (1891–1951)

M.P. (Con.) Brigg, 1931–5.

Mrs C. M. Hunter has a number of press cuttings and papers relating to her late husband's career. Details are not available. Enquiries should be directed to Mr M. H. Hunter, Escley

House, Michaelchurch Escley, Hereford.

HUNTER, Sir Thomas (1872–1953)

M.P. (Con.) Perth, 1935–45.

Messrs Sneddon Campbell & Munro, solicitors of Perth, have lost contact with Sir Thomas's heirs and they know of no papers.

HUNTER, Thomas*

M.P. (Sinn Fein) Cork Co. N.E., 1918–22.

HUNTINGDON, 15th E of
Francis John Clarence Westenra Plantagenet Hastings (1901–   )

Joint Parliamentary Secretary, Ministry of Agriculture and Fisheries, 1945–50.

The Earl of Huntingdon says he did not retain any of his political papers.

HUNTINGFIELD, 5th B
Sir William Charles Arcedeckne Vanneck (1883–1969)

M.P. (Con.) Eye, 1923–9.
Governor, Victoria, 1934–9.

Neither Lord Huntingfield nor Group Captain Hon. P. B. R. Vanneck (sons) could be contacted.

HURD, Baron
Anthony Richard Hurd (1901–66)

M.P. (Con.) Newbury, 1945–64.

A collection of papers is in the possession of Lady Hurd (widow), The Old Oxyard, Oare, Marlborough, Wilts. The papers chiefly relate to Lord Hurd's agricultural interests and to his parliamentary work.

HURD, Sir Percy Angier (1864–1950)

M.P. (Con.) Frome, 1918–23; Devizes, 1924–45.

Lady Hurd (daughter-in-law), The Old Oxyard, Oare, Marlborough, Wilts, has a small collection of papers, mainly relating to her father-in-law's parliamentary election campaigns in Frome and Devizes.

HURST, Sir Gerald Berkeley (1877–1957)

M.P. (Con.) Manchester Moss Side, 1918–23 and 1924–35.

There are six volumes of press cuttings currently with his daughter, Mrs Stubbs, Crowell Cottage, Northside, Hutton Rudby, Yarm, Yorkshire. In addition, another daughter, Mrs Felicity Elphinstone, of 3 Enterpen Hall, Hutton Rudby, Yarm, Yorkshire, has engagement diaries and a privately circulated supplement to his autobiography, *Closed Chapters*. Mrs Elphinstone believes that any other papers were destroyed on completion of the autobiography.

HUTCHINSON, Sir Charles Frederick (1850–1907)

M.P. (Lib.) Rye, 1903–6.

No information was secured. Major A. G. N. Hadden-Price, grandson of Sir Charles's executor, was unable to be of assistance.

HUTCHINSON, Geoffrey Clegg, see ILFORD, Baron

HUTCHINSON, Hugh Leicester (1904–   )

M.P. (Lab.) Manchester Rusholme, 1945–50.

HUTCHINSON, Maurice Robert Hely- (1887–1961)

M.P. (Con.) Hastings, 1937–45.

Family records have survived and enquiries should be directed to Mr Henry Hely-Hutchinson, 99 Aldwych, London WC2B 4JS.

HUTCHISON, 1st B
Sir Robert Hutchison (1873–1950)

M.P. (Lib., later Lib.Nat.) Kirkcaldy Burghs, 1922–3; Montrose Burghs, 1924–32.
Paymaster-General, 1935–8.

Hazlehurst and Woodland, p. 78, found no papers.

HUTCHISON, Sir George Aitken Clark (1873–1928)

M.P. (Con.) Midlothian North, 1922–3 and 1924–8.

There are a number of press-cuttings books relating to Sir George's General Election campaigns, 1906–24, in the possession of his son, Sir George Ian Clark Hutchison.

HUTCHISON, Sir George Ian Clark (1903–   )

M.P. (Con.) Edinburgh West, 1941–59.

Sir George has retained several volumes of press-cuttings books relating to the various municipal and general election campaigns he fought between 1935 and 1955.

HUTCHISON, Sir James Riley Holt, 1st Bt (1893–   )

M.P. (Con.) Glasgow Central, 1945–50; Glasgow Scotstoun, 1950–9.
Parliamentary Under-Secretary and Financial Secretary, War Office, 1951–4.

Sir James has kept certain papers which he is using to write his autobiography. These include records of wartime service in North Africa and France, etc. The papers are not generally available for inspection.

HUTCHISON, William (d. 1924)

M.P. (Con.) Glasgow, Kelvingrove, 1922–4.

Information available at Somerset House was not sufficient to trace members of the family.

HUTCHISON, William Gordon Douglas (1904–75)

M.P. (Con.) Romford, 1931–5.
Actor.

HUTTON, Alfred Eddison (1865–1947)

M.P. (Lib.) Morley, 1892–Jan 1910.

It was not possible to trace Hutton's children.

HUTTON, John (1847–1921)

M.P. (Con.) Northallerton, 1868–74; Richmond, Yorkshire, 1895–1906.

It was not possible to trace any of Hutton's descendants. His wife was the elder daughter of the 2nd Lord Teignmouth. The present Lord Teignmouth was unable to provide any further information.

HYDE, Baron, see CLARENDON

HYDE, Sir Clarendon Golding (1858–1934)

M.P. (Lib.) Wednesbury, 1906–Jan 1910.
Member of numerous Government Committees, 1909–23.

Neither Mr Anthony Hyde (great-grandson) nor Mrs Seton Lloyd (granddaughter) know of any papers.

HYDE, Harford Montgomery (1907–)*

M.P. (Ulster Un.) Belfast North, 1950–9.
Author and barrister.

Churchill College, Cambridge, has seven boxes of papers. The material consists of the manuscript of books and associated papers, concerning Mr Montgomery Hyde's work with British Intelligence during World War II. The material remains under restriction. Other papers of political interest remain with Mr Montgomery Hyde and these will be placed in due course in the Public Record Office of Northern Ireland. The papers include correspondence with the 8th Marquess of Londonderry and Lady Londonderry, when Mr Montgomery Hyde was private secretary to the Marquess as Secretary of State for Air and Lord Privy Seal (1930s), and there is correspondence kept while he was a Member of Parliament.

HYLTON, 3rd B
Hylton George Hylton Joliffe (1862–1945)

M.P. (Con.) Wells, 1895–9.
Lord in Waiting, 1915–18.

The present (5th) Lord Hylton, Ammerdown, Radstock, Bath, Somerset, believes that records relating to his grandfather have survived. However, the material in his care is unsorted and unavailable at present. A quantity of estate and family papers has been deposited in the Somerset Record Office, but the material includes only a few incidental letters relating to the 3rd Lord Hylton.

HYND, Henry (1900–)

M.P. (Lab.) Hackney Central, 1945–50; Accrington, 1950–66.

HYND, John Burns (1902–71)

M.P. (Lab.) Sheffield Attercliffe, 1944–70.
Chancellor of the Duchy of Lancaster and Minister for Germany and Austria, 1945–7. Minister of Pensions, 1947.

The papers, most of which are in the care of Hynd's widow, Mrs J. B. Hynd, 18 Lakeside, Enfield, Middx., are described by Hazlehurst and Woodland, pp. 78–9. Further correspondence on colonial affairs can be found in the records of the Fabian Colonial Bureau, Rhodes House Library, Oxford.

IDRIS, Thomas Howell Williams (1842–1925)

M.P. (Lib.) Flint Boroughs, 1906–Jan 1910.

ILFORD, Baron
Geoffrey Clegg Hutchinson (1893–1974)

M.P. (Con.) Ilford, 1937–45; Ilford North, 1950–4.

Lord Ilford did not retain any papers relating to his political career.

ILIFFE, 1st B
Sir Edward Mauger Iliffe (1877–1960)

M.P. (Con.) Tamworth, 1923–9.

The present (2nd) Lord Iliffe, Basildon House, Lower Basildon, nr Reading RG8 9NR, states that his father left many diaries, papers and a collection of press cuttings covering most of his career. Probably the most important papers and letters concern Lord Iliffe's part in the development of his trade and technical publishing house.

ILKESTON, 1st B
Sir (Balthazar) Walter Foster (1840–1913)

M.P. (Lib.) Chester, 1885–6; Ilkeston, 1887–Dec 1910.

ILLINGWORTH, 1st B
Albert Holden Illingworth (1865–1942)

M.P. (Co.Lib.) Heywood, 1915–18; Heywood and Radcliffe, 1918–21.
Postmaster General, 1916–21.

Hazlehurst and Woodland, p. 79, provide details of the papers remaining with Lady Illingworth, 2 York House, Kensington Church Street, London W8.

ILLINGWORTH, Percy Holden (1869–1915)

M.P. (Lib.) Shipley, 1906–15.
Junior Lord of the Treasury, 1910–12. Parliamentary Secretary, Treasury, and Government Chief Whip, 1912–15.

Dr Cameron Hazlehurst found that a selection of Illingworth's letters and a collection of press cuttings and private ephemera has survived in the possession of his son, Mr Henry Illingworth, Tornbeck House, Carron, Morayshire.

INGLEBY, 1st Vt
Osbert Peake (1897–1966)

M.P. (Con.) Leeds North, 1929–55; Leeds N.E., May–Dec 1955.
Parliamentary Under-Secretary, Home Office, 1939–44. Financial Secretary to the Treasury, 1944–5. Minister of National Insurance, 1951–3. Minister of Pensions and National Insurance, 1953–5.

The present (2nd) Viscount Ingleby, Snilesworth, Osmotherley, Northallerton, North Yorkshire, has a collection of his father's papers. These are unsorted and not available. Records of the Leeds Conservatives can be found in the local association's offices. There is an assortment of press cuttings in the City Library Local History Department and executive and other committee minutes (1923–30) of the Leeds Conservatives in the City Archives Department.

INGLEBY, Holcombe (1854–1926)

M.P. (Con.) King's Lynn, Dec 1910–18.

Mrs S. Alexander-Stevenson (granddaughter) states that family records were probably destroyed when her parents left Norfolk in 1957. However, Mr R. J. Busby, who was undertaking research in the mid-1960s, saw a series of four diaries containing pertinent and personal comment on people and events connected with politics, London social life and the Athenaeum Club. These were in the care of the late Mr C. R. Ingleby, Mrs Alexander-Stevenson's father.

INGLEWOOD, 1st B
William Morgan Fletcher-Vane (1909–)

M.P. (Con.) Westmorland, 1945–64.
Joint Parliamentary Secretary, Ministry of Pensions and National Insurance, 1958–60; Ministry of Agriculture, 1960–2.

Lord Inglewood has retained a collection of personal papers. Some of his personal papers, together with estate papers, have been deposited in the Record Office, Carlisle. They contain no significant political material.

INMAN, 1st B
Philip Albert Inman (1892–   )

Lord Privy Seal, 1947.

Lord Inman retains some papers, details of which appear in Hazlehurst and Woodland, pp. 79–80.

INSKIP, Sir Thomas Walker Hobart, see CALDECOTE, 1st Vt

INVERFORTH, 1st B
Andrew Weir (1865–1955)

Minister of Munitions (later Supply), 1919–21.

A small group of papers with the present (2nd) Lord Inverforth and material in the Public Record Office (Mun/4/6467–6644), and (Mun/4/6651–6868) are described in Hazlehurst and Woodland, p. 150.

IRVINE, Sir Arthur James (1909–)

M.P. (Lab.) Liverpool Edge Hill, 1947–
Solicitor-General, 1967–70.

IRVING, (David) Daniel (1854–1924)

M.P. (Lab.) Burnley, 1918–24.

Items of correspondence (1905, 1906) concerning Irving can be found in the Labour Representation Committee Archive, together with a letter (1914) from him concerning employment in the cotton trade. Some records of the Social Democratic Federation, for which he was an organiser, are described in *Sources*, Vol. 1, pp. 236–7. The Burnley District Central Library has only copies of local newspapers which cover Irving's career. His family could not be traced.

IRVING, William John (1892–1967)

M.P. (Lab.) Tottenham North, Dec 1945–50; Wood Green, 1950–5.

W. J. Irving's sister-in-law, Mrs N. Rook, has a folder of testimonial and formal letters, but knows of no other papers.

IRWIN, 1st B, see HALIFAX, 1st E of

IRWIN, Lord, see HALIFAX, 2nd E of

ISAACS, George Alfred (1883–   )

M.P. (Lab.) Gravesend, 1923–4; Southwark North, 1929–31 and 1939–50; Southwark, 1950–9.
Minister of Labour and National Service, 1945–51. Minister of Pensions, 1951.

Mr Isaacs kept no papers (Hazlehurst and Woodland, p. 80). Southwark Borough Libraries have a collection of press cuttings relating to him.

ISLINGTON, 1st B
Sir John Poynder Dickson-Poynder (1866–1936)

M.P. (Con.) Chippenham, 1892–Jan 1910.
Governor, New Zealand, 1910–12. Under-Secretary of State, Colonies, 1914–15. Parliamentary Under-Secretary, India, 1915–18.

A collection of papers survives in the care of Mr John Grigg. These are not political papers, but mainly letters written by Lord Islington to his wife and other letters to Lady Islington. The papers of H. H. Asquith, Lord Hardinge and Austen Chamberlain contain an assortment of Lord Islington's letters.

ISMAY, 1st B
General Sir Hastings Lionel Ismay (1887–1965)

Served India, Somaliland, etc. Assistant Secretary, Committee of Imperial Defence, 1926–30; Deputy Secretary, 1936–8. Military Secretary to Viceroy of India, 1931–3.
Chief of Staff to Minister of Defence (W. S. Churchill), 1940–5. Deputy Secretary (Military), War Cabinet, 1940–5; and Additional Secretary (Military), 1945. Chief of Staff to Viceroy of India, 1947.
Secretary of State, Commonwealth Relations, 1951–2. Secretary General, North Atlantic Treaty Organisation, 1952–7.

A collection of papers covering the whole of Ismay's career has been deposited at the Liddell Hart Centre for Military Archives. The papers include personal correspondence and material written for an autobiography. The Cabinet Office has a further collection of personal lecture notes at the Staff College, Quetta; papers on the Anglo-French meetings of 1940; notes for Prime Minister's speeches, and on post-war defence organisation; correspondence with Chiefs of Staff, Commanders-in-Chief and Military Representatives (1922–46). Some correspondence with Col. C. Walker concerning East Africa (1927–35) is in the Walker papers at Rhodes House Library, and correspondence with Admiral Keyes is at Churchill College, Cambridge.

IVEAGH, 2nd E of
Rupert Edward Cecil Lee Guinness, Vt Elveden (1874–1967)

M.P. (Con.) Haggerston, 1908–Jan 1910; Essex S.E., 1912–18; Southend-on-Sea, 1918–27.

The present (3rd) Earl of Iveagh, Saint James's Gate, Dublin 8, has a collection of his grandparents' papers. These are being sorted and collated.

IVEAGH, Gwendolen, Countess of (d. 1966)

M.P. (Con.) Southend-on-Sea, 1927–35.

See above.

JACKSON, 1st B
William Frederick Jackson (1893–1954)

M.P. (Lab.) Brecon and Radnor, 1939–45.

There was no contact with Lady Jackson (widow).

JACKSON, Charles Lionel Atkins Ward- (1869–1930)

M.P. (Con.) Leominster, 1918–22.

C. L. A. Ward-Jackson is believed to have continued the family tradition of keeping a diary. A diary covering his early years (1869–75) and written by his father is in the County Library, Middlesbrough, but none written by C. L. A. Ward-Jackson himself can be traced. There exist, however, at least two bound typescript copies of a book 'Extracts from letters written in France during the Great War by Major C. L. A. Ward-Jackson to his wife, 1915–18' (731 pp., with index). This covers the period Jul 1915 to Feb 1918, during most of which he was Camp Commandant to the VII Army Corps. Copies are in the possession of Mr William Ward-Jackson, 7 Kensington Court Gdns., London W8, and Mr Peter Ward-Jackson, 8 Walton Place, London SW3.

JACKSON, Sir Francis Stanley (1870–1947)

M.P. (Con.) Howdenshire, 1915–26.
Financial Secretary, War Office, 1922–3.
Chairman, Conservative and Unionist Party, 1923–6.
Governor, Bengal, 1927–32.

Lord Allerton, nephew of Sir Francis Jackson, knows of no surviving papers. It has not been possible to trace Jackson's daughter-in-law. Mrs H. S. L. Jackson, whom Lord Allerton believed to have information concerning Jackson's papers.

JACKSON, Sir Henry, 1st Bt (1875–1937)

M.P. (Con.) Wandsworth Central, 1924–9, 1931–7.

JACKSON, Sir John (1851–1919)

M.P. (Con.) Devonport, Jan 1910–18.
Contractor for public works.

JACKSON, John Arthur (1862–1937)

M.P. (Con.) Whitehaven, Jan-Dec 1910.

A nephew, Mr E. D. Jackson of Iwerne Minster, nr Blandford, Dorset, has only a few press cuttings, and he does not know what happened to any other papers kept by his uncle.

JACKSON, Joseph Cooksey (1879–1938)

M.P. (Con.) Heywood and Radcliffe, 1931–5.

Messrs Oglethorpe, Sturton & Gillibrand, solicitors of Lancaster, who acted for members of the family, know of no papers.

JACKSON, Richard Stephens (1850–1938)

M.P. (Lib.) Greenwich, 1906–Jan 1910.

JACKSON, Robert Frederick (1880–1951)

M.P. (Lab.) Ipswich, 1923–4.

Jackson's widow, Mrs R. Jackson, was in 1973 resident at 79 Beechcroft Road, Ipswich. No contact could be established. The Ratcliffe collection at the Suffolk Record Office (Ipswich Branch) contains a considerable amount of material relating to the Ipswich Labour movement.

JACKSON, William Lauries, see ALLERTON, 1st B

JACOB, Albert Edward (1858–1929)

M.P. (Con.) Liverpool East Toxteth, 1924–9.

Mr B. R. K. Hunton, Chairman of W. and R. Jacob & Co. (Liverpool) Ltd, has been in touch with Mr A. E. Jacob's two daughters. They have no papers, apart from one or two press cuttings relating to their father.

JACOBSEN, Thomas Owen (1864–1941)

M.P. (Lib.) Hyde, 1916–18.

Miss E. E. Jacobsen (niece) died in 1973. Her representative states that only a second cousin is now alive, and that none of T. O. Jacobsen's papers are likely to have survived.

JACOBY, Sir James Alfred (1852–1909)

M.P. (Lib.) Mid Derbyshire, 1885–1909.

No member of the family could be contacted. Neither the solicitors, Wells & Hind, nor the Lace Makers Society of Nottingham provided any relevant information.

JAGGER, John (1872–1942)

M.P. (Lab.) Manchester Clayton, 1935–42.
General President, National Union of Distributive and Allied Workers, 1920–42.

The late Sir Joseph Hallsworth, who was Jagger's executor, had no information regarding his papers. The records of the NUDAW, forming part of the archives of the Union of Shop, Distributive and Allied Workers, are described in *Sources*, Vol. 1, pp. 270–1. Mr T. D. W. Reid, who has written on Jagger for the *Dictionary of Labour Biography*, was unable to locate any family papers.

JAMES OF HEREFORD, 1st B
Sir Henry James (1828–1911)

M.P. (Lib.) Taunton, 1869–85; Bury, 1885–6; (Lib.Un.) Bury, 1886–95.
Solicitor-General, 1873. Attorney-General, 1873–4 and 1880–5. Chancellor of the Duchy of Lancaster, 1895–1902.

Hereford and Worcester Record Office has an important collection of papers which is described by Hazlehurst and Woodland, pp. 81–2.

JAMES, Wing Commander Sir Archibald William Henry (1893–)

Military career, and R.A.F.
M.P. (Con.) Wellingborough, 1931–45.

Sir Archibald has given his papers to Churchill College, Cambridge. One box of papers contains Royal Flying Corps memoirs, and papers on R.A.F. expansion, 1931–6. A few further war records survive in the Imperial War Museum. There is a scrapbook, entitled 'The War of 1914', containing various documents, photographs, cards, press cuttings, etc., relating to service in the Army and R.F.C. The material includes Sir Archibald's logbook, 1915–18, and printed charts. Details of any papers relating to his parliamentary career are not available.

JAMES, Hon. Cuthbert (1872–1930)

M.P. (Con.) Bromley, 1919–30.

Mr T. James, the only son of Hon. C. James, states that his father did not keep any papers. Mr James kindly provided a short biographical account of his father.

JAMES, Sir Leifchild Stratten Leif-, see RHAYADER, 1st B

JAMES, Admiral Sir William Milbourne (1881–1973)

Naval career; served in World War I. Chief of Staff, Atlantic Fleet, 1929–30. Deputy Chief of Naval Staff, 1935–8. C.-in-C. Portsmouth, 1939–42. Chief of Naval Information, 1943–4.
M.P. (Con.) Portsmouth North, 1943–5.

According to information received by the Liddell Hart Centre for Military Archives, the Admiral retained no papers. The original of his diary used in his published works has apparently been mislaid.

JAMESON, Lieutenant-Colonel John Eustace- (1853–1919)*

M.P. (Irish Nat.) Clare West, 1895–1906.

JAMESON, John Gordon (1878–1955)

M.P. (Con.) Edinburgh West, 1918–22.

There was no contact with Jameson's daughter, Mrs Alexa Dixon, The Wynding House, Bamburgh, Northumberland.

JAMIESON, Lord
Douglas Jamieson (1880–1952)

M.P. (Con.) Glasgow Maryhill, 1931–5.
Solicitor-General, Scotland, 1933–5. Lord Advocate, Scotland, 1935.

Neither Lady Jamieson nor her solicitors know of any surviving papers.

JANNER, Baron
Sir Barnett Janner (1892–)

M.P. (Lib.) Whitechapel and St George's, 1931–5; (Lab.) Leicester West, 1945–50; Leicester North West, 1950–70.
President, Board of Deputies of British Jews, 1955–64, etc.

Lord Janner states that he has a considerable amount of correspondence and documents. Details are not available.

JARDINE, Sir Ernest, 1st Bt (1859–1947)

M.P. (Lib.Un.) Somerset East, Jan 1910–18.

Mrs K. P. O'Connell, The Dogs, Wincanton, Somerset (granddaughter) has a small collection of press cuttings relating to her grandfather's career. These deal mainly with his business and parliamentary activities but in addition there are a number of obituary notices describing his life and work.

JARDINE, Sir John, 1st Bt (1844–1919)

M.P. (Lib.) Roxburghshire, 1906–19.
Civil Service and judicial career, India.

Mr Lionel Jardine (son), 4 Balfour Mews, London W1, states that he has a few papers only: obituary notices, and one or two articles. Sir Ian Jardine, Bt knows of no papers.

JARRETT, George William Symonds (1880–1960)

Organiser, National Service League, 1913–15; National Democratic Party, 1917–20.
M.P. (Constitutional). Dartford, 1922–3.

Papers of the National Service League are described in *Sources*, Vol. 1, p. 186, and some records of the National Democratic party are detailed on p. 32. No family was traced.

JARVIS, Sir (Joseph) John, 1st Bt (1876–1950)

M.P. (Con.) Guildford, 1935–50.

Lady Lyle of Westbourne, Bakersgate, Pirbright, Woking, Surrey, has a series of six volumes of press cuttings which relate to her father's parliamentary work and especially to work in Jarrow during the depression. Sir Francis Williams, Bt, Llys Meirchion, Denbigh, Clwyd, Sir John Jarvis's son-in-law, has one or two papers, articles, speeches and notes. Records of the Guildford Conservative Association are held in the local offices.

JAY, Douglas Patrick Thomas (1907–   )

Journalist, later Civil Servant with Ministry of Supply, Board of Trade and Prime Minister's Office.
M.P. (Lab.) Battersea North, 1946–
Economic Secretary, Treasury, 1947–50. Financial Secretary, Treasury, 1950–1. President, Board of Trade, 1964–7.

Mr Jay refers only to his published books, his pamphlets, and articles in the *Daily Herald*. He mentions no unpublished papers which he has kept.

JEBB, Sir Richard Claverhouse (1841–1905)

M.P. (Con.) Cambridge University, 1891–1905.
Regius Professor of Greek from 1889.

His classical notebooks are in the Amherst College Library, Amherst, Mass., U.S.A. Any surviving personal material may be with Mr Lionel Jebb, The Lyth, Ellesmere, Salop.

JEFFREYS, 1st B
General Sir George Darell Jeffreys (1878–1960)

Military career.
M.P. (Con.) Petersfield, 1941–51.

Enquiries should be addressed to the present (2nd) Lord Jeffreys.

JEFFREYS, Arthur Frederick (1848–1906)

M.P. (Lib.) Basingstoke, 1887–1906.
Parliamentary Secretary, Local Government Board, 1905–6.

Enquiries should be addressed to A. F. Jeffreys's great-grandson, Rt. Hon. Lord Jeffreys, Marden Grange, Devizes, Wilts. His daughter, Mrs E. Charrington, lives near Basingstoke.

JEGER, George (1903–71)

M.P. (Lab.) Winchester, 1945–50; Goole, 1950–71.

Miss Jennifer Jeger, c/o The Hansard Society for Parliamentary Government, 12 Gower Street, London WC1E 6DP, states that her father left a number of papers. These are unsorted, but the material includes documents, letters etc., relating to the Spanish Civil War and the Gibraltar question.

JEGER, Dr Santo Wayburn (1898–1953)

M.P. (Lab.) St Pancras South East, 1945–50; Holborn and St Pancras South, 1950–3.

Enquiries should be directed to Mrs Lena Jeger, M.P. Records of the Socialist Medical Association, of which S. W. Jeger was one of the founders, are described in *Sources,* Vol. 1, pp. 240–1. Constituency records, from 1948, are held in Transport House Library.

JENKINS, Arthur (1882–1946)

M.P. (Lab.) Pontypool, 1935–46.
Parliamentary Secretary, Ministry of Town and Country Planning, 1945; Ministry of Education, 1945.

The Rt. Hon. Roy Jenkins, M.P., son of Arthur Jenkins, states that only a few papers survive. These include some diaries and a few press cuttings. The material remains with Mr Roy Jenkins.

JENKINS, John (1852–1939)

M.P. (Lab.) Chatham, 1906–Jan 1910.

There was no sign of the family. Jenkins was one time President of the Cardiff Shipbuilding Society.

JENKINS, Roy Harris (1920–   )

M.P. (Lab.) Southwark Central, 1948–50; Birmingham Stechford, 1950–76.
Minister of Aviation, 1964–5. Secretary of State for Home Affairs, 1965–7 and   1974–6. Chancellor of the Exchequer, 1967–70. Deputy Leader, Labour Party, 1970–2.

Mr Jenkins states that for the time being he prefers to keep confidential the details of his own personal papers.

JENKINS, Sir William (1871–1944)

M.P. (Lab.) Neath, 1922–44.

Messrs Walter P. David & Shape, solicitors of Bridgend, South Glamorgan, suggest that enquiries should be addressed to Sir William's son, Mr David Jenkins, 2 Mount Pleasant, Cynmer, nr Port Talbot, West Glamorgan. Details of papers have not been secured.

JENKINS, Sir William Albert (1878–1968)

M.P. (Nat.Lib.) Breconshire and Radnorshire, 1922–4.

Mr H. L. Jenkins, 7 Glenmore Avenue, Thornton, Blackpool FY5 4NY, states that most of his uncle's papers were destroyed before his death. Mr Jenkins does, however, have a small collection of photographs and press cuttings relating to the period when Sir W. A. Jenkins was Mayor of Swansea, 1947–9.

JENNINGS, Sir Roland (1894–1968)

M.P. (Con.) Sedgefield, 1931–5; Sheffield Hallam, 1939–59.

Contact with Lady Jennings was not established, and Messrs Jennings, Johnson & Co., chartered accountants, of Sunderland, have no relevant papers.

JEPHCOTT, Alfred Roper (1853–1932)

M.P. (Con.) Birmingham Yardley, 1918–29.

JERSEY, 8th E of
George Henry Child Villiers, Vt Grandison (1873–1923)

Lord in Waiting, 1919.

The Jersey family papers are being transferred to the Greater London Record Office (Middlesex Records). Those of the 8th Earl consist of various box files, all labelled. There is one box file labelled 'Political and various, 1911'. Access is granted for bona fide students to see the papers, but the permission of the present Earl is necessary before any material may be published.

JESSEL, 1st B
Sir Herbert Merton Jessel, 1st Bt (1866–1950)

M.P. (Con.) St Pancras South, 1896–1906; Jan 1910–18.

The present (2nd) Lord Jessel knows of no surviving papers relating to his father's career.

JESSON, Charles (b. 1862)

M.P. (Nat.Dem./Co.Lab.) Walthamstow West, 1918–22.

It was not possible to trace Jesson's family, and the Musicians' Union, for which he was an organiser, has no personal collection. Records of the Musicians' Union are described in *Sources*, Vol. 1, pp. 165–6.

JESSON, Thomas Edward (1883–1958)

M.P. (Con.) Rochdale, 1931–5.

JEWSON, Dorothy (1884–1964)
Mrs Campbell Stephen

M.P. (Lab.) Norwich, 1923–4.

Member, National Administrative Council of the Independent Labour Party.

It was not possible to locate any papers of Dorothy Jewson. Some Jewson family papers are housed in the Norfolk Record Office but none relate to her. The records of the ILP are described in *Sources*, Vol. 1, pp. 109–11, and the records of the Norwich Constituency Labour Party on p. 139.

JEWSON, Percy William (1881–1962)

M.P. (Lib.Nat.) Great Yarmouth, 1941–5.

A diary recording Percy Jewson's trip to Russia as a member of a parliamentary delegation in 1945 has been deposited by his son, Mr Charles Jewson, in Norfolk Record Office. Family scrapbooks, 1908–62, and a volume of press cuttings relating to Percy Jewson's work as Lord Mayor of Norwich, 1934–5, are retained by Mr Charles Jewson, Horsford Hall, Norwich NOR 84X. A copy of the latter volume is also available in the Local History section of Norwich Central Library.

JODRELL, Sir Neville Paul (1858–1932)

M.P. (Con.) Mid Norfolk, 1918; King's Lynn, 1918–23.

Members of the family could not be traced; the firm of solicitors who were named in the will could provide no information. The will assigns certain family papers to Sir Neville's cousin, C. E. Jodrell, of Brisbane, Australia.

JOEL, Dudley Jack Barnato (1904–41)

M.P. (Con.) Dudley, 1931–41.

Mr Stanhope Joel of Perots Island, Southampton, Bermuda (D. J. B. Joel's last surviving brother), could not be contacted.

JOHN, Edward Thomas (1857–1931)

M.P. (Lib.) Denbighshire East, Dec 1910–18.

The University College of North Wales, Bangor, has a collection of E. T. John's papers (Mss 20456–62). The material includes some records (1924–7) of the Peace Society. A further collection of papers can be found in the National Library of Wales, including correspondence, press cuttings, etc.

JOHN, William (1878–1955)

M.P. (Lab.) Rhondda West, 1920–50.
Comptroller, H.M. Household, 1942–4. Junior Lord of the Treasury, 1944–5.

Miss S. O. Rosser, niece of William John, knows of no papers. The *Dictionary of Labour Biography*, Vol. I, p. 195, gives a short account of John's career.

JOHNSON, Howard Sydney (1911–   )

M.P. (Con.) Brighton Kemp Town, 1950–9.

Mr H. S. Johnson has retained no papers relating to his parliamentary career.

JOHNSON, James (1908–   )

M.P. (Lab.) Rugby, 1950–9; Hull West, 1964–

JOHNSON, Johr (1850–1910)

M.P. (Lab.) Gateshead, 1904–Jan 1910.

It was not possible to trace members of the family. The *Dictionary of Labour Biography,* Vol. I, pp. 195–6, refers to no papers.

JOHNSON, Sir (Louis) Stanley (1869–1937)

M.P. (Con.) Walthamstow East, 1918–24.

Persons mentioned in the will and act of probate could not be traced. Sir Stanley was Mayor of Hackney, but the Hackney Libraries Department have only a few press cuttings.

JOHNSON, Hon. Sir Reginald Powell Croom-, see CROOM-JOHNSON

JOHNSON, William (1849–1919)

M.P. (Lib.Lab., then Lab.) Nuneaton, 1906–19.

The Labour Party archive contains some correspondence (1910–14) including letters from W. Johnson, regarding his relations with the Labour Party. The *Dictionary of Labour Biography,* Vol. II, pp. 209–10, refers to no papers. The Nuneaton Divisional Librarian suggests that Mrs M. K. Johnson of 35 Black Bank, Bedworth, Nuneaton, may have photographs and a few papers only concerning Billy Johnson. Many old papers at the Bedworth Miners' Offices were destroyed.

JOHNSTON, Hon. Lord
Douglas Harold Johnston (1907–   )

M.P. (Lab.) Paisley, 1948–61.
Solicitor-General, Scotland, 1947–51.

JOHNSTON, Sir Christopher Nicholson, see SANDS, Lord

JOHNSTON, James Wellwood (1900–58)

M.P. (Con.) Stirlingshire East and Clackmannan, 1931–5.

Mrs J. Wellwood Johnston states that her husband left no political papers. Personal diaries were destroyed.

JOHNSTON, Malcolm Campbell (1871–1938)

M.P. (Con.) East Ham South, 1931–5.

Efforts to contact close relations were not successful. Mr Colin Campbell-Johnston of Brighton, whose father was a first cousin of Malcolm Campbell Johnston, knew of no papers.

JOHNSTON, Thomas (1881–1965)

M.P. (Lab.) Stirlingshire West, 1922–4, 1929–31, and 1935–45; Dundee, 1924–9. Parliamentary Under-Secretary, Scottish Office, 1929–31. Lord Privy Seal, 1931. Secretary of State for Scotland, 1941–5.

A collection of records exists at the National Library of Scotland. This consists of notebooks, addresses, correspondence and papers, 1904–57.

JOHNSTON, William (1829–1902)*

M.P. (Con.) Belfast South, 1868–78, 1885–1902.

Johnston's diaries are held in the Public Record Office of Northern Ireland.

JOHNSTONE, Harcourt (1895–1945)

M.P. (Lib.) Willesden East, 1923–4; South Shields, 1931–5; Middlesbrough West, 1940–5. Parliamentary Secretary, Department of Overseas Trade, 1940–5.

The Lords Derwent, Blakenham and Listowel, all members of the family, know of no papers, and the solicitors, Messrs Turner Peacock, could provide no further information.

JOHNSTONE, John Heywood (1850–1904)

M.P. (Con.) Horsham, 1893–1904.

Mrs A. Johnstone (daughter-in-law) states that none of her father-in-law's papers were kept.

JOHNSTONE, Joseph (1860–1931)

M.P. (Co.Lib.) Renfrewshire East, 1918–22.

JOICEY, 1st B
Sir James Joicey, 1st Bt (1846–1936)

M.P. (Lib.) Chester-le-Street, 1885–1906.

The Joicey family papers are in the care of the present Lord Joicey, Etal Manor, Berwick-on-Tweed, Northumberland. Amongst these are papers relating to the 1st Baron, including yearly pocket diaries containing personal memoranda, notes of engagements and appointments, private and business accounts, etc., 1865–9, 1871, 1874, 1875; and press-cuttings albums concerning Joicey's parliamentary candidatures, his political work, and his business activities. A catalogue of the Joicey papers is available at the Northumberland Record Office. Lord Joicey reserves the right to refuse access to the papers in his care. Papers relating to the mining interests of the family are deposited in Newcastle-upon-Tyne University Library. Papers of the Ford and Etal estates are in the care of the Northumberland Record Office.

JOLIFFE, H. G. H., see HYLTON, 3rd B

JONES, Arthur Creech (1891–1964)

M.P. (Lab.) Shipley, 1935–50; Wakefield, 1954–64.
Parliamentary Under-Secretary, Colonial Office, 1945–6. Secretary of State for the Colonies, 1946–50.

The extensive collection of papers which is in Rhodes House Library, Oxford, is described by Hazlehurst and Woodland, p. 82.

JONES, Aubrey (1911–)

M.P. (Con.) Birmingham Hall Green, 1950–65.
Minister of Fuel and Power, 1955–7. Minister of Supply, 1957–9. Chairman, National Board for Prices and Incomes, 1965–70.

Mr Aubrey Jones has retained a number of his papers, including an intermittent diary, correspondence and files of press cuttings. These are not currently made available.

JONES, Sir (Charles) Sydney (1872–1947)

M.P. (Lib.) Liverpool West Derby, 1923–4.
Lord Mayor of Liverpool, 1938–42.

The solicitors who acted in the estate, and also the Liverpool Record Office, know of no collection of papers left by Sir Sydney Jones. Sir Sydney was a partner in the shipowning concern of Alfred Holt & Co; he left no heirs. The papers of the 17th Earl of Derby, at the Liverpool Record Office, include correspondence with Sir Sydney as Lord Mayor of Liverpool, Nov 1938–Oct 1940. The Liverpool Record Office also has a few other papers, and a collection of newspaper cuttings (1929–47) relating to Sir Sydney.

JONES, Sir David Brynmor (1852–1921)

M.P. (Lib.) Stroud, 1892–5; Swansea, 1895–1914.

Sir David Brynmor Jones was survived by two step-children, neither of whom is still alive. Neither Mr R. Maine, great-nephew of Sir D. B. Jones, nor a great-niece know of any surviving papers.

JONES, David Thomas (1899–1963)

M.P. (Lab.) The Hartlepools, 1945–59.

Mrs A. Jones has no papers relating to her husband's parliamentary career. The Lord Champion, who was his executor, remembers that he destroyed a large amount of the material which he had kept while in Parliament.

JONES, Sir Edgar Rees (1878–1962)

M.P. (Lib.) Merthyr Tydfil, Jan 1910–15; (Co.Lib.) 1918–22.
Controller of Priority Department, Ministry of Munitions, 1915–18.

The Library of University College, Swansea, has a collection of material relating to Merthyr politics. This includes material relating to the affairs of the local Liberal party. No surviving member of Sir Edgar's family could be traced.

JONES, Sir Evan Davies, 1st Bt (1859–1949)

M.P. (Co.Lib.) Pembrokeshire, 1918–22.

It was not possible to contact Sir E. D. Jones' daughter in Canada.

JONES, Sir (Frederick) Elwyn, see ELWYN-JONES, Baron

JONES, Frederick Llewellyn- (1866–1941)

M.P. (Lib.) Flintshire, 1929–35.

Dr Mona Llewellyn-Jones (daughter), Clwydfa, Ruthin Road, Mold, Clwyd, fears that her sister destroyed all papers relating to their father.

JONES, George Morgan Garro, see TREFGARNE, 1st B

JONES, Sir George William Henry (d. 1956)

M.P. (Con.) Stoke Newington, 1918–23, 1924–45.

Messrs Bishop & Co., solicitors, state that all Sir George's near relatives have died. Miss D. M. Burt, a friend of the family, could provide no information regarding papers, and the North

East London Conservative Group has no papers for the period when Sir George Jones was in Parliament.

JONES, Sir (Henry) Haydn (1863–1950)

M.P. (Lib.) Merioneth, Jan 1910–45.

The Gwynedd Area Record Office at Y Lawnt, Dolgellau, has only three letters (1929–39) from Sir Haydn Jones to the headmaster of Towyn Council School, and records of the Merioneth Liberal Party (*Sources*, Vol. 1, p. 150) which relate to the M.P. No member of the family was traced.

JONES, John Emlyn Emlyn- (1889–1952)

M.P. (Lib.) Dorset North, 1922–4.

Mr Alun Emlyn-Jones (son), 64 Danycoed Road, Cyncoed, Cardiff, has retained many of his father's papers. The collection includes some correspondence, notebooks, drafts of articles and speeches, press cuttings, and papers relating to the coal trade and Emlyn-Jones's business activities. It is possible that the collection will be deposited in the Glamorgan Record Office.

JONES, John Henry (1894–1962)

M.P. (Lab.) Bolton, 1945–50; Rotherham, 1950–62.
Parliamentary Secretary, Supply, 1947–50.

J. H. Jones' widow knows of no surviving papers. A collection of press cuttings relating to his work as M.P. for Rotherham is available in Rotherham Public Library.

JONES, Sir (John) Henry Morris- (1884–1972)

M.P. (Lib.) Denbighshire, 1929–31; (Lib.Nat., later Nat.Lib.) Denbighshire, 1931–50.
Junior Lord of the Treasury, 1935–7.

Papers of Sir Henry Morris-Jones have been deposited on loan with the Clwyd Record Office at Hawarden. The collection includes diaries (1911–18, 1925–44), describing service in World War I and in the Liberal Party, and leading figures in parliament. There are also pocket diaries for 1912–19 and 1930–62, and personal notebooks, 1941–62. The autobiography, *Doctor in the Whips' Room* (1955), drew extensively on these diaries. Some correspondence (1923–63) is also extant, and this relates mainly to engagements, minor administrative matters, replies to congratulations, etc. Correspondents include Stanley Baldwin, L. Hore Belisha and David Lloyd George. The collection also includes pamphlets, notes, etc., on his family (1896–1945); parliamentary papers (1941–9), mainly on Welsh affairs; papers and photographs concerning the parliamentary delegation to Buchenwald concentration camp (April 1945); press cuttings, photographs and drafts, etc., of published works.

JONES, John Joseph (1873–1941)

M.P. (Lab.) Silvertown, 1918–40.
General Organiser, National Union of General and Municipal Workers.

There was no trace of members of the family. An autobiography, *My Lively Life*, has appeared. The G.M.W.U. records are described in *Sources*, Vol. 1, pp. 193–4.

JONES, John Lees- (1887–1966)

M.P. (Con.) Manchester Blackley, 1931–45.

Mr J. R. Lees-Jones (son) says that his father left no papers relating to his parliamentary work.

JONES, Rev. Josiah Towyn (1858–1925)

M.P. (Lib., later Co.Lib.) Carmarthen East, 1912–18; Llanelly, 1918–22.
Junior Lord of the Treasury, 1917–22.

It proved impossible to trace Mr Arthur Jones (nephew and sole executor), formerly of Llain, Penbryn, Dyfed.

JONES, Sir Lewis (1884–1968)

M.P. (Lib.Nat.) Swansea West, 1931–45.

Enquiries should be addressed to Sir Lewis Jones's son, Lt.-Col. O. L. Jones, O.B.E., of Jericho Cottage, Castlemartin, Dyfed.

JONES, Liefchild Stratton Leif-, see RHAYADER, 1st B

JONES, Llewellyn Archer Atherley- (1851–1929)

M.P. (Lib.) Durham N.W., 1885–1914.

Butt & Bowyer, solicitors who acted in the estate, had no relevant information. Atherley-Jones's wife predeceased him, and it was not possible to trace the son.

JONES, Morgan (1885–1939)

M.P. (Lab.) Caerphilly, 1921–39.
Parliamentary Secretary, Board of Education, 1924 and 1929–31.

According to information supplied by Mr D. Sutton of the Caerphilly Constituency Labour Party, Morgan Jones's sister at Bargoed has some of her brother's papers, but no other material is with other surviving members of his family. Mr Sutton has collected secondary materials relating to Morgan Jones and to the Caerphilly C.L.P., records of which are deposited in the Library of University College, Swansea.

JONES, Philip Asterley (1914–   )

M.P. (Lab.) Hitchin, 1945–50.

Mr Jones has retained no papers.

JONES, Sir (Pryce) Edward Pryce-, 1st Bt (1861–1926)

M.P. (Con.) Montgomery District, 1895–1906; Dec 1910–18.

Neither Mr David Pryce-Jones (great-nephew) nor Lady Pryce-Jones (daughter-in-law) know of surviving papers relating to Sir Edward's political career. Lady Pryce-Jones, The Manor House, Great Ryburgh, Norfolk, has a press-cutting book relating to Sir Pryce Pryce-Jones, Sir Edward's father, concerning Sir Pryce's last election campaign in 1895.

JONES, Robert Thomas (1874–1940)

M.P. (Lab.) Caernarvonshire, 1922–33.
General Secretary, North Wales Quarrymen's Union, 1908–33.

Mr E. Lloyd Jones, solicitor of Bangor, was R. T. Jones's sole executor. He confirms that at the time of his death there were no documents extant that could be of any interest or historical value. Records of the North Wales Quarrymen's Union, formerly at the National Library of Wales (*Sources*, Vol. 1, p. 265), are at the Gwynedd Record Office, Caernarvon. This material includes papers about R. T. Jones and his parliamentary career.

JONES, Thomas Isaac Mardy (1881–1970)

M.P. (Lab.) Pontypridd, 1922–31.

JONES, W. Kennedy (1865–1921)

M.P. (Con.) Hornsey, 1916–21.
Editor, *Evening News,* 1894–1900.

No member of the family was traced, and the Associated Newspaper Group Limited could provide no information.

JONES, William (1860–1915)

M.P. (Lib.) Caernarvonshire North, 1895–1915.
Junior Lord of the Treasury, 1911–15.

The papers are deposited in the Library of the University College of North Wales, Bangor (ref. 5446–86) and consist of diaries and notebooks, letters, cuttings and memoranda. The papers cover Jones's private life up to 1895 and thereafter, and his political work, including constituency correspondence, his papers as a Whip, papers relating to the Disestablishment controversy, to the Welsh National Liberal Council and to his various other political activities.

JONES, William Elwyn Edwards (1904–   )

M.P. (Lab.) Conway, 1950–1.

JONES, William Nathaniel (1858–1934)

M.P. (Lib.) Carmarthen, 1928–9.

JONES, Sir William Samuel Glyn-, see GLYN-JONES

JORDAN, Jeremiah (1830–1911)*

M.P. (Irish Nat.) Clare West, 1885–92; Meath South, 1893–5; Fermanagh South, 1895–Dec 1910.

The Northern Ireland Public Record Office has a collection of papers (D 2073), which includes family and political correspondence; drafts of speeches; newspaper cuttings and photographs. Some material relates to the 1885 election, to local railways and to the history of Fermanagh.

JOWETT, Frederick William (1864–1944)

M.P. (Lab.) Bradford West, 1906–18; Bradford East, 1922–4 and 1929–31.
1st Commissioner of Works, 1924.

Only a few papers in Bradford City Library have survived. Details are given in Hazlehurst and Woodland, p. 83. There are, however, some of Jowett's letters in the Labour Representation Committee archive (1901–6); in the Labour Party general correspondence for 1906–7; in the Labour Party War Emergency Workers'National Committee files; and in the Parliamentary files for 1929. The Independent Labour Party archives are described in *Sources,* Vol. 1, pp. 109–11.

JOWITT, 1st E
Sir William Allen Jowitt (1885–1957)

M.P. (Lib.) The Hartlepools, 1922–4; Preston, 1929; (Lab., later Nat.Lab.) Preston, 1929–31; (Lab.) Ashton-under-Lyne, 1939–45.

Attorney-General, 1929–32. Solicitor-General, 1940–2. Paymaster-General, 1942. Minister without Portfolio, 1942–4. Minister of Social Insurance (later National Insurance), 1944–5. Lord Chancellor, 1945–51.

Hazlehurst and Woodland, p. 83, state that the papers are held by Earl Jowitt's daughter, Lady Penelope Wynn-Williams, The Hall, Wittersham, Isle of Oxney, Kent.

JOYCE, Michael (b. 1854)*

M.P. (Irish Nat.) Limerick, 1900–18.

KABERRY, Sir Donald, 1st Bt (1907–)

M.P. (Con.) Leeds North West, 1950–
Assistant Government Whip, 1951–5. Parliamentary Secretary, Board of Trade, 1955.

Sir Donald states that all his constituency files were kept at the House of Commons and they were destroyed in the bomb incident there in June 1974. He does retain some papers, including details of his inquiries into the overspending and prosecution of the Yorkshire Electricity Board and its Chairman (1951–2).

KARR, Sir Henry Seton (1853–1914)

M.P. (Con.) St Helens, 1885–1906.

Documents at the Principal Probate Registry refer only to Sir Henry's widow. It was not possible to trace the family.

KAVANAGH, Walter MacMurrough (1856–1922)*

M.P. (Irish Nat.) Carlow County, 1908–10.

KAY, Sir Robert Newbald (1869–1947)

M.P. (Lib.) Elland, 1923–4.

Mr Thornton L. Kay, c/o Newbald Kay & Son, 26 Lendal, York YO1 2AG (son), knows of no surviving papers relating to his father's parliamentary career. Mr Kay does have, however, three volumes of press cuttings and photographs relating to Sir Robert's tenure as Lord Mayor of York, 1924–5.

KEARLEY, Sir Hudson Ewbanke, see DEVONPORT, 1st Vt

KEATING, Matthew (1869–1937)*

M.P. (Irish Nat.) Kilkenny South, 1909–18.

The Northern Ireland Public Record Office has some 28 documents (D 1919), including press cuttings, photographs and correspondence with Joseph Devlin.

KEATINGE, Sir Edgar Mayne (1905–)

M.P. (Con.) Bury St Edmunds, 1944–5.

Sir Edgar has retained a large number of press cuttings, covering his political campaigning in 1938–9, and during his by-election campaign in 1944 and the subsequent two years.

KEDWARD, Rev. Roderick Morris (1881–1937)

M.P. (Lib.) Bermondsey West, 1923–4; Ashford, 1929–31.

Neither Kedward's widow nor the solicitor mentioned in the will could be traced.

KEELING, Sir Edward Herbert (d. 1954)

M.P. (Con.) Twickenham, 1935–54.

Inquiries should be directed to Sir Edward's son, Mr Christopher Keeling, c/o Fenchurch Insurance Holdings Ltd, Cornwall House, 12 Coopers Row, London EC3.

KEENAN, William (1889–1955)

M.P. (Lab.) Liverpool Kirkdale, 1945–55.

It is understood that Mrs C. Keenan (widow) lives in Bootle, Merseyside. Contact was not secured.

KEENS, Sir Thomas (1870–1953)

M.P. (Lib.) Aylesbury, 1923–4.

Mr P. F. Keens, c/o Messrs Keens, Shay, Keens & Co., 295 Regent Street, London W1, has his father's surviving papers.

KEIR, Thelma Cazalet- (1899–   )

M.P. (Con.) Islington East, 1931–45.
Parliamentary Secretary, Ministry of Education, 1945.

Mrs Thelma Cazalet-Keir has retained certain papers in her care.

KEKEWICH, Sir George William (1841–1921)

Secretary, Board of Education, 1900–3.
M.P. (Lib.) Exeter, 1906–Jan 1910.

At the BLPES, there is a guardbook containing letters to Sir George and press cuttings of his speeches, etc., on his retirement from the Board of Education and during his subsequent political career. Letters from Sir G. W. Kekewich (1909–15) are also held in the Independent Labour Party papers at BLPES.

KELLAWAY, Frederick George (1870–1933)

M.P. (Lib.) Bedford, Dec 1910–22.
Parliamentary Secretary, Ministry of Munitions, 1916–21. Deputy Minister of Munitions, 1919–21. Parliamentary Secretary, Department of Overseas Trade; Additional Parliamentary Under-Secretary, Foreign Office, and Additional Parliamentary Secretary, Board of Trade, 1920–1. Postmaster General, 1921–2.

Hazlehurst and Woodland, pp. 83–4, describe the papers which are held by Kellaway's daughters, Mrs King, Hunts Green, Bradford Road, Sherborne, Dorset, and Mrs Beckley, Withermere, Burwash, Etchingham, Sussex.

KELLETT, Lieutenant Colonel Edward Orlando (1902–43)

M.P. (Con.) Birmingham Aston, 1939–43.

The Hon. Mrs William McGowan states that she has some of her late husband's papers and press cuttings. However, these have little relevance to Colonel Kellett's parliamentary career. For much of the years 1939–43 Colonel Kellett was on active military service.

KELLEY, Major Sir Frederic Arthur (1863–1926)

M.P. (Con.) Rotherham, 1918–23.

KELLEY, George Davy (1848–1911)

M.P. (Lab.) Manchester South West, 1906–Jan 1910.
General Secretary, Amalgamated Society of Lithographic Printers, 1879–1911.

The *Dictionary of Labour Biography*, Vol. II, pp. 211–14, refers only to a number of published materials relating to G. D. Kelley. No members of the family were traced.

KELLY, Edward J. (b. 1883)*

M.P. (Irish Nat.) Donegal East, Jan 1910–22.

KELLY, John T.*

M.P. (Sinn Fein) Dublin College Green, 1918–22.

KELLY, Thomas*

M.P. (Sinn Fein) Dublin St Stephen's Green, 1918–22.

KELLY, William Thomas (1874–1944)

M.P. (Lab.) Rochdale, 1924–31 and 1935–40.

Persons mentioned in the will could not be traced. The Rochdale libraries know only of local press references to Kelly.

KEMP, Sir George, see ROCHDALE, 1st B

KEMSLEY, 2nd Vt
(Geoffrey) Lionel Berry (1909–)

M.P. (Con.) Buckingham, 1943–5.
Deputy Chairman, Kemsley Newspapers Ltd, 1938–59.

KEMSLEY, Sir Colin Norman Thornton- (1903–)

M.P. (Con.) Kincardine and Aberdeenshire West, 1939–50; Angus North and Mearns, 1950–64.

Sir Colin has made a habit of returning his working papers to the appropriate bodies. Thus the papers of the Conservative policy committee on planning which he chaired are housed at Conservative Central Office, London; and his constituency papers were returned to the North Angus and Mearns Conservative Association. The papers he retained include some correspondence (letters received and copies of out letters); notes on telephone conversations; material on the Polish question, 1945–57; correspondence on the duties of the Monarch in the Commonwealth, 1952; and some press cuttings. These have been deposited on long loan with Aberdeen University Library. Reference should also be made to C. N. Thornton-Kemsley, *Through Winds and Tides* (1974).

KENDALL, (William) Denis (1903–   )

M.P. (Ind.) Grantham, 1942–50.

Mr Kendall destroyed the mass of newspaper cuttings, diaries and private papers which he had retained, and all that now survives is a small collection of press cuttings and testimonial letters.

KENNAWAY, Sir John Henry, 3rd Bt (1837–1919)

M.P. (Con.) Devon East, 1870–Jan 1910.

Sir John Kennaway, 5th Bt (grandson), is unable to locate any of his grandfather's papers. Many papers appear to have been destroyed during World War II. Family papers, for the nineteenth century, have been listed. (NRA 9463).

KENNEDY, Alfred Ravenscroft
His Honour Judge A. R. Kennedy (1879–1943)

M.P. (Con.) Preston, 1924–9.

Wing Cdr. G. F. Kennedy, Springbank Cottage, Defford, Worcester, Judge Kennedy's nephew, has a very few papers concerning his uncle's career. These mainly comprise press cuttings relating to his appointment to the County Court bench in 1929, as Commissioner of Assize in 1934, and his death. He also has an election manifesto and one or two photographs.

KENNEDY, Myles Storr Nigel (1889–1964)

M.P. (Con.) Lonsdale, 1922–3.

It was not possible to contact Mrs M. S. N. Kennedy (widow), in Ulverston, Cumbria.

KENNEDY, Patrick J. (b. 1864)*

M.P. (Irish Nat.) Kildare North, 1892–5; Westmeath North, 1900–6.

KENNEDY, Thomas (1876–1954)

M.P. (Lab.) Kirkcaldy, 1921–2, 1923–31 and 1935–44.
Junior Lord of the Treasury, 1924. Parliamentary Secretary, Treasury, 1929–31.
General Secretary, Social Democratic Federation, and editor of *Social Democrat*.

Surviving records of the Social Democratic Federation are described in *Sources*, Vol. 1, pp. 236–7. Thomas Kennedy's family was not traced.

KENNEDY, Vincent P. (b. 1876)*

M.P. (Irish Nat.) Cavan West, 1904–18.

KENNET, 1st B
Sir Edward Hilton Young (1879–1960)

M.P. (Lib.) Norwich, 1915–23, 1924–9; (Con.) Sevenoaks, 1929–35.
Financial Secretary to the Treasury, 1921–2. Parliamentary Secretary, Department of Overseas Trade, 1931. Minister of Health, 1931–5.

Kennet's papers, in the care of his son, the 2nd Baron Kennet (Mr Wayland Young) are described in Hazlehurst and Woodland, pp. 156–7.

KENT, David Rice*

M.P. (Sinn Fein) Cork County East, 1918–22.

KENWORTHY, Hon. Joseph Montague, see STRABOLGI, 10th B

KENYON, 4th B
Lloyd Tyrell-Kenyon (1864–1927)

Lord in Waiting, 1900–5 and 1916–18.

The present (5th) Lord Kenyon, Gredington, Whitchurch, Salop, states that his father kept very comprehensive scrapbooks and a number of letters, some of which are of political significance. These papers remain with Lord Kenyon.

KENYON, Barnet (1853–1930)

M.P. (Lib.) Chesterfield, 1913–29.
President, Derbyshire Miners' Association, 1896–1906.

Messrs W. & A. Glossop, solicitors to the executors, know of no papers. Records of the Derbyshire Miners' Association are with the National Union of Mineworkers, Saltergate, Chesterfield, Derbs. The *Dictionary of Labour Biography*, Vol. I, pp. 208–9, mentions no private papers.

KENYON, Clifford (1896–   )

M.P. (Lab.) Chorley, 1945–70.

KENYON, Hon. George Thomas (1840–1908)

M.P. (Con.) Denbigh Boroughs, 1885–95 and 1900–6.

The Rt Hon. Lord Kenyon, Gredington, Whitchurch, Salop, has the surviving papers of his great-uncle, the Hon. G. T. Kenyon. They include a volume of obituary press cuttings, and papers ranging through his career from Harrow to his death. They are not numerous. Kenyon's letters to Lord Rendel are in the National Library of Wales.

KENYON, James (1846–1924)

M.P. (Con.) Bury, 1895–1902.

The papers of Kenyon's firm, James Kenyon & Son Ltd, have been deposited in Lancashire Record Office. However, these contain no parliamentary papers, and are mainly concerned with business matters. The only exception is a cuttings book (DDX 823/6/4) containing copies of Factory Acts and a few circulars and notices concerning child labour, 1876–87. Mr J. C. Kenyon, M.B.E., T.D., James Kenyon's grandson, knows of no other papers, and believes it likely that any papers were disposed of after his grandfather's death. C. A. Muir's book, *The Kenyon Tradition*, was published in 1964.

KER, James Campbell (1878–1961)

Indian Civil Service.
M.P. (Con.) Stirlingshire West and Clackmannan, 1931–5.

A copy of J. C. Ker's document on terrorism, *Political Trouble in India, 1907–17* (Calcutta, 1917) can be found at the India Office Library. Mr J. D. C. Russell, Broomfield, Hunterston Road, West Kilbride, Ayrshire, who is Mr Ker's great-nephew, has two books of press cuttings. This material covers in some detail Mr Ker's activity as prospective parliamentary candidate for Stirlingshire West in the later months of 1930 and early in 1931.

KERR, Charles Iain, see TEVIOT, 1st B

KERR, Sir Hamilton William, 1st Bt (1903–74)

M.P. (Con.) Oldham, 1931–45; Cambridge, 1950–66.
Parliamentary Secretary, Ministry of Health, 1945.

The following papers survive: several volumes of an occasional diary of events, dating from the 1920s: volumes of notebooks containing personal reflections on life, religion, philosophy, etc.; some notes for speeches with occasional copy letters; a small folder of letters from the young Hamilton Kerr at school to his mother; various photographs; an album containing photographs of his paintings; a folder of press cuttings; and an unpublished autobiography (Mss copy, and two typescript copies). These are to be deposited in the Fitzwilliam Museum, Cambridge, which has other material relating to Sir Hamilton Kerr, including scrapbooks.

KERR, John (b. 1852)

M.P. (Con.) Preston, 1903–6.

KERR, Professor Sir (John) Graham (1869–1957)

M.P. (Con.) Scottish Universities, 1935–50.
Zoologist.

His papers are in the Glasgow University Archives. There are approximately 1230 letters in the collection, as well as photographic negatives, South African prints and photographic albums. The papers relate (*inter alia*) to his academic interests, to the University of Glasgow, his foreign tours, broadcasts, war camouflage (letters, 1914–41), and the Mid Scotland Ship Canal. There are no files relating in particular to parliamentary affairs:

KERR, Philip Henry, see LOTHIAN, 11th M of

KERRY, E of, see LANSDOWNE, 6th M of

KERSHAW, 1st B
Fred Kershaw (1881–1961)

Lord in Waiting, 1949–51.

Hon. D. A. Kershaw (son) believes the papers were destroyed.

KESWICK, Henry (1870–1928)

M.P. (Con.) Epsom, 1912–18.

Mr David Keswick (son) knows of no papers relating to his father's parliamentary career.

KESWICK, William (1835–1912)

M.P. (Con.) Epsom, 1899–1912.

Mr David Keswick (grandson) knows of no papers relating to his grandfather's parliamentary career.

KETTLE, Thomas Michael (1880–1916)*

M.P. (Irish Nat.) Tyrone East, 1906–Dec 1910.

KEY, Charles William (1883–1964)

M.P. (Lab.) Poplar, Bow and Bromley, 1940–50; Poplar, 1950–64.
Parliamentary Secretary, Ministry of Health, 1945–7. Minister of Works, 1947–50.

A small collection of papers is held at the Bodleian Library. Details appear in Hazlehurst and Woodland, p. 85.

KEY, Sir Neill Cooper- (1907–)

M.P. (Con.) Hastings, 1945–70.

Sir Neill has retained certain papers but details are not available.

KEYES, 1st B
Admiral of the Fleet Sir Roger John Brownlow Keyes, 1st Bt (1872–1945)

M.P. (Con.) Portsmouth North, 1934–43.
C.-in-C. Mediterranean, 1925–8; Portsmouth, 1929–31. Special Liaison Officer to the King of Belgium, 1940. Director of Combined Operations, 1940–1.

Lord Keyes's papers are deposited in the Library of Churchill College, Cambridge. The collection has been arranged into the following main groups: Personal, Naval Career, Political Career, General. The Personal papers date from the 1890s and include correspondence between Keyes and his wife, and appointments diaries. The naval papers again date from the 1890s, and cover all Keyes's major interests and activities, including papers on submarine construction; his active service during World War I, including correspondence concerning the Dardanelles Expedition, papers relating to the Zeebrugge and Ostend operations; his naval career during the inter-war years; and papers relating to the Fleet Air Arm. The Political papers include constituency material, 1934–42; copies of speeches made by Keyes; a considerable amount of correspondence, and newspaper cuttings; and papers relating to Keyes' activities during World War II. These are supplemented by material, including correspondence, relating to the variety of Lord Keyes' interests, in the general files. Many of these papers are not open to general inspection and application to see any of them should be made beforehand to the Archivist, Churchill College, Cambridge. There are some other Keyes letters in the National Library of Scotland, and letters to Sir Julian Corbett on the Dardanelles campaign in the Corbett collection.

KIDD, James (1872–1928)

M.P. (Con.) Linlithgowshire, 1918–22 and 1924–8.
Parliamentary Secretary, Scottish Board of Health, 1922–3.

Miss Margaret Kidd, Q.C., daughter of James Kidd, knows of no papers or diaries left by her father. Letters written from the House of Commons to his wife were destroyed after her death in 1930.

KILBRIDE, Dennis (1848–1924)*

M.P. (Irish Nat.) Kerry South, 1887–95; Galway North, 1895–1900; Kildare South, 1906–18.

KILEY, James Daniel (1865–1953)

M.P. (Lib.) Whitechapel, 1916–22.

The solicitors, Coode Kingdon Somper & Co. (incorporating Stikeman & Co., who acted in J. D. Kiley's estate), could provide no information. There was no trace of Kiley's widow, who was his sole executor.

KILLANIN, 2nd B*
Hon. Martin Henry Fitzpatrick Morris (1867–1927)

M.P. (Con.) Galway, 1900–1.

KILMANY, Baron
Sir William John St Clair Anstruther-Gray, 1st Bt (1905–   )

M.P. (Con.) Lanark North, 1931–45; Berwick and East Lothian, 1951–66.
Assistant Postmaster General, May–Jul, 1945. Chairman of Ways and Means and Deputy Speaker of the House of Commons, 1962–4. Chairman, Conservative Members' ('1922') Committee, 1964–6.

Lord Kilmany says he has retained a collection of diaries and correspondence.

KILMUIR, 1st E of
Sir David Patrick Maxwell-Fyfe (1900–67)

M.P. (Con.) Liverpool West Derby, 1935–54.
Solicitor-General, 1942–5. Attorney-General, 1945. Secretary of State for Home Affairs, 1951–4. Lord Chancellor, 1954–62.

Churchill College, Cambridge, holds the surviving papers. Details appear in Hazlehurst and Woodland, pp. 57–8.

KIMBALL, Lawrence (1900–71)

M.P. (Con.) Loughborough, 1931–45.

Shortly before Major L. Kimball went abroad in 1946, he destroyed all papers in his possession at that time.

KIMBER, Sir Henry, 1st Bt (1834–1923)

M.P. (Con.) Wandsworth, 1885–1913.

The papers of Lord Hardinge, at Cambridge University Library, include correspondence of Sir Henry Kimber, 1910–15. Efforts to contact the present baronet, Sir C. D. Kimber, were unsuccessful.

KIMBERLEY, 3rd E of
John, Lord Wodehouse (1883–1941)

M.P. (Lib.) Mid-Norfolk, 1906–Jan 1910.

Efforts to contact the present (4th) Earl of Kimberley (son) were not successful.

KINDERSLEY, Major Guy Molesworth (1877–1956)

M.P. (Con.) Hitchin, 1923–31.

A collection of papers is held by Mr Edmund Kindersley, The Lodge, New Castle, Ballymahon, Co. Longford, Ireland. The material includes an unpublished 'History of the Zinoviev Letter', and correspondence (1924–8) between Major Kindersley and Donald Im Thurn relating to the Zinoviev Letter. These details are published in Lewis Chester, Hugo Young *et al.*, *The Zinoviev Letter* (1967). Mr Kindersley also has a collection of press cuttings relating to his father's constituency activities.

KING, Alfred John (1859–1920)

M.P. (Lib.) Knutsford, 1906–Jan 1910.

Information given in the will and act of probate was insufficient to trace members of the family.

KING, Evelyn Mansfield (1907–   )

M.P. (Lab.) Penryn and Falmouth, 1945–50; (Con.) Dorset South, 1964–
Parliamentary Secretary, Town and Country Planning, 1947–50.

Mr King has retained no papers which he considers to be of historical importance.

KING, (Henry) Douglas (1877–1930)

M.P. (Ind.) Norfolk North, 1918–22; (Con.) Paddington South, 1922–30.
Junior Lord of the Treasury, 1922–4. Financial Secretary, War Office, 1924–8. Parliamentary
Secretary, Board of Trade (Mines Department), 1928–9.

There was no trace of persons mentioned in the will.

KING, Sir (Henry) Seymour, 1st Bt (1852–1933)

M.P. (Con.) Hull Central, 1885–1911.

Messrs Halsey Lightly and Hemsley (of London) were the solicitors who acted in the estate.
Apart from Mr C. A. M. Lightly of that firm, it was not possible to trace the executors. According to his will, Sir Seymour King left all manuscripts relating to the King family to his
cousin, Richard King. Lady King's niece, Ms Brenda Florence Mattice, received all her diaries
and manuscripts. It has not been possible to trace these persons. Sir Seymour King's banking
firms have now been amalgamated with Lloyds Bank, whose archivist knows of no records of the
firm Henry S. King and Co.

KING, Horace Maybray Maybray-, see MAYBRAY-KING, Baron

KING, Joseph (1860–1943)

M.P. (Lib.) Somerset North, Jan 1910–18.
Author.

According to information provided by Mrs King's representative, Joseph King's diaries were
burned in accordance with the directions of his will.

KING-HALL, Baron
Sir (William) Stephen Richard King-Hall (1893–1966)

Naval career.
M.P. (Independent National) Ormskirk, 1939–44.
Author.

The Hon. Miss A. King-Hall, 11 North Side, Clapham Common, London SW4, has her father's
surviving papers. These are unsorted.

KINGHORN, Squadron Leader Ernest (1907–   )

M.P. (Lab.) Great Yarmouth, 1945–50; Yarmouth, 1950–1.

KINGSMILL, Lt.-Col. William Henry (1905–71)

M.P. (Con.) Yeovil, 1945–51.

Mrs D. Douglas (widow) states that her late husband kept no diary, but an assortment of press
cuttings and papers is in existence. Inquiries should be made to Messrs Gordon Dadds, 80
Brook Street, London W1.

KINLEY, John (d. 1957)

M.P. (Lab.) Bootle, 1929–31, 1945–55.

No members of the family were traced, and no information was secured from an appeal to the *Bootle Times Herald*.

KINLOCH, Sir John George Smyth, 2nd Bt (1849–1910)

M.P. (Lib.) Perthshire East, 1889–1903.

Sir John Kinloch, Bt, Northlands, Warnham, Horsham, West Sussex, has a scrapbook of press cuttings among papers relating to his grandfather.

KINTORE, 9th E of
Sir Algernon Hawkins Thomond Keith-Falconer (1852–1930)

Lord in Waiting, 1885–6 and 1895–1905.
Governor and C.-in-C., South Australia, 1889–95.

The Rt Hon. Earl of Kintore, D. L., Keith Hall, Inverurie, Aberdeenshire AB5 OLD, has a collection of family records including documents and albums of press cuttings relating to the 9th Earl.

KIRBY, Bertie Victor (1887–1953)

M.P. (Lab.) Liverpool Everton, 1935–50.

Members of the family could not be traced, and the Liverpool Record Office knows of no papers.

KIRKPATRICK, William MacColin (1878–1953)

M.P. (Con.) Preston, 1931–7.

Inquiries should be addressed to W. M. Kirkpatrick's son, Mr Reginald C. R. Kirkpatrick, of White Hart Cottage, Compton, Guildford, Surrey, or to Mr Colin Kirkpatrick, 106 Reliance House, Cnr. Speke Ave./Moffat St., Salisbury, Rhodesia.

KIRKWOOD, 1st B
David Kirkwood (1872–1955)

M.P. (Lab.) Dumbarton Burghs, 1922–50; Dunbartonshire East, 1950–1.

The Hon. James S. Kirkwood, B. Arch., A.R.I.B.A., F.R.I.A.S., J.P., c/o Wright Kirkwood & Partners, 9 Woodside Place, Glasgow G3 7QF, Lord Kirkwood's son, has collected and preserved a considerable amount of correspondence, political and private, and many newspaper cuttings. These papers have been listed by the NRA (Scotland).

KIRKWOOD, Major John Hendley Morrison (1877–1924)

M.P. (Con.) Essex South East, Jan 1910–12.

Efforts to contact Sir Robert Kirkwood, Major J. H. M. Kirkwood's son, were unsuccessful.

KITCHENER OF KHARTOUM, 1st E
Field-Marshal Sir Horatio Herbert Kitchener (1850–1916)

Commander, Dongola Expeditionary Force, 1896; Khartoum Expedition, 1898. Chief of Staff, South Africa, 1899–1900. C.-in-C., South Africa, 1900–2, and India, 1902–9. Agent and Consul General, Egypt, 1911–14.
Secretary of State, War, 1914–16.

A collection of Kitchener's papers has been deposited in the Public Record Office (PRO 30/57). The papers relate to the period up to 1914, World War I, and personal and estate matters; there is also a series of papers collected by Sir George Arthur for his biography of Kitchener. The collection is supplemented by a small Private Office series (1914–16), again at the Public Record Office (WO 159), and by the papers at the India Office Library among the Birdwood Collection. The British Library holds a collection of correspondence (Add. Mss 52276–8), mostly between Kitchener and Lt.-Col. R. J. Marker, his aide-de-camp in India. Details appear in Hazlehurst and Woodland, pp. 85–6. Many letters by Kitchener can be found in the collections left by his correspondents, e.g. Lords Cromer, Hardinge, Milner, Morley and St Aldwyn.

KITSON, Sir James, see AIREDALE, 1st B

KNARESBOROUGH, 1st B
Sir Henry Meysey-Thompson, 4th Bt (1845–1929)

M.P. (Lib.) Knaresborough, 1880–5; (Lib.Un.) Brigg, 1885–6; Birmingham Handsworth, 1892–1905.

On ceasing to be a member of the House of Commons, Lord Knaresborough destroyed a large amount of papers and correspondence which he had retained. Certain of them which Lord Knaresborough felt to be of interest were first printed in book form as *A Small Selection of Papers and Speeches by Lord Knaresborough*. The subjects include 'South African Affairs', 'Government of Ireland Bill', 'Land Tenure Bill' and 'Bimetallism'. Copies of the book are in the possession of the Hon. Lady Richmond Brown, (daughter), Leppington House, Leppington, Malton, North Yorkshire.

KNATCHBULL, Hon. Michael Herbert Rudolph, see BRADBOURNE, 5th B

KNEBWORTH, Vt
Edward Anthony James Lytton (1903–33)

M.P. (Con.) Hitchin, 1931–3.

Lady Hermione Cobbold, sister of Viscount Knebworth, has only a collection of personal correspondence relating to her brother. Nothing relates to his parliamentary career.

KNIGHT, Eric Ayshford (1863–1944)

M.P. (Con.) Kidderminster, Jan 1910–22.

Messrs Fisher Dawson & Wasbrough, solicitors in the estate, have no knowledge of the whereabouts of any papers. There was no trace of E. A. Knight's son, Mr Richard Ayshford Knight.

KNIGHT, G. W. Holford (1877–1936)

M.P. (Lab.) Nottingham South, 1929–31; (Nat.Lab.) Nottingham South, 1931–5.

Mrs C. H. Knight (widow) could not be traced. Nottingham City Library has minute books and papers 1919–38, of the Nottingham South C.L.P.

KNIGHTS, Henry Newton (d. 1959)

M.P. (Con.) Camberwell North, 1918–22.

A son-in-law, Mr J. D. Sangway of Banstead, Surrey, could not be contacted.

KNOTT, Sir James, 1st Bt (1855–1934)

M.P. (Con.) Sunderland, 1910 (Jan–Dec).

KNOX, Major-General Sir Alfred William Fortescue (1870–1964)

Military career. Military attaché, Petrograd, 1911–18. Chief of British Military Mission to Siberia, 1918–20.
M.P. (Con.) Wycombe, 1924–45.

Lady Nye, the General's niece, knows of no papers.

KNOWLES, Sir Lees, 1st Bt (1857–1928)

M.P. (Con.) Salford West, 1886–1906.

Mr T. G. Evans, Lady Knowles's cousin and chief beneficiary, knows of no papers except for an exchange of letters between Sir Lees Knowles and Neville Chamberlain. The British Library has Sir Lees Knowles's edition of family letters, 1809–13 (Add. Mss 39956).

KYLSANT, 1st B
Sir Owen Cosby Philipps (1863–1937)

M.P. (Lib.) Pembroke and Haverfordwest, 1906–Dec 1910; (Con.) Chester, 1916–22.

The Hon. Mrs Fisher-Hoch, Plas Llanstephan, Carmarthen, Dyfed, states that her father kept no diaries or correspondence, but did retain some family press cuttings. A recently published paper on his work in the shipping industry can be found in *The Trade Makers - Elder Dempsters in W. Africa 1852–1972* by P. N. Davies.

Appendix I
A note on archives
relating to Ireland

A search for the records of Irish M.Ps elected to sit in the Westminster Parliament has posed particular problems. In the first place, it has proved beyond the resources of this survey to attempt to locate the descendants and heirs to M.Ps who lived and died in Ireland. The readily available reference works and the facilities of the Principal Probate Registry (Somerset House) which ease the search for M.Ps for constituencies in Great Britain are less relevant to conditions in Ireland. The events leading to the partition of Ireland in 1922, the establishment of the Irish Free State and the Parliament of Northern Ireland, the Civil War and ensuing political developments, broke political continuity and have often made it very difficult to trace political papers. An additional problem, of course, has been that the Sinn Feiners elected in 1918 did not take their seats. Hence biographical information is often difficult to obtain.

The second factor is that until recently no systematic attempt has been made in Ireland to conserve records. Fortunately very considerable advances are currently taking place in Ireland to assist the work of discovering and conserving records of all kinds. In particular, the foundation in 1970 of an Irish Society for Archives (*Cumann Cartlannaiochte Eireann*), a body devoting its energies to discovering and saving historical records, provided a focus for those wishing to press for new legislation to ensure the preservation of public records. The advent of the *Irish Archives Bulletin* also marked an important new development.

A number of published aids to the location of manuscript sources now exist. The most important is the eleven-volume *Manuscript Sources for the History of Irish Civilisation* (Boston, 1965), edited by R. J. Hayes, the former director of the National Library of Ireland. This publication, produced by the photographic reproduction of index cards, contains detailed information of holdings, both in Ireland and other countries, of manuscripts relating to Ireland. It serves in effect as a catalogue of the National Library's own holdings, but is also the most comprehensive guide available to worldwide holdings of Irish material. Its contents are arranged under many different categories and a perusal of its volumes is the most effective starting-point for a search for particular records available. It should be noted that an unpublished appendix of manuscripts catalogued in the National Library since the publication of Hayes, up to 1970, is available. ('Shelflist of Additional MSS. catalogued since publication of *Manuscript Sources for the History of Irish Civilisation*' (typescript, 1970), referred to hereafter as 'Shelflist of Additional MSS'.) It may be consulted in the manuscript room of the National Library in Dublin, and a copy is also available in the Bodleian Library, Oxford. The other major sources of information about Irish records are the *Reports* of the Deputy Keeper of the Records in Northern Ireland, which are published at periodic intervals by the Northern Ireland Government and give detailed information about accessions of manuscripts in the Public Record Office, Belfast.

For certain periods of modern Irish history, published material provides the only available source; special importance therefore attaches to James Carty's two-volume *Bibliography of Irish History* (Dublin, 1936),

In the note which follows an attempt is made to bring together information relating to the papers of both individuals and organisations which can throw light on the developments in

Ireland up to 1922, and on the activities of Northern Ireland M.Ps in the Westminster Parliament since 1922. For convenience this note also appears in Volume 4 of this series. A fuller version of this note can be found in *Sources*, Vol. 1, pp. 293–305.

Archive Repositories

Many of the most important manuscript collections are already in archive repositories in Ireland. The most important of these are the National Library of Ireland, the State Paper Office, and the Public Record Office — all in Dublin — and the Public Record Office of Northern Ireland in Belfast. The various university libraries in Dublin, Cork, Belfast and Galway also contain useful manuscript material, and the Linen Hall Library in Belfast and the Royal Irish Academy in Dublin also have manuscript holdings. In addition, the Public Record Office, London, holds a considerable quantity of Irish material, although some of this is subject to a special hundred years restriction. It should be noted that most official records of political significance which have been kept in Dublin are in the State Paper Office in Dublin Castle, and that there is little of political importance in the Public Record Office in Dublin, many of its records being destroyed in 1922. (See Herbert Wood: 'The Public Records of Ireland before and after 1922'. *Royal Historical Society Transactions*, 4th ser., XII (1930) 17–49; and Margaret Griffith: 'A Short Guide to the Public Record Office of Ireland', *Irish Historical Studies*, VIII (1952–), 45–58.) Students wishing to use any of these institutions should write beforehand to enquire about conditions of access.

Irish Parliamentary Movement

The movement which, from the 1870s until 1918, attempted by means of involvement in Westminster politics to wrest from Britain a measure of Home Rule for Ireland consisted of no single or continuous organisation, although there were strong organisational and individual links which provided an element of continuity. The party led by Charles Parnell in the 1880s was a very different body from Isaac Butt's Home Rule Party of the 1870s, while after 1890 dissension among Parnell's followers led to a multiplication of different organisations, all ostensibly in pursuit of Home Rule. After 1900 the party led by John Redmond, although claiming a line of descent from Parnell, operated under quite new conditions and was in many respects a new body. There were also a number of splinter groups from the main-stream of the parliamentary party. The most important of these was the Cork-based All-for-Ireland League which, between 1910 and 1916, sought to find a basis of compromise between the parliamentarians, Sinn Fein and the Unionists. But for archival purposes these are all best dealt with in one category.

The biggest gap in the Irish Parliamentary Party's archive resources is for the period before 1890. The papers of Isaac Butt, chairman of the party in the 1870s, are in the National Library, but they consist principally of correspondence and personal papers. There are, however, no Parnell papers, and so there is little of an authoritative nature on the internal affairs of the party in the 1880s. Indeed, even the papers of Parnell's associates, often voluminous for later periods, contain very little for this earlier period. The leaders of the party were at this time often in conflict with the police and the pattern of their lives was very unsettled; it is therefore not surprising that they left very few written records behind them.

It is after 1890, and especially after 1900, that the papers of certain key members of the party provide what amounts to a very full record. Of particular importance are the papers of John Redmond, leader of the Parnellite party in the 1890s and of the reunited party from 1900 until his death in 1917. This collection contains very extensive correspondence between Redmond, other Irish Nationalists, British politicians and Ministers, and many individuals and organisations throughout Ireland. The collection includes correspondence and papers relating to the day-to-day functioning of the Parnellite party before 1900, including assessments of the party's viability, both financially and in terms of political support. After 1900 the collection has very extensive material on the organisation of the whole party, including considerable correspondence before 1904 with Laurence Ginnell and John O'Donnell, who between them were largely responsible for the functioning of the Dublin office of the United Irish League, and important correspondence after 1907 with John Muldoon on party organisation. This collection is probably the most consistently comprehensive record of the party's history. It is held in the National Library of Ireland, and it can also be seen on microfilm in the Bodleian Library, Oxford. A detailed list of the collection is contained in the National Library's 'Shelflist of Additional MSS'.

The papers of John Dillon contain many significant party records for the 1890s, arising from Dillon's involvement with and eventual leadership of the anti-Parnellite section of the party. His papers contain many volumes of minutes and of other records of the party and of its various national organisations. These include the minute book of the Executive Committee of the Irish National Federation, 11 March, 1891 – 31 January 1899; the minute book of the Council of the Federation from its first meeting on 9 January 1893 until 19 January 1898; and the scrapbook containing press reports of the public meetings of the Federation from 16 November 1892 until 19 January 1898. The Dillon papers are also rich in correspondence and papers about the affairs of both the anti-Parnellite party in the 1890s and the reunited party after 1900, of which he became the last chairman for a brief period after Redmond's death. His papers are particularly valuable for administrative detail and for personal relationships within the party, and they reflect the crucial role that Dillon played in the party's affairs in the 1890s and up to 1918. The papers are still held by the Dillon family.

The papers of William O'Brien, a prominent figure in the Nationalist movement from the early 1880s until 1918, are a further indispensable source. O'Brien's papers were divided by his widow into two parts, one of which she gave to the National Library of Ireland and the other to the Library of University College, Cork. In the National Library is O'Brien's correspondence with more important national figures, as well as some selected, more general correspondence and papers. Included is his correspondence· with Michael Davitt (MSS, 913–14), Lord Dunraven (MS. 8554), John Dillon (MS. 8555), T. M. Healy (MS. 8556) and John Redmond (MS. 10,496). There are also more general groups of papers, and a manuscript work by Mrs. Sophie O'Brien 'Recollections of a Long Life' (MS. 4213–17), contains many copies of O'Brien's letters. From an organisational point of view, however, the O'Brien papers in Cork are more significant. They include correspondence and papers relating to the history of the party in the early 1890s, including the Parnell crisis of 1890–91 and the disputes among the anti-Parnellites between 1892 and 1896; but their greatest importance lies in papers relating to the development of the United Irish League between 1898 and 1900. In eight boxes of correspondence for this period a detailed picture emerges of the origins and establishment of this new body, of its methods of organisation, the character of the agitation that it engendered, its relations with the established Nationalist politicians, and its eventual part in the reunion of the parliamentary party in 1900. The collection also contains material about the disputes among parliamentarians after 1903, the establishment and functioning of the All-for-Ireland League after 1910, and considerable information about the running of newspapers with which O'Brien was concerned, especially the *Irish People* and the *Cork Free Press*. (For a description and list of this collection see P. J. Bull 'The William O'Brien Manuscripts in the Library of University College, Cork', *Journal of the Cork Historical and Archaeological Society*, LXXV (1970) 129–41.)

J. F. X. O'Brien held central positions in the parliamentary party, and his papers reflect his administrative importance to the party. He occupied the position of treasurer of the parliamentary party and was also secretary of the party's organisation in Great Britain. His papers include minutes of the committee of the anti-Parnellite party, 1892–95 (MS. 9223), account books and ledgers relating to the party's parliamentary fund between 1886 and 1896, and two letter books containing copies of correspondence relating to the Irish National League of Great Britain, 1896–1905 (MSS, 9224–25). There is also extensive correspondence between 1879 and 1905 relating to the administration and general affairs of the party.

Some other collections are also of special relevance. In particular, the papers of T. C. Harrington in the National Library contain material on the 1880s and are also particularly informative on the attempts to reunite the party in the late 1890s. The papers of Ed- ·

ward Blake in the Public Archives of Canada are particularly valuable for party discussions on the second Home Rule Bill and on the affairs of the anti-Parnellite party generally in the 1890s. A microfilm of this collection is held in the National Library. The papers of Michael Davitt are also an important source for the history of the party from the 1870s onwards. They are in the possession of Professor T. W. Moody of Trinity College, Dublin, but are not yet available for research. The papers of T. P. Gill in the National Library (MSS. 13,478–526) contain material on the Plan of Campaign in the 1880s, on the Parnell crisis of 1890–91 and on more general political matters. The National Library also contains smaller collections and individual items belonging to other Nationalist politicians. A few papers of T. M. Healy have recently been placed in University College, Dublin.

Records of a kind not normally associated directly with a political party assume importance in the case of the Irish parliamentary party because of its special relationship to certain other institutions. In particular, the close association of the party with the Roman Catholic Church, especially in the 1880s, gives significance to certain ecclesiastical archives in relation to the administration and policy of the party. Particularly important are the papers of Archbishops Croke of Cashel and Walsh of Dublin, who were the two bishops most closely associated with the parliamentary party. The Croke papers, in the archiepiscopal archives at Cashel, are accessible, normally by means of microfilm in the National Library of Ireland. The Walsh papers are in the Dublin diocesan archives.

The unusual relationship of the Irish parliamentary party and the government makes certain other records of importance to its history. The surveillance kept by the police and other government bodies over the activities of the party and of its associated organisations resulted in the compilation of extensive files and records of great value to the historian. The most important of these are among the Chief Secretary's Office Papers in Dublin Castle and in the Irish Office Papers in the Public Record Office, London. The close liaison between the party and the Liberal Government after 1905 gives significance to the papers of various Ministers and administrators, particularly those of James Bryce in the Bodleian Library and the National Library and those of Sir Antony MacDonnell, Augustine Birrell and Sir Matthew Nathan, all in the Bodleian Library.

Finally, mention should be made of two important and largely untapped sources of information about the functioning of the Irish parliamentary party, especially in particular localities. Many Irish local newspapers, usually published weekly, had strong associations with the party or with one of its sections. They are therefore very useful for information about the activities of the party and its individual members in particular areas. In particular, such newspapers often give an indication of tensions and disagreements at a local level which often found more indirect expression in national politics. The parliamentary party also controlled, as a consequence of the Local Government (Ireland) Act of 1898, large areas of local government in Ireland. The records of the county councils and other local authorities have not been easily available in the past. However, such records could throw light upon the local character of the parliamentary party.

Sinn Fein and the Republican Movement

The body known after 1906 as Sinn Fein had its origins in the late 1890s among a group of Nationalists who, although defenders of Parnell, were disillusioned with the idea of parliamentary representation as a means of securing Irish independence and who sought to infect Irish nationalism with a stronger sense of Irish cultural developments. The principal architect of its policy was Arthur Griffith, who espoused what came to be known as the 'Hungarian policy', which envisaged a solution of Ireland's constitutional problems by means of a dual monarchy. Sinn Fein was not therefore Republican in policy and it was a quite separate organisation from the Irish Republican Brotherhood, which then represented the Fenian tradition in Irish politics. Moreover, the later development of revolutionary policies which emerged in 1916 was only indirectly connected with Sinn Fein. But after 1916 the destinies of Sinn Fein and the Republican organisation merged under the impact of the Easter Rising and subsequent events; they are therefore treated here together.

By the very nature of these organisations they have left very little in the way of institutional records, although the climate of opinion in Ireland has led to a careful preservation of items relating to the history of the revolutionary bodies. Manuscript relics of Sinn Fein, the Irish Republican Brotherhood, the Irish Volunteers, the Irish Republican Army and other bodies are therefore quite extensive, but fragmentary in character. Great importance therefore attaches to a close examination of various lists of manuscripts, especially Hayes *op cit* which mentions under a number of different headings small items which together make up a moderately substantial archive for Sinn Fein and other revolutionary and Republican organisations.

The actual institutional records for Sinn Fein which have survived include minutes of the Standing Committee of Sinn Fein, January 1918 – March 1922; minutes of the Sinn Fein Publishing Company, 1906–12; and audited accounts for the Sinn Fein Publishing Company for 1912. All these records are in the National Library of Ireland, as are a number of other collections which contain significant material about Sinn Fein. In particular, a collection of letters, circulars, accounts and other papers relating to Sinn Fein, collected by Miss D. Barton and known as the Barton papers, contains considerable material on the Sinn Fein organisation, especially in Counties Wicklow and Wexford, and Dail Eireann, 1917–27. The National Library also holds a number of miscellaneous items which have been collected from various sources and which relate to the activities of Sinn Fein; they include a miscellaneous collection of circulars and other documents, 1917 and later (MS. 10,916).

Other sources may also be used to throw considerable light on the work of the Republicans. One such case is the Irish Volunteers. Established in 1913 in response to the formation of the Ulster Volunteer Force, eventually they provided the military basis for the revolution after 1916. The ranks of this organisation were split in 1914 when Redmond successfully gained control of the organisation in the interests of the parliamentary party and a minority of its ranks broke from the main body, retaining for themselves the original name of the Irish Volunteers. The majority, which became known as the Irish National Volunteers, was eventually superseded as an organisation with the decline of the parliamentary party, although many of its numbers and resources were merged with the by then ascendant Irish Volunteers. There is considerable archival material for the history of the Volunteers, much of which throws light on the activities of the more secretive Irish Republican Brotherhood, for which few records survive. The most important of these materials are in the papers of Colonel Maurice Moore, who was active in the volunteers from its inception, became Inspector-General of the Irish National Volunteers, and maintained close contact with the military sector of the Republican movement in subsequent years. This collection is held by the National Library of Ireland and includes correspondence as well as administrative material. The papers of The O'Rahilly, still in private hands, contain material not only on the Volunteers, but also on Sinn Fein in general. A copy book of Miss Grace O'Brien in the National Library (MS. 4482) contains the names and particulars of dependants of Volunteers deported after the rising of 1916.

Material of importance to the history of the Volunteers and the Republican movement is contained in the papers of Bulmer Hobson in the National Library. They contain letters and papers relating to the Easter Rising and other subjects, and they include letters of Roger Casement, Eoin MacNeill, P. H. Pearse and others. Various miscellaneous items in the National Library relate to the Irish Republican Army. There are also a number of personal collections of papers in the National Library which contain useful information on the Republican movement. The papers of Art O'Briain, who was envoy of Dail Eireann in London, contain correspondence with the British Government, including correspondence leading up to the Treaty; minutes, correspondence and other documents of the Irish National Relief Fund, London, 1916–22; and correspondence relating to Irish political prisoners in Great Britain, to the Irish Republican Prisoners' Dependants Fund, and to the Irish Self-Determination League, 1916–25. The papers of J. M. Plunkett contain considerable material on the Republican movement in general and on the organisation of Sinn Fein between 1917 and 1921 in particular. The papers of Roger Casement consist of family papers and documents on his Nationalist activities, including his journeys to the United States and to Germany, and his trial. Further material is contained in smaller collections of papers of Michael Collins, Diarmuid Lynch (a member of Dail Eireann and Sinn Fein Food Controller) and Eamonn Ceannt. The papers of Erskine Childers are still held by his family, although a microfilm of some of them is held by the National Library. There is also material of interest about the Republican movement in the papers of Eoin Neeson, also privately held, but with microfilm in the National Library. The J. J. Hearn papers, in the National Library, contain material about the Irish Republican movement in America in the 1920s.

The papers of the Dublin trade unionist, William O'Brien, which are in the National Library of Ireland, contain considerable material relevant to the Republican movement. They include many of James Connolly's own papers and papers relating to many Republican bodies, to the Irish Citizen Army, the Irish Neutrality League, and to various events in the history of the Republican movement.

Irish Unionism

The most important repository of records relating to the history of Irish Unionism is the Public Record Office of Northern Ireland in Belfast. For this reason, a close perusal of the various *Reports* of the Deputy Keeper of the Records is the most effective way of obtaining up-to-date information on the records of Unionist leaders and organisations. Collections of private papers of various individuals are important sources. In particular, the papers of Lord Midleton in the Public Record Office, London, contain material relating to his involvement in Unionist politics, especially in the south of Ireland. These papers are especially valuable for developments after 1916, and particularly for the growing divergence between southern Unionists and those of Ulster. The papers of John Henry Bernard and W. H. Lecky, in the Library of Trinity College, Dublin, should also be consulted for information about the activities of Unionists in general. On Ulster Unionism, the papers of Sir Edward Carson, Sir James Craig and Sir Wilfred Spender, all in the Public Record Office, Belfast, provide useful material.

As with the Nationalists and Republicans, the records of Unionist organisations provide important relevant material. The Irish Unionist Alliance, known from 1885 until 1891 as the Irish Loyal and Patriotic Union, was most active among Unionists outside Ulster, although it was ostensibly an all-Ireland organisation. Many of its records are now in the Northern Ireland Public Record Office. The collection includes correspondence with Sir Edward Carson, the correspondence and papers of J. M. Wilson, reports of Richard Dawson of the London Committee of the Irish Unionist Alliance, and papers relating to the split in the Alliance in 1918–19 and to incidents affecting Loyalists during the Anglo-Irish and civil wars.

The records of the Ulster Unionist Council provide the most important source for specifically Ulster Unionism; they are also held in the Belfast Public Record Office. The Ulster Unionist Council was established in 1905 to draw together disparate Ulster Unionist bodies and it eventually became the central policy-making body of the Northern Ireland Unionist Party. Many of the records of the Ulster Volunteer Force are also held in the Public Record Office, Belfast. Some of these, including the minutes of the Headquarters Council, 1914–20, and the minutes of the County Down Committee, were among the records of the Ulster Unionist Council. Many other items were deposited in response to an appeal in 1961 by the late Viscount Brookeborough, then Prime Minister of Northern Ireland, for the preservation of papers relating to the Home Rule crisis, and particularly to the activities of the Ulster Volunteer Force. There are, in addition, many small accessions to various repositories in Ireland which form an essential part of the archives of Irish Unionist organisations. The lists issued by these institutions should be carefully consulted. This is particularly so of the Northern Ireland Public Record Office, which has acquired very considerable numbers of miscellaneous items, such as minute books, membership lists and photographs, relating to various local Unionist organisations. These include records of the Armagh constituency, together with records of Antrim.

Irish Labour Movement

The history of organised labour in Ireland has been a fragmented one. The trade union movement has been greatly affected by the bitter industrial disputes of the early 20th century, and the subsequent divisions between those following the more revolutionary traditions established by leaders such as James Connolly and James Larkin and those pursuing the more limited objectives of trade unionism; moreover, the division of Ireland politically, created by the establishment of Northern Ireland, has further fragmented both union activity and political action. Such a development has necessarily affected the extent to which records have been preserved, and it is still difficult to know how extensive such records are and where they are to be found.

The most significant collection of papers for the history of Irish trade unionism and the labour movement in general is that of William O'Brien, the Dublin trade unionist, whose life was devoted to the service of the Irish Transport and General Workers' Union. After his death in 1968, O'Brien's papers were given to the National Library of Ireland. They include extensive material on his own political career in the labour movement and in association with various Republican bodies. Many of the papers of James Connolly came into O'Brien's hands, and these are included in the collection; they are an important source for the earliest period of the Irish Labour movement and of Irish Socialism in general. The National Library also holds other relevant items. These include some further records of the Irish Transport and General Workers' Union, in particular relating to the annual conferences of the union (1922–39); there is also a roll book of the union from about 1915 (MS. 3097). The National Library also holds seven volumes of records of the Dublin Trades Council, 1893–1932 (MSS. 12,779–85) and miscellaneous fragmentary papers of Charles Diamond, an Irish trade unionist in Glasgow, 1919–23 (MS. 1,540).

The Northern Ireland Public Record Office holds a number of papers of interest for the history of the Irish Labour movement. These include four volumes of diaries kept by R. McElborough, in which he comments on his experiences in the gas industry and his dealings with trade unions, 1884–1949 (D. 770), and the papers of Patrick Agnew, trade unionist and Labour M.P. for South Armagh in the Northern Ireland Parliament from 1938 to 1944, which include two minute books of the Armagh branch of the Northern Ireland Labour Party, 1933, 1946–7, two personal diaries, 1955–6, and correspondence (D. 1676).

An important recent deposit is that of the records of the Northern Ireland Labour Party, dating from c. 1940.

An Irish Society for the Study of Labour History has recently been founded, and watch should be kept for its publications.

Other Relevant Material

Certain organisations, though often not ostensibly political, have enjoyed considerable political influence and their records provide additional sources for research.

Gaelic League (Connradh na Gaedhilge)

The League was founded in 1893 with a twofold aim; to preserve Irish as the national language of the country and promote its spoken use; and to promote the study and publication of Gaelic literature, and to encourage a modern Irish literature. It was intended to be politically neutral, but this became difficult during the ensuing years. It split in 1915 over the question of Irish independence, and in 1918 was declared an illegal organisation, together with Sinn Fein. Since independence the League has continued its work to preserve and promote the Irish language.

Many of the extensive records of the League have been deposited in the National Library of Ireland. These provide an excellent source for the history of the League up to and beyond the establishment of the Irish State.

Orange Order

This organisation, and various Lodges associated with it, provided for Ulster Unionism some of the organisational and cultural backing which for the Nationalists derived from the Gaelic League, the Gaelic Athletic Association and the Ancient Order of Hibernians.

The Northern Ireland Public Record Office holds a number of records of particular Orange Lodges. These include correspondence, accounts and pamphlets of Cookstown Orange Lodge and of County Tyrone Grand Orange Lodge, mid-19th century to 1944.

Irish Co-operative Movement

The co-operative movement in Ireland was very largely the creation of Sir Horace Plunkett, a moderate Unionist politician, who wished to resolve many of the problems of rural Ireland by means of co-operation. The movement's aims were mildly political in the sense that it was concerned with many of the same issues as were politicians, but its relations with politicians were not always easy.

The Horace Plunkett papers, which are at the Plunkett Foundation for Co-operative Studies in Oxford, are the most significant collection of papers, although these are not as comprehensive as they would have been had many of them not been destroyed by fire during the civil war in Ireland. They include Plunkett's diaries, with their detailed comments on his everyday activities in Ireland and on discussions with political leaders and others. There is also considerable correspondence, both with British politicians and with individuals in Ireland, and there are other records relating to the Irish co-operative movement.

T. P. Gill, at one time a Nationalist M.P., spent the greater part of his life in non-political activity in Ireland, most of this with the Department of Agriculture and Technical Instruction, of which Plunkett was for many years the head. Gill's papers at the National Library of Ireland contain considerable material on his work at the Department, intertwined as it was with the advocacy and establishment of co-operatives, especially in the dairying industry.

There are a number of records relating to various co-operative organisations in the papers of William O'Brien, the Irish trade unionist. These are in the National Library of Ireland and include papers of the Irish Co-operative Clothing Manufacturing Society (MS. 15,650) and the Irish Co-operative Labour Press (MS. 15,651).

Irish Convention, 1917–18

The Irish Convention, convened by Lloyd George in an attempt to find an agreed solution to the problem of Irish government, was more widely representative of Irish opinion than any other political activity in Ireland's recent history. The Convention, under the chairmanship of Sir Horace Plunkett, has left a number of papers relating to its proceedings. These include the notes of J. P. Mahaffy, Provost of Trinity College, Dublin, which are in the Library of Trinity College, and agenda papers of the Convention which are in Trinity College and in the State Paper Office.

Appendix II
Postal addresses of libraries and record offices cited in the text

The following is an alphabetical list of libraries mentioned in the text. It has attempted to provide, where possible, the most up-to-date addresses. The reorganisation of local government areas in the United Kingdom has resulted in a reorganisation of record and library authorities, and efforts have been made to incorporate changes of designation and address in this list. At the time of writing the most up-to-date list of relevant libraries in the United Kingdom is that produced by the Royal Commission on Historical Manuscripts, *Record Repositories in Great Britain* (5th ed., 2nd impression, H.M.S.O., 1976).

Aberdeen University Library, Manuscript and Archives Section, University Library, King's College, Aberdeen AB9 2UB.

All Souls College, Oxford.

Amherst College Library, Amherst, Mass. 01002, U.S.A.

Avon County Record Office, Avon House, The Haymarket, Bristol BS99 7DE

Ball State University, Muncie, Indiana, U.S.A.

Balliol College, Oxford.

Bangor: University College of North Wales, Department of Manuscripts, The Library, Bangor, LL57 2DG Gwynedd.

Bath City Record Office, Guildhall, Bath BA1 5AW.

Battersea District Library, 265 Lavender Hill, London, SW11.

Bedford County Record Office, County Hall, Bedford MK42 9AP.

Belfast Public Library, Royal Avenue, Belfast, Northern Ireland; Local History Dept., Templemore Avenue, Belfast 5.

Berkshire Record Office, Shire Hall, Reading RG1 3EE.

Birmingham Public Libraries, Birmingham B3 3HQ.

Birmingham University Library, P.O. Box 363, Edgbaston, Birmingham B15 2TT.

Bodleian Library, Oxford OX1 3BG.

Boston Public Library, Boston, Mass., U.S.A.

Bradford Central Library, Prince's Way, Bradford BD1 1NN.

British Library, Department of Manuscripts, Great Russell Street, London WC1B 3DG.

Buckinghamshire Record Office, County Hall, Aylesbury, HP20 1VA.

Burnley Central Library, Grimshaw Street, Burnley, Lancs.

California State University, Northridge, California, U.S.A.

Cambridge University Library, West Road, Cambridge CB3 9DR.

Cardiff Central Library, The Hayes, Cardiff CF1 2QU.

Centre of South Asian Studies, University of Cambridge, Laundress Lane, Cambridge.
Cheshire Record Office, The Castle, Chester CH1 2DN.
Christ Church, Oxford.
Churchill College, Cambridge CB3 0DS.
Cleveland Archives Department, 81 Borough Road, Middlesbrough TS1 3AA.
Clwyd Record Office: The Old Rectory, Hawarden, Deeside, Clwyd CH5 3NR; 46 Clwyd Street, Ruthin LL15 1NP.
Coleg Harlech, Harlech, Wales.
Co-operative Union Library, Holyoake House, Hanover Street, Manchester M60 0AS.
Cork: University College Library, Cork, Republic of Ireland.
Cory Library, Rhodes University, Grahamstown, South Africa.
Cumbria Record Office, The Castle, Carlisle CA3 8UR.
Derbyshire Record Office, County Offices, Matlock DE4 3AG.
Devon Record Office, Concord House, South Street, Exeter EX1 1DX.
Dorset Record Office, County Hall, Dorchester DT1 1XJ.
Douglas Library, Queen's University, Kingston, Ontario, Canada.
Duke University Library, Durham, North Carolina 27706, U.S.A.
Dundee City Library, Dundee DD1 1DB.
Durham County Library, Darlington, Co. Durham.
Durham County Record Office, County Hall, Durham DH1 5UL.
Durham University Library, Oriental Section (Sudan Archive), Elvet Hall, Durham DH1 3TH.
Dyfed Archives, County Hall, Carmarthen SA31 1JP.
East Riding County Record Office, now Humberside County Record Office, County Hall, Beverley, North Humberside HU17 9BA.
East Sussex Record Office, Pelham House, St. Andrews Lane, Lewes BN7 1VN.
Edinburgh University Library, Department of Manuscripts, George Square, Edinburgh EH8 9LJ.
Edward Grey Institute of Field Ornithology, Alexander Library, St. Cross Road, Oxford.
Essex Record Office, County Hall, Chelmsford CM1 1LX.
Fawcett Library, 27 Wilfred Street, London SW1E 6PR.
Fitzwilliam Museum, Trumpington Street, Cambridge.
Friends House Library, Euston Road, London NW1 2BJ.
Gateshead Central Library, Prince Consort Road, Gateshead NE8 4LN.
Glamorgan Record Office, County Hall, Cathays Park, Cardiff CF1 3NE.
Glasgow University Library, Glasgow G12 8QQ.
Greater London Record Office (London Section), County Hall, London SE1 7PB; (Middlesex Records) 1 Queen Anne's Gate Buildings, Dartmouth Street, London SW1H 9BS.
Guildford Muniment Room, Castle Arch, Guildford GU1 3SX.
Guildhall Library, Aldermanbury, London EC2P 2EJ.
Gwent County Record Office, County Hall, Cwmbran NP4 2XH.
Gwynedd Archives Service:
  Caernarfon Area Record Office, Caernarfon LL55 1SH.
  Dolgellau Area Record Office, Penarlâg, Dolgellau.
  Llangefni Area Record Office, Shire Hall, Llangefni, Anglesey.
Hammersmith Public Libraries, Archives Department, Shepherds Bush Library, Uxbridge Road, London W12 8LJ.
Hampshire Record Office, 20 Southgate Street, Winchester, Hants SO23 9EF.
Hanley: Stoke-on-Trent City Libraries, Bethesda Street, Hanley, Stoke-on-Trent ST1 3RS.
Haringey Libraries Department, Bruce Castle, Lordship Lane, London N17 8NU.
Harvard University, The Baker Library, Cambridge, Mass. 02138, U.S.A.
Hastings Public Museum, John's Place, Cambridge Road, Hastings, Sussex.
Hereford and Worcester County Record Office, Shire Hall, Worcester WR1 1TR.
  County Record Office, The Old Barracks, Harold Street, Hereford HR1 2QX.
Hertfordshire Record Office, County Hall, Hertford SG13 8DE.
House of Lords Record Office, London SW1A 0PW.

Huddersfield Central Public Library, Huddersfield HD1 2SU.

Hull University, The Brynmor Jones Library, The University, Hull, Humberside HU6 7RX.

Humberside County Record Office, County Hall, Beverley, North Humberside HU17 9BA.

Huntingdonshire Record Office (now part of Cambridgeshire Record Offices), Grammar School Walk, Huntingdon PE18 6LF.

Imperial War Museum, Department of Documents, Lambeth Road, London SE1 6HZ.

India Office Library, European Manuscripts Section, 197 Blackfriars Road, London SE1 8NG.

Inner Temple Library, London EC4Y 7DA.

Institute of Agricultural History, University of Reading, Whiteknights, Reading, Berks RG6 2AG.

Institute of Economics and Statistics, St. Cross Building, Manor Road, Oxford.

International Institute of Social History, Herengracht 262–6, Amsterdam, Netherlands.

Keighley Public Library, Keighley, West Yorkshire.

Kent Archives Office, County Hall, Maidstone, Kent ME14 1XQ.

Kent: University of Kent at Canterbury, Canterbury, Kent.

Lancashire Record Office, Bow Lane, Preston PR1 8ND.

Leeds City Libraries, Archives Department, Sheepscar Branch Library, Chapeltown Road, Leeds LS7 3AP.

Leeds University, Brotherton Library, Leeds LS2 9JT.

Leicester Museum and Art Gallery, New Walk, Leicester LE1 6TD.

Leicestershire Record Office, 57 New Walk, Leicester LE1 7JB.

Library of Congress, Washington DC 20540, U.S.A.

Liddell Hart Centre for Military Archives, King's College, Strand, London WC2R 2LS.

Lincolnshire Archives Office, The Castle, Lincoln LN1 3AB.

Liverpool Record Office, City Libraries, William Brown Street, Liverpool L3 8EW.

Liverpool University Library, P.O. Box 123, Liverpool L69 3DA.

London Library, 14 St. James's Square, London SW1Y 4LG.

London University Library, Senate House, Malet Street, London WC1E 7HU.

McGill University Library, Montreal, Canada.

Manchester Central Library, St. Peter's Square, Manchester M2 5PD.

Manchester: John Rylands University Library of Manchester, Deansgate, Manchester M3 3EH.

Marx Memorial Library, Marx House, 37A Clerkenwell Green, London EC1.

Merioneth Record Office, now Gwynedd Archives Service, Dolgellau Area Record Office.

Middle East Centre, St. Antony's College, 137 Banbury Road, Oxford OX2 6JE.

Middlesbrough: Teesside Public Libraries, Central Library, Victoria Square, Middlesbrough, Teesside TS1 2AY.

Ministry of Defence Library (Navy), Empress State Building, Lillie Road, Fulham, London SW6.

Mitchell Library, Macquarie Street, Sydney, New South Wales 2000, Australia.

Mitchell Library, North Street, Glasgow G12 8QQ.

Modern Records Centre, University of Warwick Library, Coventry CV4 7AL.

National Army Museum, Royal Hospital Road, London SW3 4HT.

National Library of Australia, Parkes Place, Canberra, A.C.T., 2600, Australia.

National Library of Ireland, Department of Manuscripts, Kildare Street, Dublin 2, Republic of Ireland.

National Library of Scotland, Department of Manuscripts, George IV Bridge, Edinburgh EH1 1EW.

National Library of Wales, Department of Manuscripts, Aberystwyth, Dyfed SY23 3BU.

National Maritime Museum, Greenwich, London, SE10.

National Motor Museum, Beaulieu, Brockenhurst, Hants.

New College, Oxford.

Newcastle-on-Tyne University Library, Queen Victoria Street, Newcastle-on-Tyne NE1 7RU.

North Riding County Record Office, now North Yorkshire County Record Office, County Hall, Northallerton, North Yorkshire DL7 8SG.

Northamptonshire Record Office, Delapre Abbey, Northampton NN4 9AW.

Northumberland County Record Office, Melton Park, North Gosforth, Newcastle-on-Tyne NE3 5QX.

North Yorkshire County Record Office, County Hall, Northallerton, North Yorkshire DL7 8SG.

Norwich Central Library, Bethel Street, Norwich.

Nottingham Central Library, South Sherwood Street, Nottingham NG1 4DA.

Nottinghamshire Record Office, County House, High Pavement, Nottingham NG1 1HR.

Nuffield College, Oxford OX1 1NF.

Open University Library Milton Keynes, Bucks.

Oxford Central Library, St. Aldate's, Oxford OX1 1DJ.

Polish Institute and Sikorski Museum, 20 Princes Gate, London SW7 1QA.

Portsmouth City Record Office, Guildhall, Portsmouth, PO1 2AL.

Powys Area Library, Ship Street, Brecon, Powys.

Public Archives of Canada, 395 Wellington Street, Ottawa, Ontario K1A ON3, Canada.

Public Record Office, Chancery Lane, London WC2A 1LR.

Public Record Office of Ireland, Four Courts, Dublin, Ireland.

Public Record Office of Northern Ireland, 66 Balmoral Avenue, Belfast BT9 6NY.

Queen's University, Douglas Library, Kingston, Ontario, Canada.

Queen's University Library, University Road, Belfast 7, Northern Ireland.

Reading University Library, Whiteknights, Reading, Berks. RG6 2AE.

Rhodes House Library, Oxford.

Rotherham Central Library, Howard Street, Rotherham S65 1JH.

Royal Air Force Museum, R.A.F. Hendon, The Hyde, London NW9 5LL.

Royal Armoured Tank Corps Museum, Bovington Camp, Wareham, Dorset.

Royal Commonwealth Society Library, Northumberland Avenue, London WC2N 5BJ.

Salop Record Office, The Shirehall, Abbey Foregate, Shrewsbury SY2 6ND.

Scott Polar Research Institute Archives, Cambridge CB2 1ER.

Scottish Record Office, P.O. Box 36, H.M. General Register House, Edinburgh EH1 3YY.

Sheffield Central Library, Surrey Street, Sheffield S1 1XZ.

Sheffield University Library, Western Bank, Sheffield, South Yorkshire S10 2TN.

Somerset Record Office, Obridge Road, Taunton TA2 7PU.

South African Government Archives, Pretoria, South Africa.

South African Library, Queen Victoria Street, Cape Town, South Africa.

South Wales Miners' Library, University College, Swansea, West Glam.

South Yorkshire Archives Service, Cultural Activities Centre, Ellin Street, Sheffield S1 4PL.

Southampton Central Library, Southampton SO9 4XP.

Southern Illinois University Library, Carbondale, Illinois 62901, U.S.A.

Southport Public Library, Lord Street, Southport, Lancs.

Southwark Central Reference Library, Kennington District Library, Walworth Road, London, SE17.

Staffordshire Record Office, Eastgate Street, Stafford ST16 2LZ.

Stockport Public Libraries, Wellington Street South, Stockport SK1 3RS.

Suffolk Record Office:
Bury St. Edmunds Branch, Schoolhall Street, Bury St. Edmunds IP33 1RX
Ipswich Branch, County Hall, Ipswich, Suffolk IP4 2JS.

Surrey Record Office, County Hall, Kingston upon Thames KT1 2DN.

Sussex Archaeological Society, Barbican House, Lewes BN7 1YE.

Sussex University Library, Brighton BN1 9QL.

Swansea: University College Library, Singleton Park, Swansea, West Glam.

Swarthmore College (Peace Collection), Swarthmore, Pennsylvania 19081, U.S.A.

Texas University Library, Box 7219, Austin, Texas 78712, U.S.A.

The Times, P.O. Box 7, New Printing House Square, Gray's Inn Road, London WCJX 8EZ.

Tower Hamlets Libraries Department, Central Library, Bancroft Road, London E1 4DQ.

Trades Union Congress, Great Russell Street, London, WC1.

Trinity College, Cambridge.

Trinity College Library, Manuscripts Room, College Street, Dublin 2, Ireland.

Tunbridge Wells Central Library, Mount Pleasant, Tunbridge Wells TN1 1NS.

Tyne and Wear Archives Department, 7 Saville Place, Newcastle-on-Tyne NE1 8DQ.

University College London Library, Gower Street, London WC1E 6BT.

University College at Buckingham, Buckingham, Bucks.

Vancouver City Archives, 1150 Chestnut Street, Vancouver, B.C., Canada.

Wadham College, Oxford.

Walsall Public Library, Lichfield Street, Walsall, West Midlands.

Warrington Public Library, Museum Street, Warrington, Lancs.

Warwickshire County Record Office, Priory Park, Cape Road, Warwick CV34 4JS.

West Bromwich, Sandwell Public Libraries, High Street, West Bromwich, West Midlands B70 8DZ.

West Sussex Record Office, West Street, Chichester, West Sussex PO19 1RN.

West Yorkshire Record Office, Registry of Deeds Building, Newstead Road, Wakefield WF1 2DE.

Westminster City Libraries:

Archives Department, Victoria Library, Buckingham Palace Road, London SW1W 9TR.

Local History Library, Marylebone Library, Marylebone Road, London NW1 5PS.

Whitehaven Public Library and Museum, Lowther Street, Whitehaven, Cumbria.

William Salt Library, 19 Eastgate Street, Stafford.

Wiltshire Record Office, County Hall, Trowbridge BA14 8JG.

Worcestershire County Record Office, see Hereford and Worcester.

York City Archives, City Library, Museum Street, York YO1 2DS.

York University, J.B. Morrell Library, Heslington, York.